France in Crisis

France is in crisis. In this provocative account, Timothy Smith argues that the French economic and social model is collapsing inward on itself, the result of good intentions, bad policies, and vested interests who employ the rhetoric of "solidarity" to prevent change. French social policy is not redistributive; indeed, Smith argues, the majority of "social" spending serves to strengthen existing inequalities. He shows how politicians, intellectuals, and labor leaders have invoked the specter of "globalization" to explain homegrown problems and delay reform. Professor Smith makes frequent comparisons with the USA, the UK, Canada, Scandinavia, Germany, and the Netherlands, and argues that change need not follow the inegalitarian US or British paths but instead can lead to a more equal society. Written in a lively style, this is an unusual blend of history, policy analysis, economics, and political commentary and will be indispensable reading for anyone seeking to understand France's current malaise.

TIMOTHY B. SMITH is Associate Professor of History at Queen's University, Ontario, where he teaches Modern European history, comparative public policy, and the history of globalization. His previous publications include *Creating the Welfare State in France, 1880–1940* (2003).

France in Crisis

*Welfare, Inequality, and
Globalization since 1980*

Timothy B. Smith

Queen's University, Kingston, Ontario

CAMBRIDGE
UNIVERSITY PRESS

9510140

PUBLISHED BY THE PRESS SYNDICATE OF THE UNIVERSITY OF CAMBRIDGE
The Pitt Building, Trumpington Street, Cambridge, United Kingdom

CAMBRIDGE UNIVERSITY PRESS
The Edinburgh Building, Cambridge, CB2 2RU, UK
40 West 20th Street, New York, NY 10011–4211, USA
477 Williamstown Road, Port Melbourne, VIC 3207, Australia
Ruiz de Alarcón 13, 28014 Madrid, Spain
Dock House, The Waterfront, Cape Town 8001, South Africa

http://www.cambridge.org

First published 2004

Printed in the United Kingdom at the University Press, Cambridge

Typeface Plantin 10/12 pt.   *System* LATEX 2$_\varepsilon$ [TB]

A catalogue record for this book is available from the British Library

Library of Congress Cataloguing in Publication data
Smith, Timothy B. (Timothy Beresford)
France in Crisis: Welfare, Inequality, and Globalization since 1980 /
Timothy B. Smith.
      p.   cm.
Includes bibliographical references and index.
ISBN 0 521 84414 2 – ISBN 0 521 60520 2 (pb.)
1. France – Social policy.   2. France – Social conditions.   3. France –
Economic policy.   4. France – Economic conditions.   5. Welfare state –
France.   6. Equality – France.   7. Socialism – France.   I. Title.
HN 425.5.S58   2004   361.6'1'0944 – dc 22   2004045814

ISBN 0 521 84414 2 hb
ISBN 0 521 60520 2 pb

The publisher has used its best endeavors to ensure that the URLs for external
websites referred to in this book are correct and active at the time of going to
press. However, the publisher has no responsibility for the websites and can
make no guarantee that a site will remain live or that the content is or will
remain appropriate.

Contents

Tables

Preface

It was a familiar scene to anyone who spent time in Paris during the period 1995 to 2003: the streets were filled with ten thousand to one million protestors, young and old, rich and poor alike. They were marching in defense of "solidarity," for higher wages, against a proposed reform of the civil service or the education system, against a partial privatization of one of the 1,500 companies the state owns in full or in part, against a proposal for a small cut to social spending. They were contesting pension reform. The protestors' banners and placards denounced the menace of "neo-liberal globalization."

What was going on? Was France's social model under attack from within, from French politicians? Was it threatened from without, by globalization? *France in Crisis* answers these questions, and more. This book traces the historical roots of France's current economic and social malaise. It looks at the French welfare state and political economy broadly conceived – its recent past, its present, its relevance as a potential counter-model to the USA and Britain, and its future in a "globalizing" world.

Some on the Left contend that states are no longer free to pursue social solidarity and full employment in an age of rising trade, open borders, and financial speculation. *France in Crisis* challenges that idea, arguing that domestic political decisions still largely determine economic success – and failure. Plenty of exit options lead from France's current economic and social problems, including the Dutch and Scandinavian paths. The French welfare state can become more equitable even as it becomes more efficient. Similarly, economic reform *can* be consistent with social democratic ideals.

High levels of labor-force participation (including part-time work) together with low levels of poverty are still possible in a globalizing economy. But these goals can be achieved only if states are willing to adapt to changing circumstances. Policy cannot remained ossified in tradition as politicians denounce changing global economic dynamics. Before France reconfigures its social and labor policies, it must make peace with globalization. France must stop blaming outside forces for its problems and it must also stop equating reform with the unattractively inegalitarian US and British economic paths.

Working in France during the late 1990s, I came to know highly educated people born during the late 1960s who had never held a full-time job. I was surprised by the degree to which they blamed outside forces, not their own politicians, for their predicament. Similarly, I was struck by the tendency of leading French intellectuals, politicians, and labor leaders to attribute France's problems to "globalization," Thatcherite "neoliberalism," and the drive toward European union. An opinion survey conducted during the mid 1990s found that 50% of the French believed that Third World competition was the most important factor explaining the unemployment crisis which had gripped France since the late 1970s. In total, three-quarters of those polled listed one or another external factor as the key cause of rising unemployment. As one writer from France's leading newspaper *Le Monde* observed in 1997, shortly after the Socialist Prime Minister Lionel Jospin took office, "in the space of a few months, globalization has become not just the cause but the explanation of absolutely everything."*

I concluded that this tendency to blame external forces for the structural problems of the French economy was largely misguided. Further, it was preventing a serious, calm public debate. Since many people presented the unattractively inegalitarian US or Thatcherite path as the only alternative to the status quo, France appeared suspended in a state of inertia. As someone who teaches courses in comparative public policy, I knew that other potential models existed – France could change, and change might even lead down the path of social democracy.

This book does not celebrate the considerable successes of French social policy – others have done this before me. In fact my first book was a sympathetic portrayal of the rise of the French welfare state between 1880 and 1940; in it, I argued that by 1940 French reformers had overcome considerable opposition and constructed a successful welfare state (by the European standards of the day), geared towards families and low-income workers. French social policy, I argued, was at its most redistributive *before* the Second World War since the wealthy paid for parts of it without receiving any benefit (in a direct way).

But today things are very different. France spends almost as much as Sweden on things "social," but France has twice the unemployment and three to four times the poverty. Drawing upon the work of French government statisticians, French economists, French newspapers, political

---

* Erik Izraelewicz, *Ce monde qui nous attend* (Paris: Grasset, 1997), p. 19, quoted in Peter Karl Kresl and Sylvain Gallais, *France Encounters Globalization* (Cheltenham, UK: Edward Elgar, 2002), p. 7.

scientists, historians, sociologists, urbanists, demographers, essayists, and comparative welfare-state literature, this book highlights the alarming social and income inequalities at the heart of the French welfare state. This is a study of the failure of French politicians to reform public policies which report after government report have shown to be manifest failures. Many of France's economic and social problems are the direct result of social, fiscal, taxation, and economic policies which are locked into protecting the upper half of the income ladder at the expense of others – youth, women, immigrants, the unemployed.

Similar critiques of "welfare states without work" have been made by Gøsta Esping-Andersen (one of the world's leading experts in the comparative study of welfare states) and also by some prominent French critics, including Alain Minc. I lay no claim to theoretical innovation. But this book – fusing policy analysis and political economy with academic and popular history – presents France's public policies in a new light. *France in Crisis* is a thematically organized, synthetic study of the failure of social policy to deliver to over one-third of the population its loudly trumpeted claim of "solidarity." And because this study compares policies across nations, the reader will (I hope) learn a thing or two about the Netherlands, Sweden, the USA, Canada, Britain, and Germany.

As a work of policy analysis, this book cannot and does not shy away from judgment, so I shall lay my cards on the table. I come to this project as a supporter of redistributive Scandinavian-style social policies. But my politics are an eclectic mix: I am also in favor of Dutch and North American-style dynamic labor markets. I believe in Keynesianism when necessary, but I am not necessarily a Keynesian. I believe that the state needs to expand in some areas, at certain times, but should be prepared to withdraw in the name of the general good. Economic change need not be the enemy of equality, but it does require a malleable social policy. The Western world did not discover the timeless and immutable laws of public policy during capitalism's Glory Age (1950–75). What worked in 1965 may not in 2005. A happy medium floats between the excesses of American favoritism for the super-rich and European favoritism for the forty-year-old and older gainfully employed (usually male) voter.

A number of concerns and assumptions inform the work that follows. First, how can states reduce inequality while returning to full employment? I believe that high unemployment is the worst social problem facing continental Europe (France, Germany, Italy, Spain, Belgium, Greece, Portugal, etc.); most continental welfare-state regimes have failed to rise to the challenge of tackling this scourge. Indeed, unemployment is a social rot upon which political extremism feeds, caused to a certain extent by the very social and labor legislation so prized by comfortably employed, vacationed, and pensioned Europeans.

Second, I believe that social spending can and should remain high, but it must adapt to the inequalities of the day. Otherwise it will find itself locked into protecting yesterday's needy. I agree with John Myles that the challenge to contemporary welfare states is to adapt to precarious labor markets and the increased risks which working-aged families face in an age of rising divorce rates and single parenthood, all the while maintaining a basic commitment to preventing old-age poverty. France, like many other nations, has succeeded in the latter but failed in the former.

If politicians wish to minimize poverty, they must ensure that social policy receives constant surveillance in the name of solidarity and regular recalibration in the name of redistribution. If "solidarity" truly is the end goal, then some barometer of inequality – some sort of "perverse outcome" smoke detector which alerts politicians to programs which are veering away from their original intent or their stated goals – must guide social policy. Much of French social policy is trapped in outdated grooves, out of touch with the current needs of society and economy. The world of work has changed dramatically since the 1970s, challenging a social security system which rests on the idea of stable employment. French public policy, despite its rhetoric of solidarity, creates or aggravates as many inequalities as it corrects. In order to reduce inequality, French politicians must first peel away the layers of ideology and misinformation masking the striking publicly subsidized privileges which widen the social divide.

The Advisory Research Committee of Queen's University, Kingston, Ontario, provided funding for travel to France, for which I am grateful. Several people have kindly assisted me with this project. In particular, I wish to thank Grant Amyot, Rosanne Currarino, Peter Hall, Michael Hanagan, Rachel Hanson, Jonah Levy, Michelle Magdelaine, Bob Malcolmson, Rebecca Manley, Ian McKay, John Merriman, David Parker, Brian Pierce, Jeremy Popkin, François Rouget, Bob Shenton, Jim Stayer, Mark Wiseman, and Isser Woloch. Michael Watson was a terrific editor and the anonymous readers for Cambridge University Press provided very useful comments, helping me to improve the book. All errors and shortcomings are, of course, my own.

1   The misunderstood French welfare state

> Globalization and the intensified competition in every market in every country are used as all-purpose justifications: for the fall in real wages, the dismantling of social welfare systems, spiralling unemployment, generalized job insecurity, deteriorating working conditions, and so on. We are told these things are inevitable and natural.
>
> Sociologist André Gorz, in *Misères du présent, richesse du possible* (1997).[1]

> The American social model threatens Europe . . . the exportation by the United States of its distinct model of deregulated capitalism constitutes a threat to European nations.
>
> Emmanuel Todd, *Après l'Empire: Essai sur la décomposition du système américain* (2002), a best-selling book in France in 2002–03.[2]

> The French social model rests at the heart of the European social model. People from other continents expect that France will maintain the flame of this [great] social model.
>
> Centrist labor leader Nicole Notat, in Jean de Belot, ed., *Quelle ambition pour la France?* (2002).[3]

The supporters of France's current social and economic model argue that the high levels of unemployment and inequality, and declining job security which have characterized the nation since the late 1970s are dangerous imports which should be stopped at the border with a social democratic Maginot Line. This book argues that these problems are made in France, the product of good intentions, bad policies, and vested interests.

Among rich Western European and North American nations, France has the poorest record of job creation and the most dramatic increase in unemployment during the last quarter of the twentieth century – but the most impressive social-spending record, the most impressive record of labor-law innovations, and the second highest level of pension increases. French government spending increased from 46% of Gross Domestic Product (GDP) in 1980 to over 54% in 1998 – but poverty increased, income inequality remained high, and unemployment shot up from 1.50 million to 3.55 million, peaking, officially, at 12.6% in 1995. The labor-force participation rate fell faster than anywhere else in the rich world.[4] Youth unemployment reached 30% (officially) and youth *under*employment was, by some accounts, 75%.[5] By 2000, there were officially 4.5 million poor people in a nation of 60 million and there were another 5 million people living on the threshold of the poverty line.[6] The "big" state in the French style is not necessarily a "socialist" state. A socialistic society spreads costs and benefits, burdens and responsibilities, in a more equitable fashion than this. France was a more socialist nation in 1980 than it was in 2000.

Such a statement might seem counter-intuitive. After all, since the Second World War the French have constructed the world's third most expensive cradle-to-grave health and welfare system. Socialist governments ruled France for fifteen years between 1981 and 2002. Social spending increased by over 8% of GDP during these years. In 2000, the World Health Organization rated the French health-care system the best in the world and many French people would apply that ranking to the entire range of their social services.[7] Today, the French are firmly committed to the idea of the big welfare state; without it, they believe, social "exclusion" will increase, as it has in the United States.[8] Just as many Americans see a tax cut as a sure device to boost job creation and economic growth, most French people believe, as an article of faith, that increased "social" spending translates into an increase in solidarity and a decrease in inequality.

Like Canadians, a majority of French people will define themselves by contrasting their social security system with a negative vision of the American system.[9] Under the Socialist Prime Minister Lionel Jospin (1997–2002), the French state itself posed as a guiding light in a dark world threatened by "neoliberal"[10] politicians, the International Monetary Fund, and the World Trade Organization. This book argues that by linking France's problems to the challenge of "globalization," French politicians like Jospin encouraged French citizens to seek the culprits beyond their borders.[11] Partly as a result of this, France is psychologically and institutionally locked into inaction.

With rising crime and an unassimilated immigrant population rejected by the state and the market alike, France is in a state of crisis. In the 2002 presidential election, five million people cast ballots for Jean-Marie Le Pen, the leader of the xenophobic National Front party.[12] Almost three million people voted for Trotskyite and other far-Left fringe party leaders vehemently opposed to globalization.[13] Many French people believe that the nation is in need of immediate social, political, and economic reform.[14] Apart from the tendency to blame external forces for France's problems, why has reform proven so difficult? A key reason is that so many comfortable people resist change.

Crisis, what crisis?

From the outside looking in, the problems appear obvious and the solutions are readily visible. Of course the situation is not so cut and dried. There are millions and millions of people – the "insiders" – who are content and see no need for radical reform. If one focuses exclusively on the roughly 60% of French adults who have secure, life-long jobs and generous pensions, one will find overwhelming support for the French model. Despite a recent spate of alarmist books announcing France's imminent demise, France is not yet in terminal decline. The French private sector is still productive (though it has slipped in recent years), still vibrant enough to support the large tax base which makes the nation such a pleasant place for a majority of the population.[15] In certain areas, France has shown that it is capable of sweeping changes: the French private sector is far more dynamic and far less constrained by statism than it was twenty years ago. And certain French social policies are undoubtedly great successes, with lessons to teach other nations.

The French welfare state generally succeeds in securing the majority of French people against the risks of modern life – losing one's job, suffering financially from a serious illness or workplace accident, falling into poverty during old age, and so on. This is no small feat. Private insurance can never provide the sorts of financial guarantees that can come only from the state – Americans who pay large medical insurance co-payment fees can surely attest to this.

Full-time salaried jobs in France are well protected by labor laws which make arbitrary dismissal virtually impossible: surely this is a fundamental advance over the bad old days when workers with several years of experience could be dismissed in the blink of an eye.[16] If you are well educated, well paid, forty years old or older, and married with children, France is a super place to live – perhaps the best place in the world. Chances are, you have a job guaranteed for life and you enjoy three or four times as many paid vacation days as your North American counterparts.[17] Even as 2.5 million of your compatriots are without work, if you hold a salaried job you receive an extra 180 hours (a full month) of vacation per year but with no pay reduction, thanks to the 35-hour work-week law phased in during 2000–02.[18] Your children go, or will have gone, to an excellent state-funded daycare facility.[19] With the exception of the universities, public institutions are well funded. You can hop on a publicly subsidized high-speed train and traverse the country at 300 km/hour, from Lille to Marseille, in just four hours. You can take the regional express train and traverse Paris in forty minutes for two dollars; in London this takes twice as long and costs twice as much.

In France you have access to the world's best system of museums and you can also stroll through beautiful, well-preserved cities. You benefit from substantial tax breaks for having a large family (defined in France as three children and more). Your health-care coverage is also excellent and at times lavish; you can still seek a 'cure' at the spa at Social Security's expense. Most of your pharmaceuticals are covered at 75 to 100%, and you consume more than twice as many of them as your British counterparts (only the Japanese consume more pharmaceuticals than the French). The hospitals are well equipped – not quite up to the lavish standards of many US hospitals, but luxurious compared with Britain's aging, overstressed facilities. Unlike in Britain and Canada, there are very few waiting lists for surgeries. Most doctors are grossly underpaid by North American standards but they are equally well trained, and they still make house calls, covered by Social Security (the "Sécu"), even on Sunday nights. You see the doctor more often than your counterparts in other large European nations – seven times per year versus five to six times. At 9 to 10% of Gross National Product (GNP), French health-care spending puts it neck and neck with Canada, Switzerland, Germany, and Luxembourg as the runner-up to the USA in the health-care spending race.

Other popular social benefits include family allowances, daycare centers, and a wide array of housing subsidies and direct housing provision which benefit over one-third of the population. French housing subsidies are surely one of the most successful social programs in the West, and have been emulated by others. (Direct provision of housing in the form of high-rise towers is another matter altogether.) One-fifth of the housing stock in France has been built using public monies; in Canada and the US this figure has never reached 1%. Virtually free higher education (of varied quality) is available to two million people. If you are one of the lucky 135,000 people enrolled in the elite *grandes écoles* and other graduate schools independent of the overcrowded general university system, you may receive a stipend for attending and upon graduation a good job-for-life awaits you in the upper echelons of the civil service or the upper ranks of France's leading corporations. Public pensions are among the most generous in the world. Most middle-aged people do not have to worry about their retired parents' finances, and surely this is a good thing. Those who survive to the age of 58.5, which is the average age of retirement, can expect to live another twenty years (men) to twenty-four years (women) on large pensions financed by current workers' payroll taxes and through the general tax system.

Outside of Paris, with its high rents, the minimum wage (SMIC) approaches a living wage for a single person; this is obviously a good thing for those who benefit from it. During the mid 1990s the minimum wage of France was over 60% of the median wage; in the USA it was only 39% and in Japan it was just over 30%. In Britain there was no minimum wage until a few years ago and in North America, during the past three decades, the minimum wage has been increased once in every five or ten years, hence its value has been eroded substantially by inflation. In France, by contrast, the SMIC is usually raised every year to offset inflation, and top-ups ("coups de pouce") are not uncommon – in election years they are *de rigueur*.[20] Working life is generally less hectic in France than in the USA, with a shorter work week and stronger legal protections against abusive or unreasonable employers. In the USA, as it is said, people live to work. In France, people work to live – and the majority live quite well.

On the whole, the French economy is, like the US economy, a success story. Just as a study of those "excluded" from the fruits of the US economy would have to acknowledge that it serves the majority of the population very well, this study of the "excluded" from the French economy and social-welfare system acknowledges that the system works very well for the majority. But the majority's comfort rests on the strained shoulders of a less fortunate (and rather large) minority. In the US, the chief source of the discomfort is the market and its apologists in government; in France, the chief source of unemployment, poverty, and inequality are problematic public policies and the nation's very system of "solidarity." Most social benefits go to the richest half of society. Nevertheless, almost everyone receives *something*, and, it would appear, everyone wants more.[21] This is one of the keys to the persisting popular support for the high-taxing, high-spending French state. Many of the people who are comfortable willfully ignore the fact that their benefits come at the expense of the needy.

Responsibility for this state of affairs rests squarely on the shoulders of French politicians. During his five-year premiership, Lionel Jospin told the public that his chief mission was to *preserve* the "social market economy" and to resist the global pressures to adopt a "market society." He vowed to fight the onslaught of US-style "jungle capitalism."[22] Jospin said nothing about homegrown policy failures; that is, he said nothing about those things he had the power to change.

The USA is indeed home to a ruthless strain of capitalism and alarming income inequality, but much of France simply "isn't working." French leaders proclaimed their wish to resist the advent of US-style "McJobs," but did it follow, then, that a "social market economy" existed already in France? In the definition I use throughout this book, a "social market economy" is a full-employment economy (unemployment no higher than 5%, with very little long-term, structural unemployment, with a labor-force participation rate of around 70%). The term "social market economy" conjures up images of a dynamic, full-employment Western Europe during the 1960s or Scandinavia today. A "social market economy" is one in which the "social" and the "economy" are not in conflict.

France has not enjoyed full employment since the late 1970s. But France has a striking record of social policy innovations, and this is one of the reasons why most French people see their polity as something fundamentally different from and unquestionably superior to the US and British models. The large majority of the French population wants more state intervention in social and economic life. Two-thirds of French citizens fear that globalization threatens the French economic and social model – and perhaps this is because during the 1990s and early 2000s both main political parties told them precisely this, arguing that globalization needed to be "mastered" by states lest it destroy the European social democratic contract.[23]

But France's problems, like the USA's problems, are for the most part homegrown. Certain French public policies are failures caught in their own contradictions, collapsing under their own weight. To be sure, most French people – perhaps up to 60% of the entire adult population – are financially comfortable and well served by the economy or the pension system. Roughly two-thirds of the French labor force – those who work full time in permanent, well-protected jobs – is better protected against the vagaries of the market than in most nations. But since only 59% of the working-age population of France actually works, in fact only about 38% of the entire working-age population, aged eighteen to sixty-four, has a well-protected job. Their benefits, coupled with the benefits of retirees, who make up another 20% of the population, have come to define the essence of the French character. Their benefits are equated with "solidarity," with the French model itself. Up to 40% of the working-age population, however, is either poor, unemployed, or underemployed with access to limited social benefits, and this is no accident. French social policy is not geared towards the interests of those stuck in poverty and the 2.5 million unemployed (officially, over 9.5% of the labor force).[24]

Where does the money go? The vast majority goes to the rich and to the middle class, to the comfortably employed "insiders" (most of them middle-aged men); very little of it goes to the "outsiders" (the unemployed, low-income workers, the poor, youth, immigrants).[25] In addition, French retirees are the richest in the world (relative to current workers) and they retire much earlier than their counterparts in other major Western nations. *They* form the core of the welfare state's supporters, and since 1980 their wishes – not those of the 1.7 million working poor, single parents, the unemployed children of immigrants, the handicapped, struggling young families faced with high rents and low incomes – have driven the social policy agenda.

The USA and Canada have serious income inequality problems, non-existent or at best weak government support for low-wage families, a growing army of working poor, and poor public services such as transportation. To be sure, North America appears to be a "winner-take-all" market society, dominated by business elites and their political allies. France, by contrast, has a loser-suffer-all labor market and a winner-take-all welfare state.

The winners are vocal and skilled in the defense of their ideals and benefits. Only 9% of the French workforce is unionized (the lowest rate in the OECD), but unions have power far beyond their numbers since their representatives have, since 1945, been firmly entrenched, by law, in the nation's dozens of publicly supported, occupation-based (corporatist), social insurance funds. And union wage settlements are usually used as the template for collective bargaining in non-unionized settings, so the vast majority of the nation's non-unionized workers have their work done for them by proxy.[26]

Roughly one-quarter of the French public sector is unionized, and these men and women have learned that they have the power to stall social security reform by paralyzing the nation with political strikes. The worst possible punishment for these strikes (which, as non-wage related strikes and unconnected to a collective bargaining session, would be illegal in many nations) is the docking of a day's pay, but this is not an automatic penalty, since governments "negotiate" this with the unions after the fact. When union leaders take to the streets – as they do so frequently – they are armed with a powerful ideology, "solidarity."

Solidarity for everyone?

Solidarity was an idea born during the egalitarian phase of the French Revolution, when legislators proclaimed they had a responsibility – a "sacred debt" – to eliminate extreme poverty. France invented the idea of a *bienfaisant* state, committed to the introduction of old-age pensions, wage supplements, widespread access to primary education, and the guarantee of a "right to work," even if this meant digging ditches. The Revolution failed to deliver on these promises, and a more traditional and fatalistic view towards poverty resurfaced during the Restoration. In 1848, in the midst of yet another political upheaval in Paris, workers seized the state and tried to honor the Revolution's anti-poverty agenda and, most ambitiously, they put the "right to work" at the top of their priorities, only to fail once again.

Solidarity finally took root during the last decade of the nineteenth century, when the first social legislation, targeted at the poor, was introduced. In its late nineteenth-century formulation, solidarity was simply another word for redistribution: from the rich to the poor, from the able-bodied to the infirm, from wealthier regions to poorer regions.[27] The final goal was to create a level playing field for men, to create equality of opportunity (again, for men only), and to help those who were not in a position to help themselves. The original definition of "solidarity" stressed the *obligations* of the comfortable and the privileged to their less fortunate compatriots – not the *rights* of the comfortable themselves. The early solidarists viewed society as an interlocking series of webs binding individuals to families, their fellow citizens, and the state.

A country which practices solidarity would, in my definition (and in the traditional French definition), require regular sacrifice for the common good. A solidaristic society is one which redistributes wealth to low-wage earners and opens up the doors of social mobility. A solidaristic society pays the price for its solidarity in the here and now, instead of leaving the bill to future generations. A solidaristic society spreads risk (and jobs) equitably, instead of allowing risk, poverty, and unemployment to fall almost exclusively on the shoulders of one or two social or demographic groups.[28]

Solidarity requires trust, transparency, and civic-mindedness. Solidarity requires trade-offs and the politics of pragmatism. Solidarity, in the Swedish, Dutch, or Danish sense of the word, has been the product of slow, deliberate, civil discussions, negotiations, and compromises. Solidarity has required a certain amount of income redistribution, and, as in the Netherlands, Canada, and Sweden, periods of wage restraint in the name of job creation.[29] In a solidaristic society, citizens would pay their taxes willingly, and the tax system would be highly progressive, taking much more from the rich than from the poor. Income taxes on the super-wealthy would be high but not so high as to kill incentives. Taxes would be higher on unearned wealth, and monetary policy would not reward rentiers as a matter of course, but there would be tax breaks for venture capitalists who deliver jobs, as there are in Sweden. Tax evasion would not be commonplace, and the penalties for it would be severe – as in Finland. There would be a relatively egalitarian distribution of wealth. There would be very few poor people.

In a solidaristic nation, one segment of society (the retired and the elderly, or those aged fifty-nine and over) would not consume over 70% of all "social" spending – as they do in France. There would be something approaching equality of opportunity, and an open, meritocratic system of elite selection. Job opportunities for all age groups would abound.

Neither politicians nor the general public would allow unemployment to hover around 10% (officially) for over twenty years. Indeed, the gainfully employed would *demand* that the state put an end to this, even at the expense of sacrificing a little bit themselves. An open, dynamic labor market would permit people with unusual career paths to ascend the corporate ladder later in life – say, beginning in their thirties or even in their forties. There would not be a narrow process of selecting the nation's upper civil servants, and they would not be consecrated with "noble" status, held above the laws of merit, efficiency, and responsibility.[30] The sons and daughters of professionals and civil servants would not have their elevated *état* confirmed by the state itself, their good fortunes fixed in stone and sealed with the wax of a diploma from an elite, state-run finishing school. The graduates of said schools would not be hard-wired into the commanding heights of the market and the bureaucracy as a matter of state policy, at the tender age of twenty-five, even as the general youth unemployment rate has been 20 to 30% since 1980. The state, in short, would not train an aristocracy hiding behind a veil of meritocracy.

This definition of soldarity outlined above does not vary too much from the vision put forth by the French Socialists themselves during the 1970s and early 1980s.[31] But today, on every score, France (plus Italy and Spain and, in some ways, Belgium, Germany, Greece, and Portugal) would fail the test of solidarity. Of course, few nations would measure up, but some – Denmark, Sweden, the Netherlands, Canada, Britain, Australia – would meet some or several criteria. And yet . . . why is it that in Canada, the USA and in the UK, many people on the Left seem to have an image of France which is at odds with reality? Why do we characterize France as a solidaristic society? More importantly, why do most French people believe that they live in such a society?[32]

To a certain extent, because they have absorbed the solidaristic catechism; they have taken the hegemonic, mythic rhetoric of "solidarity" at face value. Politicians may rename the social affairs ministry the Ministry of National Solidarity, ex-cabinet ministers such as Elisabeth Guigou may declare her steadfast support for "solidarity" as she marches in the streets to defend the public sector's unfunded pensions (as she did in November 2002), and even the chameleon Jacques Chirac may declare the issue of "la fracture sociale" to be a key concern of his government (as he did during the 1995 presidential election and once again in October 2003), but this does not necessarily mean that "solidarity" is practiced.

Today the most vocal defenders of "solidarity" are public-sector workers and the members of the "special" pension funds (discussed in Chapter 2). The language of "solidarity" has been appropriated by the comfortably employed "insiders" – the very people who oppose reforms which might make a space for the outsiders. "Solidarity" talk bears little resemblance to its original nineteenth-century formulation and it does not correspond with the rhetoric and goals of the early 1980s.

Today solidarity usually means "security." Continued security, that is, for the one-quarter of the workforce (state employees) which has lifelong job security and "special" social benefits financed by the general, regressive tax system. From roughly 1980 to 2000, people seeking jobs lived in a Depression-style world, whereas gainfully employed people enjoyed comfortable raises, longer vacations, and a degree of job security most people can only dream of.[33] Since jobs became so well protected during the 1980s, employers found it easier to squeeze more productivity out of existing workers than to hire additional ones. This involved raising the drawbridge and digging a moat around those already in employment. Until recently, healthy economic growth was not translated into job creation.

French "solidarity" is better understood as state-mandated job protection and insurance. This is an entirely different thing than the redistribution of wealth. The post-transfer poverty rate in the EU in 2000 was highest in France, Britain, and Ireland, but job security in France was much higher than in these nations.[34] Job security, of course, is a great thing – provided that it can be delivered to the vast majority of people and provided it does not come at the expense of the very people who do not enjoy it. There is a trade-off, but it is seldom discussed by French intellectuals and politicians. French leaders have not been candid with the populace about the costs, by-products, and unintended consequences of "solidaristic" social policy.

The crisis of long-term unemployment and youth unemployment

The key unintended consequence of French social and economic policy is high unemployment. Long-term unemployment (a bout of joblessness lasting over one year) is an overlooked but key source of inequality. The scope of the problem is staggering.[35] In 1995, the French long-term unemployment rate was 45% (meaning that 45% of the unemployed had been so for at least one year), or six to nine times the Canadian and US rates of 8 and 5%, respectively.[36] Between 1985 and 1995, more than twenty percent of the unemployed of France had been out of work for a period of more than two years.[37] In North America, long-term unemployment has not exceeded 20% (of the unemployed population) since the Great Depression of the 1930s. Long-term unemployment of the French sort would be politically unacceptable in Canada, the USA,

Britain, Denmark, Switzerland, Japan, the Netherlands, and Sweden – nations which put a higher social value upon work.[38]

Unofficially, the real unemployment rate in France was probably in the neighborhood of 15 to 20% during the mid 1990s, as the labor-force participation rate plummeted. French politicians on the Left and Right alike blamed external forces for this. Labor leaders and intellectuals constructed a false dichotomy between "good" French-style jobs with high unemployment and "bad" US-style jobs with lower unemployment.

The situation was (and is) far more complex than this. From 1972 to 1996, the overall labor-force participation rate was on the rise in Canada, Norway, the Netherlands, Australia, and Denmark. These nations include some of the most "neo-liberal," "turbo-capitalist," and "solidaristic," egalitarian nations in the world. More people were working in these nations, and more work-hours were being clocked, even as unemployment was falling throughout the 1990s. France, by contrast, witnessed the complete opposite scenario, yet discussion of these nations is rare in France, as political elites prefer to hold themselves up to an American mirror.[39] It is not difficult to engage in self-congratulation when the USA is your yardstick for social solidarity. In light of the Swedish, Dutch, and perhaps even the Canadian experience, French social policy is much less effective at decreasing inequality and providing jobs.

Yet the French economy is not as sclerotic as Right-wing Anglo-American critics have portrayed it over the past decade. In fact, economic growth has been, on average, 2% per year since 1980, with some years witnessing growth below 1%, others seeing growth of almost 3%.[40] If high unemployment persists in the context of an economy which is indeed growing, then the fruits of economic growth are not being shared, and something is preventing that newly created wealth from being translated into new jobs.[41] In many ways, the French economy is dynamic and innovative, but a large portion of the population is excluded from the fruits of growth.

France did, however, become less and less productive during the 1990s: economic output per capita was eighth in the world in 1990; by 2002 it had slipped to eighteenth.[42] Most of the new social spending during the 1990s went to pensions and health care (two-thirds of health care is spent on the retired). Neither of these programs contribute as much to productivity as do family allowances and education, which saw substantial cuts. New monies were indeed devoted to job creation and subsidies (discussed in Chapter 4) but they made only a tiny dent in the unemployment crisis and they were overshadowed by spending on pensions and health.

If more and more money is being spent on things "social" (and, mainly on the upper-half of the income ladder) even as the economy is failing to deliver the goods to those most in need, then there is a problem.[43] As Amartya Sen writes in *Development as Freedom* (1999),

Given the massive scale of unemployment in contemporary European economies, the concentration on income inequality only can be deceptive. Indeed, it can be argued that at this time the massive level of European unemployment constitutes at least as important an issue of inequality, in its own right, as income distribution itself. An exclusive focus on income inequality tends to give the impression that Western Europe has done very much better than the United States in keeping inequality [in the widest sense] down . . . If unemployment batters lives, then that must somehow be taken into account in the analysis of economic inequality.[44]

The unemployment crisis is not addressed effectively by France's large welfare state; in any given year since the mid 1980s, 40 to 50% of jobless people have not qualified for unemployment insurance. Half of all those unemployed during the 1990s were aged twenty-one to thirty.[45] Neglected by market and state alike, many youth and immigrants and their children are tempted by vandalism and petty crime; this, in turn, plays no small role in stoking the fires of the far Right. Immigrants and their children are the most likely to be unemployed. They are the last hired and the first fired. They are also the most likely to live in public housing estates. They are a "problem" to many of the supporters of Jean-Marie Le Pen's racist National Front political party only insofar as they are linked to the unemployment crisis and the rise in "insecurity."

If France had a dynamic labor market it could absorb its immigrant population into the workforce, as it did during the 1920s, 1950s, and 1960s. Full employment would certainly not eliminate all racism in France, but it would obviously steal some of the wind out of the far Right's sails. If France had had an unemployment rate of 5 or 6% instead of the official rate of 9 to 10% in the early 2000s, vandalism and crime would have dropped as young men would have turned to work. Le Pen's fifteen years of fame (and 15% of the vote) would have dried up.

The French model itself is the leading cause of the current economic and social crisis. It has served not to diminish inequality and unemployment, but rather to institutionalize these scourges on both class and racial lines – a point which was admitted, in a roundabout way, by Prime Minister Lionel Jospin in a letter appended to an obscure 1998 government report on unemployment and labor costs in France. As Jospin wrote, "this tax on labor, most notably on low-skilled labor, probably constitutes a disincentive to the creation of jobs in our country."[46]

If Jospin had made hundreds of speeches and written dozens of newspaper articles on *this* topic (and on others, including red tape, high deficits which crowded out investment and made high interest rates necessary, an overvalued currency, wage inflation, and tight labor laws, which are discussed in the chapters which follow), instead of concentrating almost exclusively on the threat that "globalization" apparently posed to the French model, he would have done his nation a better service. The Left has washed its hands of any responsibility for France's current problems and set the terms of the debate in such a way that reform seems to threaten "civilization"; the Right has done little to change things, equally fearful of alienating the comfortably employed middle class, the "insiders." As Sophie Meunier has argued, the Right is equally responsible for a certain "double-talk" on globalization and a failure to reform. The extremists on both sides enter into the void.[47]

The origins of France's economic problems, then, have been well known to politicians for many years but they have not relayed the message to the public and set about correcting it.[48] In order to help the minority (a rather large minority) of the population trapped in unemployment, the comfortable majority would have to give up some of its comforts, including regular wage increases which, over the past twenty years, have outstripped the European and North American average. Later chapters argue, with French economist Denis Olivennes and journalist Alain Minc, that France *chose* high unemployment as a "solution" to domestic struggles for resources; the problem was not imposed from without French borders.[49]

Continental solidarity: a mirage?

European popular critics like Will Hutton (a Brit) are so determined to discredit the US model by concentrating on income inequality that they neglect to consider the lack of a market income as a key form of inequality in its own right (and critics like Hutton assume that all of those "excluded" from employment in Europe are helped with a generous system of unemployment insurance, but this book demonstrates that this is not the case).[50] Likewise, for two decades French (and German) state and labor leaders have operated under the assumption that no new jobs but high "social" spending is better than low-paid "McJobs" and lower state spending. It is an article of faith on the European Left and Right alike that the US economic model is far less egalitarian; therefore the dynamism associated with the US model should not be pursued.

This thinking is wrong on at least three counts: first, the USA has no monopoly on economic dynamism; second, dynamism and social cohesion are not mutually exclusive; third, France has a structural inequality problem which is invisible in studies of *income* inequality. Under 59% of French working-age adults work.[51] By contrast, the labor-force participation rate is over 73% in Sweden and the USA, and over 70% in Canada, Norway, Denmark, the Netherlands, and several other European nations, most of which have lower unemployment rates than France.[52] Today, the proportion of French people seeking work, as a percentage of those aged eighteen to sixty-four, is at an all time low, proving that the unemployment crisis is not the result of more women seeking to enter the workforce, and certainly not the result of the presence of immigrants, as some have claimed.[53]

To be sure, those who work in France tend to have high wages and better working conditions than in many other nations. But what if their high wages and job security come, to a certain extent, at the expense of high unemployment and the withdrawal of several million people from the labor market? If this is the case, then official measurements of inequality are inadequate. France's low participation rate points to the subject of later chapters, the unsustainability of the French welfare state: fewer and fewer people are working yet they are asked to assume the burdens of more and more dependent people.

Despite these obvious problems with the French model, to most Europeans it still seems preferable to (their understanding of) the Anglo-American alternative. To most people on the European Left (and to many on the Right as well), France and other European nations seem to have constructed more humane, less frenetic, and more generous labor markets than in North America and Britain. During the late 1990s and early 2000s, many French politicians presented themselves as a protective shield against the bad influences of "globalization" and American-style "neoliberalism."[54] The Left held regular conferences, as in Paris, in November–December 2003, at which they debated how to preserve "solidarity" in light of the US-led neoliberal agenda. Anti-globalization activists presented high public spending as a social good in its own right, *point final*. In late 2003, Philippe Frémeaux, the editor of *Alternatives économiques*, a leading magazine devoted to social issues and the anti-globalization movement, wrote, "any reduction in taxes will inevitably come at the expense of a reduction in the quality of public services or a lower level of solidarity towards the weakest" members of society.[55]

This book challenges this line of thinking. If redistribution is your goal (and it *is* the official goal of the French Left), the important thing is not the level of spending; it is the *type* of spending that matters most. The operating principle of the French Socialist party today – national (or European) "solidarity" versus global "neoliberalism" – is a false choice.

We might join the editors of *Alternatives économiques* and *Le Monde Diplomatique* and criticize the USA incessantly, but this will not help us to understand France's problems, nor will it solve them.[56] This book argues that if France wishes to tackle structural unemployment, it must indeed make sweeping changes, but it need not take a leaf from the US story. France might look instead at what the Dutch, the Swedes, the British, the Finns, the Canadians, and even the Germans have done recently. France can reform its welfare state, cut red tape, further reform its labor laws, increase its competitiveness, return to full employment, and poverty need not increase by a single person. But labor laws will have to be changed and social spending will have to be *reshuffled, reoriented*. And perceptions within France will have to change radically.

The marketplace tamed?

This sort of argument is never found on the French Left and only rarely is it heard on the Right. Since the market is such a distrusted entity, any critique of the state or of "the social" seems like a form of tacit or even direct support for its unattractive antithesis.[57] Since labor-market reforms originated in Thatcher's UK, change is associated with an unpopular foreign model. "Raffarin, c'est Thatcher," read the banners in the streets of Paris during 2003.

Many on the Left possess an urgent need to believe that the French version of solidarity constitutes a more humane alternative to the unequal Anglo-American way. In this view, Germany, with its "Rhineland," or "stakeholder" form of consensual capitalism placing long-term corporate interests and workers' interests ahead of stock market driven "short-termism," is also an exemplary alternative.[58] This book is not a study of Germany but there is a significant amount of comparative material on several nations, including Germany itself. With 12% unemployment in 2003 and an ossified labor market, the German model, which is very much like the French (and the Italian), also collapsed inward on itself during the 1990s. To a greater extent than in France, however, German politicians have been willing to discuss the shortcomings of their model, to commission a report which was highly critical of labor-market regulations, and to act, with positive results, in 2003, on (some) of its recommendations.[59] Germany is home to many of the world's leading Leftist critics of globalization, such as Ulrich Beck. But Beck's brew of globo-pessimism does not seem to have influenced the German Left to the same extent as French anti-globalist rhetoric swayed the Jospin government.[60]

Europeans' reflexive dislike of the US model, grounded in self-congratulatory clichéd views, leads to an equal and opposite misunderstanding of the European model itself. Many academic studies of European social policy accentuate the positive and ignore the negative. In this blurred vision, America (where 65% of all retirement income comes from Social Security, where over 40% of medical expenses are borne by Medicare and Medicaid, where public universities are the best in the world) is the barren desert landscape; Europe is the social garden of plenty. The typical French person on the street thinks that *all* social provision is in private hands in the USA, when in fact 55 to 60% of it is.[61] (By contrast, 15 to 30% of social provision is in private hands in Europe.) Many Europeans believe that *all* higher education in the USA is private; in reality only 20% of students are enrolled in "private" institutions (some of which obtain over one-third or even one-half of their revenues from public sources). Social policy nationalism is a clever ploy, distracting the European population from homegrown economic problems.[62]

With their public services crumbling at their feet, their health-care system starved of funding since the 1970s, and inequality on the rise, British critics can be forgiven for casting envious eyes across the Channel. Likewise, the US Left wing (what survives of this endangered species) displays the same tendency when it studies France and Germany.[63] According to several popular critics of North American political economy, European labor law and social policy have slowed down the apparently destructive side-effects of unregulated "turbo capitalism," thereby sparing the continent much of the social and familial breakdown which characterizes the USA, and which is apparently the result of American-style, dynamic capitalism, with its thin protection for workers.[64]

By contrast, centrist French economists like Edmond Malinvaud and Charles Goldfinger paint a picture of suffocating labor laws and excessive disincentives to work (welfare traps and high unemployment benefits available to some ex-workers).[65] Right-wing British and American editorialists liken the French welfare state to a runaway gravy train. Critics point to the exodus of 150 high tech and/or start-up, entrepreneurial firms to Southern England during the late 1990s, who fled in order to take advantage of lower payroll taxes, lower capital gains taxes, fewer government regulations, and, above all, more flexible labor laws.[66] Up to 300,000 French citizens live in Britain in order to avoid French capital gains taxes and various regulations on investment – or simply to find work, as is the case with most young French workers living in London. During the dot.com boom, over 45,000 French people worked in Silicon Valley. Symbolically, in 2002, Marianne herself (the supermodel Laetitia Casta, whose bust is the official symbol of the French Republic) took flight to London.[67]

The fear of playing into the Right's hands[68] prevents the European Left from being more self-critical and it has led to a dogmatic defence of the failed status quo. Just as the US Right has preached more market, more deregulation, less state as the solution for all problems, so too has the

French Left preached more state spending, more labor regulation, and more "solidarity" as the great panacea. Both camps have taken refuge in ideology.

No essential link connects low public spending and low unemployment – high-spending, low unemployment Netherlands and the Nordic countries (discussed in detail in Chapters 3 and 4) prove this point. I do not advocate a Right-wing, US-style "solution" to Europe's problems. Countries *can* have it both ways if they are willing to tolerate job destruction and then show a little creativity in helping with the retraining and reinsertion of workers.[69] And the big spending state *can* coexist with a dynamic economy open to world trade – witness the Netherlands and Sweden.[70] The important thing is what the big state is doing. Is it held captive by vested interests? Is it pursuing an active labor-market policy geared towards high levels of participation or is it paying people of working age to stay at home (France, Italy)? Is it trying to slow down the wheels of capital with constrictive labor laws (France, Germany, Italy), or does it tolerate the churn of capitalism and then seek to reintegrate the victims of corporate downsizing and technological change with an expensive, activist, and effective job placement and retraining system (Sweden, the Netherlands)?

Why France matters

A book which faults a nation for not being more like other nations is unlikely to find an audience – nor would it deserve one. Every country is different, with different political traditions and economic conditions. These variables are indeed considered in the pages that follow. If this book takes French politicians to task for failing to redistribute income it is because it measures the French welfare state against the high rhetoric of its supporters. French social policy is wrapped up, with much fanfare, in the seductive language of "solidarity," so any critique must engage with these assumptions.

The stakes are high: the problems are so serious that they threaten the short-term political stability and the long-term economic future of the French nation. France has the second largest economy in the European Union and the fifth largest economy in the world. France's problems can be found in many continental Western European nations. Indeed, it might be possible in several sections of this book to substitute "Germany" or "Italy" for France and the story would be much the same.[71] The crisis of the French welfare state, then, is tied up with a more general crisis of the entire European project. If France fails to reform, other nations will be more likely to procrastinate.

Long-term unemployment, rising child poverty, the looming crisis of insolvent pay-as-you-go pension systems, intergenerational inequality, and "special social rights" (an oxymoron *par excellence*) for some members of society are common European problems outside of Scandinavia and Britain.[72] Recent street protests against pension and labor-market reform in Greece, Portugal, Austria, and Italy illustrate the general continental European trend.[73] Today, most European nations have unfunded pension promises (pension liabilities) which equal the debts they had in the years following the First World War. But today taxes are so high in Europe (at 40 to 50% of GDP as opposed to 15 to 25% of GDP in 1918) that they cannot be raised substantially, as they were during the 1920s, to pay for these debts. Hence the urgency of reform.

Reform is not a sure recipe for increased inequality but it will certainly require that people who for decades have enjoyed publicly subsidized privileges give some of them up in the name of the common interest.[74] This is precisely what most French labor leaders have failed to support, as witnessed by the strikes against Prime Minister Raffarin's timid reforms of 2003.

Almost everyone receives something from the European welfare state – this is indeed its great strength. In most Western nations, universalism (from stingy US Social Security to generous Swedish solidarity) has been the price required to bring the wealthy on board the welfare train. In France, far too many poor people receive much less than they need and many wealthy people take far more out of the welfare state than they put in. Rectifying this situation need not lead down the path of targeted, stigmatizing, residual US-style social programs. The universalist welfare state, providing benefits to all, can be retained: it might also be reoriented in the name of *solidarity*, by introducing sliding-scale universalism, whereby everyone receives something, but the poor receive more than the rich and the middle class. In order to achieve this, the power of the "social partners" must be challenged.

As Chapter Two argues, many of today's funding problems can be traced back to the 1940s, when the ambitious reforms proposed by men like Pierre Laroque were blown off course. During the 1940s, French leaders flirted with British-style universalism and Swedish-style redistributive solidarity only to be outflanked by the insular, selfish representatives of corporatism. In 1945, the French movement for social democracy reached a potential turning point and failed to turn.

2   Corporatist welfare states: the residue of the past, or the wave of the future?

As the nation grew objectively richer, it felt subjectively poorer. Why? If government is "poor," if it is unable to "afford" things, that is because of its inability to unlock resources from entrenched claimants and reallocate them for new needs. It is not poor; it is paralyzed. It is not malnourished; it is maladaptive. It is trapped in its own past, held there like Gulliver in Lilliput by a thousand ancient commitments and ten thousand committed clients . . . Not only are programs virtually impossible to kill, but once put in place they are also hard to change. Every wrinkle in the law, every grant formula and tax loophole, produces a winner who resists subsequent reform, unless "reform" happens to mean more money or benefits for the lobbies concerned.

Jonathan Rauch, commenting on the USA,
in his book *Government's End* (1994).[1]

Today, there are three Frances. First, there are those whose jobs are guaranteed for life and who don't do much of anything . . . let alone create any wealth for the nation. These are the functionaries, who have replaced the aristocracy of years gone by. Naturally, they are as frightened as the nobles must have been on the eve . . . of August 4 [1789, when the nobility's privileges were abolished]. Then, there are those who have a job, who work, who create wealth. Finally, there are all those who are "excluded" from everything, the unemployed, the illiterate, foreigners, those on welfare, those forgotten and despised.

Thierry Desjardins, *La décomposition française* (2002).[2]

The idea of rights implies that my rights are equal to yours. If rights aren't equal, they wouldn't be rights, just a set of privileges for separate groups of individuals.

Michael Ignatieff, *The Rights Revolution* (2000).[3]

During the last fifteen years, sociologists and political scientists, have, following the lead of Gøsta Esping-Andersen, drawn maps of Western welfare states.[4] In this conceptual universe, there are three main galaxies of welfare-state regimes, although recently some experts claim to have discovered a fourth.[5] The most egalitarian group is comprised of the social democratic, universalistic welfare states of Scandinavia, where the ideal of solidarity shines brightest. These nations are characterized by high income taxes, social services of the highest common denominator provided to almost all citizens on equal terms, low levels of income inequality, virtually no poverty, low levels of unemployment, and high levels of female participation, usually in the public sector. The public purpose is geared towards the prevention of poverty and the employment of everyone who wishes to work. As we shall see in Chapter 4, to this end, the Scandinavian (and Dutch) people have accepted the need for the regular reconfiguration of their social and economic policies, whether this has taken the form of more part-time work, government spending cuts, wage restraint, partial privatization of the health-care system, or the introduction of supplementary private pensions.

The other extreme is the North American liberal-residual welfare state regime which uses social policy at the fringes, as a measure of last resort. The labor market is relatively unfettered and private interests provide more "social" benefits (pensions, daycare, medical insurance). In short, public policy is geared towards dissuading working-age people from relying on the state. Taxes are lower, labor laws are weak, inequality is higher, but jobs are abundant. The public purpose is geared towards economic growth but the distribution of that growth is left to chance – or, as of late, rigged in favor of high earners, who see their taxes cut year after year.

In the middle group stands France, along with Austria, Italy, and Germany, the other "corporatist"[6] or "continental conservative welfare states" (Spain, Greece, Portugal, and Belgium share many of the traits of this model as well). Some argue for the existence of a fourth, distinct group of "Mediterranean" welfare-state regimes, distinguished by heavy indebtedness, overspending on pensions, low spending on the family, high levels of youth unemployment, and a large black market. There is considerable overlap between these "Mediterranean" welfare-state regimes and the French model.

In the corporatist/continental conservative and Mediterranean model, social benefits and labor laws solidify status distinctions. Unlike in Canada or the UK, most social services are not administered by a single provider (the national or provincial government) on equal terms to all citizens; rather, they are provided by intermediary bodies (corps) and are in some way linked to one's occupational status, or to a particular insurance fund with which one is affiliated. "Corporatism" also denotes a system of labor relations in which business interests, state officials, and labor meet regularly, in an extra-parliamentary setting, to negotiate wages, social benefits, and other issues.[7] France does not fall into this particular category, but the term "corporatism" is indeed used widely by the French themselves due to the existence of occupation-based social funds, therefore I retain the term in this text.

In the corporatist/continental conservative welfare states, taxes and spending are almost as high as in Scandinavia, but unemployment is much higher, income inequality is substantially higher, and female labor participation is lower (especially in Germany and Italy). In some ways, the corporatist model is geared towards the prevention of the social disruption caused by rapid economic change. This is an admirable ideal but in practice it has often translated into the protection of existing workers at the expense of aspiring ones.

In the French system, benefits are indeed widespread but not universal in nature; different occupations have bargained (and gone on strike) for more favorable deals within the welfare state: the self-employed, civil servants, teachers, highly paid professionals or *cadres*, farmers, miners, merchant sailors, train conductors, and so on. Since they consist of a multitude of separate but unequal social insurance funds, corporatist welfare states run the risk of being hijacked by the most powerful, vocal, or disruptive interests in society, the skilled and organized male workforce, the solidarity aristocracy.

A key assumption in much of the literature on comparative welfare-state typologies is that French-style corporatism is a *self-financing* system of "professional solidarity," to use the words of one critic.[8] The various special pension regimes are closed clubs, indeed, but only where benefits are concerned: they are financed by outsiders through annual taxpayer bail-outs. This runs counter to any notion of *solidarity*, and smacks more of corporatist privilege, of rent-seeking.

Generally speaking, income redistribution is not the guiding principle of corporatist/continental conservative welfare states even if the rhetoric of redistribution is commonly heard. This is not an iron law – Germany manages to redistribute more national income than France – but a general pattern discernable in other nations (Italy, Spain). The distinguishing feature of the model since the 1980s has been unusually high long-term, structural unemployment which hits youth, women, and immigrants hardest, high benefit levels for middle-aged men (with, apparently, the assumption that they will share these benefits with their unemployed family members), and a reduction in the labor-force participation rate through early retirement. The corporatist/continental conservative model defies the traditional notion of an efficiency–equality tradeoff since it often fails on both counts.[9] The French welfare state "maintains incomes more than it redistributes them."[10]

For those concerned with reducing *risk*, this is, of course, better than nothing. It is certainly better than the US model. Without publicly supported and supervised health-care insurance, for instance, many French people would probably have trouble gaining access to costly medical care. But other nations provide such basic public services to protect against life's risks, and they do it in a far more efficient and egalitarian manner, and through a far more progressive taxation system. As in Canada, they do it on simple, transparent, privilege-free terms.

When *privileges* are won, they are, by definition, won by the most powerful (and/or potentially disruptive) members of society: the people with the power to stop the trains and turn out the lights. The 4.5 million poor people of France have no privileges. The key purpose of French (and Italian, and German) social policy is to ensure status continuity and to protect the "droits acquis" of those born before 1950. The French welfare state is a middle-and upper-middle-class welfare state, not a working-class welfare state. It is a pensioners' state, not a pro-youth state. It is a protection system for those already employed, not a full-employment state. It is concerned primarily with protecting jobs, not in allowing or helping the market to create (and destroy) them in the first place.

The rebirth of the old regime: corporatist welfare states

The protection of one-quarter of society at the expense of the rest is not redistributive solidarity in practice. The fact that the source is "the public" (which generally has good connotations in France) instead of "the private" (which is generally distrusted) does not necessarily mean that the general good is served. In fact, the special pension regimes and the public sector's "special" social benefits are a drag on the French economy, a burden on the highly taxed, modestly paid private-sector workers who must subsidize them. The special regimes violate the idea of equality of citizenship.[11]

Indeed, since the 1940s, the French welfare state has resurrected a society of privileged *corps*, with separate and unequal categories of citizens, anchoring "social" privilege at the very heart of the nation's political economy.[12] But if one opens most historical textbooks on modern France, one will see no trace of this corporatist residue.

For at least two generations, historians have taught that the French Revolution swept away the old corporate order, with the workers' guilds and the special privileges of the nobility being two of the greatest losers. They argue that the Revolution inaugurated the world of nineteenth-century laissez-faire liberalism, in which legal privilege was gone, in which labor and capital were bound only by the cash nexus, in which the "medieval rubbish" which had gummed up the economy was swept clear, once and forever. This is certainly accurate in the general sense, and the nineteenth century was indeed the highwater point of laissez-faire capitalism. But scattered cells of corporatism survived and during the 1940s they recombined and implanted themselves at the heart of the expanding social services. The post-war welfare state violated several of the cardinal tenets of the French Revolution: equality under the law, equality before the taxation system, and an end to special categories of citizens. With our eyes fixed on the past, the historical profession has been blind to the present: the *Ancien Régime* is alive and protesting in the streets.[13]

The key difference is that today the people who enjoy privileges have cloaked them with a universalistic ideology. The corporatist welfare-state model, like the liberal laissez-faire model, is grounded in a fiction: the privileges of a minority are presented as potential benefits for all – do not criticize the American millionaire, you might become one yourself; do not begrudge the special benefits of the French upper-level *cadre*, post-office clerk or railroad worker, they stand at the avant-garde of all things social, a model for others around the world seeking solidarity. This book challenges this line of thinking. What instruments we have agree: the distance separating Sweden and France is greater than that which separates France from the USA. A brief discussion of the special benefits enjoyed by the public sector will illustrate what I mean: in no other nation is the public sector so privileged.

Solidarity for the special

Some 25 to 30% of the French retiree population belongs to the public sector pension fund or to the various "special regime" pension funds like that of the RATP (Paris' bus and metro system), the SNCF (the national railway system), and the Bank of France. The three dozen major "special" funds are all insolvent. Some of them have one contributor for thirty pensioners (the general tax system and the private-sector pension fund bails out these regimes).

The 30% slice of the population affiliated with the public sector and special regimes consumes 60% of the nation's annual pension costs, twice their share in a world of truly equitable pension disbursements. The remaining 70% of the retired population, affiliated with the main pension fund for private-sector workers, accounts for only 40% of pension costs, but it has been subsidizing the insolvent special regime pension funds for decades. In general, whether one belongs to the special regimes or to the main public- or private-sector fund, professionals and other workers on the upper third of the income ladder tend to be the best protected.

Similar inequalities can be found in the nation's unemployment insurance funds, which favor older, better-paid workers over the young and the low paid; in the nation's family benefits, which favor the wealthy with large families over poor, single-parent households with one child; and in the tax system in general, which is riddled with loopholes for the wealthy.[14] Some of the other special "rights" at the heart of French social policy include special family allowances, free or subsidized housing and extra pension credits for civil servants, and free supplementary medical insurance for some workers. For decades, EDF (the national electricity company) workers have enjoyed access to up to fifty supplementary forms of payment and bonuses, upon which social security taxes are not levied: these include a two-month salary bonus for employees who marry and a 95% reduction in employees' electricity bills. EDF goes to great pains to *hide* these publicly funded privileges from the public eye, which proves that the company is aware of their anti-solidaristic nature.

SNCF (railroad) workers can stay in ski chalets in the Alps owned by the company's labor council (*comité d'entreprise*) for about one-fifth the cost of a normal vacation plus their trip via rail is free (including the fares of relatives and children). SNCF employees are entitled to eighteen free trips within Europe per year. The SNCF's annual debt, paid by taxpayers, is equivalent to 1% of GNP; this is equivalent to the salaries of 650,000 workers paid the minimum wage.[15] Bank of France employees benefit from low-interest mortgages and low-rent apartments.[16] Several cities own apartments which they provide at highly discounted rents to their upper-level employees. The Parisian transit system's *comité d'entreprise* owns a château, twenty vacation centers, twenty-four restaurants, and two vacation parks.

The absentee rate in the public sector is twice as high as the private sector. Salaries are typically 20 to 30% higher in the civil service (except at the very top levels of management) and civil servants benefit from a wide array of tax exemptions.[17] The French public sector is the European leader in strike days: whenever a government proposes trimming costs, vested interests wrap themselves in the language of solidarity and resist reform. The streets fill with marchers hoisting banners vowing to defend a certain "French-style public service." The "public" is presented as "social," no matter how egregious the perks involved, and many people are convinced. If France is a "blocked society" here is the reason.

Overall, and in comparison with similar nations (Germany, for example) there are an estimated 500,000 to 1,000,000 too many public-sector workers in France. It is impossible to fire a French civil servant. The public sector in Sweden is slightly larger than the French, but the jobs in Sweden tend to be useful in that most of them meet a real social need and these jobs are funded, in the first place, by highly progressive taxes, not French-style regressive taxes. The French public sector, by contrast, is awash in sinecures. Typical is the Ministry of Agriculture, which increased its workforce by 3% between the late 1980s and late 1990s, even as the number of farmers fell by 500,000 over this period. The Bank of France has twice as many employees per capita than the central banks of every other large OECD nation.[18] Any proposal to cut the public sector is presented by the unions like FO and the CGT as an attack on "solidarity." Where does this sentiment originate?

During the 1930s, unions expanded rapidly in the public sector and they bargained (and struck) for better "social" benefits. By the 1940s, the public sector had become the spiritual home of solidarity. At this time, the private sector had become so thoroughly discredited, so guilty by association with the Depression and the failure to withstand the Germans, that the public sector came to embody the very spirit of the nation. Today, this ideal has been perverted beyond recognition, since the public sector no longer stands at the avant-garde of economic progress. But the state is still associated with the economic glory days, the *trente glorieuses*, so proposals which seem to threaten "the public service" are still seen, as Jacques Chevallier reminds us, as "acts of sacrilege."[19] Since France's unusually expensive public sector requires high taxes and deficits to sustain it, it bears down on the over-taxed, over-regulated private sector and contributes to the high unemployment rate.

There are a startling number of redundancies: for example, French taxes are assessed by one agency and collected by another. No other European nation does this. A proposal to fuse the two agencies during the late 1990s caused an uproar, so it was abandoned. The cost of collecting taxes in France is *six times higher*, as a percentage of GDP, than in Sweden and the USA. Several ministries resist computerization and remain highly overstaffed and inefficient.[20] The trains run on time (provided they are running at all) but the labyrinth of bureaucracy in France can hardly be considered efficient. Red tape keeps bureaucrats employed and business expansion stalled. The public sector airs its disputes in the street, while the weak parliament stands on the sidelines. The general public is the loser.

A brief historical sketch

How has corporatist privilege become so strong, so firmly embedded in French economy and society? No one alive in 1914 could have predicted it: the debates over social insurance in France prior to 1914 were grounded in a widespread distrust of German-style special social legislation for workers, which, critics claimed, targeted certain categories of citizens for special treatment. According to the republican vision of the French Revolution, intermediary bodies (*corps*) should not intervene between state and citizen. Only those deemed to be less-than-full citizens (women, children) might conceivably be singled out for special treatment, and indeed they were, as of the 1870s. By the 1890s, indigent men were added to this formula. But prior to 1930, there were no significant social programs singling out male workers – as there were in Germany since the early 1880s and in Britain since 1911. Unlike these two nations, France never had a national poor law, and during the nineteenth century many French politicians prided themselves on this. In 1920, the social programs of several American states, including New York, Massachusetts, and Wisconsin, were more advanced and effective than those of most French departments (the ninety political-territorial units somewhere between a county and a region in size).[21]

Between 1893 and 1913, legislation was passed providing medical assistance to the indigent at the local level and modest pensions for the elderly indigent, accident insurance for industrial workers, maternal leave benefits for working women, and bonuses to large families. A 1910 pension law failed due to worker opposition and court challenges. In 1914, France's social programs reached only a fraction of the population and they were not expensive by any means. There was one key exception: in the realm of child and maternal welfare, France was a pioneer. A few large cities constructed maternalist welfare states – but all of this took place within the context of a state which spent one-fifth as much GNP as it does today.

France was not a laggard, but simply an average European spender on social welfare. The French surpassed the European average for social welfare spending in 1933 and they caught up with the British by roughly 1939, but they were still far behind the Germans.[22] In 1950, only Denmark, Britain, Sweden, and Norway covered at least 70% of the population with a comprehensive social umbrella, including health insurance, pensions, unemployment insurance, accident and disability insurance, and so on. France reached this stage during the early 1970s. Until the 1960s, France's traditional, residual poor-relief networks funded by cities and departments were very active.[23] National unemployment insurance appeared in France only in 1958, twenty years after it appeared in the USA and Canada, and fifty years after it appeared in Britain. (For a list of France's major social legislation between 1893 and 2003 see the Appendix.)

Two decades of scholarship by revisionist historians has succeeded in dispelling the notion that France lagged behind other European nations with similar levels of wealth, urbanization, and proletarianization. By the same token, the unusually big welfare state in France is scarcely thirty years old – hardly a national institution rooted in the deepest recesses of the French spirit. Fears that reorienting, recasting, or even simply cutting social spending by a few points of GNP will threaten the French social contract are not grounded in an accurate reading of recent history.

The burden of war

After the First World War, Europe entered a new social policy universe. Over 1.4 million French lost their lives to the war. To a much greater extent than in North America, the survivors of the battlefields and the dependents of the dead would now have to be provided for by the state. Invalided veterans already enjoyed the right to medical care and pensions, but they gained considerable benefits at this time. In total, one million invalided soldiers and civilians plus their 630,000 dependents, 680,000 widows, and 760,000 *orphelins de père* were provided with costly medical–social programs. By 1939, 10% of the French population received a war-related pension, representing 16% of national tax revenues. In Germany, war pensions consumed almost one-third of the national budget by 1925.

As in Germany, social solidarity in France was born of suffering, simple necessity as well as idealism. The First World War brought privation and misery to the lower-middle class; this, coupled with France's weak private insurance industry, would cause them to seek the security of the state. *La charité d'hier c'est la justice d'aujourd'hui*: as the urban poor benefitted more from social assistance during and immediately after the war, others realized that perhaps they might have an interest in gaining similar benefits. The erosion of lower-middle-class economic power was not, of course, a singularly French problem. The problem was far more acute in Weimar Germany.[24] Between the Two World Wars, European nations opened their social umbrellas wider, making space for more and more citizens.

By 1920, prices had risen 400% over 1914 ones, ruining lower middle-class savings and fixed incomes. The task of reinserting unemployed demobilized soldiers into the workforce was not an easy one, especially in light of industrial and agricultural stagnation. Labor unrest rose, and while many elements of the organized labor movement gained as a result, this had the effect of driving a wedge between organized workers and the "new poor" living on stagnant or declining incomes.

A stronger, albeit splintered, socialist labor movement entered the political arena and put pressure on all political parties to deliver the social goods. The class conflict accelerated and became institutionalized as the Socialist party became a potent political force during the 1920s. But the Left was divided (as it would be right up to the 1980s) even as the majority of French voters chose a Left-wing deputy from the late 1920s right up through the 1970s. Moderate politicians attempted to buy "social peace" with social legislation. Municipal and national civil servants succeeded in bargaining for more generous pensions and for family allowances between the wars, setting a precedent for occupation-based social insurance and setting the tone for the post-Second World War period.[25] As labor unions entrenched in the public sector gained special benefits between the wars, they made it more likely that, in the postwar era of nationalized industries, these benefits would spread as the state expanded into various sectors of the economy.

French employers set up family allowance programs for a variety of reasons: out of a paternalistic Social Catholic sense of justice or social order; out of a fear of depopulation; in the hope that such programs might divide labor unions, relieve wage pressures, shore up the labor supply and/or forestall national, compulsory programs. In the end, voluntary programs, whether company-led or *mutuelle*-led, were the genie let out of the bottle: they would raise expectations and show the nation that nationally mandated, compulsory programs were possible.

The decline in the French birth rate coupled with fears of another war with Germany eased the passage of national family allowance legislation in 1932. Concerns over sexual equality were secondary; assistance to mother-workers would help to boost the size of the workforce, which suffered from chronic labor shortages, and allowances might also help to reconcile French women with work (the female labor participation rate was unusually high in France). Whatever the inspiration, French family policy blazed new trails, and firmly established itself as the cornerstone of the welfare state for the next three decades.[26] In 1932, French family allowances were among the world's most generous.

Between the wars, social reformers enjoyed their first successes at the local level, as cities dominated by center-left and socialist politicians built up mini-welfare states.[27] The next step was to translate these successes to national legislation. Interest groups ranging from Catholic pronatalist associations to the national association of mayors, and the new national association of hospitals emerged as allies to champion important causes like health insurance for workers, family allowances, and public housing, and they succeeded in convincing politicians of all political stripes to spend more. Mutual aid societies run by workers at the local level and by workers' parties themselves jumped into the fray, claiming a key spot in the administration of new social programs, establishing the basic framework for the post-Second World War social security administration (i.e., a fragmented, occupation-based one, with insurance funds, or *mutuelles*, run by unions and led by elected union representatives).

Hospital care was extended by several French municipalities during the mid-1920s on the grounds that the war had created "new poor," victims of war-induced inflation who could afford neither a medical visit nor a stay in a clinic.[28] State-mandated insurance was seen as an instrument to "reliev[e] the misery of the middle class."[29] This lies at the heart of the origins of the ambitious 1928 law and can explain its success and its extension to millions more people by 1940. The same phenomenon occurred in the United States and Britain during the 1930s, only it was the spread of private health insurance which helped parts of the American and British middle class cope with rising medical costs.[30]

By the beginning of the Second World War, over twenty million Frenchmen and women had medical insurance – over 50% of the entire population. New hospitals were built and old ones were renovated using general tax revenues. Where medical insurance is concerned, France was now on par with Britain, if not ahead, given that workers' dependents were also covered by the bill – a glaring omission in the 1911 National Insurance Act. Although the new program was a far cry from universal health insurance and it had many critics at the time, it was a significant step: only 6% of the population (2.2 million people) had ever qualified for state-funded health care, of any sort, before 1914.[31]

The health insurance system was financed mostly out of employer/ employee payroll taxes, not out of general tax revenues. Still, the state was now using general tax revenues to train thousands more doctors and tens of thousands of new nurses, and to establish important new public health clinics and various other municipal social institutions. For instance, half a million people were treated annually by Paris' public health clinics by 1925; this constituted an important form of redistribution. Some cities paid for one-quarter of patients' out-of-pocket expenses.[32]

In a sense, this was the highwater point of social and income redistribution in French history: several social services were being provided to only one-half the population, but the entire nation was contributing towards them through the various forms of taxation of the time. To be sure, taxation was overwhelmingly regressive in nature (meaning it took a disproportionate share of the poor's income), but the tax system remained so during the 1940s and 1950s as the social security system was expanded. The Interwar period was indeed a time when the middle class and the upper-middle class were willing to pay for, but not benefit directly from, the nation's emerging social programs and public health facilities. Their generosity (or, perhaps, *complacency*, in the face of governmental actions) would evaporate at the end of the Second World War. Once the working class and lower-middle class were covered by the law, it was only a matter of time before those above them on the income ladder would see a good thing and ask to join – on their own terms.

Administrative complexity

Between the hatching of the insurance bill in 1920 to 1921 and the implementation of the program in 1930, interest groups intervened to redirect the course of reform. The social insurance bill passed in April 1928 and was put into effect two years later after it had been amended to mollify the mutual aid sector, doctors and business leaders, all of whom put up fierce opposition.[33]

The social insurance law was the Magna Carta of the French welfare state. As Paul Dutton argues, after 1945 reformers "had little choice but to build their edifice on top of [its] foundations. They could use new materials, build higher, and add many more rooms, but the outlines of the old structure would always be visible."[34] The state accepted the French medical profession's sacred "charter," drawn up in 1927, and still in force today. The charter states that French health-care policy rests upon the principle of "médecine libérale" – that is, freedom of physician choice, freedom to prescribe medications, fee-for-service payment, and direct payment by the patient to the doctor for (most) services rendered. To this day, no French government has been able to alter these four commandments.

The health insurance law came with a great deal of red tape attached. Here were planted, inadvertently, the seeds of administrative complexity which bedevil French governments today in their efforts to curb costs. The 1928 law created a corporatist, German-style system of micro-bureaucracies, providing benefits according to one's spot in the occupational order of things – one's profession, one's *corps*. Today, this would strike many people, born into a world of NHS and Canadian Medicare-style single-payer health systems, like a costly, byzantine way to run a health-care system, and indeed it was. (Today, there is one general health fund, the Sécu, but there are still dozens of supplementary medical insurance funds, the *mutuelles*, and there is still a great deal of administrative complexity, with no clear lines of demarcation and no firm government control, in the British fashion, from the top.)

Under the authoritarian Vichy regime, each and every major social program of the Interwar years was expanded, particularly those targeted at the family (although Vichy had a guide in the form of the pronatalist

Code de la famille passed shortly before the war began). Under Vichy, the number of *assurés sociaux* increased by over one million persons.[35] Vichy also passed legislation which opened the public hospitals up to all citizens, no matter their wealth, and this legislation remained on the books – and was trumpeted by politicians – after the war.

This, then, is a rough sketch of the state of affairs when France emerged from the Second World War. France had a solid, entirely normal (by European standards) welfare state. France had a fiscally sustainable social service sector in 1945 and even as late as 1960. Prior to 1970, the welfare state was a complement – not a competitor – to the marketplace, since it built up human capital and helped to grease the wheels of capitalism. How and why have the French come so far so fast? From a historian's perspective, seen in the *longue durée*, an unusually large and expensive system of social welfare is not firmly rooted in the French past.

Looking abroad, looking ahead

During the 1940s, French social reformers sought to catch up with other nations, looking abroad for positive models to emulate. The Beveridge Report of the UK (a 1942 policy blueprint which sold 800,000 copies and inspired social policy reformers around the world) "was a constant reference-point in the French debate." Beveridge called for the British state to maintain full employment (3% unemployment or lower), to provide family allowances, decent pensions, to expand access to secondary education, and to provide a national health service. The French Resistance, including the followers of de Gaulle, such as Pierre Laroque (soon to be France's leading social reformer), and Alexandre Parodi (future Minister of Labor), were in London during the war, where they imbibed Beveridge's heady idealism and the even more potent ideals brewing in the British Labour Party. Parodi addressed the Consultative Assembly in July 1945: "all the countries of the world . . . are striving to set up a system of social security for their workers and sometimes even for their entire populations. France must also prepare such a system. . . ." The Socialist party, pointing to Beveridge, warned that France "should not be left behind."[36] In the end, the direct influence of Beveridge's plan on French legislation was minimal, but the knowledge of the ambitious British reforms surely reminded the French just how far they would lag if they did not reform in one way or another.[37]

Like their counterparts in other major European nations, French reformers such as Ambroise Croizat hoped that universalistic social policy (with its equal treatment of poor and middle class, not to mention the administrative streamlining and economies of scale that come with such systems) would be an important element in the postwar settlement. Within three years, their hopes were dashed.

Professionals, the self-employed, skilled workers centered in the public sector, and the middle class in general torpedoed legislative attempts at Beveridge-style universalism and Swedish-style redistribution. In 1947, Roger Millot founded the *Comité national de liaison et d'action des classes moyennes* for the sole purpose of uniting professionals and the self-employed in an effort to thwart redistributive, universalistic social legislation. Baldwin writes: "Universalist reforms in France . . . were motivated by ambitions to aid the poorest directly at the expense of the better-off. The resistance marshaled by those negatively affected was more than a match for the political muscle of reformers."[38]

In a sense, French reformers like Laroque tried to graft the high ideals of the universalistic welfare state onto a particularistic, insular workforce, still colored by its corporatist past, and this British import was soundly rejected by the chief organs of the labor movement and professional associations alike. Group after occupational group resisted the call to universalistic, redistributive solidarity – then, at a later date, joined on terms as favorable as possible to themselves. Layer upon layer of occupation-based regimes were established, including the ones for *cadres* (their insurance fund dates from 1947), artisans, liberal professions, and *commerçants* (1948), and farmers (1951), who got their own special pension regimes when they realized that their own self-interests could be best served by pooling together in a state-sanctioned and supported, occupation-based insurance fund. The model inspiring all of this was not Beveridge-style universalism, nor was it a Swedish-style redistributive form of universalism. The model was, on the contrary, the special benefits enjoyed by upper-level French civil servants.[39]

When attempts to introduce redistributive universalism had clearly failed, French reformers would have to settle for one main health insurance fund and the supplementary *mutuelles*, plus dozens of separate occupation-based pension funds. The law of 17 January 1948 called for a system of separate and unequal pension systems for the various categories of the self-employed.[40] Several occupational categories held out until the 1960s and 1970s before they joined.[41]

Very few people gave up anything in 1945–48. Income was not redistributed the way it was in other nations. Progressive income taxes were the product of the 1940s in Canada, the USA (where the top marginal rate hit 70% by the 1970s), Britain and Sweden (where top marginal rates hit 90%), but not France, where the income tax on the wealthy had about one third as much bite. Pre-war corporatist perks enjoyed by the French civil service remained, and indeed grew stronger, and were won by other privileged groups, including the workers of many of the newly nationalized firms and industries of the 1940s.[42]

The UK's new welfare state was not, of course, some form of social paradise. Flat-rate, 1940s Beveridge-style benefits were seductively solidaristic at first sight, but decidedly bourgeois and non-redistributive upon closer examination, since they also entailed flat-rate contributions. Nevertheless, flat-rate universalism, à l'anglaise, was and is a more transparent, more efficient, less privilege-ridden way than French-style corporatism to administer social policy. Coupled with Britain's progressive income taxes, this was a small but clear step in the direction of egalitarianism.

In France, all were taxed more, but the tax system remained fundamentally regressive in every way. Elites gained from the expansion of pre-war benefits. Workers generally gained insurance against risk but they were lucky to break even when benefits received were measured against taxes paid.[43] Workers generally benefitted from redistribution only if they had two children or more.

A pro-family welfare state, 1945–1960

Women's equal status under the law as well as the principle of equal pay for equal work were enshrined in the Fourth Republic's constitution. These principles were observed mainly in the breach. The new order emphasized the state's duty to *protect* women's family roles. The preamble of the constitution read: "The Nation shall ensure to the individual and family the conditions necessary to their development. It shall guarantee to all, especially to the child, the mother, and aged workers, the protection of their health, material security, rest and leisure."[44] The rhetoric of sexual equality proved to be empty words; married French women were without equal civil rights until 1965–70, when the last residue of the Napoleonic Code was finally wiped from the books, along with the concept of the *chef de famille*.

The chief form of sexual inequality was surely economic in nature: as in other nations, women had unequal access to higher education and to the professions; the notion of equal pay for equal work was decades away from being contemplated. Two of the *grande écoles*, the Polytechnique and the Ecole des Mines were closed to women until 1964; the others had admitted a token handful by that time.[45] Pension plans announced shortly after the war generally served to plant seeds which would bear inegalitarian fruit during the 1970s and 1980s. Given that most people who retired during the 1940s and 1950s received no more than 40% of their pre-retirement income, the pension benefits won during the 1940s were promises of future largesse, not immediate, unbearable costs. Nevertheless, the male worker-centered, occupation-based social policy of the 1940s cemented sexual inequality at that time and into retirement. This was the general pattern of continental European social policy of the day.

There was, however, one distinct feature to the postwar welfare state in France. Between 1945 and 1960, France chose to construct the world's most advanced pro-natalist welfare state. To many contemporaries, this was the keystone in the social edifice, its crowning success.

Family allowances were the costliest social program in France and a few other nations during the 1940s and 1950s, and only partly due to the baby boom. Benefits were at an all-time high *vis-à-vis* the average wage; they peaked during the 1950s at roughly the equivalent of US $350 per month (in 2000 dollars, which was double their value in the year 2000). During the early years, in the late 1940s and early 1950s, spending on French family policy accounted for 40 to 50% of the total social budget.[46]

During the 1950s, foreign observers immediately noted the unusually generous family benefits available to parents.[47] France had its eyes fixed on the future, and the country was prepared to invest in it. By 1961, towards the tail end of the baby boom, France still devoted 33.4% of its social security expenditure to family benefits, 29% to pensions and disability, and 29% to sickness.[48] The three main policy foci were in balance. By 1970, after the baby boom, the nation still devoted over 25% of the social budget to the family. Health and pensions were claiming more for themselves, but the balance was still there. Support for the family has faded from the picture. It now represents only 9% of all social spending. Taking into account the slight drop in the birth rate since 1970, and all other things being equal, it should still represent 20 to 25%.

Universalism vanquished; corporatism triumphant

Is corporatist social policy a "natural," inevitable product of French history, as its defenders today proclaim?[49] Twenty-five years after he had failed in his efforts to introduce a British-style, universalistic welfare state to France, Pierre Laroque lamented that "the spirit of fraternal solidarity which marked the end of the war was broken very quickly, as the particularisms of professional [and occupational] identities re-emerged with a new force."[50] Had the possibilities for universalism ever been strong in a nation as socially fragmented as France?

Solidaristic, universalistic reform was indeed a tall order in such a heterogeneous socio-economic order, but it was not impossible. After all,

the British medical profession, friendly societies, and insurance companies hardly greeted universalism with open arms. Solidaristic reform
succeeded in Britain, which was, to be sure, a much more urbanized
and proletarianized society. The workers' movement had by 1914 united
around one party, the Labour Party. Although there were seemingly endless gradations of status and class in Britain, the basic economic and occupational structure was far more uniform than in France, where large-scale
production and concentration had not progressed as much.

French independents, the self-employed, were far more numerous and
important than in the UK. The slow development of large-scale enterprise
in France had served to fragment workers' identities; as late as 1900
some 60% of workers still worked in units of under ten employees.[51]
Occupation-specific identities, redolent of the old corporate order of the
eighteenth century, were much stronger in France (and even stronger in
Germany, Italy, and Austria, where corporatism also triumphed). This
militated against universalistic pensions and other social benefits, not
to mention the idea of one uniform, public hospital system. In other
words, the French nation's more complex demographic and occupational
makeup was indeed reproduced and mirrored in its health-care and social
security system.

Workers in nineteenth-century France lived outside the pale of the constitution. At least twenty thousand workers were killed during the Paris
Commune; strikes were repressed brutally by the state; workers were singled out through the *livret* or internal passport which monitored their
political behavior right up to 1890; labor law was unabashedly biased
in favor of bosses, and so on. Bitter from the bloody legacy of their
struggle with the French state, workers harbored a long-standing suspicion of state-controlled social programs. Accordingly, they torpedoed
the 1910 pension law, and, once won over (partially) to the idea of social
insurance, they tended to fight for a large administrative role in any new
social program which emerged, such as the 1928/1930 health insurance
plan. Similarly, in 1945–50, those who already had favorable pension
systems (public employees, miners, the military, railroad workers, etc.)
resisted the idea of joining a universal system. Neither these groups, nor
the independent workers, nor better paid *cadres* wished to be coupled
with unskilled workers and others in a global pension system, as reformers proposed.[52] Class resentments, social snobbery, distrust of reform,
and sheer self-interest were the motivating factors. The same was true of
the workers of newly formed state-owned companies, such as the EDF
(Electricité de France).[53]

Any reforms and/or new institutions introduced during the 1940s
would have to include workers' representation – this was the message

of French unions during the mid 1940s and this idea carried the day.[54] But workers did not unite around one single party, as their British counterparts did, and this served to fragment the social security system and reduce its universalistic and redistributive potential. The relatively weak and faction-ridden French parliament was (and is) a less effective vehicle for universalistic reform. Coupled with a relatively less "programmatic" party structure, French reformers faced vested interests from a weaker starting point than the Labour government in the UK.[55]

France's half-dozen major unions were now firmly ensconced within the post-Second World War welfare state's administrative machinery, giving them power (mainly, in later years, the power to frustrate reform) far beyond their numbers. This very "embeddedness" would, in an indirect way, militate against a more uniform approach to social issues. Corporatism was the result of a splintered but militant labor movement, and not necessarily the reflection of a vibrant associative sector. Universalism, by contrast, as Baldwin and Gourevitch have shown, was the product of the emergence of broad coalitions. In Scandinavia, farmers and urban workers united in favor of universalism.[56] In Britain, the majority of the working class and middle class alike supported the political class's centralizing postwar social vision, which hinged on Beveridge's Report and was made possible by the strong British parliament. The war certainly forged a sense of common purpose in Britain; the German occupation may have had the opposite effect in France.

To be sure, "Laroque's appeal for all citizens to enroll in a single social security *caisse* for the sake of national solidarity had no history," and therefore it was less likely to succeed.[57] But Britain had no history of Beveridge-style universalism (indeed, the stigmatizing Poor Law was its very antithesis) and yet Britons adopted Beveridge's vision and many lower-middle-class workers abandoned their old private insurance schemes when they realized that the public programs now on offer were a better bargain. During the Interwar years, Britain had a publicly funded but targeted, worker-based health insurance system which had grown out of an even stronger mutualist tradition than the French, but which was transformed under Clement Attlee's Labour government (1945–51) into a universal one.

Path dependency was indeed a powerful force in postwar France, but as the British case shows, the past can be overcome. The French *chose* to accept a complex, fragmented, corporatist welfare state which reproduced class divisions and mollified private and public vested interests. Today France is paying a very high price for this choice. It is too reductionist to portray the emergence of corporatism as the inevitable outcome of its social and occupational structure.[58] The special pension regimes did not spring, inevitably, from a certain French *terroir*; their elimination would be difficult but it would not constitute some sort of crime against France's social heritage. In fact, the elimination of the special regimes might herald a more egalitarian social order.

Before this happens, politicians must arm themselves with a reformist rhetoric to match the seductive rhetoric of solidarity. Certain sectors of the French economy, but particularly the public sector, the special pension regimes, and the union leaders who run the social funds, are masters of public relations. During the past decade, they have succeeded in cloaking their narrow interests with the rhetoric of solidarity.

Reform *manqué*: the right-not-to-work movement of 1995–1996

In November and December 1995 and, again briefly in January 1996, millions of French workers and elite *cadres* alike affirmed the nation's commitment to the various benefits associated with the big welfare state (if not their willingness to pay for them in the here and now), taking to the streets of Paris and other large cities to defend a few of their cherished social programs against the budgetary tweezers of Prime Minister Alain Juppé.[59] France was paralyzed for six weeks; public transit was shut down, many businesses closed, and hundreds of prominent Parisian intellectuals jumped into the fray, leading the charge against Juppé. With their appearances on television shows, their speeches delivered on the streets of Paris, their battle cries shouted at train stations, and their full-page petitions in the major newspapers, French intellectuals issued a collective "J'accuse" to Juppé. Nothing like this had been seen in France since May 68, when the nation staged the world's largest and longest general strike. The world took note of this vast "social movement," and many observers misunderstood it.[60]

Many foreigners believed that the French were serving notice of their commitment to "solidarity," their steadfast refusal to bow down before the dictates of US-led neoliberal globalization. The upper-middle class of France, some thought, was willing to go to the wall to defend "solidarity." The economist Dani Rodrik argued, with reference to the French strikes and to protest movements against globalization in other nations, on the first page of his widely read book, *Has Globalization Gone too Far?* (1997): "the international integration of markets for goods, services, and capital is pressuring societies to alter their traditional practices, and in return broad segments of these societies are putting up a fight."[61] Likewise, many

French people themselves saw Juppé as a sort of French Thatcherite. The leaders of the strikes presented their actions as "the first great movement against globalization."[62]

Here was a mass social movement, to be sure, but one which was geared towards the *maintenance* of costly benefits which served not to diminish inequality but rather to widen the social divide. The most comfortably employed workers of France were hoping to retain their corporatist privileges. They invoked the specter of globalization in order to discredit their opponents. The need to control spiralling health and pension costs was a domestic issue – nothing more, nothing less. The main health care fund was 67 billion francs (roughly 10 billion euros) in deficit in 1995, with an accumulated debt of over 250 billion francs. Several of the key pension funds were also in debt, as they had been since the 1970s. But now the baby boomers were getting set to retire and Juppé was trying to prepare for this.

In total, France was running an annual budget deficit of 200 to 300 billion francs (roughly 30 to 50 billion euros). This was an unsustainable situation, fuelled by high public spending of all sorts, health-care inflation, higher pension costs, and an unusually low retirement age (fifty to sixty). Juppé attempted to address some of these serious problems.[63] Juppé's opponents charged him with tearing up the very social fabric of the nation. In fact Juppé was trying to save the nation from its unsustainable course.

Juppé would be a centrist Democrat on the American political spectrum, a "red" Tory or a centrist Liberal in Canada, and he would be comfortable in the British Labour Party. Juppé was motivated by two pressing concerns: 1) he believed it was high time to control runaway non-redistributive social spending before it further harmed the economy; 2) he had to trim the annual budget deficit from 6% to 3% of GDP in order to meet the requirements imposed by France's decision to join the European Monetary Union (EMU) – the precursor to the adoption of the euro currency.[64] Only Sweden and Italy were in worse financial shape, but Sweden was well on its way toward a wholesale reform of its budget and welfare state and even Italy managed to implement a (partial) reform of its costly pension system.

The last thing on the minds of French protestors was income inequality and unemployment; they were marching against a government they did not trust and in favor of a romanticized vision of the public sector. *None of Juppé's cuts targeted the poor.* Civil servants were objecting to the idea that they would have to wait until the age of sixty to retire. Doctors were protesting the idea that they might have to accept limits on their ability to prescribe drugs and treatments. The vast majority of the cuts would have affected skilled men (and relatively few women) over the age of fifty; most of the people affected were in the upper half of the income ladder. Protestors were marching for themselves, either because their special benefits were at risk or they feared theirs might be next.

Some of the SNCF's perks were and still are quite remarkable. Some employees enjoy the "right" to retire at the age of fifty with a full pension. (The normal age of retirement in the private sector is sixty and it is fifty-five in the general public sector. Thanks to Raffarin's reform, in 2008, things change, as the public sector will be aligned with the private and people must contribute for forty years before they are eligible for a full pension. As of 2012, forty-one years will be required in both sectors. But the special regimes like the SNCF have not yet been reformed; it is still possible to retire on a full pension with only 27.5 years of contributions.)

Juppé wanted to eliminate retirement at age fifty to fifty-five in the SNCF, which is financed by raiding the general (private sector) pension regime and the treasury to the tune of 2.8 billion euros per year. He also wanted to move towards a more egalitarian, rationally administered and cost-efficient system of social benefits, with fewer privileges for corporatist interests in general, and with fewer separate insurance funds.[65] Juppé's goal was equal benefits for equal contributions.

Juppé's plan also included a concrete proposal to *extend* health care coverage to the 1% of the population which still did not have access to it. This was hardly a "neoliberal" reform plan. In fact, this proposal, in and of itself, was one of the most truly solidaristic social reforms of the previous twenty years. Juppé's Socialist successor, Lionel Jospin, carried out this very reform five years later, and when Jospin departed from politics in 2002, the leading, center-Left[66] newspaper Le Monde hailed this measure as his crowning achievement.[67] Taken as a whole, Juppé's reforms would have steered France closer to Scandinavia than to the USA, since he proposed treating people *equally* and he proposed cost containment through *universalism* – not through mean-spirited cuts for the poor. In fact Juppé had increased the minimum wage by 4% (even as he had increased regressive sales taxes) prior to launching his reforms. Juppé's targets were the comfortable, not the low paid, not the marginalized. This is precisely why the protests were so loud.

Juppé erred in invoking Maastricht to justify reforms which were necessary regardless of trade, regardless of Europe. President Chirac had been elected in May 1995 on a platform which vowed to heal the "social fracture." And now he and Prime Minister Juppé seemed to be reneging on this promise. To Juppé, the expensive corporatist perks were plain to see; to the general public, the public sector is the embodiment of solidarity.

Juppé might have focused on the unsustainable course of French finances, regardless of the outside world. Juppé failed to provide a coherent intellectual justification for his reforms. Instead, unable or unwilling to make this sort of argument (perhaps because by the 1990s the French public had adopted such a cavalier attitude toward public debt), he invoked the need to cut spending in order to meet EMU criteria. As a result, the public believed that the French way of life was being threatened by outside forces.[68] France, a proud nation with a long history of nationalistic curricula teaching that French institutions and values are socially just, avant-garde and a model for the rest of the world, could see no reason why the outside world should impose limits on *solidarité*.

Redistributive solidarity, however, was not under attack. The fact that millions of people (50 to 60% of the population, according to opinion polls) supported the strikes may simply mean that the French share a disdain for the private sector and tend to distrust any reform which is associated with its (apparent) dictates. In other words, protesting social spending cuts was a way of expressing distaste for a government associated with the EU or American-led "neoliberal" agenda. Or, the widespread support for the strikers may simply indicate that the public was unaware of the magnitude of the SNCF's perks. Finally, there were millions of people (30% of the working population, including public-sector workers) who hoped to retain *their* own "special regime" insurance and pension funds. An attack on one branch of the welfare state was probably considered an attack on all. If the various special pension regimes fell to "neoliberalism," surely other social programs would follow, in domino fashion. Alas, the "neoliberal" threat was contained, and a powerful message was delivered to would-be reformers in the years to come.

With the exception of his semi-successful efforts to contain hospital costs, and the passage of a law which now gives the French parliament power to vote the annual health-care budget (in practice this has not lived up to its promise), Juppé did not have his way. The special pension regimes were not reformed; civil servants' pensions were not touched (until Raffarin succeeded in 2003). In 1997, Juppé's government was rejected in the snap parliamentary elections called by President Chirac. Juppé took the fall, and Jospin picked up the pieces.

Five years of Socialist rule (1997–2002) followed, with no attempt at a major overhaul of the Sécu or the special pension regimes. Jospin's five years in power were a great missed opportunity. To be sure, Jospin was haunted by the anti-Juppé strikes, but with his official commitment to fight neoliberal globalization, Jospin might have reformed French labor law and pensions (indeed he commissioned several reports which called for sweeping reforms in these areas) and it would have been difficult to taint him by association with the unpopular US or Thatcherite path. This is precisely how French intellectuals, labor leaders, and Socialist and

Communist politicians had succeeded in demolishing Juppé's legislative agenda.

Led by the renowned late sociologist Pierre Bourdieu and by the novelist and critic Viviane Forrester, French *bien pensant* opinion came up with no shortage of excuses to explain their (significant) role in killing Juppé's reforms: "he was too arrogant"; "he was too cold, too technocratic"; he "did not consult us first."[69] Indeed, Juppé was all of this and more. But at the end of the day, a reasonable reform package designed to address serious problems and introduced in an orderly, parliamentary fashion by a democratically elected government was defeated by costly strikes (roughly 0.5% of French GNP went down the drain) and no alternative was proposed.

Juppé fought against a strong current of public support for social security: in 1983, a major French polling company found that 85% of the population felt that the abolition of social security would be "very serious," yet only 81% said the abolition of the right to vote would be "very serious" and 70% believed that the freedom of the press fell into this category. Only 2% believed that social security was "not important" or "not at all important."[70]

To the Lyon station

The French have come to define themselves in terms of their social security net, in all its byzantine and inegalitarian forms, and Juppé disregarded this to his peril. On 12 December 1995, Pierre Bourdieu made the hazardous passage from the Left Bank to the Gare de Lyon in order to defend the *cheminots* and in the hope of launching the revolution against neoliberalism. He delivered a remarkable speech to a large crowd at the train station:

I have come to offer support to everyone who has been fighting for the last three weeks against the destruction of a civilization, one associated with public service, with the republican [idea of] equality of rights . . . this crisis is a historic chance for France and for all those who refuse the new alternative: liberalism or barbarism . . . In fighting for their social rights, the strikers are fighting for everyone's rights.[71]

Since the early 1980s, this type of rhetoric has been common among French writers, artists, professors, teachers, and, of course, Socialist and Communist politicians. Bourdieu's December Theses should go down in history as an example of the degree to which the French intellectual class had committed itself to resisting reform – of any sort – during the 1990s.

At the time Bourdieu issued this statement, the chief medical insurance fund was 60 billion francs in deficit ($10 billion) and the crisis of the pension system had been the subject of over fifteen major government reports during the fifteen previous years. The SNCF train drivers had some of the most generous publicly subsidized benefits in the world. Yet the opponents of Juppé's plan to *modify* this situation succeeded in denying the need for reform and in shifting the blame onto others. To Bourdieu, France was at risk of succumbing to "the tyranny of World Bank and IMF-style experts who impose the dictates of the new Leviathan, financial markets. . . ."[72] In this vision, France was falling victim to a vast, international Right-wing conspiracy.

Bourdieu presented France's solidarity aristocrats, the "seigneurs du rail"[73] (as some of their own colleagues call them), as the defenders of "civilization," of equality. In reality, these people were defending their expensive "right" to retire at fifty on the public dime, even though life expectancies had increased by over ten years since the time at which the "right" to retire at fifty had been established.[74]

Many people were simply motivated by fear: the fear of change, the fear that reform would bring about a sort of Thatcherization of France. When distinguished men of letters like Bourdieu argued that France need not reform, that the *cheminots* were on the right track, he helped to steel the public's resolve to resist Juppé. Standing in the midst of the strikes, the *New Yorker* writer Adam Gopnik observed: "Though the strike has developed a quasi-revolutionary momentum, it doesn't have anything like a quasi-revolutionary ideology; the slogan of the government functionaries at the heart of the strike is, essentially, 'Status quo forever.' The tone is entirely middle class; it suggests a vast petit bourgeois ghost dance, trying to summon up, by its fervor and intensity, a certainty that the future will be like the *trente glorieuses*, the glorious thirty years of French prosperity that ended in the late seventies."[75]

The French media (and Juppé himself) failed to convey the gravity of the nation's problems to the public. Somehow, Juppé seemed to underestimate the power of the crowd, the street protest, even though this is a basic tradition in France. Despite the regular protests of the previous fifteen years – against conservative and Socialist governments alike – Juppé thought he could succeed. He also erred in ignoring the fact that the French parliament is weak and does not carry the same sort of legitimacy as, say, the British or Canadian parliament. Since legislation in France is produced in a top-down, cabinet-driven manner, and generally does not spring from civil society, from Dutch, German, or Swedish-style tripartite (government–business–labor) negotiations, or from parliament itself, ambitious reformers must be careful to consult with the people and with the various social insurance fund directors before they introduce important or controversial reforms.[76] Juppé did none of the above.

As Paul Pierson, Martin Rhodes, Jonah Levy, and others have noted, welfare-state expansion is a simple process, especially in a state-centric policy environment like France.[77] But cutting costs is hard to do; welfare-state retrenchment is a thankless process. It requires the "politics of blame avoidance" (rather than credit claiming) on the part of those doing the cutting. In nations with long traditions of state–business–labor negotiations, "social pacts" can be hammered out, with a slice of blame served up to each party – and hence to no one in particular. This makes reform easier. In France, by contrast, corporatist interests are relatively weak in that they are not accepted by the strong state as equal players (the way they are in Germany). But corporatist interests in France are strong in one way: the union leaders at the head of the social insurance funds resent their lack of input into regular decision making, and, partly as a result of this, they are radicalized. Their strength springs from their ability to tap into solidarity ideology and destroy government reforms by coordinating strikes with the labor leaders at the head of public-sector unions.

When his ambitious reform package was unveiled in parliament in the autumn of 1995, almost no one outside the cabinet knew what had gone on behind closed doors. Juppé had the temerity to boast that fewer than ten people had laid their eyes on the bill before he tabled it! This, political scientist Bruno Palier reminds us, was Juppé's key error.[78] Just as Juppé claimed all the credit for the brilliance of his reform package, he would take all of the blame.

Having said this, once Juppé's plan became public knowledge, its opponents preferred to engage in demagoguery rather than with the facts. Jean-Jacques Dupeyroux, the doyen of French social security law and the editor of the influential journal *Droit social*, observed several months after the December 1995 strikes: "Regarding the Juppé Plan, the French were bombarded from all directions with slogans . . . But to my knowledge, not one single television show attempted to discuss, in a serious fashion, without *brouhaha*, the major lines of the plan."[79] In one of the sharpest analyses of the December 1995 strikes, *Le grand refus* (1996), the leading sociologist Alain Touraine argues,

in the economic realm, French society has taken refuge in its corporatism; at the ideological level, in its republicanism; and at the cultural level, in its past. In doing so, it transfers to the next generation the burdens of artificial protections [i.e., corporatist protections against economic change] and the non-decisions, behind which it tries to hide from the world in which it lives . . . Those who are the most protected contribute to French society's failure to adapt and therefore they increase the risks towards those who are the least protected.[80]

Touraine believes that the selfishness of the "protected sector" (i.e. the public sector and others with corporatist benefits), prevents the government from undertaking reforms which would help marginalized people gain a foothold in the economy.[81]

The street protests of 2000 to 2003

This pattern of strike activity continues to this day. In late September 2000, a disruptive strike of SNCF (state railway) workers and Parisian metro/bus workers (the RATP) shut the city down for one day. Like millions of Parisians, I experienced the defense of "solidarity" first hand, as I wove my way through one of France's regular "social movements." The streets were filled with workers brandishing banners vowing to protect a certain "French style of public service" from "neoliberal globalization."

In September 2000, the RATP was protesting the slowness of negotiations over salary increases. The root of the conflict? The notorious 35-hour work-week law, introduced by Martine Aubry and Lionel Jospin in 1998, which promised jobs for all, but with no corresponding pay cuts, no sacrifices of any sort. (The 35-hour law was supposed to induce companies and public bodies like the RATP to hire new workers, thereby reducing the general unemployment rate.) At a time when payroll taxes on private sector workers were near an all-time high,[82] when the unemployed numbered in the millions, RATP workers continued to benefit from a "right" to retire on a full pension at the average age of fifty-three, even though they had contributed less than one-half the average worker's lifetime contributions to his/her pension. RATP workers' wages are 30% more than those of their private sector counterparts with equal qualifications.

The RATP's pension fund has been insolvent to the tune of over 2.5 billion euros each year during the late 1990s and early 2000s (employees paid only 0.5 billion per year in contributions, the company paid 1.1 billion, and the taxpayer bailed out the rest: 2.5 billion euros). These are significant sums, given the relatively insignificant portion of the workforce these 150,000 employees and the slightly larger number of retirees represent. The total payment by taxpayers and the company was over 20,000 euros per retiree per year.[83]

The RATP was protesting what looked like a pay raise of slightly more than 1%.[84] Having supported the 35-hour work-week law in the name of "solidarity" towards the unemployed, RATP workers were disappointed that they would have to help pay for the creation of new jobs in the form of lower-than-anticipated raises and new, more flexible work schedules. RATP workers have been as successful as millionaire Republicans in the USA in misrepresenting their own narrow interests as the general public interest.[85] Once again, the RATP succeeded in thwarting reform.

The French marched in the streets, once again, in January 2001, November 2002, and throughout 2003, to defend what they see as their hard-earned "droits acquis," or "social rights" – in this case, a twenty-year-old "right" to retire, thanks to current workers' payroll contributions and subsidies from the general tax system, on a full pension, as early as the age of fifty to sixty. Even as the French were (and are) living longer and longer, and as other nations are raising the retirement age back up to sixty-five (Germany, Italy) or even to sixty-seven (as in Denmark and the USA) or seventy (as in Japan), middle-aged French workers dug in their heels.

Street protests in France (and in Italy) are almost always geared towards the maintenance of privileges funded via regressive taxation systems. They are not protest movements in favor of poverty reduction, redistribution, full employment, or equality in face of the tax system.

Corporatist welfare states and the challenge of reform

And the reason for this is obvious: the greater the privileges, the more there is to lose as states contemplate cuts. *This* is why France, Italy, Spain, and Germany have led the charge against "neoliberalism's" threat to "solidarity" – it has not emanated from the Netherlands (a corporatist-universalist hybrid), Denmark, Finland, and Sweden, four nations which have been cutting and reorienting social spending towards the most needy as well as increasing the labor-force participation rate for two decades. The anti-Juppé strikes form part of a long continuum of protest, from the 1968 strikes to the 1,460 official street demonstrations in favor of better pay, working conditions, job security, and the like in Paris alone during 2001, to the anti-Raffarin strikes of 2003.[86]

As Giuliano Bonoli, Bruno Palier, and Gøsta Esping-Andersen have argued, the corporatist social-welfare model is unsuited to adapting to socio-economic change since it tends to use stable employment in the first instance as the primary basis for social benefits, as opposed to a more flexible needs-based route or a more open-ended, umbrella-like, citizenship-based route. "Since entitlement to benefits must be earned [even, I would add, if the benefits themselves need not be 'earned' in full] those who are most in need are often unable to gain access to provisions." A "ring-fenced labour market" excludes the weakest members of society. "High benefits for workers" are defended by those already comfortably employed, and these people – from EDF to the SNCF to the high-paid managers of the Banque de France, Air France, and the RATP – "are generally unwilling to trade some of their privileges in order to create more jobs for those excluded from the labour market." The French welfare state is "frozen" in time, with governments trying to "defrost" it but succeeding only in taking tiny chips away from the solid core of work-based benefits and distributing crumbs to the excluded.[87]

These facts have been well known in policy circles for years. In 1989, an important social security review panel reported on the many short-comings of the system. As the Commissariat Général du Plan noted, the world of work had, already in 1989, changed completely since the imme-diate postwar era, when the welfare state was expanded: "[it is] . . . a sys-tem founded essentially upon professional [or occupational] solidarity, in the context of a full-employment economy, in which the archetypal job was the full-time, permanently salaried position. This . . . demonstrates the excessively cloistered nature of our social protection system, and it helps to explain why it has had such difficulty in adapting to the [new] types of [economic] risks against which it should now be insuring."[88] Finally, the Commissariat recommended that the principle "à droits égaux, efforts contributifs identiques" (equal contributions for equal ben-efits) be observed.[89] In other words, two hundred years after the French Revolution had abolished social and legal privilege, the Commissariat called for an end to publicly subsidized "social welfare" privileges.

How corporatist welfare states block job creation

As corporatist privileges are melded into a universalistic system, social inequality will necessarily fall. Similarly, as corporatist barriers to eco-nomic change fall, employment levels will rise. If governments, in turn, choose to monitor income distribution and adjust social spending accord-ingly, inequality need not rise.

In the short term, corporatist welfare states ensure the continuing com-fort of certain powerfully represented economic interests. But in the long term, corporatist welfare states are the most harmful to the economy since they tend to hinder economic rationalization and change in general. The comfort of the few comes at a cost to the many.[90] Corporatist continental conservative welfare states cement strong bonds on an industry-wide basis between, say, all construction workers in one region, or most metal workers in one city (or, as in Germany, the entire country). Corporatist welfare states stand for high wages and a complex, protective layer of labor legislation which makes firing and above all hiring difficult. They reveal the fundamental tension of the modern economy: the tension between workers, whose natural inclination – who can blame them? – is toward stability, toward job security; and between employers, whose chief interest is the economic survival of their firm, and with keeping up with technological change and the competition.

In the absence of a Dutch or Swedish style of universalistic discourse, stressing common sacrifice, common benefits, the need for regular industrial and institutional change and a concern for equality,[91] corporatist welfare arrangements give rise to some of the most expensive, inegalitarian, male-dominated, and inflexible labor forces in the world: those of France, Germany, Italy, and Belgium. These nations also suffer some of the highest unemployment rates in OECD nations. This is a perverse outcome, given the ostensible concern for jobs and "solidarity" which characterizes these nations.[92]

Diversity does have the benefit of strongly rooting the various social insurance systems into the nation's polity, but it also makes quick and widespread reform difficult.[93] Unlike in Sweden, the UK, or in any given Canadian province or American state, the ability to effect sweeping reforms in France, be they expansionary or constrictive, is frustrated by the numerous vested interests present on the scene. The French state is undoubtedly massive and expensive to run, but in certain realms, such as social security, its authority is very fragmented. Most of the insurance funds are legally independent entities, although for decades they have been subsidized using general tax revenues and they have always been subject to the administrative scrutiny of the Ministries of Health and Labor. Parliament has the authority to renegotiate the terms of its *tutelle* over the funds, but this is easier said than done: regular street protests make this so.

Since the social welfare system is so fragmented, it is virtually impossible to reform several funds at once because the various "social partners" must be consulted. Reform, therefore, tends to be carried out (or, more commonly, simply contemplated) in small measures.[94] Reform, in turn, tends to be seen as a zero-sum game. So people cling to their piece of the pie and they are sympathetic when another group wraps its own interest in the flag of solidarity. As Gérard Moatti, editor of the journal *Sociétal*, argues,

Everyone for himself, and the State for everyone: in France, the majority of issues of collective interest are considered through a dialogue between the state and each particular category concerned – and very rarely through a dialogue between the various categories. This legitimizes corporatisms: with the rules of the game set in this manner, each group is justified in defending its own interests . . . Every public expense is seen as being redistributive. This "quant-à-soi" corporatism . . . prevents governments from openly criticizing any particular category.[95]

The resilience of corporatism and the privileged civil service

Corporatist welfare states gain widespread public support from their richly woven, complex fabric, but this also entails a multiplication of vested interests who will oppose reform. When you have a welfare state which consists of dozens of insurance funds co-administered by elected union representatives, funded mostly by payroll taxes, firmly rooted into the nation's political soil, with numerous social welfare offices in every town, with mutual insurance funds in every region, with a social affairs committee in every factory, with several hundred thousand administrators, then it will be harder to reform it. There will be too many people with too much to lose.[96]

Some critics charge that universalistic welfare states waste resources on the middle class, but the scenario which unfolded in France was worse from a financial point of view. Universalism has the benefit of treating all citizens equally – whether this means equally generously, as in Sweden, or equally stingily, as in Britain and Canada today. Everywhere it exists, universalism reduces bureaucracy and administrative costs. And universalism can, in conjunction with progressive income taxes, redistribute from the rich to the poor.[97]

Since the French health, pension, unemployment, and family allowance systems are not funded out of general income taxes, as most provincial health-care systems are in Canada, but primarily through current workers' payroll taxes (which generally cover 65% of the costs) which are visible and politically symbolic, and through the smaller CSG tax and the VAT tax, the public's sense of entitlement is stronger. When resources flow into and stem from a progressive income tax system, one's sense of individual ownership is diminished, and one will probably be more inclined to see benefits and sacrifices as things that stem from or are imposed by the collectivity. Hence when politicians tighten the fiscal belt, fewer people will protest and those that do will not have power sufficient to block reform.

When Margaret Thatcher wanted to squeeze or contain social spending, she needed only to consult her cabinet to do so. There were no "social partners" to placate. Admittedly, her cabinet was divided but this obstacle was less formidable than the various obstacles to reform in France. Canada's Prime Minister as well as the provincial Premiers have the same power to cut or expand. There is one unemployment regime covering all of Canada: this made reform quick and easy during the mid 1990s. The power of officials in Denmark to allocate social spending at will is perhaps without parallel: since over 80% of all social security revenues come from income taxes, high earners have been less inclined to obstruct reform.

By contrast, the corporatist nature of France's welfare state makes cost cutting (or re-allocation towards the poor) much more difficult. Responsibility is more diffused.[98] Opportunities for dissent and obstruction are greater. In theory, this sounds more democratic than the British and Canadian scenarios. In practice, the French system has led to far more serious fiscal problems. History shows that powerful bureaucrats of the Swedish or British sort (in the 1940s–60s, at least), armed with the ideology of universalism and operating in a progressive income tax environment, do a better job of delivering redistributive solidarity than worker-co-administered, payroll-tax based, corporatist insurance funds in the French style.

By the mid 1980s, when proposals were in the air to simplify and unify the various social insurance funds, the Ministry of Social Affairs conducted a wide-ranging study on the lack of coordination in the social security system(s). It concluded that this would be a daunting task: each year, 3,000 new pages of legislative texts, regulations, ministerial circulars, and so forth, were added to the 115,000 pages of text which constituted the country's social security guidebook.[99] Here is a system so complex, so byzantine, that it makes the 2,500 page US federal tax code look simple by comparison. The principal private sector pension fund has over 190,000 agents installed in 400 different locations across the nation. There are over 100,000 hospital administrators and another 332,000 administrators in the regional offices of the *Caisse nationale de l'assurance maladie des travailleurs salariés* and other social welfare insurance agencies. Health administration costs are twice as high as in Britain.[100] The chief medical insurance fund has some 145 local and regional branches. Although it covers 80% of the population, there are eighteen other major funds. Usually, those people who are affiliated with the special pension funds are also affiliated with a special, work-related health fund. Each pension fund is like a fiefdom, and in 1995–96 Alain Juppé learned the hard way that their directors and beneficiaries will go to battle to defend their turf.[101] Other politicians took note.

Reform threatens the nation's hundreds of thousands of social sector workers. Many of them still work in offices which are not computerized.

Because these people deal in "solidarity," and not, say, widgets, they are able to represent their own interests as being the public interest. But every now and then they let down their guard and speak with candor. As one representative from the labor union Force Ouvrière (FO) admitted in a 1994 interview, any reform in the direction of a Swedish-style or Canadian style single-payer insurance system, funded from general income and sales taxes, would be opposed for the following reasons: "We oppose the tendency towards shifting financing from contribution [payroll taxes] to [general] taxation. The transfer of financial obligations to the state will imply the transfer of decision-making power, and we are against that."[102] As one senior civil servant with the Ministry of Social Affairs put it that same year: "The financing system based on social contributions has generated a system of discussion between people who *believe* they are the representatives of employees and employers. Such a system has resulted in much abuse . . . The social security system is locked by lobbies who do not want the system to change."[103]

As Ashford notes, "special interests abound, each with its own organization, administrative and political access, and often its own publications and research support."[104] During the 1980s and 1990s, the cumulative pressure of these numerous vested interests was a disincentive for governments to contemplate widespread, meaningful reform. Governments of the Left and the Right tried to wrestle control from the "social" partners and they succeeded in one small way: they introduced a new tax (the CSG) which is levied on *all* forms of income, and which is earmarked for social spending. By the late 1990s, the CSG brought more into French coffers than the traditional income tax. The CSG – opposed bitterly by the unions and social partners – may well be the thin edge of the wedge which eventually pries control from the corporatist social funds.[105]

The lure of the state

Another key obstacle to reform is that the youth of France generally does not understand the nature of the unemployment crisis. They usually attribute the current economic blues to the all-explanatory, amorphous process of "globalization" and the American-style corporate sector. Research conducted during the mid 1990s suggested an almost complete ignorance on the part of French youth of the demographic profile of the nation.[106] Rather than eliminating the special regimes, most young people looked forward to the day when they too might benefit, like their parents and grandparents. The same sort of logic upholds the inegalitarian distribution of wealth in the USA.

Most young Frenchmen and women do not begrudge the privileges of the (middle-aged-dominated) public sector; perhaps they see no need to beat it and would prefer to join it. Indeed, the more the state sapped the vitality of the market during the 1980s and 1990s, the more likely people were to seek employment in the security of the public sector. It was a vicious circle indeed. In 1990, there were six candidates for each public sector job which appeared; in 1996, there were fourteen.[107] A far greater percentage of French youth than British, Canadian, or American youth express a desire to join the civil service.[108] To a greater extent, perhaps, than in any other rich nation, the best and the brightest go into the public service.[109] The result is that there is no countervailing power to the public sector in France (just as there is no countervailing power to the private sector in the USA). As Vivien Schmidt emphasizes, France lacks a "legitimizing discourse" for social welfare reform and general reform of the public sector.[110]

France is in desperate need of such a discourse. A recent study estimates that 57% of the adult population are either civil servants themselves, or the children, parents, or spouses of civil servants.[111] Over the past five years, a similar proportion of people – usually 50 to 60% – have supported public sector protests over pension reform.[112] Fully one-half of the French population is dependent on the state: either they receive a pension from it or they work for it. If one adds the unemployed and those on social assistance, one reaches a figure of over 55%. This yearning for secure public employment and this quest for *rentier* status, of course, is not unique to France – it can be found in Spain, Italy, Greece, Portugal, and throughout Latin America. Likewise, the economic problems associated with this ethos are universal.

France, then, is not alone: from Paris to Rome to Athens to Lisbon to Berlin, labor markets have frozen and the social welfare edifice has become rigid, unaffordable, out of touch with current economic and demographic realities. The corporatist/continental conservative welfare state has not addressed the problems of the post-industrial world: how to provide jobs to those who are displaced as technological change shrinks the blue-collar class, how to adapt social policy to the new, lower-wage service economy; how to adapt to new single-parent family models; how to balance the increasing claims of an aging society on state coffers with the need to prepare for the future; how to address the problems associated with youth poverty; how to ensure that the brunt of the country's economic problems are not shouldered by young women and immigrants, who are the most likely to be unemployed.[113] Each and every one of these problems is domestic in origin.

If things are to change for the better, the state must wrestle funds from strong, vocal, and sometimes militant vested interests who, like the millionaire Republican in the USA, arm themselves with a powerful ideology and present their narrow interests as the national interest. Taxes have reached their limit, and even the Socialists admitted this in the summer of 2000, cutting them by almost two points of GDP over the next two years. But the French state still spends twenty-one more points of GDP than the American state (53% vs. 32% in the early 2000s, all levels of government included). The French state suffers from solidaristic overstretch. In order to reduce poverty, France need not increase spending; it must, however, reshuffle it.

Can expensive corporatist benefits be extended to everyone?

The idea that the privileges of the French railroad system's workers (low age of retirement, generous additional family benefits, generous supplementary medical insurance, extra vacation days, etc.) could be universalized is out of the question. Nonetheless, when presented with the bleak financial scenario of the French pension system(s), most French union leaders will avoid engagement with numbers and put capitalism itself on trial.

When the newspaper *Le Parisien* asked Force Ouvrière leader Marc Blondel in December 2002: "Despite the financial problems with their pension regimes, will you continue to support the advantages of functionaries?", he argued that "our social rights cannot be questioned. If they were, then there would be no limit to social dumping. On the contrary, we must proceed towards an alignment towards the top."[114]

With 9.5% unemployment and 4.5 million poor people in need of more spending *on them* (whether in the form of boosted family benefits, housing credits, or payroll-tax reductions, etc.), Force Ouvrière proposed the following: raising pension contributions by 0.3% of GNP per year, every year, until 2040, and allowing everyone to retire after 37.5 years of contributions – instead of the forty-one years now required in the wake of Raffarin's 2003 reform.[115] If enacted, Blondel's proposals would lead to budget deficits of at least 10% of GDP and public spending equal to 60% of GDP. Pension spending would rise to 23% of GNP. But none of this new spending would have anything to do with poverty reduction, revealing the social partners' anti-social goals. Presumably some money would be left over for family allowances, health, housing, and education. Supporters of this type of thinking, like the authors Jean-Jacques Chavigné and Gérard Filoche, argue that French public-sector pensions stand at the "avant-garde" of global social policy, a model for all aspiring solidarists.[116]

In Germany, the USA, Denmark, and Japan, workers will soon have to wait until they are aged sixty-five, sixty-seven, or seventy to receive a full pension. For two decades, French pension policy has been out of step with other rich nations.[117] Raffarin's recent reform will merely have the effect of raising the average age of retirement back towards the age of sixty-three. The French public is firmly committed to retirement as early as possible: *Le Parisien* found that 78% of the people it polled in January 2001 supported the demonstrations and strikes taking place at that time against the business community's proposal – not the Jospin government's – to gradually raise the retirement age back up to sixty-five. Even many young Parisians, in their early twenties, support the idea of retirement at sixty or younger – like their more militant fifty-five year-old compatriots, they have been conditioned to expect this as their "right."[118] And they have bought into the myth that the withdrawal of an older worker from the workforce will necessarily create a position for a younger worker.

At a time when France may be on the verge of a social crisis to rival May '68 or December '95, with racial tension rising and unemployment remaining high, the need to switch back to a full-employment society has never been greater. But a significant chunk of the electorate, in alliance with several labor and political leaders, seems more interested in defending expensive, non-redistributive "social" benefits than in allowing the nation to change, to adapt, to create new jobs in the private sector. Calls for social policy restraint and reform have become entangled with an entirely different issue – "globalization," creating an intellectual impasse, a cultural cul-de-sac.

3 The "treason of the intellectuals": globalization as the big excuse for France's economic and social problems

The whole aim of practical politics is to keep the populace alarmed (and hence clamorous to be led to safety) by menacing it with an endless series of hobgoblins, all of them imaginary.

H. L. Mencken

A few years ago, it was Europe that was being presented negatively by a large part of the French political elite: the euro was going to destroy jobs, and the loss of sovereignty would be terrible for the French economy. All of this was false. Today, we are looking for another devil – one who now has the face of globalization.

Denis Kessler, the vice-president of the French employers' association (MEDEF), 2000.[1]

The French are trapped in the illusion that they are in no way responsible for their problems. Neither in the general nor in the particular. Responsibility is hell, therefore it is other people. The scapegoats have been refashioned over the years: Les "gros," les "patrons" [the wealthy, bosses], les "puissances d'argent," le "capitalisme", "les Boches" [Germans] and "les deux cents familles" have given way to "globalization," Maastricht Europe [the city where the EMU and the euro were agreed upon], to "elites."

Journalist François de Closets, in Le Compte à rebours (The Countdown) (1998).[2]

Since the 1960s, social politics in France has been colored by much more than the traditional class debate.[3] Solidaristic overstretch dates back to the Right's time in power during the 1960s and 1970s. The two main Rightist parties, the Gaullists and the Giscardians, "were competing for middle class votes, while both feared the rise of [a] united Left."[4] As in other rich nations, spending more on "the social" made good electoral sense; at a time when productivity and economic growth were at historic highs, when government coffers were overflowing with money, people's expectations of what the state could achieve were high. Between 1945 and 1995, the French social security system grew two-and-a-half times faster than national wealth.[5] Under President Giscard d'Estaing (1974–81) social spending and wages increased at an unprecedented rate.

Since the 1980s, there has been a peculiar French twist: "beyond the political battles, there is a distinct nationalist strain" to French social politics.[6] The French define themselves today by contrasting their social security system with a negative vision of the American system.[7] A strong social welfare system and public sector in general has come to occupy a central component of the French national identity.[8] This is not simply the dogma of the French intellectual or Left-wing politician: this sentiment is widespread. In the midst of the anti-G8 Summit protests in Evian in 2003, a forty-three-year-old French teacher on strike to protest pension reform and the reorganization of the education system told the newspaper *Le Figaro*: "Globalization and the threat to the public services: it's all linked."[9] By the early 2000s, 72% of French people told pollsters that they were "suspicious" of globalization, 65% identified it as "a direct cause of" rising social inequality, and 55% believed it was a threat to French companies and jobs. Only 12% were enthusiastic about it.[10] A majority of French people view globalization as the negation of their distinct social-economic-cultural model, a model their politicians tell them should be embraced around the globe.

"Most French people see the market as a jungle, to be feared if it cannot first be tamed by the state."[11] *Le Monde*, the leading French newspaper, printed 2,375 articles on "globalization" in 1999 and 2000. The *New York Times*, a larger production with far more space in which to fit the news it prints, published only 705 articles during the same period. President Chirac, a "conservative,"[12] gave no fewer than 163 speeches on globalization (many of them alarming speeches) between 1995 and 2000.[13] No surprise many French people think globalization explains so much.

Opinion polls show that most French people have a negative view of the USA, even as they consume American products and attend Hollywood films as frequently as the citizens of other European nations. Prime Minister Jospin himself declared that he was against "the dangers of unbridled globalization driven by jungle capitalism" – which, in the context of his speech, was an obvious attack on the USA.[14] Since lower public spending is associated with the USA, necessary reforms, which would call for lower "social" spending in *some* areas or simply less spending on the "protected people," are frustrated by this political rhetoric.[15]

The *mur de grandeur*

French pride in their distinct model prejudices them against adopting certain aspects of foreign models and changing. But pride can be overcome: the Swedes have basked in their peculiar national identity, the *folkhemmet* (the people's home, as in the land of the people, of equality), for many more decades than the French have embraced "solidarité." Sweden cleansed the stables during the 1990s; France did not.

French reformers, burdened by heavy historical baggage, must scale the *mur de grandeur*. From Michelet – who wrote in *Le peuple* (1846): "When France remembers that she was and must be the saviour of the human race, when she gathers her children about her and teaches them France as faith and religion, then will she rediscover her vitality . . . Only France has the right to project herself as a model, because no people has merged its own interest and destiny with that of humanity more than she" – to Charles de Gaulle, who wrote in his *Mémoires de guerre* (1954) that "France cannot be France without grandeur," the quest for grandeur lies at the core of French history.[16] And today it is at the root of France's problems. As the historian of the EU, John Gillingham, notes, "the chimera of grandeur is the source of France's current malaise. The quest for this elusive prize has trapped France in the coils of commitments it cannot meet and ends it cannot reach, raised expectations it has no chance of fulfilling, and deferred frank confrontation with the important challenges it faces. A pervasive *morosité* is the result."[17]

By opening up to the world and further loosening labor restrictions (all the while doing a better job of targeting social spending on the victims of change and the holders of new, less-than-ideal jobs), France can become, like the Dutch and the Swedes, *more solidaristic*. As Philippe Lemaître wrote in *Le Monde* in May 1997, when the Jospin government came to power, "[all the while] demonizing the American model, Europe has forgotten that it already has the faults, but none of the positive features" of the USA.[18] In equating all "social" spending with the good, and all cuts and all change with the bad, French intellectuals during the 1980s and 1990s led the nation into an intellectual impasse. The rise of political extremism is one result.

When intensely defensive nationalism mixes with public policy, the prospect of rational debate and calm dialogue is surely diminished. Perhaps in no other Western nation is the intellectual class so involved in such serious debates, but without bringing much empiricism or moderation to the table. Intellectuals have tended to see social welfare as a symbol of a certain type of "civilization" they prefer, hence they have rarely bothered to concern themselves with inconvenient details like the practical effects or unintended consequences of "social" spending.

To many people, the existence of high unemployment in the context of high social spending and an official commitment to "solidarity" is baffling; it leads them down the road of demagoguery and scapegoating. If France was experiencing an economic and social crisis, surely the rising tide of neoliberal-driven world trade was largely to blame, as many people were told throughout the 1990s and early 2000s by leading French newspapers and magazines like *Le Monde*, *Le Monde Diplomatique*, *L'Humanité*, *Libération*, *Politis* and *Alternatives économiques*.[19] As Philippe Manière writes in his book *La vengeance du peuple. Les élites, Le Pen et les Français* (2002), "Brussels and Washington have become, in the dominant political discourse of our elites, the new Sodom and Gomorrahs, the two capitals of anti-France."[20]

The Left has never accepted that reform is necessary for its own sake; the Right has not taken this case to the public in a convincing manner and it has occasionally pandered to the public's fears over globalization. Over the past fifteen years, significant reforms have indeed been made in some crucial areas, including the dismantling of much of the postwar statist apparatus. As Vivien Schmidt showed in her landmark study, *From State to Market? The Transformation of French Business and Government* (1996), during the 1980s and early 1990s French businesses changed beyond recognition. Schmidt argues that "the dirigiste state, so carefully built up during the postwar period, was effectively dismantled."[21] Schmidt's argument is compelling.

As Sophie Meunier and Philip Gordon have recently argued, these sweeping reforms (and those under Jospin during the late 1990s) were introduced by stealth, with no intellectual justification for them, no political reward or credit sought by the very people who carried them out. Imagine Reagan or Thatcher failing to take credit for their efforts to deregulate the economy: this is precisely what has happened in France since the late 1980s. Since the move away from *dirigisme* was not presented as something which was a good thing to do regardless of outside forces, extremist critics have been able to point to globalization as the driving force behind these seemingly sinister changes. The failure of French elites to offer a consistent political and intellectual justification for their reforms constitutes a failure of leadership and is directly responsible for the rise of extremism. For over a decade, politicians on both sides of the spectrum have been speaking out of both sides of their mouths, telling the public that they would defend the big welfare state even as they quietly demolished the *dirigiste* apparatus.

On the one hand, important efforts have been made to deregulate the economy. But the interventionist impulse is alive and kicking in matters social: consider the 35-hour work week, the "emplois-jeunes" program and the various other statist social innovations of the Jospin government. Some critics, like Erik Izraelewicz, have argued that during the 1990s the French Socialists operated under the assumption that either: a) what the rest of the world did was irrelevant since the French labor model was superior and other nations were pursuing a misguided quest to refashion themselves along American lines; or b) eventually the rest of the world would come around to embrace the French model.[22] In either case, here was a fatal conceit which justified a status quo characterized by life-battering long-term unemployment.

At times it seems as if many French leaders have forgotten that it was the dynamic economy – not the state, not labor laws, not pensions, not family allowances – which created the very prosperity upon which so much rests today. Indeed, many French intellectuals, politicians, and labor leaders are convinced that the essence of European civilization is the welfare state itself – and the US market model represents the other, negative half of this binary world-view. Ignacio Ramonet, an editor with *Le Monde Diplomatique* and author of several widely read books on international affairs and political economy, has, along with his colleagues, managed to focus the entire public debate on the defence of existing spending. The very market which pays for social policies in the first place is ignored, since it is mistrusted or simply despised:

Europe invented the Welfare State. Like nowhere else in the world, the citizens of the Fifteen [the EU's core 15 nation-members] benefit from a pension system, health insurance, family allowances, unemployment benefits, and labor law [protections]. This arsenal of socio-economic guarantees, conquered by the workers' movement, constitutes the heart of modern European civilization. Above all, this is what distinguishes the European Union from other geopolitical zones, most notably from its economic competitors Japan and America.[23]

There are several problems with this line of thinking. First, it is a myopic, ahistorical view which denies the fundamental similarities uniting the USA and Europe: they are rich, democratic, open, capitalist societies. Capitalism is the "heart of European civilization," and has been for several centuries. Second, the welfare state was indeed born in Europe – in authoritarian Germany. Since the early 1990s, the mythic "social democratic" interpretation of the rise of the welfare state, which ascribes success to strong worker movements and socialist parties, has been challenged (rather effectively, in my view) by historians such as Peter Baldwin (France, Britain, Germany, Scandinavia), David Vincent (Britain), and Penny Bryden (Canada).[24] Finally, Europe has welfare states precisely because Europe is rich and capitalist, and not the other way around. In Ramonet's view, the welfare state is required for prosperity in the first place, and therefore the defence of "the social" is his exclusive focus. This type of cart-before-the-horse thinking is one of the things that got France into its current economic problems. The failure of the intellectual class to accept change, coupled with the failure of political leaders of all stripes to offer a consistent intellectual justification for their actions, has allowed economically illiterate essayists and sheep farmers to capture the public discourse.

The "economic horror" and the Bové phenomenon

In 1996, Viviane Forrester penned an alarmist diatribe against the USA and globalization. The book sold over 350,000 copies in France alone and won one of the nation's most prestigious book awards.[25] In *The Economic Horror*, Forrester invoked the specter of American-led "globalization" in language full of passionate intensity but devoid of factual accuracy. She spoke of the "economic genocide" being brought on by globalization. This was great for book sales, but terrible for the general level of public debate on a serious issue. The impact of books like *The Economic Horror* should not be underestimated: dozens and dozens of similarly polemical, lazily researched *libelles* have been published since the early 1990s.

Forrester attributed virtually every economic and social problem in France, from high youth unemployment, rising inequality, racial segregation, and rising crime, to "globalization." A literary critic for *Le Monde*, Forrester was clearly in over her head, with no understanding of the concept of comparative advantage, no sense of the history of the developing world, no grasp of the vast literature on globalization, technological change, trade, and inequality. And yet, with her simplistic screed, she somehow set the very parameters of the debate on globalization.[26] As Kresl and Gallais argue in *France Encounters Globalization*, although *The Economic Horror* was "written in elegant prose, the analysis is inspired by *élan vital* rather than by either data or theory, the mainstays of social scientists."[27] "What the social scientist finds lacking is establishment of a causal relationship between what could conceivably be considered two parallel series of events."[28]

At the grassroots level, the demagogic anti-globalization leader José Bové was made into a national celebrity by the nation's media, which is overwhelmingly anti-American.[29] This one-time Californian dreams of a world free from the tyranny of fast food outlets. This jovial, mustachioed *militant* from Millau has been active for many years, but it was the US duty on Roquefort cheese which led him to a higher stage of anti-imperial activism. He urges the French to shun *la malbouffe* (lousy fast food). He vandalized a McDonald's restaurant under construction, destroyed GM crops, spent a few months in prison, and received the support of a slim majority of the French population. Prime Minister Jospin legitimized Bové in the public eye, taking him out to a highly publicized dinner, during which they agreed that they did not care too much for McDonald's – and the level of public discourse rose to Olympian heights.

Bové and the nationalist-protectionist school of anti-globalism care so much about the developing world that they want to keep its products off French shelves.[30] When Bové addressed a crowd of 200,000 "anti-neoliberal globalization" activists in Larzac, France in August 2003, he declared that his goal was to "bring down the WTO and bring about a more equal distribution of wealth in the world." By this he meant he wished to tax wealthy financial speculators – he was not vowing to share *his* income with the poor of the developing world; he was proposing to use other people's money.[31]

During the 1990s, globalization was commonly blamed for the problems of the developing world as well as France's own problems. Typical was the intensely nationalistic, anti-American Jean-Pierre Chevènement, who, as a minister in Mitterrand's governments, pushed for policies which led to high unemployment. Throughout the 1990s, he failed to take responsibility for this, preferring instead to campaign against "l'Europe libérale et la mondialisation" (a key election slogan), putting the blame for many of France's homegrown social and economic problems on globalization.[32] Chevènement has faded from the scene, but many of the key architects of France's economic crisis during the early 1980s remain and some have risen to the top of the Socialist Party. Their invocation of the threat of "globalization" has prevented a full historical disclosure of their errors.

The fear of change

The underlying fear of the anti-globalists may well be the fear of change, broadly conceived. French intellectuals have a long history of decrying rapid industrial/social change. In the nineteenth century, English-style urban growth and industrial change was the great demon. The entire public debate on social assistance in France during the nineteenth century was framed by the negative Other, the English, their excessively fast economic and urban growth, their horrible slums, the wide gap between the rich and the poor, and their cruel, self-defeating Poor Law.[33]

A major World Values Survey of 1990 found that 41.9% of Canadians "welcome change" and 15.0% "worry" about it. By contrast, only 30.5% of French "welcome change," and 19.2% "worry" about it. In Canada, 19.1% responded that "new" ideas were better than old and the European aggregate for this question was 18.6%; in France, only 12.8%.[34] As usual, de Gaulle has left us with a gem: the ". . . tendency of Frenchmen, whatever their occupation, [is] to clamor for progress while hoping that everything will remain the same."[35] More recently, the technology writer Virginia Postrel has argued in *The Future and its Enemies* (1998), that the technocrat's nightmare is dynamism – dynamism which he or she has not planned, for which he/she can claim little or no credit.[36]

A whole generation of French leaders, many of them trained at the same two or three graduate schools, has been accultured into the belief that the French state is by definition good and wise, and that it has a primordial mission to tame, to civilize, to manage the very nature of society. Prime Minister Jospin's statements regarding the nature of the ideal society reflect this interventionist impulse. France, he argued, shall be a "social-market society, not a market society." In June 2001, he articulated his vision at a conference of European socialist politicians: "If we have accepted the market economy, we do not accept any sort of market economy . . . We resist the commodification of the world. The economy must serve man and not vice versa. The market must be a servant; it must not be a master."[37]

Since the 1980s, a large section of France's intellectual and political class has retreated into rhetoric like Jospin's.[38] The result is that serious debate on important questions like international trade and pension reform, free from extreme ideological, self-righteous *prises de position*, has become difficult. Discussion of significant "social" spending cuts (or reshuffling) is taboo, and is equated with a wholesale assault on the philosophical underpinnings of the welfare state, of "solidarity" – even of "civilization."[39]

Pension reform: is there really a link to globalization?

The fear of "globalization" often gets wrapped up in the opposition to domestic reform, hindering politicians' efforts to save France from its self-destructive pension policy and souring the debate. Critics who invoke changing demographics and the low retirement age are accused of "catastrophisme." Today, the magazine *Politis* links its official mission statement – "the rendez-vous for anti-neoliberal globalization, for the solidaristic economy, and for the defense of the environment" – with its commitment to "save our solidaristic pensions."[40] In fact the imperative to reform pensions in order to save them from outright bankruptcy is entirely domestic in origin. And one cannot "save" what does not exist.

Like much of what is written in the French academy, discussions of French social problems need to come back down to earth.[41] Thoughtless, non peer-reviewed 100-page books published by presses which live off government subsidies appear regularly with entirely misleading arguments and titles such as *Les retraites au péril du libéralisme*; these books do nothing to enlighten the public on a serious issue.[42] (In fact, there is absolutely no danger of the French converting to financially solvent, fully funded private pension funds. But there is the very real danger that the current pay-as-you-go pension systems will bankrupt the country and send it into further political turmoil.)[43] Apparently serious books on the pension crisis issue appear regularly (and sell quite well) with titles like *Pension Funds: The Trick of Con Artists* – the title is supposed to allude to American- and British-style private, capitalized pension funds. Another bestseller was called *La Bourse ou la Vie: La grande manipulation des petits actionnaires* (2000).[44] The point of these books is to distract attention from the homegrown problems and to offer up a false choice: French-style "solidaristic" pensions or the neoliberal Robert Maxwell- Enron-style alternative.

Reform will be rendered even more difficult since it has been tainted by association with Thatcherism and the American New Right. Tony Blair is commonly portrayed as a sort of socialist sellout, a sneaky Bernsteinite. The country's main unions, including the CGT (a communist stronghold) and FO (until 2004 led by the militant Marc Blondel) have portrayed pension reform as a Right-wing, World Bank-dictated conspiracy. Leafing through *Force Ouvrière*'s weekly newspaper is to enter an unreconstructed Marxist time warp, a world of sinister plots hatched by a New York–London axis of financiers bent on the destruction of European public sector pensions.[45] In 1999, Prime Minister Jospin expressed his disappointment with Germany's Chancellor Gerhard Schroeder when he published a joint declaration with Blair regarding the "Third Way."[46] Eyes rolled in 1998 when Blair made a speech (in French) to the French Parliament, in which he exhorted his hosts to tune into his message, drop their dogmatic commitment to statism, and follow him into the Third Way. Blair's project never had much appeal in France.[47]

Jean-Luc Cazettes, the head of the nation's chief pension fund during the late 1990s, the CNAV, opposed the proposal that France might follow the German and Swedish path and introduce partial capitalization, or supplementary, private, self-funded, 401k (USA) or RRSP-style (Canada) pensions, on the grounds that the stock market is nothing but a "marché de dupes."[48] The deceptive language of solidarity was readily apparent in the backlash against the publication of the 1999 "Charpin Report" on the impending pension crisis, issued by Jean-Michel Charpin of the Commissariat Général du Plan. Charpin recommended that eligibility for pensions in the private sector should come only after 42.5 years of contributions, and not as a right of citizenship available to all those who turn sixty and/or have contributed for forty years, as it has been since 1982. This report was met with widespread denunciation by the country's leading newspapers, the intellectual class, and the unions.[49]

Newspapers like *L'Humanité* and *Libération* opposed Charpin's "neoliberalism." This report was commissioned by the Jospin government in all likelihood in order to have an (apparently neutral) civil servant deliver the bad news and take the fall. It was widely read and discussed in the media. It has provided the framework for debate ever since its publication. Immediately, it provoked vocal opposition, couched in the most misleading and even apocalyptic terms, as witnessed in the May 1999 article in *Le Monde* entitled, "Le Rapport Charpin, c'est la rupture programmée du contrat social."[50] In fact, the report was not a deliberate attempt to break the current social contract – it was, rather, an attempt to *save* French society from being broken by its unsustainable pension promises.[51]

The misleading rhetoric which flowed from the "social partners" during the 1990s went unchallenged by most politicians, who, like their American counterparts, lived in fear of powerful seniors' organizations and, above all, the militant and disruptive French public sector. A key negotiating tactic (if it can be called so) of French unions was to threaten a repeat of December 1995, when the nation was brought to a standstill by strikes.[52] The very language used by the "social partners" is a smokescreen, a powerful ideological and political tool, for it helps to squeeze out alternatives and to limit the parameters of debate. According to the labor leader Claude Debons, of the CFDT, "behind the apparent *bonhomie* of [Prime Minister] Raffarin is a rampant Thatcherism." Raffarin's questioning of the 35-hour law was grounded not in a concern for the fuzzy math behind this policy, but rather out of a "liberal and inegalitarian" logic.[53] Likewise, Raffarin's pension reform, which brought at least one million people into the streets on 13 May 2003, was perceived as a neoliberal inspired piece of trickery.[54] The issue of finances was of no concern to the protestors; "Raffarin: l'Américain," read the headlines in the main leftist newspapers in 2003. Raffarin the "demolition man," the "destroyer" of the welfare state, read the titles of media releases and pamphlets produced by ATTAC (the pro-Tobin Tax, anti-globalization pressure group) in 2003 in order to discredit the prime minister's timid reforms. This literature is full of references to "Trojan Horses" and plots: "One 'reform' may hide within it another," writes Michel Husson of ATTAC. ATTAC portrays Raffarin's reforms as some sort of aristocratic plot against true France, as an attempt to "dismantle" a certain French "civilization."[55]

Denmark, Sweden, Japan, the USA, Canada, Britain, Australia, Germany, and Italy made important reforms to their public pension systems during the last ten years but somehow their "civilization" carries on. These reforms received, if anything, cursory coverage in the back pages of *Le Monde*: the result was an impoverishment of political discourse. When a partial reform finally came, in 2003 under Raffarin, its cost had risen considerably. Ultimately, Raffarin succeeded by invoking, *ad nauseam*, the funding shortfall and the alarming demographic scenario. He also succeeded in emphasizing that reform was not an attack on any particular group, but something which was in the best interests of all French citizens – something Juppé had failed to do.

Anti-globalization talk and the rise of political extremism

Globophobia does far more than stall the reform of the French social security system; it is linked to the rise of political extremism. As Sophie Meunier reminds us, France is one of the leading beneficiaries of globalization: from Danone (which owns Evian) to LVMH, Paribas, Sodexho Alliance, L'Oréal, TotalFina Elf, Peugeot, Suez, Pernod Ricard, Michelin, and Lyonnaise des Eaux, French companies are now second only to US ones in the pantheon of multinationals.[56] Champagne, claret, and cognac is consumed around the world, from London to Bombay. French cuisine inspires the Iron Chefs in Japan and Bobby Flay in the USA. French engineers build hydroelectric dams across Asia; French oil companies operate around the globe. French agricultural produce is sold throughout Europe. French weapons, perfumes, pharmaceuticals, planes, trains, and automobiles are sold around the world. By 2001, France had become the third most attractive location for Foreign Direct Investment (FDI) in the world. Foreign firms accounted for 15% of employment in France. Yet, as Meunier notes,

in spite of this key role played by France in promoting globalization and by globalization in modernizing France, the country seems to have locked itself up in an anti-globalization discourse . . . On the left as on the right, the public discourse of most of the political parties emphasizes the scandals (Vilvoorde) [the auto plant which was closed] and debacles (Vivendi) of globalization rather than its success stories (LVMH or Paribas). They have created an atmosphere of distrust of the globalization process so widespread that the French now appear to share a *pensée unique* on globalization. Yet this schizophrenia about globalization, innocuous as it may seem, has real political consequences. The inability of the Jospin government to be upfront about the challenges of globalization and to align its rhetoric with its actions helps explain the shocking results of the 2002 presidential election, in which a far-right candidate, Jean-Marie Le Pen, outpolled Jospin and passed into the second round.[57]

As Vivien Schmidt argues, some time during the mid 1990s, "globalization" ceased being a challenge and instead became a threat.[58] It came to be seen more and more as an American-led cultural assault instead of an economic opportunity. Instead of celebrating – or simply acknowledging – the major *désétatisation* which has taken place since the mid 1980s, instead of telling the public that France has in fact *gained* from a less regulated, more privatized, more open economy, French politicians (Jospin in particular) shedded several skins of state by stealth, hoping the public would not notice.

But the extremists on the Right and on the Left fringe noticed. And, since no French politician had taken the case for de-*dirigisme* to the public, small wonder the extremists presented the wave of privatizations and the retreat from *dirigisme* under Jospin and his predecessors as being forced upon France by the outside world. The splintering of the Left into various extremist anti-globalization parties, such as those led by Jean-Pierre Chevènement and Olivier Besancenot (who presides over the Ligue Communiste Révolutionnaire), created the opening for Le Pen, allowing him to win five million votes and enter into the second round of the 2002 presidential election.[59] The fear over globalization was a key issue in the election. For the Left-Bank intellectual, it was *the* key issue. Globalization (*mondialisation*) is omnipresent in the French political discourse and a common topic of conversation in cafés and restaurants. There is, of course, nothing peculiarly French about this sort of national obsession: each nation tends to have one. Just as a proposed increase in taxes will be presented by American conservatives as a threat to American civilization, any proposed reduction in "solidarity" seems like a threat to French civilization, and will bring throngs of professors into the streets of the fifth and sixth *arrondissements* of Paris.

Is there something peculiar about French institutions which might explain why a large proportion of French intellectuals seem to be obsessed with this issue? My view is that the national educational system imparts such a profound reverence for French *culture* that economic issues are more likely to be seen through cultural lenses. Does the proposed new pension formula conform to the French cultural model or threaten it? This is the type of question French intellectuals, labor leaders, and Socialist politicians will ask when they contemplate pension reform proposals. Does it spring from *our* distinct cultural model or does it emanate from The Other, from the neoliberal world? The question: does it make our bankrupt system affordable? is rarely posed. To intellectuals, where pensions are concerned, talking about numbers is the language of the Right.

As the historian Tony Judt has shown in his critique of the post-Second World War intellectual climate in France, the French intellectual's tendency to dismiss transparent facts with the heavy hand of ideological posturing dates back at least several decades, if not centuries.[60] Judt argues: "Ever since the statutes of the University of Paris (AD 1215) required of them that its scholars work to found a 'comprehensive theory of the world,' the dominant characteristic of French intellectual discourse has been the drive to organize and contain knowledge within a single frame," leading, in the past, to a search for "all-embracing metahistories." Judt argues that this habit of thought is transmitted from generation to generation via "a remarkably unbroken urban culture, that of the Parisian community of writers and scholars, unique in the Western experience."[61] This leads to the widespread adoption of "cultural fads" and abstract "universalist visions."[62] Abstraction triumphs over empiricism; One Big Idea strikes down all others, crowding out more nuanced views of complex issues. "From such heights, everything is clear, but not very much is visible."[63] The French welfare state has become so thoroughly interwoven into the national fabric, so thoroughly identified as a rampart against globalization, that its reform seems to require going back to a sort of social Stone Age – or forward to a future the French fear . . . America.[64]

Why many French people fear cultural globalization

Cultural globalization, often equated with the spread of American culture, is surely an important phenomenon, and many prominent French intellectuals, artists, and politicians are haunted by it. Veteran broadcast and print journalist Alain Duhamel estimates that 20% of the French population is militantly opposed to globalization.[65] As with many other people around the world, the French (not all of them, of course, but a significant minority and probably a majority of intellectuals) resent the USA's economic success, its scientific prowess, its riches, and military power out of all proportion to its 4% share of the world's population, its sometimes arrogant and inconsistent projection of its power and ideals around the world.[66] Unlike most other peoples, the French, heirs themselves to a great Revolution, believe that *their model* is also a potential gift to the world. This is why the French clash with the USA more than the Danes do. When the French engage in good old-fashioned *schadenfreude*, the USA is usually the target. "Anti-Americanism indulges France's fantasy of past greatness and splendor." Anti-Americanism "became the uncontested ideology of French public life" during the 1990s and early 2000s. As Jean-François Revel argues, anti-Americanism is *the* French national obsession.[67]

When French anti-globalists, particularly intellectuals and Leftist politicians, say they are opposed to cultural globalization what they usually mean is that they are opposed to the excessive spread of *American* culture. Like anti-Americans around the world, French anti-globalists regard US pop culture as base and vulgar, a culture of the lowest common denominator.[68] In this vision, if the French radiate good taste, artsy films, and fine food around the world, the USA pollutes the airwaves with Hollywood trash and it assaults the "traditional" cuisines of the world with fast food.

As Richard Kuisel argues in *Seducing the French: The Dilemma of Americanization* (1993), "The French feel culturally superior and destined to enlighten the globe."[69] Kuisel continues: "the French response to America in the twentieth century derives, in large measure, from an assumption that the New World is a social model of the future."[70] Very few French citizens have ever been comfortable with this thought. French opposition to "globalization" cannot be understood without reference to the common French fear that America is the chief threat to a distinctively French, manifestly superior form of *civilisation*.

The French state, Tyler Cowen reminds us, spends upwards of $3 billion per year, employing "twelve thousand cultural bureaucrats, trying to nourish and preserve their vision of a uniquely French culture."[71] When the USA tried to put cultural industries on the table during the 1993 Uruguay Round of the GATT negotiations, a raw nerve was hit, and French foes of globalization seized the moment to rally support against the idea that culture was just another merchandise.[72] Joined by Canada, which also contains a hard core of anti-American cultural protectionists, France led the movement to exempt "culture" from free-trade agreements. French success in killing the Multilateral Agreement on Investment in 1998 was probably a great victory for democracy (as well as proof that companies are indeed arrogant but not as powerful as critics claim); this episode launched Prime Minister Jospin to the unofficial position of leading head of state opposed to globalization.[73] The French protest movement against genetically modified crops and the use of hormones in the US beef industry catapulted José Bové into international stardom. Jospin delivered keynote addresses at international No Globo conferences. He attended the annual anti-globalization meeting in Porto Alegre, Brazil. In Rio, he blamed globalization for the rise in inequality in France and in Brazil itself.[74]

In these speeches, and in the op-ed pieces he wrote for newspapers, Jospin always made this link without ever making an empirical case for his argument. He rarely mentioned the impact of technological change on low-skilled workers, which, several academic studies have suggested, is far more threatening to low-skilled workers than trade. Jospin never seemed aware of (or willing to acknowledge) research conducted by the French statistical bureau INSEE or the important scholarly work by Cline, Iversen, Wren, and Cusack which suggests that the transition from a high-wage blue collar, manufacturing economy to a service economy might be the most important cause of "exclusion" and the rise of the working poor.[75] Jospin never mentioned the overvalued franc or high real interest rates which were largely the result of deficit spending, and the only time he mentioned the onerous red tape which regulates French business, the 35-hour law, and the Auroux Laws, was when he suggested that they should provide a model for a new "Social Europe."[76] (In other words, what had failed in France could succeed only if projected to Europe as a whole.)[77]

The French state spent eight more points of GDP in 1995 than it did in 1980 (70% of this extra spending going to "the social"), but poverty and unemployment increased. Domestic policy failures and the misallocation of new spending to the already comfortable are the root of this; globalization has very little to do with it. The French state is not being prevented from engaging in the old poverty-eradicating *dirigiste* policies of the post-Second World War era precisely because *dirigisme* probably had little to do with poverty reduction in the first place.

From Colbert to welfare state?

Globalization is such a threat to many French elites because they see it as a wild, untamed force – "jungle capitalism," in Jospin's words – poised to bury every remnant of *étatisme*. If many French politicians were willing to jettison *dirigisme* they will go to the wall to defend the big welfare state and the big public sector. Since the French have retreated from statist economic planning by stealth, with no public avowal on the part of those who ordered the retreat, many people on the Left still see a return to statism as a viable alternative to "neoliberal globalization." In the minds of the majority of French Socialists and Communists, and even a slim portion of the moderate Right, statism is so inextricably linked with the *trente glorieuses*, France's thirty glory years of economic growth (1945–75), that its apparent antithesis, full-blown deregulation, seems like a threat to a tradition dating back to Colbert. Posing the issue in such stark terms makes further reform more difficult.

Colbert has little to do with modern France. One of the greatest myths surrounding the French is that their current fondness for the big state can be traced all the way back to the seventeenth century, when Louis XIV's minister Jean-Baptiste Colbert developed the nation's transportation networks, introduced tariffs, and promoted key domestic industries.[78] In 1999, for example, Jean-Luc Lagardère, the late great arms magnate, said: "The role of the state has been fundamental since the 17th century, something I greatly admire."[79] The common view of a straight, inevitable line from Colbert's statism of the seventeenth century to the

Table 3.1 *French government
spending,% of GDP*

1870	12.6	1960	34.6
1913	17.0	1980	46.1
1920	27.6	1990	49.8
1937	29.0	1996	54.5

Source: "The World Economy," *The Economist,*
20 September 1997, p. 8. From an IMF survey.

heavy-handed statism of the post-1945 era is held in France and overseas alike. The Colbert to Welfare paradigm locates a recent, politically
created situation (the huge, *dirigiste,* high-spending, post-Second World
War French state) within the deep recesses of French history, thereby
making it seem inevitable, natural, set in stone. This view is historically
inaccurate.

Having said this, ideas matter, even if they are not grounded in historical truth. Historical myths can help to create an imagined reality which
will influence policy. Myths can help to seal off debate, to limit the parameters of discussion. If, as many French people believe, statist approaches
to job creation and high social spending are "normal" in France, then
proposals to move cautiously, gradually, in another direction appear to
threaten the French national identity. Such proposals might even seem
unFrench.

The Colbert to Welfare myth springs from an ahistorical appeal to
history. It overlooks the nineteenth and early twentieth centuries, when
the French state was a less effective, less interventionist, less professional
entity than its British and German counterparts. And this view confuses
the *ideal* of the big, interventionist state with the big state itself. It equates
talk and theory with influence and practice.[80]

In fact the road to the welfare state in France had to be cut through the
bedrock of laissez-faire liberalism that was nineteenth-century elite opinion. As Richard Kuisel has demonstrated, well into the 1930s, diehard
liberals dominated the universities, the influential Paris Law Faculty, the
grandes écoles, and *bien pensant* opinion.[81] There was nothing resembling
concerted economic planning before the First World War – and, arguably,
before the 1940s. British government spending was a full six points of
GDP higher than French during the early 1930s.

As the French emerged from the Vichy era, humbled and humiliated,
they, like the proud and victorious British, seized upon social security and
economic planning as a means to rebuild their world, to relegitimize their

political order, to deliver the goods to an eager populace. Economic and social laissez-faire were deemed guilty by association with the spineless Third Republic; accordingly, these ideas were dealt a death blow, replaced with the Fourth Republic's new religion of planning and social security. In 1940, the spirit of the late nineteenth-century political economist Paul Leroy Beaulieu, the high priest of French liberalism, still stalked the corridors of the academy and the assembly; at war's end, his corpus was given a quick burial.

French academics and politicians now put their faith in Keynesian economics, which was taught to the small army of missionary-like technocrats (and future prime ministers) being trained at the new Ecole Nationale d'Administration (ENA).[82] In his book *L'Etat en France de 1789 à nos jours*, Pierre Rosanvallon argues that the war had a decisive cultural impact on the French, which led to a widely held paradigmatic shift in social and economic thought.[83] Before the war the state had been less interventionist, less concerned with full employment, than the American and British states; after the war, the French converted to Keynesianism, to *étatisme*, to the idea of full employment, with full force.[84]

"Modernization or decadence"

"The state must hold the levers of command," declared General Charles de Gaulle, the head of the provisional government of France, in 1945. But there was more: "the privileged classes," he said, had "disqualified themselves."[85] This was a slight exaggeration: the new bosses were for the most part the old bosses (at least, they were drawn from the same sorts of social milieux). But de Gaulle did indeed set the postwar era's intellectual tone towards business. Business leaders were declared guilty by association with interwar economic stagnation and the defeat at the hands of the Germans.

After the war, a profound break with this past was required for both economic and psychological reasons. The new Commissariat Général du Plan would help to set targets and priorities, to provide direction for private business and the nationalized sector alike. Politicians and the general public alike deemed the laissez-faire capitalist system of the interwar years narrow-minded, backward, and timid. Indeed this view had more than a kernel of truth to it: in 1939, the average age of French industrial machinery was four times that of their American counterparts and three times older than their British counterparts. At the core of the postwar critique of French capitalism was the damning verdict that a backward economy had allowed the Germans to roll over the nation in a matter of weeks.

Nationalized industries – the banks, the transport industry, the energy industry – would serve as the spearheads in the postwar economic battle. They would help to "relaunch" France as a great economic power. Nationalization would assist the modernization process, build up investment, and consolidate excessively fragmented industries (1,730 companies were involved in the production and transmission of electricity in 1939). Nationalization would also integrate a hostile working class movement, represented by the powerful Communist Party, into the heart of the postwar economic order.[86] (At times the party had the second highest number of votes, but it was outgunned by rightist coalitions.) By 1950, the French state had a major role in most of the key sectors of the economy and the Plan provided 50% of the nation's total capital investment.[87] The state industries accounted for 50% of all economic activity. By the early 1980s, the state owned or had a controlling interest in over 4,000 firms (today the figure is closer to 1,500).[88]

During the 1940s, the French were caught up in a life or death struggle – or so men like the planning commission's founder, Jean Monnet, told them – and the nation's very ethos was geared towards "the politics of productivity."[89] With the battle cry "modernization or decadence," Monnet distilled a complex array of economic issues into a readily digestible slogan. The expansion of the social security system figured at the center of the postwar modernization program. At this point, a significant number (but a clear minority) of people began to view social spending as an *a priori* good, regardless of economic conditions, regardless of fiscal constraints.

The welfare state and the "end of history"?

Despite the initial flaws of the new social security edifice, despite the failure of universalism, there was a whiff of triumphalism in the air after the war when critics took stock of the new social security system. Dr Pierre Theil ushered in the New Year in January 1947 with a leader in the journal he edited, *Les Annales de la médecine sociale*, with the following remarkable statement: "Isn't it wonderful that in the midst of a total war, such a destructive war, we have seen the gestation of a vast social movement whose first buds had only to wait for the Armistice to open? France, England, the United States of America, various European nations and others are all witnessing the birth of plans for Social Security . . . which will, one by one, color the map of the world."[90]

Like many of his compatriots at this time, Theil viewed the welfare state as nothing less than a higher form of civilization towards which all nations were marching inexorably. The red flag of solidarity would be hoisted around the world, to the betterment of all. His thinking was neatly encapsulated in the motto: "monde social – forme moderne de la civilisation."[91] This is the type of heady optimism that underlay the massive social spending of the postwar era. Never had the French nation promised so much to so many.[92]

The Liberation was seen by many as a time to right the wrongs of the past, to move the country forward, along the (seemingly inevitable) international path of social and economic justice. The right to welfare – and, one hundred years after it was first proclaimed during the 1848 Revolution, the right to work – was enshrined in the constitution of the new, Fourth Republic: "It shall be the duty of all to work, and the right of all to obtain employment." As elsewhere in the West, the French state was invested with an almost sacred duty to ensure full employment.

During the 1950s, the French began to define their social services as against a negative American model.[93] This was probably some form of compensation for the fact that the French were now seeking to learn from the USA in all realms economic, sending teams of advisors to US factories and universities to learn the most modern forms of management. Immediately after the war, the state performed an educative role as it launched business down the path of modernization: the état instituteur would, as Rosanvallon argues, treat businesses much as the republican state of the 1880s treated the public in general. With the zeal of the missionary it would spread the word and attempt to change the very essence of the nation.[94]

Since the state became enormous at precisely the time that the French economy was enjoying its glory age, many people cannot imagine prosperity without a large state. As Gordon and Meunier argue in *The French Challenge*,

Because the 1950s and 1960s also saw a large increase in state benefits, like social security and generous health care and pension benefits, many French people remember *dirigisme* fondly (often attributing to it more importance than it deserved) . . . This favorable judgment – in contrast, for example, to Great Britain, where many people had judged their interventionist state a failure by the 1980s – would later contribute to France's difficulty in adapting to the requirements of globalization. Why, many French people felt (and continue to feel), fix something that is not fundamentally broken?[95]

The problem with this popularly held assumption is that, although the French state did grow rapidly during the boom years of the 1950s and 1960s, it was a much smaller state than today's. When the bubble burst during the mid 1970s, the French state spent considerably less on social policy than it does today – a full ten points of GDP less. Overall state spending was fifteen points lower than today. Spending kept on rising as the economy was slowing, but this certainly did not help to bring back the glory years.

The rosy view of French *dirigisme* links two parallel phenomena without establishing an empirical link. We will probably never know for sure the extent to which economic planning was responsible for economic growth. In any case, the big state was the response to unusual circumstances: the need to rebuild a war-torn, psychologically crippled nation. Today, the failure of political elites to convey the message that what worked during the 1950s and 1960s need not continue to be relevant has allowed the splinter parties to yearn for a return to the supposedly good old days of *dirigisme* and it has made social security and labor-law reform even more difficult. When an unprofitable French state-owned company is partially privatized, critics will see this as an attack on the very essence of the social order.

Germany did not engage in French-style economic planning but it grew just as spectacularly as did France. Canada boomed as well, becoming the second richest nation in the world by 1960, but the federal and provincial governments combined spent less than half the amount of the typical European state during the 1950s and 1960s. The root of postwar prosperity in France, as elsewhere, was the greatest burst of productivity growth in world history, coupled with a one-time shot in the arm (in the form of a huge wave of low-wage rural migrants to French cities and a huge spurt of infrastructure expansion), not state direction of the economy *per se.*[96]

Planning did indeed revive a few areas crucial for overall growth: banking, the transport industry, and the energy sector, providing essential oils for commercial intercourse. Planning helped to coordinate scarce capital and to allocate Marshall Plan aid efficiently. At a time when French infrastructure in general lagged far behind that of its competitors, the state played a key role in helping to close this gap. But what worked during the 1950s, during a distinct historical epoch, need not provide a timeless model.

I am not positing a sort of "separate sphere" view of economy and state; I am well aware that there is a symbiotic relationship between the two. I *am* attempting to put the horse before the cart. State spending is a bit like infrastructure in general: you can build it, and the positive economic spin-offs will come, but you cannot continue to build indefinitely, in excess of annual tax revenues. At a certain point the law of diminishing returns kicks in. France reached this point some time during the 1980s.

From France and Italy during the 1950s and 1960s, to Japan during the 1960s and 1970s, to Singapore and Taiwan during the 1970s and 1980s, to China from the mid 1980s to the present, one-off, exceptional inputs – infrastructure expansion, the shift from agriculture to a factory and service-based economy, productivity explosions caused by rapid expansion of higher education, and the spread of skills and female education – typically result in growth rates of 5 to 9% for two or three decades. But these cards can be played only once: eventually the game is over as some sort of plateau of skills is reached, and the rural exodus comes to a halt. Eventually the housing construction market settles down as only 200,000 new units are added per year instead of 500,000 (as in France in 1988–95 compared with the boom years of 1968–75), the universities have been established and the new hospitals have been built, the highways have been constructed, the telephone systems have been expanded, the spread of female education slows as all girls and many young women receive a good education, and economic growth settles down to 1 to 3% per year, to reflect regular productivity increases as opposed to one-off infrastructure inputs.[97] This model applies to countries with big states and small states; it works for Korea and Japan (with very small welfare states, even today) and for Sweden (with its huge welfare state). It works for countries which nationalized industries (France, Italy) and those which did not (Singapore, Japan, Germany, Canada before the 1970s).

Until recently, French politicians, with their strong pride in their distinct economic model, seemed blind to this reality. Like others around the West, they confused these one-off inputs with the apparent efficacy of economic planning itself. As the dispensers of subsidies and social programs, politicians have been very happy to tell the public that *they* were the bringers of jobs – not the marketplace, not productivity growth, not the Marshall Plan, not the rise of Germany as a trading partner, not the world trading system in general. So when the system they built broke, small wonder many of them blamed outside forces: the EU, Maastricht, "neoliberal" globalization, and not the true culprits – themselves, their misguided policies.

Basic investments in social capital are obviously a key function of the modern state. Without a well-educated and healthy population, prosperity is impossible. But a significant portion of the French Left assumes, as an article of faith, that the post-Second World War economic boom would have been impossible without the big, high-spending state. If this holds true, then only similar approaches will work in the future. This view has been analyzed and refuted by the French economist Daniel Cohen.[98] The prosperity of the *trente glorieuses* made the big state possible, not the other way round.

A quick glance at Canada and the USA shows that unprecedented economic prosperity took place in nations which did not follow the *dirigiste*

Table 3.2   *The marketplace (not social policies), the root of postwar prosperity (and poverty): changes in the composition of the active French population, 1954–88*

	Percent of French population				
Occupational category	1954	1962	1975	1982	1988
Farmers & agricultural laborers	21.0	15.5	7.5	6.5	6.0
Business, shopkeepers, artisans	13.0	10.5	8.0	8.0	8.0
Upper management, liberal professions	3.0	4.5	7.0	8.0	11.0
Middle management, white collar	9.0	11.5	17.0	18.0	20.0
Clerical white collar	17.0	18.5	24.0	26.5	27.0
Industrial workers	37.0	39.5	36.5	33.0	28.0

Source: Henri Mendras and Alistair Cole, *Social Change in Modern France* (Cambridge: Cambridge University Press, 1991), p. 35. For similar statistics see Roger Price, *A Concise History of France* (Cambridge: Cambridge University Press, 1993), p. 289.

French path and which did not have big welfare states. The Great Wage Compression of the 1940s to 1970s, which saw the North American and European working class gain relative to the middle and upper classes, was the result of productivity increases and a full employment environment: with labor scarcity comes greater bargaining power. Union strength was also important, but not a critical element, given that the unionization rates in Canada and the USA never hit 50% (and the same is true for France, where unionization never reached 30%). Table 3.2 shows how fundamental market growth was to the Glory Years. Full employment, moderately inflationary monetary policy, and low real interest rates which spurred growth: each one of these factors is more important than state planning in explaining the overall success of Western economies during the Glory Years of capitalism.

To a certain extent, the growth of the public welfare state was responsible for the expansion of the white-collar categories (see Table 3.2). But nurses, hospital workers, technicians, and the like are not very well paid in France. And besides, this phenomenon would have occurred with or without public-sponsored insurance (as in the USA, and as in Canada, which did not have state health care until the late 1960s). The point is that the *market* created good jobs during the 1950s and 1960s, and it created the general prosperity that made possible the unprecedented expansion of public clerical and white-collar positions. These jobs, after all, were funded by the larger tax base of these boom years.

Many French politicians view the *trente glorieuses* through rose-tinted lenses. They forget that the economic boom came with labor mobility, migration, business expansion and contraction, and flexibility unheard of in France today. The *trente glorieuses* were not so glorious for the artisan and self-employed class, a couple million of whom were rendered redundant by technological change and changing patterns of distribution and consumption. The labor market was far more flexible in the mid 1960s, when unemployment was under 2%, than it was by 1995, when unemployment hit 12.5%. And the Glory Years were not so glorious for the millions of low-paid workers who lived in garrets, one-room apartments, rooming houses, and shanty towns. As the minimum wage was increased dramatically during the 1970s and 1980s, low-wage work was priced out of the nation. There was a trade-off, but it is rarely appreciated by critics today.

During the *trente glorieuses*, French society was on the move as never before: 1.3 million people left agriculture between 1949 and 1958, and another 1.7 million left between 1958 and 1990 – most of them during the 1960s. Between 1958 and 1972 alone, agricultural employment fell from 22 to 11% of the workforce. In the midst of all this social dislocation, this geographic mobility, this flux in every sense, unemployment was never a problem. The economy and society adapted to new times, and this is precisely why unemployment never became a problem, even as taxes and social charges were rising.[99]

The labor-force participation rate was three points higher in 1965 than in 1995.[100] And people worked longer days. They had less than one-third of the vacation time workers enjoy today. French industry was more firmly in the control of the state during the 1960s, but the labor force was not nearly as rigidly protected by legislation. People came and went from jobs at twice the rate of the 1990s. Today, most on the French Left (and many on the Right as well) seem to want it both ways: they yearn for the full employment of the Golden Age, but they do not accept that full employment requires a more flexible labor force – even more flexible than reforms during the past fifteen years have made it. As a later chapter will show, the vast majority of the discomfort associated with new half-measures promoting labor market flexibility has been borne by young, female part-time workers.

Between 1959 and 1979 – the most successful period in the history of the French economy – French exports rose from 12.8% of GDP to 20.7%. Exports grew at twice the rate of domestic production in general. France boomed as a result of more open European borders. Greater competition kept businesses on their toes, leading to productivity gains and to outlets for French goods.

As Cohen has argued, during the period 1980–94, even as French *society* was becoming more and more polarized between the comfortably employed and pensioned and the "excluded," the French *economy* as a whole was not "in crisis." The economic "crisis" was only a *relative* decline, a *relative* "problem"; the French had become accustomed to 1960s growth rates of 5% per year, when in fact the average rate of growth of the economy since 1850 is closer to 1.5%. If the *trente glorieuses* (1945–75), with its spectacular economic growth rates, had never taken place, the period since 1975 would still be the most successful in the history of the French economy and the world economy alike.[101] To be sure, European competition has been on the rise since the 1980s and all nations have had to readjust following the oil crises and deindustrialization. Some nations *chose* better paths than others.

Despite the slower but still healthy growth rates since 1980, there is a general sense of malaise in France caused chiefly by chronic, long-term unemployment and expectations of social spending which have outstripped the economy's ability to pay. Trade plays only a small role in this story. It affects a few visible sectors (the clothing and steel industries) but has little negative impact on the general economy.[102] But in general French industry *is* competitive, and is not under attack. But one would never know this from reading the leading newspapers *Le Monde*, *Le Monde Diplomatique*, or *Libération*. The very language used to describe the economic woes of France during the 1980s and 1990s was often misleading and self-exculpatory. "La crise," the popular media and the Left argued *ad nauseam*, had tied the hands of politicians. According to this argument, unemployment levels of 12.5% were regrettable, but unavoidable – or else imposed by hostile outside forces.

The growth of the state in the global era?

As Jonah Levy argues in his study of recent French political economy, *Tocqueville's Revenge* (1999), "whatever else one might say about the French state, it would be hard to describe it as 'withering.'"[103] The state has changed dramatically and retreated in several areas but it has not shrunk.[104] Even after the wave of privatizations under Prime Minister Chirac during the 1980s (and, more recently and more ambitiously, under Jospin during the late 1990s), one in four workers continues to work for the state – in the other OECD nations (excluding Scandinavia) the state employs 11 to 18% of the workforce. Privatization was indeed a significant step away from *dirigisme* but it was not accompanied by a general retreat in state spending or a reduction in the size of the civil service. Inefficiencies in the public sector weigh heavily upon the treasury and dig deep into the common person's pocketbook. Subsidies to French farmers add over six hundred euros to the annual grocery bill of each French family. Tight labor laws and high minimum wages ensure that jobs for low-skilled workers do not appear quickly enough to absorb those who have been affected by deindustrialization. Each and every one of these problems is domestic in origin.

The French Left, however, thinks that globalization has impoverished France's low-skilled workers.[105] Under François Hollande, the Socialist Party has recently taken a turn to the far Left. The party is now posing as the only viable "altermondialiste" option; the anti-globalization agenda is at the heart of its platform.[106] If the French Socialists failed to deliver jobs during the 1980s and 1990s (before the short-lived expansion of 1999–2001, that is), then the outside neoliberal world was to blame. After all, job creation figured at the core of public policy, as the Party claimed.

Indeed, this is true. Has not the French state, since the mid 1980s, subsidized over two million jobs in the form of new positions created in the public sector, tax credits which "exonerate" businesses of a certain portion of the high payroll taxes which come attached to low-wage jobs, and subsidies for part-time jobs of "limited duration" (the CDDs)? The answer to all of the above is a resounding yes. The problem is that the French state also chose – under Mitterrand's Socialists and Chirac's RPR alike – to adhere to certain policies (deficit spending on the wrong sorts of things, high interest rates, an overvalued currency, inflationary wage policies, high payroll taxes, tight labor laws governing the hiring and firing of full-time workers, some of the rich world's most byzantine regulations inhibiting business start-ups) which, taken together, have killed more jobs than the various make-work schemes ever created. And these subsidized jobs are not ideal by any stretch of the imagination: by 1997, three-quarters of those benefitting from a CES (Contrat d'emploi solidarité) were working half-time (twenty hours per week) with limited social benefits.[107] France is trapped in a sort of "Keynesian unemployment" quagmire: a situation characterized by continued high public spending (which, in the original formula, was seen as a good thing for job creation), reasonably healthy economic growth (2.0%), *and* high unemployment.[108]

Job-creation schemes cannot be considered in a vacuum and offered up as proof that the state did everything possible in order to reduce unemployment. My argument, developed in more detail in the next chapter, is that French politicians (and labor leaders) did everything they could – given their ideological opposition to wholesale labor market reform and given their unwillingness to ask the gainfully employed portion of the population to sacrifice in the form of wage restraint and general state spending cuts. And globalization has little to do with any of this; domestic political failure has everything to do with it.

Race to the bottom?

If one opens the pages of *Le Monde Diplomatique*, one will read that globalization is leading states to slash income-tax rates on high earners in order to prevent tax flight. One will read that redistribution is increasingly difficult in an age of globalization. These fears are exaggerated: the vast majority of Europeans have no interest in moving to another nation. Only five million Europeans, out of almost 400 million, work outside their country of birth, and most of these are international men of management and those who speak the readily translated languages of medicine, engineering, or high tech. Many are border-hopping Alsatians working in Germany, French living just inside Swiss borders, Belgians working in northern France or Luxembourg, and so on. What appears to be tax flight is often "job flight"; people leave stagnant economies in search of greater opportunities, as young Greek and Italian professionals do.

Brain drains occur mainly when nations, like Spain, underfund research and development and put up barriers to entrepreneurialism. But the solid core – indeed, more than 98% – of taxpayers will continue to stay put, tied to their home and native lands by bonds of tradition, language, and culture. Tax flight is an important but sector-specific, exaggerated phenomenon: states still have ample room in which to engage in redistribution.[109] As trade has increased during the last thirty years and as tariffs have fallen tenfold between rich countries, overall state spending and taxation have *increased substantially*, across the EU.[110] Public spending in France has increased by eight points of GDP since 1980. The average OECD nation spent 43% of GDP in 1980 but 48% in 2000.[111]

But, generally speaking, spending on the poor did not increase. Is globalization to blame for this?[112] No. *We* are to blame: that is, the middle-class electorate of most (not all) Western nations is to blame. Popular critics like Naomi Klein, Ulrich Beck, Noreena Hertz, George Monbiot, and Viviane Forrester are simply wrong to argue that globalization has limited states' abilities to engage in social redistribution; deregulation of financial markets and the lifting of capital controls have not affected pension and health-care spending, which continue to rise and rise across Europe and North America too. Critics of what Charles Derber calls "corporate mystique" and "corporate ascendancy" confuse the (admitted) resurgence in corporate hubris and corruption during the 1990s with corporate domination writ large.[113] Corporations are indeed succeeding, here and there, in rewriting some labor, investment, and regulatory legislation in their favor. But this is an altogether separate phenomenon from generalized state retreat: there is no necessary link between corporate ambition (consider the MAI treaty that failed) and state rollback.

The far Left and far Right alike portray the EU as a force for the neoliberal revolution. Things are not so black and white: freer trade comes with strings attached. The EU had fewer than 2,000 legal acts in force in 1973; by 1996 there were more than 23,000. During the last thirty years there has been a convergence of state spending, taxation, and regulation *toward the top*. As Eastern European nations join the club, they too will spend more and more on social services, just as Ireland, Spain, Greece, and Portugal – social policy backwaters only twenty-five years ago – do today.[114]

Low-skilled workers face greater competition for resources *from within* France than from without its borders: taxation and redistribution of income still take place within national borders, even in an age of rising trade. Rising trade has not forced the French state to keep job-killing payroll taxes at over 40% of the cost of labor nor has globalization forced the French (and the Germans and Italians) to devote over 70% of social spending to those over the age of fifty-nine. The allocation of the vast majority of domestic spending to the upper half of society is at the root of many of Europe's social problems. If the critics of "globalization" directed their energies to *this* issue, they could eliminate poverty.

Many states are indeed reshuffling their social spending, cutting "welfare" and education spending here, cutting family allowances there, but increasing spending on retirement homes, pensions, and health care everywhere. Demographics, medical inflation, and pensioneering have squeezed out more redistributive forms of spending, in the process creating more inequality within Western nations than "globalization" has ever done. Likewise, the failure of France to share its wealth with the poor, with the unskilled – jobs being the key form of wealth to be shared in a market economy – is a homegrown issue.

Have open borders harmed French workers?

France was until recently the least vulnerable of major European nations to foreign trade.[115] French exports, while rising steadily throughout the 1980s and 1990s, accounted for only 21.4% of Gross Domestic Product (GDP) in 2002. French imports represent a slightly smaller portion of GDP, resulting in a healthy trade surplus. In total, exports and imports accounted for just over 40% of GDP during the mid 1990s, and now closer to 50%.[116] By all accounts, French companies are thriving on the international stage.

In Canada, Sweden, the Netherlands, and several other nations, exports alone represent 40 to 60% of GDP.[117] And in these nations, unemployment is one-third to one-half the French rate. Trade (exports and imports) represents over 70% of some Western nations' GDP. According to the journal *Foreign Policy*, in 2002 the Netherlands was the world's 8th most trade-dependent nation and Sweden was 21st but France was 46th.[118] Overall, Sweden was ranked the world's third most "globalized" nation, and the most affected by FDI (foreign direct investment). And Sweden is one of the most egalitarian nations in the world. Given that trade is not nearly as significant for France as it is for several other nations, it cannot be the crucial element explaining the alarming rise in unemployment and inequality since 1980. Domestic political decisions ensure that Sweden is, at once, one of the most globalized, open economies and one of the most egalitarian in the world.

Likewise, domestic factors explain the dramatic rise in *inequality* in the USA. Trade – exports and imports combined – account for only 25% of US GDP. The key factors in the US inequality crisis are tax cuts for the super-rich; the shift from a higher-wage manufacturing sector to a lower-wage service sector; technological change; the decline in union membership; the rise of regressive payroll taxes on low incomes; an unusually low minimum wage at a time when full-employment conditions could have tolerated an increase; the official turning of a blind eye to the near slave-wages paid to a reserve army of black-market immigrant labor, which drives down the wages of others; an overvalued dollar during the 1980s which hurt low value-added exports produced by low-skilled, low-paid workers; the lack of social support for poor families; a general corporate culture of greed; the decline in the proportion of young Americans attending university, which increases the "value" of those who do have a diploma; tight monetary policy aimed at choking inflation which also choked job creation in low-margin industries dominated by low-wage workers, and so on. These things, James K. Galbraith reminds us in his landmark book, *Created Unequal: The Crisis in American Pay* (1999), are largely to blame for the rise in inequality in the USA. But try selling this complex laundry list to the public in a nuanced election platform. Small wonder Right-wing critics in the USA like Pat Buchanan prefer not to bother with minor things like facts; instead they squeeze all the complexity of the world into a catchy anti-globalization slogan and roll it towards the electorate in an overwhelmingly demagogic fashion.

Prime Minister Jospin knew – he admitted in a 1998 report – that internal factors were also to blame for the problems of France's low-skilled workers, but he chose to focus on the threat of globalization.[119] Trade and exchange rate volatility have the potential to seriously undermine the sovereignty of small, politically and economically weaker nations in the developing world – say, a sparsely populated former French colony dependent upon a single cash crop like cocoa or vanilla. France itself cannot invoke this excuse.

Globalization is indeed an unsettling force for many nations, but the nations most at risk are the not-so-developing ones racked by debt, burdened with the legacy of imperialism and/or corrupt local leaders, lacking strong political and economic institutions, decades behind Europe in the technology race, and unable to fully exploit their comparative advantage in low value-added sectors due to European and American tariffs.

French farmers and auto workers are shielded from overseas competition thanks to the EU. No surprise that a good deal of the opposition to "globalization" stems from these very sectors. Opposition to "globalization" is often nothing more than a thinly veiled effort to support a rigged system of competition, working in favor of French workers and against non-European workers. In other words, we are speaking of plain old protectionism masquerading as "solidarity."

France is the world's second largest exporter of agricultural goods, but you cannot buy many things taken for granted by North Americans: inexpensive Central American fruits, cheap grapes from Chile, cheap grapefruit from Florida, inexpensive meats from South America.[120] The second richest nation in Europe, France is a net taker from European coffers. Europe's farmers receive subsidies amounting to 36% the value of their products; the US figure is 23% and the Canadian figure is under 10%.[121] France takes the majority of the CAP payments (farm subsidies). Even the Netherlands, with one-quarter the French population, contributes three to six times *more* (in absolute terms) to the EU budget. The EU has been an overwhelming benefit to the French economy, not a drain on it. And in any case the French have been the leaders in pushing for greater European integration.[122] Now that Europe is finally seeking to create a truly level playing field, it threatens to expose certain sectors of the French economy (the public sector such as *La Poste* and EDF) to competition. But the majority of the French workforce faces no such threat.

Trade is increasingly important, but in the good sense. Rising intra-EU trade, as the economist Jean-Hervé Lorenzi has demonstrated, has served as an outlet for French goods and services. In each and every year since 1992, France has had a large trade surplus. It was 40 billion euros in 1997, 30 billion in 2001.[123] The French economy as a whole, economist Patrick Artus concludes, is not in terminal decline.[124] Between 1990 and 2002, GNP growth per capita was 45% versus 65% in the USA and only 30% in Germany. France is still a rich country, but it has slipped: in 2000, British GNP surpassed that of France, reversing a thirty-year-old trend.

How globalization *has* changed things

There is no doubt that increased international competition is leading *some* Western nations to deregulate labor markets, embrace freer trade and let lame duck industries die a natural death instead of hooking them up to costly and futile life-support subsidies. States are indeed trimming *some* types of spending and privatizing *some* sectors of the economy.[125] There is some evidence of this in Sweden and in Canada. Twenty years ago, the Left in New Zealand embarked on a radical program of economic reform out of a fear of being left behind by global markets, yes, but primarily because the nation had self-destructed due to terrible economic management.[126]

But there is very little evidence of this for France, Germany, or Italy. There have been "realignments" within the welfare state, but not a wholesale assault on government spending in the widest sense. As Paul Pierson concludes in a comparative study of welfare state "retrenchment," "what is striking is how hard it is to find *radical* changes in advanced welfare states."[127] With a few notable exceptions (the Netherlands, Canada), government spending around the Western world has stayed constant or risen significantly since 1980, even as globalization was on the rise. Not even Reagan and Thatcher managed to "dismantle" the welfare state: using "salami tactics," they took small slices here, only to give more there.[128]

States are still free to intervene in the form of a redistributive, progressive tax system (one that takes much more from the rich and the middle class than from the modestly paid). States are still capable of giving regular and reliable funding to education (something the French state has failed to do over the past twenty years). States retain the power to fund generous family support systems (which have declined by 50% in real terms over the past forty years in France); if they choose to, states can still maintain strong universal public health-care systems (here the French have indeed succeeded). States are free to fund pension systems in the name of eliminating old-age poverty (here the French succeeded but then went too far).

To be sure, in a few important areas, the pressures of the outside world grew during the 1980s and 1990s: foreign direct investment (FDI) rose and a brain drain of French researchers and computer industry professionals occurred as French universities and basic research and development were underfunded. The ability of nations (especially heavily indebted ones) to strike out on their own and pursue pseudo-Keynesianism-in-one-country diminished.[129] Mitterrand's flirtation with this path is a well-known story of failure, taken up in detail in the next chapter. By the 1980s, the tools of domestic macroeconomic policy were indeed subjected to unprecedented scrutiny by outside forces. But the impact of those very outside forces was potentially much stronger in the UK, where FDI inflows were $80 billion per year during the period 1995–2000 (twice the French figure), and also in tiny, sparsely populated Sweden, where FDI, at $50 billion, was $10 billion more than in France.[130]

Today, *financial* deregulation, which is certainly on the rise, is often confused by French critics with a wholesale assault on the welfare state. No such assault is taking place. Restrictions on certain types of corporate financial activities have indeed been lifted. Over 1.5 trillion dollars moves around the world electronically each day. Currency speculation was not possible to the same extent under the old Bretton Woods System, which pegged most Western currencies to the US dollar and the US dollar to gold; today speculation makes billionaires out of men based in the Bahamas. But overall state spending has not been trimmed.[131]

If poverty rose during this period, if low-skilled workers fared worse, then Western states have only themselves to blame: they failed to allocate resources to the most needy; they failed to "unlock" resources from middle-class and wealthy constituents, they failed to loosen up labor markets (and then give income supplements to low earners). Today welfare states are "in transition," not in decline.[132] Welfare states are "captured" by the affluent, under threat from within, as health-care and pension spending squeeze out other forms of spending; they are not under threat from without. As Linda Weiss, Layna Mosley, and others have shown, the idea of the "powerless state" is a myth; there is still "room to move"; welfare states can still grow, nations can continue to tax at high levels, provided they do not go into high levels of debt.[133]

Martin Rhodes concludes that "in continental Europe, governments, employers and labor unions have more or less agreed that the price of adjustment should be shouldered by the unemployed, comprised largely of younger, female and older workers."[134]

"Globalization" did not dictate that one in four French workers be a state employee – indeed, it would seem to call for a dramatic downsizing of the bureaucracy, but there are no signs of this.[135] Different social and economic models are still possible in an age of globalization. Outside forces did not force an economic crisis or income inequality on Sweden, which was far more vulnerable to the withdrawal of foreign investment during the 1990s, and far more dependent upon trade than France. To be sure, during the early 1990s, Sweden had a deficit and unemployment crisis (7% GDP deficit; 7%+ unemployment). But with quick reforms the Swedes turned the beat around, returning to under 5% unemployment within a few short years all the while reining in public spending.[136]

The common currency adopted by twelve EU nations, the euro, requires that budget deficits be under 3% of GDP and that the national debt be under 60% of GDP. But France and Germany have recently thumbed their noses at these rules with impunity.[137] The euro may indeed rob member-states of the ability to pursue full-employment *monetary* policy but this is a problem for the future, not a primary cause of unemployment in the past. And, as the next chapter will show, there are other ways of operating economies at full steam.

As Geoffrey Garrett has argued in a cross-national survey of trade, taxes, and state spending, during the 1990s globalization generally did not force states to trim their welfare states.[138] But, he concludes, globalization probably did punish heavily indebted nations seeking to continue to carry high public debt by requiring them to raise interest rates. As Schmidt, Scharpf, and Swank conclude, only when public debt has been unusually high (above 100% of GDP), as in Belgium, Italy, and Canada, has the threat of capital mobility and other pressures of globalization led directly to cuts in domestic spending.[139]

Having said this, outside forces do not decide *which type* of spending should be cut: domestic states still retain that power. Thus Canada, which focused its cuts on the poor and the young during the 1990s, *chose* to do this. Nothing prevented the Canadian Liberals from cutting costlier, non-redistributive spending (unfunded public pensions for the wealthy, for example). As Vivien Schmidt concludes in her sweeping study of European political economy, *The Futures of European Capitalism* (2002): "There is no convergence in the welfare arena."[140]

Even if the pressures of the outside world do indeed make chronic budget deficits more difficult for smaller, indebted nations to sustain, this book will not shed a single tear over this issue; how the Left (from France to Italy to Canada) has managed to turn the practice of running up massive annual deficits, year in and year out, into a cardinal virtue of social democracy is surely one of the unsolved mysteries of recent political history. This phenomenon is doubly curious, given that the vast majority of deficit spending in Europe during the 1980s and 1990s went towards *non-redistributive* current social programs, not poverty-reduction ones, not increased education spending, not long-term investments in infrastructure.

The idea of reducing deficits springs from purely homegrown imperatives; the EU's 3% rule is merely a scapegoat and nothing more, invoked by leaders afraid to alienate vested interests and wrestle spending back down to earth. And if the 3% rule does indeed force France's hand, we must put this new constraint in historical perspective. A deficit of 3% of GDP was unheard of in France before the early 1980s; not even the high spending Giscard governments managed to go so far in debt. Further-more, we might ask what causes these large deficits in the first place. For the most part, lavish pensions, a low retirement age which bears no rela-tion to longer life expectancies and low birth rates, inefficient health-care spending (such as excessive pharmaceutical consumption) and Europe's largest public sector, overstaffed by an estimated 500,000 to 1,000,000 workers: these are the roots of French deficits.[141] Finally, even without an EU prohibition of large deficits, France (or any other nation) would pay a price for profligacy. If governments cannot convince citizens to pay for spending they seem to cherish, then this is a domestic problem in the first instance.

Blaming international bond-raters, currency speculators (before the euro), or the EU for the failure to pay for solidarity in the here and now is not a convincing argument. As Prime Minister Raffarin introduced a (partial) reform of France's pension system in 2003, the Socialist party called for new taxes on stock trades, currency speculation, and various other financial transactions associated with deregulated capitalism to fund the homegrown pension shortfall, showing how "neoliberal globalization" and pension reform are linked in the minds of the French Left. Introduc-ing a "Tobin Tax" on financial transactions and currency speculation is probably a good idea on its own merits, but the link to the pension crisis is by no means clear. Proposals such as these cloud the main issue: the underfunded pension systems which are no longer sustainable given the low retirement age and the aging population, the already high payroll tax burden bearing down on businesses.

Similarly, there is nothing progressive about leaving huge deficits, incurred to pay for current, non-redistributive spending, to future gener-ations. When France had a budget deficit of 6% GDP in 1995, street protests focused their energies on the external "neoliberal" threat to France's domestic priorities – protestors did not seem to think that the 6% figure was a problem in and of itself. As François Charpentier reminded us in his monumental encyclopedia of French social welfare programs, the French state consumed over 53% of GDP in 2000; there was no good rea-son why poverty should persist in light of spending of this magnitude.[142]

The architects of crisis: French politicians

The French economy, in the widest sense, has been reasonably healthy, but it has failed to share its riches with job seekers. Globalization has had little to do with this.[143] Studies by the official French government statistical bureau INSEE in the mid and late 1990s (under both socialist and conservative rule) suggested that only 2 to 3% of the entire French workforce had been directly affected by Third World competition. Paul Krugman estimates the figure for the USA to be 5%; others put it a bit higher at 6%.[144] To be sure, downward pressure on the wages of 5% of the population may lead to ripple effects throughout the economy, but this is not an intractable problem: states still have the freedom and the resources to set about correcting it – and some states (Sweden, Denmark, the Netherlands) have indeed chosen to do so. The states which have chosen not to do so, which have become paralyzed by vested interests (France, Italy), incapable of reshuffling resources to the most needy, are precisely the states in which extreme anti-globalization rhetoric is strongest.

At the most, as INSEE concluded, 300,000 French jobs had been lost to "globalization" in the two decades leading up to the mid 1990s, but there were over 3.5 million people without jobs in 1997 alone. To be sure, here was a problem, but a relatively minor one compared to homegrown ones which, I will argue in the next chapter, killed many more jobs.[145] These facts have never prevented scores of politicians and intellectuals from making a career out of opposing globalization. It is an easier sell, a simple idea. It is the Big Excuse.

Real wages in France increased by 40% between 1980 and 1994. Since payroll taxes also rose, after-tax incomes in the private sector increased by 0.5% per year during this period. Public-sector workers fared the best, and public pensions were increased at the rate of 4% per year in real terms. During the 1980s and 1990s, plenty of new wealth was created, taxed, and distributed. If there was a "crisis" in France during the 1980s, it was not caused by a decline in the nation's wealth (as it was during the 1930s, for example); it was caused by the misallocation of resources to comfortable people and by rising expectations whipped up by governments afraid to restore the link between growth and spending. As we will see in the next chapter, by the late 1990s, almost two million jobs were subsidized by the state in one form or another, but the overall employment rate fell, since the private sector did not create new positions. Globalization had very little to do with this. Since the rhetoric and the efforts of the governments of the 1980s suggested that France was doing all that it could to help the unemployed, people were more likely to point their fingers at "globalization" as they took stock of France's problems.[146]

4   France's break with socialism

A country like ours, with 1,500,000 unemployed, ceases to be a free country.

Presidential candidate François Mitterrand, in a televised address to the nation, late 1980 (when he left office in 1995, there were 3.5 million unemployed).[1]

If you are elected, unemployment will rise due to the measures you will take and which will weigh down upon businesses.

President Valéry Giscard d'Estaing, to Mitterrand, television debate, 5 May 1981.[2]

Between 1981 and 1995, the Socialist President, François Mitterrand, and his various governments ruled except for two periods when the Right dominated the legislature, during 1986 to 1988 (when Jacques Chirac served as Prime Minister), and during 1993 to 1995 (when Edouard Balladur was Prime Minister). President Chirac took power in 1995, and ruled with Prime Minister Alain Juppé until 1997. The Left, led by Lionel Jospin, regained the prime minister's office during 1997. Since 2002, Prime Minister Raffarin has ruled with a large conservative legislative majority.

Although the Socialists ruled France for fifteen years between 1981 and 2002, it would be too simple to lay the blame for France's economic problems solely on their doorstep. When Chirac was Prime Minister in 1986 to 1988, unemployment hovered at around 10%. Chirac's policies to remedy this situation were not substantially different than those of Prime Minister Fabius before him. Both leaders attempted to relieve some of the barriers to private sector expansion but they also raised taxes in order to pay (partially) for more social spending. When conservative Prime Ministers Balladur and Juppé held power, the unemployment rate rose to record highs, taxes were increased, budget deficits increased, and interest rates were higher than at any other period in twentieth-century French history.

During the 1980s, a basic consensus emerged regarding social policy: first, it should be used as a cushion to protect older workers victimized by de-industrialization and de-*dirigisme*; and second, any significant cuts to social spending would constitute a sort of *regression sociale*, a backpedalling away from the *trente glorieuses*, away from "solidarity." During the 1995 and 1997 election campaigns, both main political parties promised to reduce social "exclusion" via increased social spending; an uninformed observer might well have imagined Jacques Chirac, a man of the "Right," to be the true guardian of the French welfare state. Since France has made such bold and sincere efforts to heal the social divide – to no avail – many people are tempted to point their fingers at "globalization." This chapter will show how the French have indeed made considerable efforts to boost employment – but they tended to pursue the wrong policies and they tended to cancel out pro-employment measures with job-killing ones.

Mitterrand and Chirac never took full responsibility for their role in creating the unemployment crisis. Both men blamed outside forces – the need to prepare the nation for European monetary union by imposing austerity measures, the rising tide of neoliberal globalization, the threat of Asian competition, Reaganism and Thatcherism, the growing influence of international investors, the "wall of money." As Mitterrand said famously in 1983: "I am torn between two ambitions: constructing Europe and [bringing about] social justice. The EMS[3] is necessary to achieve the former, and it limits my ability to [bring about] the latter."[4] By this he meant that the pressures imposed by the terms of the European monetary system to keep inflation low and deficits under control had forced him to "turn" in 1983 and prevented him from delivering the redistributive social agenda he had promised during the 1981 election campaign. Similarly, twelve years later the conservative Alain Juppé tried to justify his select cuts to the civil service by invoking the need to meet EMU criteria.

This chapter challenges the "European alibi." The "Great U-Turn" of 1983 was only a partial turn; it did not freeze overall spending, it slowed its growth. The U-Turn was necessary due to domestic failures, not outside constraints. It did not entail a total reversal of strict labor laws and red tape which continue, to this day, to hinder job creation. And by 1995, French deficits were running at 6% of GDP – proof that the U-Turn was a temporary detour on the road to chronic deficits. Social spending continued to grow after 1983, but, at 2% in real terms instead of the 5 to 6% rate of 1981–82, not as quickly as planned.

The state continued to intervene in the labor market throughout the 1980s and 1990s, to the point where, by 2000, over two million jobs were subsidized, in one way or another, by taxpayers; this might conceivably be cited as an example of the state's commitment to eliminating unemployment. But such an argument stands only if the state did not do other things which prevented the private sector from creating jobs itself. Overall, unemployment increased because the private sector was crippled by fiscal and macroeconomic policies which choked investment and raised the cost of doing business. Most of France's efforts to ease the transition away from a manufacturing-based economy and to avoid social conflict (through early retirements, deficit spending, the raising of the minimum wage, laws protecting jobs, public-sector make-work projects, higher taxes to fund more social spending) have proven counter-productive since the low-wage, private service sector has been prevented from absorbing the jobs lost to technological change.

No major French politician told the public during an election campaign or at any other time that higher "social" spending was not necessarily a positive thing. No politician told the public that spending levels were adequate and that a reshuffling of existing spending was required (regardless of external pressures such as European integration). As we will see towards the end of this chapter, Dutch leaders told this to their electorate in the 1980s and Swedish leaders did as well during the 1990s. During the early 1980s, the two main French political parties disagreed over things like the nationalization of industries, but little else. Politicians pledged to "share work" but they never proposed the sharing of wages. Politicians protected the disposable incomes of the middle class at the expense of those seeking to find a job in the first place.

The basic argument between Left and Right throughout the 1980s was not how to trim non-redistributive social spending, but rather which types of taxes should be raised in order to save programs cherished by the middle-class French electorate. Throughout the 1980s and 1990s taxes increased, under both political parties. Jospin tended to increase taxes on higher earners, Chirac and Balladur preferred to raise regressive sales taxes and payroll taxes, Mauroy raised taxes on everyone. As Bruno Palier reminds us, every eighteen months a "rescue plan" emerged from parliament, and both sides of the spectrum presented themselves as the more reliable guardian of solidarity.[5]

The net result in either case was to stifle job growth. By the 1990s, payroll taxes added 50% to the wages of low-skilled workers, pricing such work out of the nation. Instead of addressing this problem, governments preferred to avoid confrontation with the vested interests in control of the social funds (who opposed the reduction of the payroll taxes which fuel their funds) and sought instead to focus job growth in the public sector.

Both political camps accepted the fallacy that the highly subsidized withdrawal of older workers would necessarily free up jobs for younger ones. Both camps failed to deliver jobs because they were unwilling to go to the general public and ask them to sacrifice in a significant way.

Plenty of new wealth has been created in France since 1980 – but an unusually high portion of it (by European standards) was devoted to state spending, social transfers, tax increases, and raises for those already employed, leaving little behind for private-sector job creation.

As a result, the costs of adjusting to the oil crisis, to de-industrialization, to the slowdown in productivity, and to the drive toward monetary union were borne overwhelmingly by the "outsiders" – those already unemployed during the late 1970s and 1980s, as well as those who would come to constitute the bulk of the unemployed in the years to come: youth, women, immigrants, and the unskilled.

Giscard's failed presidency

The script written by Giscard d'Estaing and later by Mitterrand and Mauroy during 1981–82 was passed along relatively intact to each and every Prime Minister during the 1980s and 1990s. Unemployment rose by four points during Giscard's seven years (1974–81), from 3% to 7%, even as "social" spending increased at an unprecedented rate, by a remarkable 6 points of GDP. The crisis reached a new level under Mitterrand, during the first five years of his initial mandate, before the first "cohabitation" with the Right, as unemployment rose by four points and the labor-force participation rate dropped by another three points, even as social spending rose by another three points of GDP (and, in total, by six points of GDP by 1995).[6] Between 1981 and 1986, the labor force contracted more rapidly than at any other time in twentieth-century France. The first Mitterrand governments led the nation down several policy paths, such as retirement at the age of fifty to sixty, which their successors (on the Left and Right alike) did not contemplate reversing until the early 2000s.

As Peter Gourevitch argues, "history has its points of critical choice, moments of flux when several things might happen but only one actually does. For years afterward, that winning alternative will preempt other possibilities, and things will seem more closed. Economic crises create one such set of points of choice."[7] Between 1975 and 1980, there had been 200,000 to 300,000 "licenciements économiques" per year (economic lay-offs). A few sectors of the economy were particularly hard hit: metallurgy, steel, coal mining, machine works, the textile and clothing industries, and small business, which was suffering from competition from larger chain stores and supermarkets.[8] Over 1.5 million people were without jobs in early 1981.

De-industrialization was a Western-wide trend, fuelled by technological change, greater competition, wage inflation, and rising oil prices.

It was visible in Ohio, the north of England, Ontario and Belgium. In France, the department of the Nord, bordering Belgium, had a 10% unemployment rate already in 1980. And unemployment was becoming more and more structural, a long-term condition: 150 days on average in 1974; 240 days in 1980. In 1971, 36% of the unemployed found a job within a month of being laid off; by 1975, only 14% did.[9]

During the 1950s and 1960s, *dirigisme* had been geared towards change, towards modernization, with all the social and economic disruption this entailed. As Jonah Levy argues, by the 1970s, *dirigisme* was redirected towards "resisting adjustment." Under Giscard, economic policy "lapsed into the worst form of conservatism" as "lame ducks swallowed resources" which might have been directed at more promising sectors or simply at tax cuts or budget compression (which would have allowed for lower interest rates, lower inflation, and higher levels of investment). Resources "were utilized, not to undertake much-needed restructuring . . . but to delay layoffs and adjustment – at least until the next election."[10] Giscard adopted the rhetoric of liberalization all the while retreating from it.

By 1976, firms needed a labor inspector's permission to fire workers (this rule stayed in place for ten years). In 1978, fewer than one dozen firms received over 75% of all state aid to industry and this money was generally used to delay lay-offs and adjustment, not to facilitate restructuring. The tough new rules aimed at preventing rash downsizings ended up scaring businesses from hiring in the first place. Precisely when the labor market needed to soften up in order to absorb the people who were losing their jobs in the manufacturing sector, Giscard made it more rigid.

Standing in the shadow of May '68, Giscard had become, as Levy argues, "extraordinarily conflict-averse"; his first reflex whenever workers or farmers or shopkeepers took to the streets was to capitulate and throw money at them. With unemployment insurance replacement rates hitting 90% for some people, France was becoming a zero-risk society – and also a zero-sum society, in the sense that the labor movement, with state approval, was taking more and more of the nation's wealth at the expense of the unemployed.

The phenomenon of excessive wage increases had begun with the Grenelle agreements, the ransom paid by de Gaulle to end the nationwide strikes in 1968. These accords boosted the minimum wage by 33%.[11] But the minimum wage was low at this point in time, and productivity growth was high, so this sudden inflationary shock to the nation's wage structure was absorbed without causing irreparable economic damage. Also, a quick devaluation of the franc less than one year later helped to offset some of the inflationary spin-offs.

The Grenelle settlement set a precedent, emboldening those who had wanted even more. It seemed to prove the existence of a great, hidden pot of money; it seemed to confirm the widespread belief that the rich were hoarding the nation's wealth, and that all the labor movement need do was strike to get more of it. The rich were indeed hoarding the nation's wealth, as they had been for centuries, but the way to correct this problem (without slowing down job growth) was not to legislate substantial wage increases and leave all other things equal; the solution was to take from the upper quarter of the income ladder and redistribute to those at the bottom. Nothing of the sort was done; instead of redistribution, French labor continued to demand inflationary measures.

In 1970, the SMIC (minimum wage) was reindexed. Whereas it used to float on the rising cost of living, henceforth it would rise with the average wage, which usually outstrips prices. In many ways this policy made good sense, but it was introduced overnight, at a substantial cost to business.[12] Since workers and politicians alike had always tried to establish a favorable ratio between average wages and pension levels, these wage settlements would have significant spin-off effects elsewhere.

By the mid 1970s, the die was cast: French public spending and wage settlements began to outpace economic growth by a factor of two. Public spending rose from 36.6% of GDP in 1973 to 42.6% in 1978; higher wages for civil servants, sweeter pension deals allowing for earlier and earlier retirement within the special regimes, substantial hikes to all pension regimes, and health-care inflation were the key causes. Only Sweden, Belgium, and Italy witnessed spending of this sort; only in Italy did wages increase faster.

As inflation rose, unions and non-unionized workers alike feared for the future and bargained for above-inflation wage settlements. The minimum wage was raised above the inflation rate and settlements in the few remaining labor strongholds were "extended" throughout the economy.

Corporations went into debt and were prevented from investing in new procedures and new ventures. Stagflation (a stagnant economic situation coupled with inflation) called for a certain period of high interest rates to stabilize prices. If nations wished to keep unemployment low *and* try to curb inflation, declining or stagnating real incomes and/or state spending cuts were necessary. President Giscard d'Estaing implemented none of the above.

In 1979–80, Giscard and Prime Minister Raymond Barre finally began to take a small measure of responsibility for their errors of the past few years. Barre's so-called period of austerity was nothing of the sort: he simply decreased the rate at which social spending rose, from 6% per year in 1978 to just 2% by 1980–81. On the eve of the 1981 election, Giscard

Table 4.1 *Real rate of economic growth,*
salaries, public spending (%), etc., France,
1971–78

Economic growth	3.0
Salaries	5.8
Investment	2.8
Social transfers	7.9
All public expenses	6.2

Source: Commissariat Général du Plan, *Rapport*
sur les principales options du VIIIe Plan (Paris: La
Documentation Française, 1979), p. 39.

and Barre were neither cutting substantially nor were they reflating the economy. Like other politicians in the Western world, they appeared rudderless.

The Socialists' plan to "break with capitalism"

François Mitterrand was not one to muddle. His voluntarism and optimism stood in sharp contrast to Giscard's haplessness. The Socialists' victory in 1981 seemed to herald a new era. Expectations were high, whipped up by Mitterrand's bold rhetoric, confident campaign slogans, and highly charged gestures such as his placing of a rose at the tomb of Jean Jaurès. Mitterrand promised nothing less than to "transform society," to make a "break," a "rupture with capitalism."[13] He promised to make good on all the unfulfilled dreams of his predecessors during the Popular Front and Liberation eras.

The French Socialists' goal to bring about a "break with capitalism" did not emerge from an intellectual or social vacuum; it had been in the works for many years. Anti-capitalist ideology was, in some ways, the logical counterpoint and in other ways an overreaction to the terrible record of employer–employee relations and workplace conditions which characterized France during the 1940s through the 1970s. The industrial accident record of French businesses was among the worst in the Western world; low trust on the part of workers was one obvious result. Small wonder that one of the key planks of the Socialists was to "democratize" the workplace, to give workers more control (as in Sweden and Germany) over the day-to-day operations at the shopfloor level. But the desire to bring about a "break with capitalism" stemmed overwhelmingly from the unreconstructed Marxism which was a prime ideological current within the Socialist Party.

In 1972, at a time of prosperity unprecedented in world history, when France had taken giant steps out of stagnation and into mass affluence, Mitterrand claimed, in the party's official program, that once in power he would attack "the economic and political system . . . on which is built an unjust and decadent society." The Socialist Party, he claimed, "does not seek the approval of the privileged, the exploiters, the profiteers: there can be no truce between the enemies of the people and the people themselves."[14] By 1981, this rhetoric was for the most part confined to the Left wing of the Socialist Party, symbolized by Jean-Pierre Chevènement. But years in the wilderness had radicalized the party as a whole and it was certainly to the left of most other European social democratic movements.

Paradoxically, unionization levels were the lowest in the Western world at a time when the French workforce had ample reason to organize. But, in keeping with a century-old tradition, the country's unions were polarized by petty doctrinal disputes, the narcissism of small differences. Distrust, suspicion, class resentments, and conflict were the the stuff of everyday life.[15] In such an atmosphere, face-to-face negotiations and gradualism were difficult. Reform did not trickle up from the provinces, from the shopfloors, to the National Assembly. There was no equivalent to a *Lands-organisation*, no IG Metall, at the head of an allied political party, deeply embedded in French industry. The Socialist Party did not have strong links to workers themselves, many of whom opted for the seemingly more authentic, less bookish Communist Party of Georges Marchais. Hence the Socialists' dreams of a "rupture" with this old world, and a top-down, legislative solution. The failure of gradualism – of Swedish-style face-to-face negotiations – was significant. It would mean a big bang was more likely in 1981. Few members of the Mitterrand cabinet had had any contact with the world of private industry, the social services, or labor unions for that matter. Never had a cabinet been so dominated by ENA and ENS-trained civil service mandarins; never had pragmatism been in such short supply.

1981: France's break with fiscal discipline

Mitterrand's bold reforms tended to be striking failures or smashing successes. His chief legacy is not his pharaonic *grands projets*. As with Giscard, his chief legacy is that he failed to be honest with the French people and begin a debate over how the nation would tighten its collective belt and adjust to the oil shock, unemployment, and technological change. By raising public expectations so high during the early years of his mandate and by swinging the pendulum so far to the side of social spending increases, statist solutions to unemployment, early retirement, extra leisure, and wage inflation, Mitterrand led the nation even further down the road taken by Giscard. Just as Clinton and Blair's agendas were limited by the radical nature of the reforms introduced by their predecessors, so too were all French politicians' hands tied by the radical nature of the social programs introduced and expanded during the early 1980s.

To be sure, some of Mitterrand's reforms should never be reversed. Without doubt, several social programs and legal changes introduced during his first government were grounded in ideals of social justice. These can be upheld and sustained over the decades to come. The death penalty was abolished, draconian military courts were shut down, as were the special civil courts used to punish Corsican separatists. State-appointed prefects were stripped of some of their powers; elected regional councils gained at their expense. Decentralization breathed some life (and more opportunities for local corruption) into municipal and departmental politics. Tougher legislation cracking down on sexual discrimination was passed, if not observed. Workers were given added protections against abusive employers. Workers' voices were integrated into company decision making – although, in many cases, this may have simply institutionalized high levels of distrust and encouraged high wage demands which limited employers' abilities to hire new workers.

Health, safety, and environmental regulations were tightened up. Tens of thousands of additional nurses and medical technicians were trained, ensuring that France does not have the severe personnel shortages which plague the British and Canadian health-care systems.[16] Immigrants were given new protections and permanent residence. One quarter of the prison population – the non-violent, for the most part – was released, easing congestion and improving (somewhat) the terrible conditions of French prisons. High spending on public transportation and the energy sector kept French infrastructure sound. Spending on "culture" and "quality of life" projects was surely excessive, but there were some positive "collateral" results. City councils around the nation cleaned up the facades of soot-stained buildings. French urban planners, armed with new subsidies, gave the world stunning new monuments and cultural centers – witness the renaissance of Montpellier, Lyon, and Paris. The fact that France is the world's most popular tourist destination is surely related to this. Unfortunately, success in matters cultural was not matched by success in matters economic.

The year 1981 might have been an opportunity to take stock of France's economic failures during the Giscard era. Giscard's seven years in power might have served notice that deficit spending and higher taxes at a time of lagging corporate profitability and falling productivity was a recipe for failure. Instead, Mitterrand charged Giscard with timidity, and proposed to administer higher doses of Giscard's medicine. Mitterrand proposed to turn the clock back, to "relance" spending to its mid 1970s rates – and he did.

(Pseudo) Keynesianism in one country

A brief look at recent public policy around the Western world would have provided many indications that deficit spending (which is really the only major prescription of Keynes followed by nations which invoked the great economist's name) was not helping nations to reduce their unemployment levels. In France itself, the manifest failure of Giscard and Chirac's Keynesian efforts of 1974–75, when pension and other social policy expenses were boosted by over 14% in real terms, was ignored.[17] The failure of Trudeau's equally impressive deficit spending and his nationalizations of large sectors of the Canadian economy was ignored. The Labour Party's abandonment of Keynes several years before Thatcher buried his books was seen not as evidence that Keynesianism was doomed in stagflationary times but as proof that others had lost their nerve. In 1981, François Mitterrand was not for turning.

Keynes had prescribed his deficit-spending remedy under the assumption that deflation would obtain in bad times (as during the 1930s). In 1981, however, inflation was running at over 13%, industrial jobs were being shed by the tens of thousands, and European competition was on the rise. Other nations were trying (and sometimes succeeding, as in the Netherlands and Britain) to contain spending, but the French government was committed to its rapid expansion. High spending and deficits on the order of 3% of GDP during 1981–85 (the accelerator) in the context of a nation which also needed to have low inflation and wanted to have a strong currency required unusually high interest rates (an even stronger brake) to bring this about. This brake on corporate investment and expansion would, in turn, slow down the private sector and increase the cost of servicing the debts businesses were already carrying. French public policy was running off in all directions, with a revved up public sector and a private sector deprived of gas and carrying a heavier and heavier tax load.

At a time when nations as diverse as Sweden, Australia, and the Netherlands were urging (or legislating) wage restraint, France did the opposite. Wage restraint in France was a temporary measure enforced for two short years, following in the wake of the 1981–82 wage explosion, and by the mid 1980s it had been abandoned. At precisely the moment when the economy was slowing down, and about to undergo a structural transformation, the government put new financial burdens upon it. According to Göran Therborn, "just as in 1936, the French Left of 1981 had three basic ideas about how to confront the crisis – all of them wrong. They were: short-term boosting of private consumption, a reduction in working time and the defence of the value of the currency."[18]

First, the Socialists chose massive and immediate reflationary government spending: a 25% (gross) and 12% (real terms) increase in 1981.[19] Total social transfer payments to households were increased by 5.8% in 1981 and by 7.8% in 1982, both in real terms. Payroll taxes went up too (but not enough to cover the new spending), so the real disposable incomes of households grew by 3.2% in 1981 and again in 1982 – but real incomes for many people were falling or stagnating in many other nations in the de-industrializing world.

Here is a partial list of added costs for French businesses: the working week was reduced to thirty-nine hours from forty, with no loss of pay to workers. In addition, workers were given a fifth week of paid vacation, adding further to business expenses. Stricter rules governing the hiring and firing of workers were introduced in 1982. Severance pay was increased. General retirement at the age of sixty went into effect on 1 January 1983. Pre-retirement schemes for those unemployed as of the age of fifty to fifty-five covered over 500,000 people by 1983 and almost one million people by the end of the decade. With the exception of the relaxation of some labor laws (making firing easier and part-time work possible) under the more pro-business Laurent Fabius and his successor Jacques Chirac, none of these policies were reversed during the 1980s.

The banking industry and dozens of other private industries were nationalized; as a result 600,000 people were added to the civil service within the space of one year.[20] In addition, hundreds of thousands of new jobs were created in the health and social service sector; they came attached with expensive public-sector pensions (this policy is now coming home to roost, with many baby boomers aged fifty-five retiring from the public service at 85% of their best six months' salary). These new employees also came attached with supplemental family allowances, shorter work weeks than the norm, more sick days and vacation days, and so on. Prime Minister Chirac privatized several state firms a few years later, but the overall size of the public sector did not shrink due to job growth in the health and social services sector. This was a leading cause of deficits.

As Peter Hall demonstrates, the nationalized firms were supposed to serve as laboratories for social reform and "relaunch" the French economy; they ended up accumulating large losses.[21] The state provided 190 billion francs in subsidies to nationalized firms and absorbed another 120 billion francs in losses by 1984. Higher spending is not always economically productive or reflationary, and here is a good example. Total state spending increased by 27.6% (gross) and over 12% (real terms) in 1982 alone; but hundreds of thousands of people were added to the unemployment rolls that same year.[22] (The nationalized firms were turned around by 1985, at a high price.)

Right away, the government raised the SMIC (minimum wage) by 10.6% and pensions by 7% (both in real terms). By 1983 the minimum wage had been increased by almost 25% (real terms). Family allowances were boosted, but this did not make up for their rapid decline during the 1970s. The government also increased housing subsidies by over 25%.[23]

The budget deficit quadrupled in 1981–82, to over 3% of GDP. But the vast majority of this spending went to those who already had jobs or were comfortably pensioned. Increased spending on "solidarity" was not paid for with the redistribution of existing wealth; it was mortgaged. There was no other way to pay for it. As Gary Freeman has argued, when the Socialist Party took power in 1981,

> it was already too late to create the kind of welfare state it wanted. The times were not propitious for bold social experiments. Economic stagnation and budgetary constraints overwhelmed the social agenda . . . Any significant steps to make the system more equitable, redistributive and uniform would require the imposition of hardships on sizeable numbers of voters who were part of the Socialist coalition [i.e., public sector workers, members of the "special regimes"]. The tax rates necessary to support the most extensive improvements in benefits would fall heavily on working-class incomes. In other words, Socialist rhetoric was badly out of step with the realities of French social welfare arrangements.[24]

A "wealth tax" was introduced but it targeted only the top 1% of taxpayers and was therefore a symbolic but insignificant drop in the *fisc*'s bucket. Although the "wealth tax" and the (unforgivable) new tax on cognac (Mitterrand himself hailed from neighboring Jarnac!) made a tiny dent in the pocketbooks of the rich, they feared that more was to come. When Mitterrand slapped the Western world's highest capital gains taxes on the French, he launched a massive flight of capital across the English Channel, a financial Dunkirk. If Mitterrand had truly wished to take from the rich, he would have taxed the upper 25% of the income ladder at a high rate, as states do in Sweden, Germany, Canada, and Denmark – not just the upper 1%.

As Freeman reminds us, the "rich" (in reality, the upper quarter) included many of the Socialists' constituents, including older professors and teachers, many engineers, many well-educated professionals, some doctors, and upper-level civil servants of all sorts. "Les riches" included a large portion of those over the age of fifty. And so the "rich" could not really pay the entire bill. Even as its leaders were inspired by the Swedish model, the French *people* were not ready to take a turn towards Sweden, with its punishing income taxes on the upper third of society, its acceptance of wage restraint (during the 1980s), its acceptance of public-sector cuts (during the 1990s).[25]

In its effort to boost consumer spending and job creation via higher social benefits, the state created deficits of an unprecedented magnitude (during peacetime). In 1981, as Germany, the USA, and Britain were fixated on slaying inflation, France was doing the opposite, injecting fuel into the economy. Predictably, this led to a trade deficit and a run on the franc. In order to defend the franc, the French would have to raise interest rates through the roof, which would crowd out investment and cripple the private sector.

As W. Rand Smith notes, gross profit margins in France had fallen substantially in France between 1974 and 1981 (down 4.6% of value added), but gross wages had increased (up 1.6%) as had employers' social security contributions (up 3.7%). Accordingly, corporate investment slipped from 17% of value added in the 1960s to 14% of value added during the 1970s. In 1980 alone, private investment fell almost 15%. French industry was falling far behind its chief competitors.[26] The rise in social security taxes set France apart from other European nations, hurting business competitiveness. Private individuals with jobs certainly benefitted from the increases to social benefits, but job creation did not result. The insiders were rewarded; the outsiders grew in number.

French companies were burdened with sudden, dramatic increases to their costs: ten billion francs of new taxes already by the autumn of 1981. The trade deficit with Germany grew by 35% in 1981 and 81% in the first quarter of 1982. Firms' net savings "fell to nearly zero in response to the high interest rates demanded by the international context and the need to defend the franc."[27] Private firms' investment dropped by 12% in 1981 alone. The trade deficit increased from 56 to 93 billion francs.

Public and private investment in research and development dropped. University research declined. Investment in the manufacturing sector increased in France by only 25% between 1980 and 1997; in the UK this figure was 100%; in the USA, 84%; in Germany, 34%.[28] Overall investment by French firms increased by only 15% during the 1990s, as against 89% in the USA. Public and private investment combined fell by 50% between 1980 and 2000.[29]

Between 1979 and 1994 social transfers increased from 20.2 to 25.1% of GNP. More than half of this increase was due to costlier pensions and the early retirement age.[30] The debt was on average 3% of GDP during 1981 to 1985. The U-Turn merely entailed "austerity" sufficient to stabilize the debt at 3%, checking, not reversing, the expansionary course set in 1981.

Zero inflation, zero job creation, or, *franc fort*, weak economy

The French state tolerated an average inflation rate of 5% between 1950 and 1973.[31] High inflation by today's standards was, to a certain extent, the by-product of (and made tolerable by) high economic growth. But there were several years when inflation (say, of 5%) was higher than the prime interest rate (say, of 4%) leading to negative real interest rates (−1%, or free borrowing). This was a great spur to job creation. This balance was broken during the mid 1970s, as wages began to outstrip economic growth.

During the late 1970s and early 1980s, price stability became a key concern of Western governments; a high pendulum swing against double digit inflation was one of the key planks of the monetarist revolution. Slaying inflation became public policy issue number one in several nations.[32] Nations which restrained public spending *and* exercised wage restraint (Britain, the Netherlands) had a shorter, less painful transition to monetarism. Nations which tried to have it both ways (deficit spending, wage increases, *and* low inflation), such as Italy and Canada (until the early 1990s) and France (for several more years) created mass unemployment.

Monetary union, David Calleo reminds us, was inspired by two key motives: the desire of post-Cold War Europe to make a big collective statement and the need to reassert monetary autonomy *vis-à-vis* the US dollar. The 1980s had witnessed a drain of European investment towards the USA, as German investment funds (in particular) funded the massive US deficits, attracted by high bond rates on offer from the US Treasury. Capital flight was indeed a problem eating away at European macroeconomic sovereignty, and it certainly tied the hands of any European government seeking to embark on a massive inflationary launch. This was no secret at the time.

The idea of the euro was born out of the realization (and hope) that there would be strength in numbers: by bonding together, Europeans might regain a semblance of control over their macroeconomic policy (at the European level, all the while abandoning it at the national level).[33] European monetary union required fiscal harmonization, and the Germans, who co-led the drive with the French, insisted on the price stability and fiscal discipline which had been at the core of their political economy for three decades.[34]

The oil shocks of the 1970s seemed to have rendered traditional devaluation measures useless: attempts to devalue currencies with an eye toward curbing inflationary pressures would only make oil imports (which had increased by 400% in price) and imports in general (which now took up 25% of GDP in several nations) more expensive, defeating the original purpose of devaluation. If this option was no longer in the cards, strict monetary discipline might reduce inflationary expectations in capital markets and might also lower the inflation premium on wages. This was the virtuous circle which had existed in Germany since the Second World War and during the late 1970s Giscard and Barre finally converted to the faith.

Mitterrand and Mauroy would prove to be quick converts, but they took a sort of "buffet Catholicism" approach to the EMS convergence criteria, picking and choosing what they wished from the formula all the while professing their unstinting faith. During the 1980s and 1990s, slaying inflation became public policy number one in France, under the Right and Left alike. But budget discipline was not adopted (as it was in Germany). And *this* was the fatal decision.

The costs of taking the German road were indeed high, but the way in which France paid them was not pre-ordained.[35] The "real" interest rate is the true cost of borrowing money. It consists of the spread between nominal interest rates and inflation. Thus a nominal interest rate of 9% with an inflation rate of 2% implies a real interest rate of 7% (the level reached in France during the late 1980s). Some nations, such as Germany and the USA, tolerated higher inflation and had real interest rates 50% below the French level; higher economic growth was the result.[36]

As the economist Jean-Paul Fitoussi has reminded us, the costs of borrowing money in France during the 1980s and 1990s were higher than at any other point in modern French history, save the 1870s–80s.[37] Nowhere else in Europe were such high interest rates maintained for so long – for fifteen years.[38] Domestic decisions taken by central bankers and politicians were far more important than global forces were in causing unemployment. By the late 1990s, a memorable phrase had emerged to describe French monetary policy during the period 1981–95: "sado-monetarism."[39]

The pain affected millions of people and the scars remain: since the debts accumulated during this fifteen-year period of high real interest rates were compounded at a much higher than usual interest rate, the negative outcomes were both short term and long term. Since the damage to the economy was so severe and so persistent, millions of people never had a chance at a stable career. Businesses put off expansion plans for a decade; youth were not hired as a result. France's national debt is at least 50% larger today than it would have been had the real interest rate been 3% instead of 6 to 7%.[40]

In 1981, France had a national debt of 1 trillion francs. By 1995, the debt was 5 trillion francs. In real terms, the national debt had almost tripled in fourteen years.[41] The debt rose under Socialists and the Right alike; Chirac and Balladur talked the talk of austerity but they never delivered it. Like the Socialists, the Right was beholden to its middle-class electorate and it lived in fear of the militant public sector, which refused to accept cuts. If leaders from Fabius through Bérégovoy and Juppé squeezed one program (family allowances in several years, public sector salaries in a couple of years), they let two others (health, pensions) rise above the economic growth and inflation rates in each and every year.

Throughout the 1980s and 1990s, this overspending was punished severely by international markets, as the franc was hit hard.[42] The government and the Bank of France (it was never fully independent of political pressure) defended the franc by raising interest rates to twice the level in other Western nations. In one month in the summer of 1995 the price was at least 50 billion extra francs in interest costs for French firms, and 30 billion extra for the state.

Today, critics argue that Europe's 3% cap on national deficits limits states' abilities to engage in solidarity. There is no logical reason why this should be so: deficits of this order are recent things. During the 1970s – even during the height of stagflation and Giscard's unprecedented spending spree – France never had a deficit approaching 3%. The average deficit under Giscard had been only 0.7% of GDP.[43] And the French state always retained the ability to decide which type of spending to squeeze: from the nuclear weapons program to cultural and industrial subsidies to social welfare spending to civil servants' salaries to the overstaffed French bureaucracy itself . . . the range of options was (and is) quite large. It is difficult to believe that a state which was spending 45 to 54% of GDP during the 1980s and 1990s and was still allowed a 3% of GDP budget deficit on top of this was prevented from eliminating poverty by outside forces. The "European alibi" was (and is) invoked by politicians Left and Right who have lacked the courage to get non-redistributive domestic spending under control.

If "Europe" placed restraints on French domestic policy, it was because France's domestic policy was wrong-headed to begin with. France was spending beyond its means in 1981–82 and, from a social democratic point of view, it was spending in the worst possible way since it was giving benefits to the "insiders" at the expense of "outsiders."

Sado-monetarism, or, "competitive disinflation"

Some elements inside the first Mitterrand cabinet, including Jacques Delors, also wanted a strong franc in order to increase business productivity.[44] Delors realized – quite rightly – that devaluation might solve France's short-term problems but that it would only serve as a crutch for industries which were, in any case, suffering from indebtedness and slowing productivity. French firms might conceivably ratchet up their production and ride the wave of a weak franc in export markets, but this was likely to be a swell with a short and unpredictable break. Such an approach would, necessarily, become a beggar-thy-neighbor policy: what would prevent other nations from adopting a similar path? And would this, in turn, unravel monetary union and cause the European project to come crashing down?

Competitive disinflation was, in a sense, a higher road to take and Mitterrand deserves credit for ignoring those like Chevènement who wished to pull France out of the EMS snake and revert to a form of 1930s style semi-autarky. The key problem was that French industry could not support higher interest rates *and* higher social charges at the same time. Politicians on the Left and Right alike failed on the employment front because they wanted it both ways.

Chirac's government later in the decade (as well as Balladur's government of 1993–95) was an even more ardent supporter of competitive disinflation.[45] As the theory went, if French firms wished to compete, they would need to become more productive (like the Germans) since they would be forced to sell their goods abroad at a high price (the benefit would come from the lower costs associated with a low-inflation business environment). There was a curious logic behind this policy: French firms, which had been so heavily taxed and regulated by 1982, were now told that the way for them to compete in Europe was not to have this fiscal and regulatory burden lifted, but rather the solution was to suffer even more punishment. Now businesses were told to overcome the world's highest real interest rates – it was, after all, for their own good.

"Competitive disinflation," as it was called, made some sense – all other things equal. But a nation which had just announced massive deficit spending, sweeping new labor laws, a sudden boost to the minimum wage (despite the fact that most companies had been operating at losses or very slim profit margins since the mid 1970s oil shock and wage inflation), and the nationalization of over forty banks and insurance companies, was a nation which scared off investors and put high hurdles in the path of businesses seeking to expand. French economic policy was caught in a vicious circle: the economy was supposed to be revived with inflationary deficit spending, but this required high interest rates in order to prop up the franc and to reassure investors that France, with its government promising a "break with capitalism," was a safe place to park their money. There was a slight contradiction between rhetoric and goals.

From 1982 through 1987 there was a direct link between the rapid, dramatic drop in inflation and the rapid, dramatic drop in employment.[46] This happened in the USA and Britain as well, but the pain was inflicted for three to five years. France experienced a mini-recovery during Chirac's tenure as prime minister, only to slide for a decade. For better or worse, during the 1980s British and American public policy was oriented in one clear direction; French public policy was confused, with the brake and the accelerator applied at the same time. Between 1980 and 1985, French exports declined from 10.4% of world market share (of the top nine exporters) to 9.0%.[47]

The French exception

To be sure, deficit spending was not a peculiarly French approach to the economic problems of the early 1980s. What did distinguish the French was their commitment to a *massive* "relaunch," a huge burst of state spending at precisely the time when several other nations were attempting to realign spending with productivity levels and growth rates (in Germany, for instance, overall social spending was cut by 1.9 points of GDP during the 1980s).[48]

With the Socialists stewing in the political wilderness for a couple of decades before their ascension to power, they failed to adapt their program to the problems of post-industrial society. As Jean-Pierre Vesperini argued in a trenchant 1993 critique of Socialist economic policy, the battles of the 1950s and 1960s were being played out in the early 1980s.[49] By 1981, the solutions proposed by the French Socialists did not correspond to the most pressing problems of the day.[50] Most gainfully employed workers were doing rather well – their wages had, after all, doubled or tripled in real terms over the previous thirty years, they had access to a wide array of social programs, and unemployment, while rising, was still "only" 7% (plus the labor-force participation rate was over 63%). The people who really needed the help were those without work in the first place. The way to help those without work was to ask those with good jobs to sacrifice.

The problems were not overwhelmingly in the well-paid blue-collar, male-dominated workforce: they were now emerging in a new low-wage service sector. But single-parent households toiling just above the poverty line were not even a faint blip on the Socialists' radar screen. Public policy during Mitterrand's first years was geared towards improving the lot of *existing* skilled, male worker-voters.[51]

Hoisting the minimum wage, lowering the boom on job creation

The decision to launch an inflationary spending spree when no other major nation with the exception of the USA dared to do so (the holder of the world's currency could afford to play by its own rules) was a fatal one. Everything else, from high interest rates to the overvalued franc, stemmed from this one decision.

In May 1981, then, as the Socialists moved into Matignon and the Elysée, even after a decade of alarming wage inflation, wage restraint was an idea associated with the apologists of capital. In this vision, since most workers were, by definition, "exploited," the answer to their problems – or, more importantly, to the problems of the unemployed – could not conceivably have been stagnant or lower wages in the name of job creation. Minister of Labor Jean Auroux declared in a speech to the International Labor Organization:

The first decision taken by our government in the social domain was to raise the minimum wage substantially. This decision speaks to our will to give priority to the least favored [members of society] . . . In the same spirit, we increased a number of social benefits substantially. But, in our view, these measures, which point towards a more just distribution of national wealth, are grounded in an equally important economic logic. In fact, we wish to prove that social progress can and must be, the essential motor of economic activity, and this truth must also find its expression internationally.

Raising the minimum wage could not have led to a more "just distribution" of wealth unless the new wealth required to pay for these added labor costs were generated – overnight – by the economy in the form of higher productivity, or unless it were redistributed from the rich to lower-paid workers in the form of a wage subsidy. The new wealth required to "redistribute" to existing workers could not have come from profits, since many French companies were operating at losses at this time.

The sudden, significant increase to the minimum wage was a gain for those who already had jobs.[52] It did not constitute a form of redistribution; it was a form of wealth hoarding for the "insiders." Unemployment rose and profits in France fell rapidly between 1981 and 1983. Company directors had protested that they could not possibly afford the higher minimum wage, but, in the context of a low-trust, anti-business political culture, they were ignored.[53] There could not have been a more inopportune time in post-Second World War France to impose costly new burdens on companies. There was no social *dialogue* taking place in France at this time – as there would be in the Netherlands in 1982. The French *patronat* opposed most of the Socialists' reforms from day one. Elites, however, can shoulder only so much of the responsibility.

"Toujours plus"

In 1981, France's chief unions were committed to the idea that capitalism itself "was basically undesirable and irreparable." A message of austerity was unlikely to win many votes.[54] So Mitterrand prescribed more and more of what had failed for eight years straight during the 1970s: deficit spending. He needed to do *something*.

There were, however, at least three ways of dealing with stagflation: 1) the North American way, which spread risk, wage stagnation, and job losses throughout most of the labor force; 2) the corporatist or continental-conservative European way, which protected the majority of securely employed people and required a large minority (chiefly women, youth, and immigrants) to shoulder the brunt of the burden; 3) the Dutch and Scandinavian way, which was a sort of middle ground between the first two options.

The idea of allowing a large chunk of the working class and middle class to experience declining real incomes was never considered during the 1980s. Neither Left nor Right was willing to convey such a message to the French people. Yet only the Left would have been trusted to deliver this bad news: had Chirac or Balladur or Juppé attempted to impose significant wage cuts across the board, the nation would have been brought to a standstill with strikes (consider the street demonstrations against Balladur's proposal in 1994 to introduce a Canadian-or Dutch-style lower minimum wage for younger workers).

Of course, payroll taxes were also increased in France during the 1980s, adding over 45% to the cost of labor by the end of the decade, so many low and modestly paid workers in the private sector received scant real pay increases. But this was better than in several nations, where rising taxes coupled with low wage increases led to large real losses in income.[55]

The social consequences of declining real incomes are probably less harmful than the problems associated with widespread, long-term unemployment. A nation with a labor-force participation rate just below 70%,

Table 4.2   *The fruits of labor: distribution of real economic growth as %, 1980–91*

	New jobs	Real wages	New taxes	Profits
France	4.4	50.8	12.3	31.6
Germany	19.7	21.3	12.2	45.0
USA	43.3	19.2	9.7	24.3

A few other minor variables are omitted from the table above.
Source: Sénat, Les Rapports du Sénat no. 504, Senator Bernard Barbier, reporter, *La persistence du chômage en Europe* (Paris: Senate of France, 1994), p. 53.

in which perhaps 30% of the population suffered a 10 to 20% decline in real income (Canada during the 1980s to mid 1990s) but only 7 to 10% of potential workers were unemployed, fared better, and chose the more "solidaristic" option than a nation (France during the same period) in which only 59% to 63% of the population aged eighteen to sixty-four worked, 9 to 12.5% (officially) of the population was unemployed, another 10% had dropped out of the labor force, and in which most workers received significant increases (up to 40%) in their real, pre-tax income.

Clearly, for many French workers, there was no "crise" to speak of during the 1980s.[56]

European wage growth in the international context

During the 1980s, in the USA real wages for workers without a university education dropped by 15%, and most other workers were lucky to see increases. But in much of Western Europe low-skilled workers saw their real wages increase by 15 to 20%.[57] Those nations with the highest increases in the unemployment rate during the 1980s and 1990s – France and Italy – also witnessed the greatest real salary increases. Those nations with the lowest unemployment rates – the USA, Canada, Switzerland – enjoyed the lowest salary gains. Although other variables were involved, there is a perfect fit, across a dozen OECD nations, between salary growth rates and unemployment rates.[58]

Large, state-mandated increases in the minimum wage, generous salary settlements in the public sector (by international standards), and the greater bargaining power that came with a more protected workforce led to higher wages in France. Across Europe, but especially in France and Italy, employers found it easier to pay existing workers more money, and squeeze more productivity out of them, than to hire new full-time workers at lower wages (the North American way) – since new workers would prove to be difficult to fire if the need should arise in the near future.[59] Higher productivity was also achieved through robotization and computerization.[60]

The French Socialists have always claimed that their significant boost to the minimum wage during the 1980s represents a major social democratic breakthrough. In a direct but limited way, this is obviously true. If one considers social and economic policies in a vacuum, and is blind to trade-offs and unintended consequences, one can make this argument. Between 1981 and 1983, the minimum wage was increased by 25% (real terms). Millions of people benefitted directly. But, indirectly, if hundreds of thousands of jobs were killed in the process, or if only 50,000 jobs were eliminated, then the picture becomes more complicated.[61] The minimum wage (SMIC) is paid to 11% of the workforce (over 2 million workers), and when it rises upward pressure is created on the wages of those just above it. The SMIC was so high in France vis-à-vis other nations that by the late 1990s economists estimated that a 1% increase in its value killed 4,000 to 20,000 jobs.[62] Each year during the 1990s the SMIC was indeed raised by 1 to 4.0%, to keep up with wages. Additional "coups de pouce" were given every second year or so throughout the 1980s and 1990s – by the Left and Right alike – and invariably during election years.

By the early 1990s, it was becoming clear to more and more people that wage growth in the context of high unemployment was a problem. In 1994, Denis Olivennes published a polemical article called "The French Preference for Unemployment" in the influential journal, *Le Débat*. He argued that high unemployment had not been an unavoidable phenomenon imposed from without; rather, it had been a conscious political choice, a solution chosen by the state, by companies, by unions, by workers. Critics like Alain Minc, today one of the directors of *Le Monde*, backed Olivennes in several articles in leading newspapers and in his widely read study, *La France de l'an 2000*.[63] The real wages of manufacturing workers in France increased at double the OECD average rate between 1974 and 1982, and during the 1980s overall wages were well above the OECD average.[64] During the 1980s, more and more people advocated the "sharing" of jobs through the shortening of the work week, but few people called for a sharing of wages as well.

One comparative study concludes that between 1980 and 1991, 50% of all value added in France went to the salaries of the already-employed. In Germany and the USA, that figure was only 20%. In the USA, 43% of value added went to job creation; in Germany, that figure was 20%. In France, only 5% of value added went to job creation. Obviously companies themselves create (or do not create) jobs and they should be held accountable. But companies operate within a climate set by politicians, who are ultimately responsible.

According to a more recent study, by the left-leaning Observatoire français des Conjonctures économiques (OFCE), 86.3% of all value added to the French economy in 1981 was taken by salary increases and payroll taxes (which funded, overwhelmingly, the benefits of the already employed and the retired).[65] By the end of 1982, with the large increases to the minimum wage, salaries alone took up 71% of all value added. This figure settled down, according to INSEE and the OFCE, at around 63% during the 1990s – but then more and more value added was taken by higher taxes. Whatever the precise figures, the conclusion is clear: French workers took significantly more of their nation's new wealth for themselves than did their northern European and North American counterparts.[66]

French politicians were so concerned about low-skilled workers' wages (and union leaders were so concerned with the already-employed) that they legislated and bargained low-wage jobs out of existence. One in four workers is unskilled, so the failure to allow new, low-wage unskilled jobs in the service sector to appear quickly enough to absorb unemployment from the manufacturing sector is a serious problem.[67]

The French manufacturing sector shed three-quarters of a million jobs between the mid 1970s and 1990. The French state was faced with a Hobson's choice of facilitating the appearance of less-than-ideal jobs versus no jobs at all. France has finally made peace (unofficially) with "McJobs" but it resisted the move during the early and mid 1980s, only to partially relax labor laws later in the decade under Chirac and Rocard. But the damage had been done. Even after part-time work became an option due to the easing of labor restrictions, the high minimum wage limited the expansion of this type of work. As the journalist Sophie Pedder argued in 1999, throughout the 1990s young, unskilled workers fled France to London to take on the types of low-wage service jobs the French state had prevented businesses from creating. As Pedder wrote, "the unspoken attitude of government seems to be: we know better than they do what is good for them." As an advisor to Martine Aubry told Pedder: "Our model is certainly very heavy and costly, but it guarantees our solidarity." The rebuttal to this type of argument has been articulated in pithy fashion by Tony Blair: "High unemployment is not social cohesion."[68] And, I would add, low unemployment and social solidarity are not mutually exclusive, as Scandinavia and the Netherlands prove.

The desire to avoid "McJobs" was matched by a desire to limit the pains of economic adjustment. Perversely, the wish to avoid unemployment and the political repercussions associated with it ensured that the problem grew worse.

The confusion of employment and retirement policy

Since 1971, the major unions, including the CGT and the CFDT, had been campaigning for retirement at sixty. But no government was willing to listen and the *patronat* refused as well. By the early 1980s, these conflicting interests had converged, and agreed that older workers should withdraw from the labor force. Right and Left alike agreed that the withdrawal of one person from the workforce would instantly open a job for another, and at no cost to the economy. The problem was that the person who withdrew from the workforce would now leave on a full pension, at fifty years of age. The *patronat* had productivity issues in mind; the unions were fighting for social "rights" and for their largest demographic group.[69]

Mitterrand and Mauroy's costly pre-retirement scheme had its origins in plans designed for an industry in decline: the mines and foundries of Longwy, in the northeast, and of Lorraine. These plans are a good example of a generalized pessimism, of Maginot Economics. A 1977 agreement hatched under Giscard provided for retirement between the ages of fifty-four and fifty-six, at 75% of salary.[70] Under Mitterrand, more and more industries were added to the formula and the departure age was reduced to fifty. By 1990, the number of pre-retirees quintupled, reaching almost one million people (mostly men).

This policy was grounded in a strong ideological current. Prime Minister Mauroy addressed the National Assembly on 15 September 1981: "[we propose] a new vision of life and work . . . a new relationship between man and work . . . [made possible by] the *notion clé* that the fight against unemployment is the *partage du travail* [sharing of work]."[71] Economists call this line of thinking the "lump of labor fallacy" – the idea that there is a finite supply of work. As economist Jean Pisani-Ferry argues, Mauroy and Mitterrand were simply tapping into a deep historical vein of economic pessimism.[72] Mauroy outlined the government's vision in a speech given in his hometown, Lille, which was threatened by rising unemployment:

And now . . . I would like to address myself to those who are the most senior, to those in this region who have spent their lives working, *eh bien, montrez, oui, qu'il faut changer la vie*, and when the hour of retirement comes, you will retire in order to give work to your sons and daughters. This is what I am asking of you. The government will enable you to retire at 55 years [politicians like Mauroy himself, well over the age of 55, were of course exempted!]. Leave at 55 with your head high, proud of your life's labor. This is what we will ask of you . . . This is our contract of solidarity. Let the oldest workers, those who have worked, leave, and make room for the youth so that everyone may have work.[73]

Sociologist Xavier Gaullier called the pre-retirement program a form of downsizing through official "social decree."[74] He accused the government of failing to acknowledge that France was undergoing a painful process of economic restructuring. He argued that the Socialists were hiding "behind slogans" like "making way for youth" ("place aux jeunes"), and this, he concluded, was preventing the French from having a full reckoning with the problems of the day.[75]

The pre-retirement program set in motion a sort of self-fulfilling prophecy – older workers were unsuited for work. And so they became; companies would henceforth be tempted to use the pre-retirement schemes as a backdoor to downsize on the public dime, to externalize business costs. The older worker who was let go was rarely replaced by a younger, less expensive worker: it was more common to replace him with a robot, a computer, a leaner and more efficient (but higher paid) workforce . . . or with nothing at all.[76]

Despite government assurances that the pre-retirement plan would be a self-financing, job-generating scheme, the exact opposite was true. In 1990, the Rocard government forgave 600 million francs in employers' social charges in order to help firms hire low-paid, younger workers but it also spent 30 *billion* francs to finance the pre-retirement packages of workers aged fifty-five and up. This sum was *fifty times more* than the tax incentives for firms to hire youth.[77] Left and Right supported this policy.

Over 86,000 jobs were shed by the steel industry during the 1970s and 1980s, but not one single steelworker was officially "laid off." Workers were let down on golden parachutes, in the form of early retirement programs that were so costly (at the price of 1 million francs per worker, or $200,000 at late 1980s exchange rates), they ate up, at one point, 75% of the expenses of France's chief unemployment insurance fund.[78] Already in 1984, one-twelfth of the private-sector workforce, 1 million of 12 million people, were benefitting from the pre-retirement programs.[79]

Over 40% of those who benefitted from the pre-retirement packages had been highly skilled, specialized workers, who had been earning high wages. The vast majority of beneficiaries were men. The total cost of this new program was, already in 1984, 45 billion francs, as against 40 billion for all other unemployment-related costs.[80] Rather than allow workers to be laid off and then spend 45 billion francs on retraining them (the

Swedish way), thereby taking pressure off the already insolvent pension systems by keeping the labor-force participation rate constant and the dependency rate lower, the French state subsidized inactivity. Given the impending pension funding crisis and the lowering of the retirement age, this reduction of the labor-force activity rate was the worst possible route to take.[81] It played a significant role in the huge deficits which began to accumulate during the early 1990s, and which resulted in the 1995 strikes. The pre-retirement plan is one of the greatest public policy errors of the past quarter century.

By 1985, only 67.8% of men aged fifty-five to fifty-nine were still working; in the USA this figure was 80.1%, in Germany, 78%.[82] By 2002, under 37% of French men over the age of sixty and under the age of twenty-four were working. Nowhere did the labor-force participation rate of youth and older workers fall so far, so fast.

As Xavier Gaullier noted in 1988, France had become:

a dual-track society, divided by age. On one side . . . the actively employed, aged twenty-five to fifty-five, monopolizing stable, salaried work, employed full-time with a career consisting of rising salaries . . . supporting the growing inactive population [retirees, the unemployed] . . . on the other side, the inactive and those in unstable jobs, aged under 30 and over 50, condemned to underemployment . . . and to leisure.[83]

By 1990, there was no other nation in the Western world outside Italy and Spain which had a more discriminatory job market against the young and those over the age of fifty-five.[84] To a large extent, state policies (supported by Chirac's conservatives as well) were responsible.

By the mid 1980s, the Fond national de l'Emploi devoted 90% of its budget to pre-retirement and only 10% to job creation.[85] By the early 1990s, this situation had changed, as the Rocard government directed more and more money to active labor market policies, but there were still so many other brakes applied to the economy (high interest rates, the *franc fort*, high payroll taxes, red tape) that these measures failed to bear fruit.

Several studies in the late 1980s concluded that the overall net effect of early retirement on job creation was neutral or even negative, and certainly not positive.[86] The best that can be said of early retirement is that it helped to contain social unrest – in the short term. And this type of approach was necessary precisely because no government was willing to deliver the bad news to the manufacturing sector and tell its workforce that a painful process of restructuring was taking over the entire industrialized world. In the absence of a universal discourse stressing common sacrifices, France became a zero-sum society and a winner-take-all welfare state. By 1990, almost one million fifty-year-olds had been granted a full pension but over one million twenty to thirty-year-olds were out of work. The high taxes associated with spending like this crippled the economy; expensive early retirement packages were paid for with unusually high youth unemployment.

The best way to make room for young job seekers (as well as to keep a space for those over the age of fifty-five, who may not be in tune with new technologies or with computers) is to maintain an economy in full employment. Everything else will follow, for all age groups, as it did throughout the West during the 1960s and in the USA during the 1990s, when Americans had by far the highest labor participation rate among those aged sixteen to sixty-four (as well as the G7's highest rate of participation among those aged over sixty-five), but also the lowest unemployment rate. As the US case shows, work is not a finite thing. Even the Netherlands, with its high level of social spending and its complex welfare state, managed to put more people to work and for *longer* work weeks during the 1990s – all the while cutting unemployment to 4%.

Today, every other OECD nation with a lower unemployment rate than France also has a longer work week and higher retirement ages. This includes nations with strong welfare states such as Denmark. Even in 1981, there were several reports available from the Paris-based OECD and from several other sources which suggested that those nations in which the labor force had grown the most during the second half of the 1970s also witnessed the lowest increase in unemployment. Canada, for instance, saw the number of unemployed grow by 5.7% between 1974 and 1984, but the labor force expanded by 33.4%. In France, the unemployment level grew by 7.1%, yet the labor force had grown by only 8.2%.[87] The idea that there was a clear link between the number of people working (or the number of hours they work) and the availability of jobs was and is a fallacy. Other factors – payroll taxes, interest rates, currency values, laws governing hiring and firing – were (and are) far more important.

From a purely economic point of view, the French situation – rapidly rising real wages in the context of very low unionization levels and very high unemployment – makes little sense, since during times of high unemployment, wages should stagnate as the bargaining power of workers declines, as in Canada during the period 1980–99 and in the USA during the period 1975–95.[88] But the high minimum wage policy ensures that low-paid workers' wages retain their real value over time, and labor law intervenes in France to "correct" the market – in favor of those already with jobs and to the detriment of those without them.[89]

French labor law

French labor law has been loosened a great deal since the restrictions on firing implemented under Giscard and since the Auroux Laws were introduced in 1982, but for the most part this means that firms are now free to hire part-time workers. Firing a full-time worker is just as costly and time consuming today (severance pay, red tape, etc.) as it was twenty years ago.[90] As a result, firms still prefer to retain expensive "insiders" rather than hire outsiders.[91]

The Auroux Laws of 1982 wrapped miles and miles of red tape around large French firms. These laws were loosened up in 1986, but large companies contemplating large lay-offs run the risk of falling under the media spotlight and becoming pawns in the electoral cycle.[92] Laid-off workers have first priority in future hires. For large, profitable companies, the decision to hire, then, is a lifelong one. Firing workers for incompetence requires several official complaint forms and juridical procedures. The process can take several months, if not a couple years.[93]

The Auroux Laws represent far more than an attempt to shield French workers from economic insecurity. Beyond this, they are the result of a common pattern in French political life: the failure to organize, the failure to engage in local, face-to-face, collective action. Today the rate of union membership in France is the lowest in the post-industrial world. The Auroux Laws were a heavy-handed, statist measure which, in essence, unionized the entire full-time workforce of France. Hence the need for unions is lower than it was twenty years ago.[94] The Auroux Laws mandated annual salary negotiations and put more power into the hands of the internal workers' committees. On the surface this may seem like a great social democratic breakthrough; in reality it is the complete opposite, for it led to labor *in*flexibility and wage inflation on a national scale, which drove up the unemployment rate. This pattern exists in several Latin American countries – there is nothing peculiarly French about it.[95] Nowhere has it succeeded. Some nations, such as Sweden, have managed to perform much better than France even when 80 to 90% of its workforce has been unionized in recent times. But this was the result of bargaining, of grassroots organizing, of face-to-face meetings and concessions arrived at between labor, management, and government.

Red tape rising

Red tape is a formidable barrier to job creation – more formidable than the Auroux Laws themselves. The French Code du Travail is thousands of pages long.[96] French laws governing social security are complex and burdensome to businesses: the basic survey of American social legislation, by Sar Levitan, is one-tenth the length of the basic French text, by Jean-Jacques Dupeyroux. Severance pay in France is at least two months and often much more (six months is not unusual). An OECD report in 2000 concluded that of twenty-one OECD nations, only Italy put up taller hurdles in the face of businesses looking to expand, contract, or simply to continue operating (Britain scored best, Canada, second-best). No other nation put as many administrative constraints on businesses as did France.[97]

Recent research suggests that excessive regulations are a significant barrier to the start-up and growth of new firms: setting up a business takes on average seven working days in the USA but sixty-six in France and ninety in Germany. There are serious consequences:

Lower start-up costs and less strict worker protection make it easier for innovative entrepreneurs in America to experiment on a small scale (hence the smaller size of new firms), to test the markets and to expand. In Europe the higher costs involved in changing the size of the workforce make all these harder. In a period of rapid technological change, greater experimentation allows new ideas to be tried out more swiftly. In such times, Europe's barriers to entry can become a barrier to growth.[98]

There were 309,000 start-up companies in France in 1990 but only 271,000 in 1997. A recent OECD study shows that Canada and the USA had a start-up rate of 6.9%; the UK and Italy had a rate of 3.4%; France, Germany, and Japan were at the bottom at 1.8%.[99]

Small wonder foreign firms have been so reluctant to set up shop in France since the 1980s. With almost one-fifth the population of the EU 15 zone, France attracted only one-tenth of foreign investment in the zone, almost all of it in newly capitalized, privatized firms, and not in the more meat-and-potato parts of industry or the service sector.[100] Investment finally began to flow back into France starting around 2000, in the midst of a mini-recovery, but much of it consisted of US pension funds moving into undercapitalized markets and buying shares in public offerings – few US firms have set up factories in France. For this, they still prefer to go to Ireland and Britain, where the barriers to entry are so few. In 2001, when Marks & Spencer and Danone became the target of demonstrations and government intervention over their plans to close plants and stores, some foreign firms were surely discouraged from expanding to France.

Employment: the French fiasco

The side effects of France's self-made economic crisis were not shared equitably. As unemployment rose to unprecedented levels, and as the labor force participation rate fell rapidly, the comfortably employed in France became even more comfortable, better paid, and better vacationed.[101] The reverse generally happened in the USA, Canada, Britain, and elsewhere, as vacation time was cut and downsizing threatened even the well educated and well paid. I do not advocate a US-style "white-collar sweatshop" as the solution to the problems of post-industrial society.[102] But I do wish to emphasize the fact that many well-educated, well-paid Frenchmen and women gained costly, publicly financed benefits at the expense of those who were excluded from those very benefits.

Jobs would not be created, in the first instance, by loosening the controls on the market (as they were in the Netherlands) or by easing the tax burden and the regulatory hurdles standing in the way – jobs would be created thanks to the logic of state solidarity. And not just any type of job was acceptable: new jobs would have to be "good" jobs, filtered through a solidaristic sieve, defined not according to the value the market put on them but according to political decisions. This sentiment persisted into the 1990s: "We want quality jobs, not low-paid ones," said an advisor to Martine Aubry, then Minister of Labor and Solidarity, in 1999.[103] During the 1990s, payroll taxes were indeed reduced by the Left and Right alike, but today they are still over 40% of wages and above the European average. The majority of the monies devoted to job creation were channeled into statist measures (which meant that other taxes would have to be introduced and existing taxes would remain high) even as the general macroeconomic climate was choking job creation in the first place. It was a vicious circle.

This half-hearted approach led the French only part-way to Sweden: in Sweden social democracy is created from the shopfloor (in the form of a compressed wage scale and high productivity) to the treasury (in the form of very high taxes on higher earners) to the social security ministries (in the form of programs which then use these tax revenues to redistribute down the pay ladder). Swedish macroeconomic policy during the 1980s and 1990s was always fixated on full employment, even at the price of cutting certain forms of state spending, even at the price of wage restraint. The pressures of monetary union did not prevent the French from taking a similar approach; the unwillingness to cut or reorient non-redistributive social spending and to urge (or impose) wage restraint prevented the French from pursuing full employment.

As John Stephens and Duane Swank have emphasized, as the Swedes were trimming overall state spending during the period 1980 to 1995 (by over eight points of GDP), they made sure that they also *increased* the social wage. Total *social* spending of the redistributive sort increased by 2% of GDP and employment increased as well.[104]

Politicians would prove willing to turn the French nationalized sector around, dumping *dirigisme* in the process. Under François Mitterrand, French capitalism was reborn, moving, in Vivien Schmidt's term, "from state to market."[105] France emerged from the 1980s, after the reforms of the Fabius, Chirac and Rocard governments, a far more dynamic, open economy – but with a large portion of the population excluded from healthy economic growth.

The French were unwilling to abandon expensive, tax and deficit-generating, statist solutions to problems like unemployment.[106] Indeed, as Levy suggests, French governments "expanded social spending" during the mid and late 1980s "to undercut resistance to measures of economic liberalization."[107] If Prime Minister Rocard was willing to continue Chirac's policy of loosening up labor markets and encouraging part-time work, he felt compelled to introduce the RMI (Revenu Minimum d'Insertion), which would come to cover almost 2 million people by the late 1990s, creating a massive welfare trap. The RMI payment was only slightly less valuable than the wage on offer in the form of part-time state-subsidized jobs. It was a classic example of how the state took one liberalizing measure only to cancel it out with another tax-generating, statist measure.

Levy argues that "many of the hopes and aspirations associated with *dirigisme* have been transferred to the social policy arena." Indeed, the 1995 presidential and 1997 parliamentary elections were "waged over social policy, with victorious candidates [Chirac in 1995, Jospin in 1997] in each instance pledging to use the welfare state to reduce unemployment and heal social divisions."[108] The idea that a revitalized private sector might constitute some form of social good in and of itself was an unlikely vote-winner. Having framed the issue of social exclusion around state intervention rather than a combination of market expansion with state supplements, French politicians of both major stripes throughout the 1980s and 1990s ensured that the tax wedge on low-paid jobs would remain among the highest in Europe. By the late 1990s, after the damage was done, Jospin recognized this error and, to his credit, reduced income and payroll taxes on low-income workers and targeted family spending at the poor. But it was too little too late.

Social spending increased from 23.5% of GDP in 1980 to 30.1% in 1995. Spending went up under each and every government, including Chirac's self-styled "neoliberal" government of 1986–88 and Balladur's government of 1993–95. But poverty and unemployment increased as well. By the 1990s, France had reached an impasse: its reformist energy had been exhausted by the painful process of moving "from state to market." But the non-redistributive, inefficient welfare state was in need of thorough reform. Reform will require a huge intellectual leap away from the old statist ways and it will require that French leaders be honest – once and for all – about the disastrous policy path chosen during the early 1980s and retained by both Right and Left alike.

By the mid 1990s, the annual deficit was 6% of GDP and the national debt was ten times larger – this does not include unfunded pension promises, which were themselves over 210% of GDP. In twenty years, the French social welfare sector grew by eight points of GDP but unemployment doubled. Only Sweden and Italy were in worse shape, but Sweden was on its way to a wholesale reform of its pension system and public spending in general.[109] As Sweden concentrated on re-integrating youth into the workforce, French youth were sacrificed as the French Socialists dug a "solidaristic" Maginot Line around their electoral constituents.[110]

Did French governments exhaust all the options at hand? No, they did not. A look to the north suggests that there was (and there remains) a Third Way, a solidaristic escape hatch – and it isn't necessarily Tony Blair's UK.

The Dutch miracle: "Jobs, jobs, and even more jobs"

During the early 1980s, the Netherlands was the Sick Man of Europe. As Göran Therborn has argued, the nation was "perhaps the most spectacular employment failure in the advanced capitalist world."[111] Unemployment was at least 12% – and much higher, given that 15% of the workforce (one million people) was on a disability pension. Overall, 27% of the working-age population was dependent on the state in one way or another. The discovery of North Sea oil was more a curse than a blessing; black gold led to attention-to-deficit disorder.[112]

The Netherlands had become a classic case of a "welfare state without work," to use Gøsta Esping-Andersen's term."[113] Labor-force participation in the Netherlands was only 52% in 1982 (the same rate, officially, in Italy today).[114] Over 34% of GDP was devoted to social transfers alone, and the Dutch state consumed, in total, 67% of GDP.[115] As in France, early retirement schemes for men were numerous in the Netherlands, but jobs were not. The concern to buy social peace with early retirement packages at a time of industrial restructuring took precedence over most other things "social." The Dutch had taken this path earlier than the French, and it was perhaps their good fortune to have pursued this policy to such an extreme that they could see the end of the cul-de-sac. Here was Europe's true "U-Turn."

The Netherlands was, in Esping-Andersen's term, a "continental conservative welfare state" regime which put the interests of male breadwinners – whether employed or pensioned or living on over-generous disability insurance – before all others, especially women and aspiring workers. As in France, increased spending on "solidarity" was nothing of the sort: it was fast becoming a disguise for state-supported structural unemployment.[116] The Netherlands had sunk to rock bottom.

What a difference a decade can make. By the mid 1990s, 66% of potential workers in the Netherlands were working, and the unemployment rate had *dropped* from 12% to just over 4% – proving that work is not a finite thing, that it need not be "shared" out by politicians in order to reduce unemployment. Income inequality in the Netherlands did not increase markedly, as in Britain or the USA. The social welfare system was not demonized and unions were not smashed, as in Thatcher's Britain. No particular group was singled out for an excessive sacrifice.[117]

The Dutch welfare state was not simply cut, its castaways left to drift in a hostile marketplace. On the contrary, social policy was cut and regeared towards integrating people back into the workforce. Cuts were not part of a grand, ideological project (as with the 1996 welfare cuts in the USA). Indeed, at the end of the day, the Netherlands was a *more solidaristic* nation in 1995 than it had been in 1980, when many more people were in receipt of some form of government payment and when "social" spending had been much higher. New jobs appeared in the Netherlands at *four to six times* the rate of its European neighbors. One million new jobs appeared in the span of one decade. This, in and of itself, was the nation's strongest social policy, for these jobs were not the much-feared US-style no-benefits jobs. Most of them were good jobs.[118]

Brave Dutch leaders such as Ruud Lubbers, the Christian Democratic (moderate conservative) Prime Minister and Wim Kok, head of the Labor Party, managed to sell the idea of wage restraint by counterbalancing it with a promise to compensate low-income workers through targeted tax reductions and strengthened family policy.[119] The Dutch welfare state was and still is a very complex corporatist-universalistic hybrid, filled with occupation-based insurance fund directors and labor interests who, like their French counterparts, indeed had the power to block reforms. But unlike their French counterparts, they chose not to do so; in fact, the power of the "social partners" within the welfare state was eroded considerably by the reforms begun in 1982.[120] This was a remarkable case of political compromise and dialogue between state, labor, and business. The 1982 Wassenaar Agreement, limiting wages and beginning a wholesale reform of social policy, set the stage for future success. There was grumbling among labor leaders, to be sure, and no keen enthusiasm for reform, but at the end of the day it was accepted. This landmark reform "created that rare social partnership that actually produced sound results."[121]

Between 1982 and 1985, real wages were cut by 9%, but the work week was also cut by 5%, so there was some compensation in the form of extra leisure time. Higher productivity made up the difference. (Jospin, by contrast, thought he could have it both ways: a shorter work week – 12% shorter – without pay cuts.) The Dutch minimum wage for adults was deindexed and allowed to drop from 80% of the average wage to 67%. The youth minimum wage fell faster and further. All told, the various social minima fell by 30% in real value between 1980 and 1996. In France, by contrast, the minimum wage was increased by 30% in real terms during the 1980s.[122] French firms were faced with rising costs during the 1980s; Dutch companies saw wages fall as a percentage of their total costs, and, in turn, they created more jobs. Dutch workers became more productive. The very ethos of the Netherlands shifted in favor of work.

The exact opposite was happening in France at this time: fewer and fewer people were working as a percentage of the working-age population, real wages were rising relatively quickly, social spending was increasing, and so too was unemployment. In France, sociologists like André Gorz were dreaming of a world free from the tyranny of work.[123] Over the course of the 1980s, the franc was not devalued substantially but the social and intellectual importance of work was.[124]

Whereas (a vulgarized form of) Keynesianism was retained in France even as it was clearly not working, the Dutch abandoned deficit spending quietly. The Germans had already abandoned it in 1974 and the British under Callaghan would follow suit a couple years later. As Terhorst and van der Ven conclude, "the transition from Keynesianism to monetarism took a longer time in the Netherlands than in many other countries [the USA, the UK, Canada], was less celebrated by its victors and less hard on its victims."[125]

In the Netherlands, wage restraint (indeed, an immediate, state-business-union agreement on a *reduction* in wages) came with public spending restraint broadly conceived. This extended to the Dutch currency, thanks to immediate state-induced devaluation and after this a free-floating guilder, its value determined purely by the market mechanism. France, by contrast, delayed devaluation for almost two years and then only partially devalued when its hand was forced.

From the mid 1980s to the late 1990s, under Left and Right governments alike, France pursued a job-killing *franc fort* policy, pegging the franc to the much stronger German mark, binding, for political motives, the French currency to that of a more productive economy, driving up the costs of French firms doing business within Europe.[126] The Netherlands was faced with the same constraints as France since it too was poised to join the euro zone. Since the Dutch were wrestling their deficits under control, they did not need to send interest rates to all-time highs. Dutch companies, in contrast to their French counterparts, found themselves more competitive within Europe; profits went up and companies poured money into research and development.

French social benefits were boosted in 1981 by 25%; Dutch social security benefits were frozen and cut the next year. In the Netherlands, several social benefits were reindexed to inflation, rather than wages, ensuring they would rise less rapidly in the future. The pain was not inflicted solely on youth, or on any particular age cohort or sector of society. The Netherlands' attractively low level of unemployment was *not* a statistical finesse job resting upon the hunched shoulders of an army of working poor. Public-sector wages were cut as were private-sector wages. Pensions were cut and so too was family support for wealthier families. Disability was cut; 150,000 people returned to work in a matter of months. Overall state spending was cut from 67% of GDP to 50% by 1998 (and down to 43% by 2002). The number of state employees was cut from 15% to 11% of the workforce but public services did not suffer from a marked decline in quality.

The private sector was revitalized, but not at the expense of the public sector, which remained strong despite cuts. The welfare state was not dismantled; it was reinvented. As Huber and Stephens conclude, "these cutbacks and structural reforms left intact the comprehensive character of the Dutch welfare state and its effective approach to lowering poverty"; they did not amount to a US-style War on Welfare.[127] Business, labor, and political elites promised to retain the essence of the Dutch social model and the public trusted their motives and their ability to succeed. The Dutch made peace with the idea of a more flexible, less ideal workplace; they did not try to cling to the good old days.

Job growth in the Netherlands during the 1980s and 1990s was four to six times higher than in France. Dutch women's employment rate rose from 50 to 60% during this period. To be sure, most women who found jobs took part-time jobs. And many of them wanted this, seeing as they were looking to balance family and work.[128] By 2000, one-third of all jobs in the Netherlands were part-time or slightly below full-time, the highest rate in the West.[129] But over 50% of part-time jobs in the Netherlands were held by youth (high school and university students primarily), so the story is not as bleak as it has been portrayed by critics. *Poverty did not increase*, even as part-time work did. In fact, by 1997, after fifteen years of cuts to "social" spending, the Dutch low income rate (those with incomes below 60% of the median income) was only 10%; after fifteen years of *increases* to "social" spending the low-income rate in France was 16%.[130]

As the French state was incurring large deficits to pay for current, non-redistributive spending during the early and mid 1990s, the Dutch somehow found the nerve to cut spending substantially. The Netherlands appeared to have the best of both worlds – strong social support systems and a strong economy.

Was this too good to be true? French critics on the Left, such as the editors of *Le Monde Diplomatique*, have portrayed the Dutch miracle as a mirage: all of this was done, they say, by creating unstable, poorly paid part-time work.[131] And, more damning than this: an unusually high percentage of the Dutch workforce remained "disabled." Fair enough, the latter criticism is valid, even to this day. There is still a certain amount of disguised unemployment in the Netherlands. One might even attribute part of the Dutch Miracle to its North Sea oil and natural gas wealth. But in the grand scheme of things these critiques miss the mark: despite the failure to eliminate *all* of the abuses of the disability insurance plans, the Dutch labor-force participation rate increased dramatically and budget deficits fell equally fast. This is the root of success: all future social spending depends on it. The Dutch succeeded in reforming expensive social welfare programs which had been locked into place by strong corporatist lobbies: *this* is the core achievement. The Dutch reforms were not paid for with North Sea natural gas; reforms required that millions of people accept real pay cuts, social spending cuts, and overall state compression. The cuts were made at precisely the moment when oil and gas prices were falling.

As the Dutch scholars Jelle Visser and Anton Hemerijck demonstrate in a balanced, comparative study, the general thrust of the French critique of the "Dutch miracle" is wrong: the gap between part-time and full-time wages in the Netherlands was only 5% in the mid 1990s. Over 80% of collective agreements provided for *pro rata* wages and fringe benefits for part-time work. Pensions and other social guarantees still came attached to part-time jobs created during the 1980s and 1990s. The Dutch reforms did not increase income inequality at an above-average rate; indeed, it rose by only 4 to 5% between 1982 and 1996, which was the European average, and well below the British and American rates of 22 and 35%, respectively.[132] Widespread part-time work is not ideal but it is sustainable and it is better than widespread unemployment and subsidized inactivity, neither of which are sustainable, especially in light of the aging population.

The Dutch succeeded because their leaders took responsibility for their errors, constructed a discourse of legitimation for reform, accepted trade-offs, and introduced sweeping changes which at first glance might have appeared "unsolidaristic."[133] There were indeed protests in favor of protecting "disability" benefits from the butcher's block, but the beneficiaries of capitalism's Golden Age did not march in the streets for five weeks straight to delay reform of *any* sort – as the French did in 1995. Today the Netherlands has stable finances, a competitive corporate sector which invests at a far greater rate than its French counterparts, a large funded system of private/complementary pensions to balance basic public ones, high levels of job creation, low youth unemployment, unusually low levels of old-age poverty, *and* a strong welfare state. Today the Dutch are more productive, per worker-hour, than the French, Germans, and the British.[134] At the end of the day, the Dutch had returned to full employment by 1995 *and* their social expenses still comprised 30.1% of GDP – which was just half a point below the German figure, two points below the French, and much higher than the British, US, and Canadian figures of 25.9%, 17.1%, and 20.8%, respectively.[135]

To be sure, racial tension and political extremism on the Right-wing fringe is now rising. The Dutch have not entirely succeeded in integrating the most recent immigrants, who suffer from high levels of unemployment.[136] (And who has in Europe? The French? The Germans?) In any case, the future of the Netherlands is far more certain than that of France or Germany. Short-term pain has translated into long-term gain and an *increase* in solidarity. To be sure, since 2001 unemployment has risen. There are still problems to be solved, but there are also jobs for most people who want them – surely this, in and of itself, is a social success of the highest order. Many of these jobs are not perfect – but which nation *has* succeeded in recreating the seemingly ideal work conditions of the 1950s? The Dutch accepted this trade-off and they are better off as a result.

Dutch pragmatism, French dogmatism

In France, during the Jospin years (1997–2002), the Dutch Miracle received widespread reporting. But the French reaction was different than in other nations: the Dutch model was an embarrassment to many French politicians and intellectuals because it proved that capable leaders and responsible citizens could indeed reform welfare states and labor markets – and not do so on the backs of the poor, the young, and the unemployed. The Dutch reforms showed that states are still free to pursue "solidarity," reform welfare states, *and* deliver full (or, as of late, near-full) employment in an age of globalization. No surprise that a great deal of the research which attempts to prove that the "Dutch Miracle" is in fact a "mirage" stems from France.[137] In attempting to discredit the Dutch model, French politicians could cleanse their consciences and comfort themselves in the thought that there was no alternative to the path they chose during the 1980s and 1990s.

Both the Netherlands and Sweden are far more integrated into global trade (and therefore more exposed to its threats and benefits) than is France.[138] Yet both nations have unemployment levels of less than one-half the French rate and their poverty rates are three to four times lower. Income is also distributed much more equitably in these two nations. The Netherlands and Sweden use social policy as a means of supporting the market – not as a means to fight it and punish it.[139] To be sure, the public sector was expanded in Sweden during the 1970s and 1980s to mop up unemployment, and the nation continues to pay for this with high taxes.[140] Parts of the Swedish public sector are indeed female employment ghettos, but there are worse outcomes, such as the unemployment ghettos of France. Swedes are not cast adrift with no help whatsoever or with a token sum of, say, 400 euros per month, but this happens to several million people in France even as millions are comfortably pensioned in their fifties. In 1995, the French statistical bureau CREDOC conducted a survey of people living below the poverty line. It found that one in ten people had no state assistance of any sort.[141] One-half of the unemployed do not qualify for insurance.

The Swedish and Dutch labor-force participation rates are high – over 70%. The activity rate of French people aged fifty-five to sixty-four is only 37% (2003); thanks to recent pension reforms in Sweden it is 65%.[142] This is one reason why the expensive Scandinavian social model is sustainable. If the French wish to continue to have 10% unemployment, a 59% labor participation rate, with 2% economic growth, they can probably continue to do so, as long as the social fabric does not continue to tear apart. Solidarity ideology is a very powerful glue: like the US ideology of self-help, it helps to contain discontent and channel it away from the true culprit.

Is social solidarity possible only in small, homogeneous states with traditions of centralized wage bargaining between business, labor, and government? Admittedly, reform is easier in smaller states with corporatist labor arrangements. "Small states in big trouble" have an easier time identifying and tackling problems, hammering out wage restraint agreements, sharing the blame for painful reforms, and so on. But Canada, a heterogeneous nation of over 30 million people inhabiting a thin strip of land spanning an entire continent, managed to reform during the 1990s, and Spain and Finland have reformed recently as well. There are "varieties of capitalism" and there can be varieties of reform.[143]

The point of highlighting the Dutch path is not to present it as some sort of reform Utopia; the point is to emphasize the fact that nations – even ones with corporatist vested interests similar to the French – are free to change. The common denominator in the countries which have reformed is strong political leadership and a discourse of common sacrifice. Politicians in these nations have dared to make unpopular reforms which emphasized the general good and a commitment to equality over corporatist selfishness. In nations which have succeeded in reforming, elites have convinced voters that reforms are necessary not only due to external constraints, but also because they are desirable in and of themselves.[144]

Countries which have succeeded in adapting to the post-industrial world have another crucial thing in common: wage restraint to offset the costs of adjusting to manufacturing job losses and the lower productivity rates of the newer service sector.[145] As John Grahl and Paul Teague remind us, incomes in Western Europe (France, Germany, Italy, etc.) increased by 50% during the 1980s and 1990s, but 8 million people were condemned to long-term unemployment in any given year. As they conclude, the continental "European social model has a future only if a conscious choice is made to reverse this process." Europe may be less tolerant than North America of low wages, but it also seems very tolerant of *no wages*.[146]

As the next chapter shows, France also has a long history of tolerating high degrees of income inequality. The concern to reduce inequality has never figured prominently in the French tax system: not during the 1940s, not during the 1960s, not during the 1980s. A nation's tax system is one of the keys to inequality. Contrary to popular myth, tax regimes are not converging towards the bottom: the Dutch, Swedish, American, and French tax systems are worlds apart and they show few signs of becoming more alike.[147] The persistence of an unusually regressive taxation system into the twenty-first century is the result of domestic political choices.

5   Persisting inequalities

[The income tax is] something anti-French, and contrary to the customs and genius of the nation.

> Leading French newspaper, *Le Temps*, 1896.[1]

We must therefore conclude that, with the same [fiscal] means available to engage in redistribution as our neighbors – that is to say, a similar tax burden . . . and with a similar income distribution *before* taxes and a level of transfers without parallel, *the redistributive results of France are inferior.* This stems . . . above all from the limited nature of progressive income taxes.

> The *Conseil d'Analyse économique*, reporting to Prime Minister Jospin, 1998.[2]

For several decades after the Second World War, many studies of the welfare state looked only at one side of the coin, at the apparently positive, "solidaristic" expenditures. They generally neglected to consider where the money used to pay for social programs came from in the first place. They also neglected to examine just who was receiving the bulk of social benefits. Was most "social spending" being devoted to the middle class? Were the poor and the working class paying more than they took out of the welfare state? Was income inequality reduced significantly? At the end of the day, was social mobility affected?

The late US economist, Mancur Olson, reminded us in his book *The Rise and Decline of Nations* (1982), that:

current orthodoxies of both Left and Right assume that almost all the redistribution of income that occurs is the redistribution inspired by egalitarian motives, and that goes from the nonpoor to the poor. In reality many, if not most, of the redistributions are inspired by entirely different motives, and most of them have arbitrary rather than egalitarian impacts on the distribution of income – more than a few redistribute income from lower to higher income people.[3]

Similarly, fifteen years ago, Gøsta Esping-Andersen challenged us to look more closely at the unintended consequences of social policy as well as the different ways in which certain occupational groups were privileged by the "welfare state." As he wrote, "the welfare state is not just a mechanism that intervenes in, and possibly corrects, the structure of inequality; it is, in its own right, a system of stratification. It is an active force in the ordering of social relations."[4]

This chapter concentrates on the failure of the post-Second World War French welfare state and the taxation system alike to redistribute income and to reduce poverty.[5] The later part of the chapter looks at the issues of social mobility and access to education, access to health care, and assistance for the disabled. I challenge the widely held notion that inequality is strongly linked to rising global competition and I conclude that domestic factors are far more important.

Social welfare spending = economic redistribution?

The very term "welfare state" may be misleading since it implies an element of social justice. For decades, French politicians have equated their commitment to high spending with a commitment to equality or solidarity. But French social policy is not overwhelmingly redistributive, and it is not financed with progressive income taxes, as in Denmark and Sweden, nor is it financed with a mix of progressive income taxes and payroll taxes, as in Germany, Canada, and Britain. As in other corporatist/continental conservative welfare states, French social spending is financed with a mix of regressive payroll taxes, regressive sales taxes, and, for a little over a decade, a smaller "general social contribution" tax (the CSG).

From the 1950s until roughly 1980 France was *the* leader in income inequality among OECD nations.[6] Whereas the British welfare state was progressive during the period 1950–75 (the top 20% of income earners received only 7.2% of transfer payments as against 47.3% going to the bottom 20%), in France the top 20% of income earners received 24% of transfer payments and the bottom 20% of earners only 18%.[7] By 1991 French social policy was slightly more progressive, but French manual workers "remain[ed] in virtually the same relative position – at about 80% of average income – after social benefits [had] been distributed."[8]

The USA, Britain, Canada, and Australia have now shot ahead of France, but France remains a highly stratified society in both the social and economic sense. The wealthiest 10% of the French income ladder are 50% richer than their Swedish counterparts and the upper quarter of the French income ladder is not brought down by the tax system the way it is in Denmark, Sweden, and Germany.[9] As the French economist Thomas Piketty concludes in his monumental 800-page study of the tax system, the French rich traversed the twentieth century largely unaffected by taxation policies.[10] In fact, today many of France's wealthy citizens occupy privileged spots at the core of the "welfare state." This is one of the key

Table 5.1 *Social security payroll taxes as % of total state revenues, select OECD nations, 1965–90*

Country	1965	1980	1990
France	34.2	42.7	44.2
Germany	26.8	34.3	36.8
Belgium	31.4	30.4	34.7
Netherlands	30.8	38.1	37.3
Italy	34.2	38.0	32.9
USA	16.4	26.2	29.5
UK	15.4	16.6	17.5
Ireland	6.5	14.3	14.8
Denmark	5.4	1.8	3.1
OECD Average	18.0	23.3	23.5

Sources: Catherine Mills, *Economie de la protection sociale* (Paris: Dalloz, 1994), p. 213; D. Cohen, A. Lefranc, and G. Saint-Paul, "French Unemployment: A Transatlantic Perspective," *Economic Policy* 25 (1997), pp. 265–93; Premier Ministre, Conseil d'Analyse économique, Edmond Malinvaud, reporter, *Les cotisations sociales à la charge des employeurs: analyse économique* (Paris: La Documentation Française, 1998).

reasons they tend to support it. France is "perpetually torn between its dream of a more just society and its reluctance to give up its old comfortable but inequitable ways."[11]

Chief among these "inequitable ways" is the historic reliance on taxing the poor and the modestly paid worker. France was the last major Western nation to introduce a meaningful income tax. Nowhere else were the debates surrounding income tax as long and as controversial. When the income tax was finally introduced just before the First World War, it was a token tax, bringing in a fraction of 1% of Gross National Product (GNP); by 1965 income taxes still amounted to only 3.3% of GNP. By 1975, this had increased to 4.0%, whereas the VAT (Value Added Tax, or sales tax) amounted to 9.5% of GNP. Today, the VAT brings in more than one-quarter of French tax revenues. This tax, which is hidden in the cost of goods and services, is 19.6% on virtually all things sold, except food, and even higher on "luxury" items.[12]

But the chief source of public revenues is payroll taxes, or taxes on jobs, paid by both employer and employee. This tax is a disincentive to job creation.

Today payroll taxes bring in closer to 40% of revenues, since the CSG tax, levied on all forms of income, was introduced in 1991 in order to ease the tax burden on jobs and businesses.[13] The CSG approaches 8% of high incomes and since it is levied on all workers (on a sliding scale), it is as important as the traditional income tax. The income tax is levied on only one-half of households, and not necessarily the richest half. The income tax itself now accounts for less than 15% of all French government revenues – by far the lowest proportion in the Western world, one-quarter the proportion of Denmark, and one-third the proportion of most "Anglo-Saxon" nations.

Before the advent of the CSG, over 80% of taxes collected in France were indirect and/or regressive in nature. Only 10% of all taxes were truly progressive; another 10% were moderately so.[14] Today these figures have changed slightly in the direction of progressivity, but France still has a more regressive tax system than any other major European nation. These factors do not show up in many surveys of inequality, but they should: market incomes as well as inputs to (and transfers from) the state affect people's standard of living.

The French tax system hurts low-income and younger workers the most. It digs deeper into the wallets of those who purchase large, durable goods (a young couple purchasing its first automobile, its first set of household appliances and furniture, etc.). Thirty years ago, the VAT was only 8%. Today, by contrast, when young people purchase the expensive things that new households need: beds, dining-room tables, sofas, kitchen appliances (which usually do not come provided in apartments in France), they pay more than double the sales tax their parents paid. And, as we shall see in a later chapter, young people's incomes have *declined* by over 25% since the early 1980s.[15]

Private vices, public vices: the hidden welfare state[16]

The French (and Italian) tax collection agencies are less efficient and less vigilant than their German, British, and North American counterparts. Occasionally a high-flying French businessman/politician like Bernard Tapie might end up in jail for one year for evading taxes, but it is extremely rare for the wealthy but unknown citizen to be sent to jail for evading taxes. The incarceration rate for egregious cases of tax evasion is lower in France than in most other OECD nations.[17]

Most people who do pay income tax lose only one-tenth of their gross income.[18] Middle-aged parents whose children have left the nest pretend that their children still live with them, allowing them to gain considerable tax breaks, or even to pay no taxes at all. People lie about the number of dependents they support in order to escape local residency taxes (this is a common problem in Paris). Tax evasion is common among independent contractors (a painter or builder), in the services (the piano repair shop owner on the Left Bank who deals only in cash), and among professionals who bill per service (lawyers, accountants).

During the late 1990s, roughly 60% of all taxes collected in France still bore no relation to the level of an individual's wealth. Whereas the regular wage earner (i.e., the salaried blue-collar and white-collar worker) took home 55% of all income in 1990, he/she paid 84% of the nation's income taxes.[19] Many nations have hidden welfare states for the wealthy, and in France it is a taxation system that saddles the average working person with a heavy and regressive tax burden, to the profit of professionals, the independently wealthy, and the self-employed, who exploit the *fisc*'s inefficient, loophole-ladened tax collection system. When the state audited a random sample of 40,000 taxpayers in 1972, it found that 50% of professionals had underreported their income.[20] An estimated 60 billion francs per year were lost to middle-class and professional tax evasion every year during the late 1980s – roughly the figure of all revenues from the nation's income tax itself. During the early 1980s, President Mitterrand attempted to redress this situation, slapping a number of (largely symbolic) surtaxes on the super-wealthy – on the top 200,000 families. Some of Mitterrand's wealth taxes were watered down once Prime Minister Chirac took office in 1986 but the surtax on "large fortunes" is still collected. In any case this symbolic tax represented only 1 to 2% of the tax revenues brought in from income tax and VAT combined.[21]

Income taxes are not an important source of government revenue because the government knows that it would lose too much money to tax evasion.[22] The weight of the past also plays a role: France taxes consumption at such a high rate today because it has been doing so for centuries. Reform would indeed be a messy process. But in the absence of a more transparent, progressive income tax collection system, France remains a "low-trust"[23] society, in which people feel the weight of the state every time they make a purchase. Low-income, regularly paid factory workers know that high-flying lawyers, brokers, independent contractors, and others who can often choose to deal in cash and fees-for-services escape a large share of their tax obligations. Understandably, those who are unable to escape the taxman resent this. When they are asked to make a sacrifice they protest.[24] The revelation that over the last four decades the nation's political leaders, top civil servants, and generals had received hundreds of millions of francs in annual tax-free cash payments (over 400 million francs or $75 million in "secret funds" each year during the period 1990–2000) confirmed what most French people had thought for ages: politicians are hopelessly corrupt. This did not help to instill confidence in the health of the polity or the fairness of the tax system.[25]

Likewise, when the press revealed that President Jacques Chirac paid 2.4 million francs in cash for several vacations during the period 1992–94 (while mayor of Paris), few people were surprised. The Chirac family spent more than five times this amount, mostly in cash, on "food" while Chirac was mayor of Paris.[26] Tax evasion has been built into the very heart of the political system for forty years and here we may have a prime example of it. In 2002, an international agency which measures corruption levels ranked France twenty-fifth. Finland topped the list as the least corrupt nation in the world. Most other major European nations were well ahead of France (only Greece and Portugal were not).[27]

The absence of trust

Low levels of social trust hinder efforts to reform. As Charles de Gaulle noted in his memoirs, after listing many of the advances in French society, including spectacular economic growth, the rapid expansion of hospitals, the advent of generous pensions and longer and longer vacation times: "Despite . . . the material progress of the French people . . . , social relationships [are] marked by suspicion and bitterness. . . . Everyone resents what he lacks more than he appreciates what he has."[28] There is a vicious logic at work: France is a "low-trust" society, in which many citizens do not fully trust the state and therefore attempt to escape its claims (i.e., pay their taxes). But the state is also seen as a potential source of generous benefits. The high level of social resentment and distrust which characterized France over three decades ago, when de Gaulle wrote these words, persists, largely because the unfair taxation system has changed little since his time.

When, in 2002, Marc Blondel, the head of the Force Ouvrière union, resisted the call of the employers' organization (MEDEF) to prolong the number of contribution years for a full pension, he avoided the issue of sustainability and finances altogether, instead deflecting attention to the privileges of the super-rich: "when I see that the salaries of some of the bosses of the [largest forty] companies represent 554 times the minimum wage" [I realize that] "everything is a question of political choices: there is a lot of wealth in this country" and therefore there is no need to cut the pensions of privileged functionaries (most FO members work in the public sector).[29] Income inequality of this sort is indeed a problem, but Blondel's linking of this issue to the pension crisis is a diversionary tactic.

If politicians introduced a more progressive income tax model, there might be more social trust and a diminished sense of grievance towards the wealthy. If there were more social trust, further reform of the unsustainable pension system, the deficit-racking health-care system, and labor laws would probably be easier.[30] Wage restraint in the name of job creation might be accepted. Moderate and reasonable reform, which has proven possible in Sweden, Canada, Germany, Spain, Denmark, and the Netherlands – might not be tainted with the misleading label of "neoliberalism."

Instead, to many people, society seems unjust and unfair, not a land of opportunity. Political elites are distrusted. Accordingly, more and more people vote for parties (the National Front, the new ultra-Left and Right fringe parties that emerged in 2000–02) which oppose some of the basic tenets of the Republic, the very existence of the EU, and/or capitalism. The 2002 elections witnessed up to 30% of voters choose an extremist political party (definitions of "extremist" vary).

Widespread distrust of the state, politicians, and business elites is well documented. In 1990, for example, at a time when per capita GDP was among the top six or seven in the world, when the French had more paid vacation time than most other people, and one of the best health care systems in the world, only 24.9% of the French responded, in a World Values Survey, that they had a "high level of financial satisfaction." The average for a group of twelve of the richest Western nations was 44.0%; in twelve poor nations, including Nigeria, India, and Mexico, it was 26.0%. Over 52% of Canadians were happy with their income, and over 58% of the Dutch were – and this was at a time when both nations were experiencing stagnating or declining real wages for a majority of the population. These two nations have more transparent pay structures and income tax systems. Political elites have succeeded in convincing the public that economic problems (and solutions) are to a large extent domestic in origin. Political corruption is also lower. Trust in elites is higher. There is probably a link.

To be sure, these types of surveys should always be taken with a healthy dose of skepticism, lest one slip down the slope of sociological stereotyping. But there is evidence from various surveys to suggest that the French may be generally less happy and less optimistic, more fearful of change, than other Europeans. And this may be well rooted in history: a 1949 international poll found that only 10% of French said they were "very happy" yet 25% of Britons and 50% of Australians claimed they were so. Similarly, France had the largest proportion of self-declared "unhappy" people – 33% as against 12% in the Netherlands.[31] French unhappiness with things financial is matched by their (apparent) general state of malaise.

The tax system breeds distrust, but the social welfare system generally does not. Since almost all French citizens receive *something* from the welfare state, there is not a widespread sense of grievance towards those who are the most privileged. Indeed, most people channel their grievances towards private business and/or the process of "globalization" when in fact many of France's most egregious inequalities stem from publicly funded perks and tax loopholes. As Béatrice Majnoni d'Intignano argued in her 1998 critique of the French public sector, the very social attitudes towards work in France have been diluted by the nation's massive state employee/rentier population, and their attitudes and aspirations:

> We no longer look to work as our key source of income, but rather we seek a "statut rémunérateur" which will protect against the risk of being without a regular income. Securing a job in the post office and marrying a teacher with [access to a municipally] subsidized apartment, gaining access to the same vacations as their children, has become an individualistic, winning strategy in the short term [for many families], but in the long run it constitutes a losing formula for society as a whole. In the new class struggle, the exploiting class consists of those who have privileged status [public sector employees and older, protected workers and retirees in general] and the proletarians are the excluded and the youth.[32]

Majnoni d'Intignano, a professor of economics, is part of a growing minority of centrist elite opinion, but her message has not been parlayed to the general public by the news media. A veil of ideology, upheld by the intellectual class and politicians of all parties, continues to ensure the public's ignorance and to obscure stark inequalities – inequalities of income, and inequalities of access to "social rights."[33]

Birth, social privilege, class advantages, an elitist system of publicly financed graduate-level finishing schools, political connections, one's sex – all of these factors remain as powerful in determining success as does pure merit. A government which spends over 50% of GDP has not managed to create a more equal society than forty years ago, when the state spent only 35% of GDP. Every other society which devotes such a large portion of its resources to "social" expenditures achieves a much higher rate of economic redistribution and social mobility.

Throughout the 1980s, the state spent more and more on "solidarity," but poverty increased because new spending was not targeted at the poor effectively and in fact most new social spending went to the middle class. In 1987, 52.3% of those who were poor at one point during the year escaped poverty later that year; by 1994, that figure had dropped to 44.3%.[34]

Income inequality

Income inequality is firmly rooted in French history. As Table 5.2 reveals, during the 1970s the bottom two income deciles in France fared particularly badly, especially in comparison with their German,

Table 5.2 *After-tax household income, as % of national wealth, decile shares, c. 1970*

Decile ->	1	2	3	4	5	6	7	8	9	10
France (1970)	1.4	2.8	4.2	5.5	7.4	8.8	9.7	13.1	16.6	30.5
W. Ger (1973)	2.8	3.7	4.6	5.7	6.7	8.2	9.8	12.1	15.7	30.6
UK (1973)	2.4	3.7	5.3	6.9	8.5	9.9	11.1	12.9	15.4	23.9
Nether. (1967)	3.2	5.9	6.8	7.7	8.3	9.2	10.4	12.1	14.5	21.8
Sweden (1972)	2.6	4.7	6.3	7.8	9.0	10.0	11.6	13.1	16.4	18.6
USA (1972)	1.7	3.2	4.6	6.3	7.9	9.6	11.4	13.2	16.0	26.1
Can. (1972)	1.6	3.6	5.2	6.8	8.3	9.7	11.2	13.0	15.8	24.7
AVERAGE*	2.2	3.8	5.3	6.7	8.1	9.4	10.8	12.7	15.6	25.4

* Average includes a few nations not listed here (Norway, Spain, Japan, Australia)
Source: Maurice Larkin, *France since the Popular Front: Government and People, 1936–1986* (Oxford: Clarendon Press, 1988), p. 212.

British, and North American counterparts (and the top decile fared rather well).

Table 5.2 shows that the upper half of the French income ladder owned considerably more than their counterparts in every other nation in this group. This pattern persisted into the 1980s.

The source of your income mattered too. Into the 1970s, the tax system provided for special treatment of some occupational categories. Low-paid workers lost half their income to various taxes; highly paid cadres lost slightly less (around 40 to 45%) of their much higher incomes. The tax burden of the independently employed was one half the burden of the salaried worker. Farmers were notorious tax shirkers, often dealing in cash for crops. Today these discrepancies are not as pronounced, but they persist.[35]

It may come as a surprise to see that the "Anglo-Saxon" world had a much more egalitarian income structure, and a more redistributive taxation system, than three of Europe's most populous and presumably more socially progressive nations: France, Germany, and Italy (see Table 5.2).[36] During the 1970s, the bottom 10% of the French income ladder suffered a *net loss* after taxes and after social transfers were factored in. In Sweden, the UK, the USA, and Canada, the tax systems were clearly aimed at sharing the top 20%'s wealth with those lower on the income ladder. France stood out as the only nation in which the eighth and ninth highest income deciles were net gainers from tax and social policy.[37]

During the 1980s, almost alone among major Western nations, France did not undertake a major reform of its taxation system. The overall payroll tax burden increased slowly and steadily (about one point of GDP per year) from 35.0% of GDP in 1973, at the dawn of the economic slowdown, to 44.6% in 1984, where it stabilized (even as social benefits increased again and again and as other forms of tax increased).[38] By the mid 1990s, the French tax system was slightly more progressive than it had been in 1975, thanks to the introduction of the CSG tax, levied on all forms of income and earmarked for social spending, but the UK, the USA, and Canada's tax systems were, by one account, twice as progressive, and Denmark and Sweden's were more than three times as progressive as the French. The Socialists failed to deliver on their promise to reduce inequality. In 2000, even after the CSG had become as important as the income tax itself, Italy had a more progressive taxation system than France.[39]

To put a human face on these statistics, consider that in 1998, the typical person earning 10,000 francs per month before taxes (or roughly $ CDN 2,230 per month or the average Canadian salary) would lose 20.6% of that to regressive payroll taxes alone. In Canada, that person would have earned the first $6,500 tax-free, then lost about 17% of income between $6,501 and $26,760, depending upon the province in which he/she resided, for a total loss of only around 13% of gross income, plus payroll taxes, for a total tax rate of 15 to 17%. This is similar to what many Americans would pay in taxes, depending of course on their state of residence. But in France, other forms of taxes, including income, property, automobile, and residential would take away even more income. Finally, a VAT sales tax of 19.6% would have eaten away further still at his or her net income.[40] The total cost in the late 1990s of the 10,000-franc (gross, per month) employee to the typical company was 14,185 francs – a significant increase. The take home pay after payroll taxes of the worker was 7,944 francs, or only slightly more than half the total cost of his/her labor.[41]

Despite overall high taxes, the wealthy are not "taxed down" the way they are in Scandinavia or in Canada. In 1980, the top 10% of the French income ladder was 3.1 times better off than the bottom 10%. By 1994, even after the introduction of the tax on "large fortunes," and including a dramatic rise in overall government spending, the top 10% of French society was now 3.3 times better off – and there were two million more unemployed people, which itself constituted a massive new form of socioeconomic inequality.

In 2000, France spent twice as much per capita as Canada on "social" services, but its poverty rate was only two to three points lower (officially) and its unemployment rate was significantly higher – four to five points higher, and perhaps ten points higher if France's low labor force

Table 5.3 *Tax revenues, some OECD nations, as % of total tax revenues, 1997*

	Income	Business	Payroll	Wealth	VAT
USA	39.0	9.4	24.2	10.7	16.7
Italy	25.3	9.5	33.5	5.1	25.9
UK	24.8	12.1	17.2	10.8	35.0
Germany	23.9	4.0	41.6	2.7	27.7
France	14.0	5.8	40.6	5.4	27.8

Note: A few minor taxes are not included (only about 97% of any given nation's tax sources are listed).
Sources: OECD statistics, cited in Jean-Marie Monnier, "Prélèvements obligatoires," in Serge Cordellier and Elisabeth Lau, eds., *L'Etat de la France, 2000–2001* (Paris: La Découverte, 2000), p. 400; "L'essor des prestations sociales," *Espace social européen* 360 (3 January, 1997), pp. 14–17.

participation rate (*vis-à-vis* Canada and in relation to the recent French past) is factored in. In 2000, the bottom fifth of the Canadian income ladder owned 7.5% of the nation's wealth and the top, richest fifth owned 39.4%. In France, those figures were, respectively, 7.2% and 40.2%. But France spent nine more points of GDP than Canada (54% vs. 45%).[42] In Scandinavia, the lowest fifth of the income ladder owns between 11 and 13% of national wealth and there is virtually no poverty.[43]

During the early 1980s, the top 1% of French society owned, in relation to the rest of the population, almost as much wealth as their American counterparts. (To be sure, the wealthy in France did not enjoy the same high market incomes as their American counterparts.) The top 1% in Britain was significantly poorer.[44]

The French do not get a good, redistributive return on their social spending. Canada's less-developed social welfare sector is compensated by its lower unemployment, its greater social mobility, and its overall higher standard of housing and living. This is why the United Nations ranked Canada, and not countries like France or Italy, number one on its quality of life index for several years running during the 1990s. (Evidently the climate is not a factor in these UN surveys.)

The key problem is the underdeveloped income tax.[45] As Table 5.3 shows, in the late 1990s, the income tax was still far below the OECD average.

Until France lowers its regressive payroll taxes and introduces a meaningful, progressive income tax which takes from the upper quarter and

Table 5.4 *"The three worlds of wealth": distribution of net income, 1985–89 (Gini coefficients. Lower = more equal)*

Finland	20.0	(most equal distribution of wealth)
Sweden	21.1	
Norway	22.2	
W. Germany	24.5	(middle-range distribution of wealth)
Netherlands	26.2	
Canada	26.9	
UK	27.8	
Australia	28.7	
France	29.0	
USA	31.8	(least equal distribution of wealth)

Sources: Göran Therborn, *European Modernity and Beyond: The Trajectory of European Societies, 1945–2000* (London: Macmillan, 1995), p. 153; Walter Korpi and Joakim Palme, "The Paradox of Redistribution and Strategies of Equality: Welfare State Institutions, Inequality, and Poverty in Western Countries," *American Sociological Review* 63 (October 1998), p. 674; Thomas Piketty, *L'économie des inégalités* (Paris: La Découverte, 1999), p. 15.

gives to the lower quarter, it will remain a highly unequal society. Globalization did not prevent the French Socialists from doing this: path dependency and the fear of alienating their own supporters, many of whom were upper middle class, prevented the Socialists from honoring this electoral pledge.[46]

All things considered, the average income tax rate right at the top of the income ladder in France is 40%.[47] This is only slightly higher than rates in the USA and the UK, and it is less than the top Canadian rate. It is offset by the regressive nature of the rest of the French tax regime and extensive loopholes.

The French state spent more than every nation listed in Table 5.4 except Sweden and Finland.[48] Where overall "social democracy" indicators are concerned, some leading scholars of comparative social welfare regimes like Esping-Andersen and Therborn have grouped France in the bottom category, along with the USA, Japan, Ireland, and two other corporatist welfare states – Italy and Austria.[49]

Furthermore, in few other nations (Italy and Spain are in the same league) are the inequalities of wealth between age groups so pronounced, and in few other nations is the tax system rigged in favor of certain occupations (farmers, professionals, and the self-employed). This, too, does not show up on income inequality statistics, but it certainly adds to the inequalities which continue to divide France.

Limited mobility as a form of inequality

Social inequality takes on various forms. Even after the much vaunted boost to the minimum wage under the Mitterrand governments, the lot of the low-paid French worker is no bed of roses. Workers tend to live in very small apartments (often just one or two small rooms), which they usually rent for life. Tenants' rights are weaker in France; many people must sign a five-or seven-year lease, limiting their freedom of mobility. Since most apartments do not come equipped with fridges and stoves (this is required by law in Canada and in most US states), washing machines, dryers, and dishwashers, these appliances must be purchased by the renter. The high cost of acquiring a driver's license makes it out of reach for many low-income people. The high price of gasoline and car insurance further limits the mobility of the low-paid worker. To be sure, public transportation is excellent in France (provided it is not on strike), but not so excellent that the wealthy opt out of car culture and all the conveniences it confers.

One oversight in the literature on inequality is that inequality in the USA takes place in the context of a nation which is 20 to 30% richer than most European nations. A lower-middle-class person in the USA (and in Canada) has a greater chance of owning a house than his/her European counterpart. He/she will typically live in a much larger apartment. The average American home is 145 m^2 but in France it is 87 m^2 and in Denmark, 110 m^2.[50] France's average home size is reduced by the large numbers of urban dwellers who live in one tiny room such as the showerless garrets of Parisian apartment buildings (where many people died during the 2003 heatwave).

French workers have more job security than their American and Canadian counterparts, but they keep less of their income. They have more security, but less freedom. If they find themselves in an unpleasant working environment, they usually do not have an exit option, given the extreme scarcity of good jobs, and the very real possibility that they will end up as part of the long-term unemployed if they quit their position. In 1995, with unemployment at 12.5% (and when 45% of the unemployed had been so for one year or longer), with youth unemployment officially at 28%, with an undeveloped (by European standards) job retraining and placement system, who would have dared quit an unpleasant job to look for a new one? Very few low-skilled workers would have chosen to roll the dice.

The ability to switch from an unpleasant job is an important form of freedom: without an exit option, workers' rights diminish as employers gain more leverage. With a mass army of unemployed waiting in the wings and competing for scarce job openings, long-term unemployment reduces the freedom and mobility of both the unemployed and the gainfully employed worker. As a recent INSEE study shows, during low points in the French economy (1984, 1993), workers were 50% less likely to switch from one job to another than they were in 1974–75 – the last year France enjoyed full employment.[51] Job mobility increased in 2000–01, close to 1974 levels, precisely when the labor market improved suddenly, as the first wave of baby boomers retired and as the economy experienced a brief surge. People left bad jobs for better ones as soon as they could. For a twenty-year period (roughly 1980–2000), usually only the highly skilled had exit options.

The welfare state and social mobility

As we saw above, in 2000, France spent twice as much per capita as Canada on social services. But social mobility is considerably higher in Canada. Indeed, the French political and economic elite is chosen from an unusually shallow talent pool. The Ecole Nationale d'Administration (ENA) and the other *grandes écoles* perpetuate a tiny, caste-like aristocracy of wealth and brains; these schools are well-worn but narrow stairways to the halls of power. During the period 1987–96, only 5.5% of the students of the ENA hailed from working-class backgrounds. Two-thirds of the students' fathers were *cadres* or members of the "liberal professions" (law, etc.).[52] In September 2001, several Parisian newspapers reported that only 9% of students at the prestigious *grande école* Sciences Po hailed from working-class or "popular" backgrounds. The vast majority were the sons and daughters of people in the top fifth of the income ladder. During the late 1990s, only 13 to 15% of students in the general university system came from working-class backgrounds. By contrast, in Canada, 25 to 30% of university students came from low-income families (admittedly, with rising tuition, this figure is falling, as it is in the USA). Tuition in Canada is typically $CDN 3,000 to 5,000 (in early 2004 the Canadian dollar traded at $0.77) per year for an undergraduate in the arts – proof that there is no essential link between free higher education and overall social mobility levels. In Table 5.5, derived from Erikson and Goldthorpe's landmark study, *The Constant Flux: A Study of Class Mobility in Industrial Societies* (1992), the lower the figure, the more fluid the society.

Table 5.5 *Social mobility, c. 1990*

Australia	−0.23	(highest mobility; most open societies)
USA	−0.20	
Japan	−0.20	
Sweden	−0.17	
England	0.09	
Italy	0.12	
Germany	0.13	
Netherlands	0.16	
Ireland	0.16	
France	0.16	
Scotland	0.19	(least mobile, least open)

Sources: Robert Erikson and John H. Goldthorpe, *The Constant Flux: A Study of Class Mobility in Industrial Societies* (Oxford: Oxford University Press, 1992). This table is derived from Therborn, *European Modernity and Beyond*, pp. 174–75.

More recent research by Erikson and Jonsson confirms this 1990 study: Sweden is light years ahead of France in its redistributive efforts, but it spends only a couple more points of GDP.[53]

Recently critics have questioned the widely held notion that the USA is the most socially mobile nation in the West. Even if this critique is accurate, it does not change the fact that several other European nations are far more fluid and open than France. Indeed, other academic studies, including those conducted by the French themselves, confirm France's relatively low levels of mobility.[54]

Solidarity in sickness but not in wealth

So far this book has concentrated on the most expensive and non-redistributive elements of France's complex social security system. In addition, by focusing on the unemployment crisis, which I see as a negative variable in any comprehensive assessment of French social policy, this book has been doubly critical. But no study of French social policy and political economy would be complete without a look at the health-care system, which can be regarded, generally speaking, as a success story.

Health-care spending has accounted for 9 to 10% of GNP in any given year since 1990. Along with four or five other Western nations, the French are in the top tier of health care – measured in terms of success and costliness. In 2000, the French public took great pride in the fact that the World Health Organisation had ranked the French health system the best in the world, whereas the USA was ranked thirty-seventh.[55]

Few Americans see a reason to take note of the French health-care system, but it is the envy of many Britons, who stare across the Channel at a seemingly lavish system which has virtually no waiting lists. Although the French health-care system is among the most effective in the Western world, there are some inequities built into the heart of it. Many of these inequities stem from the very nature of modern, class society, and they can be found readily in almost every other Western nation.

Since the 1980s, class divisions in the realm of medical care have increased in the UK and Canada, with the private sector competing with the public for the care of the wealthy. France has escaped this trend by continuing to spend a great deal of money and by accumulating annual deficits of billions of euros on its health system.[56] The health-care deficits of France, then, represent an administrative failure but they also reflect the Western-wide phenomenon of medical inflation. The way in which the French have coped with medical inflation has ensured that the wealthy have not broken away from the main system, and, from a social democratic point of view, this would have to be considered a success.

The success of the French medical sector is a recent phenomenon. Having slipped into a slumber between the wars, French medicine was finally revived with a series of cash infusions during the 1950s to 1970s. But the decline of top-level medical research was dramatic: no Nobel prize in medicine or physiology was awarded to a French scientist between 1928 and 1965, and after that date the French received only one-third as many Nobels per capita as the Germans, the British, and the Swiss. A government committee investigated this state of affairs in the mid 1950s, spearheaded by Dr Robert Debré (of the Debré political clan). The 1958 ordinance creating university-hospitals and research centers and reforming medical education helped to get France back on track. The French constructed dozens of avant-garde hospitals in the 1960s and 1970s, and the Pasteur Institute, the French equivalent to the American NIH, began to reestablish the nation as a medical powerhouse. A nation once tolerant of widespread health problems, including one of Europe's highest tuberculosis death rates into the 1950s, became a nation of widespread medical consumption. Medical inflation in France was higher than in most OECD nations: 22% per year (gross) during the 1970s.

Today the hospital sector employs over 1.1 million people. This is double the 1970 figure.[57] Hospitals now consume over 55% of health-care costs, up from only 35% in 1967.[58] This is above the international average. The hospital sector is still somewhat stratified, with posh private clinics, small hospitals, and spas accessible to those with the best complementary insurance. The SNCF's medical service, for example, is a virtual health-care system within a system. Private hospitals account for one-third of the nation's hospital beds. Some modestly paid people have access to these institutions, many of which are located in sylvan settings in the South, but many people do not. There is no NHS in France. Then again, the French are spared the solidarity of the NHS's surgery waiting list.

Most private hospitals are non-profit organizations. They receive the insured and are reimbursed with public funds. Whereas the wealthy of Britain opt out of NHS hospitals to be served at their own expense (or their company's expense) in private for-profit institutions, in France the manual worker's payroll deductions (as well as general tax revenues) subsidize the private clinics frequented by the *cadre*. Thirty years ago, the disparities between the public and private hospital sector were significant; today they are negligible, limited to varying levels of comfort and not quality of surgical care or medical practice. In any case, the most complicated surgical procedures are performed only in public university teaching hospitals, which prevents a clear bifurcation of the hospital system along class lines.[59]

Until the 1980s, *cadres* were much more likely to be treated in a private hospital and *cadres supérieurs* were twice as likely to be hospitalized in a clinic than in a public hospital.[60] They were also twice as likely as a manual worker to see a specialist.[61] Manual workers alone, who made up over 30% of the working population, accounted for only 12.8% of the private sector's clientele.[62] But these are minor problems: the French health-care system is today one of the very best in the world – if you are a patient, that is. (Poorly paid family doctors and nurses might beg to differ.) As the World Health Organisation noted in its *World Health Report 2000*, the poor have good access to prenatal and postnatal health care.

Easy access to less vital services is, however, one of the chief problems. France is not as well poised to contain spiralling health costs as some other nations. Costs rose by over 6% in 2000. The deficit for 2002 was 6 billion euros; for 2003 it was in the neighborhood of 10 billion.[63] If cost containment is the Achilles heel of the health sector, the key success is the general availability of good health-care services to low-income workers – the types who tend not to have insurance in the United States. Success stories such as this one should serve as a reminder of French social policy's mixed record.

Due to the considerable amount of autonomy individuals have to maneuver, the result of the corporatist, fragmented nature of the system, cost containment is difficult and in some cases impossible. Unlike pensions, however, rising health-care costs are the product of a service which is, in theory, available to all French citizens, no matter what their age, no matter what the size of their wallet, no matter if they work for a state firm which has good corporatist benefits, or a small pizzeria, which has no such benefits. Although the elderly use the health system at a rate of three or four times that of workers in their twenties, this happens in all rich nations.[64]

Until 2000, roughly 1% of the population had no legal right to medical care. These people were served by charitable organizations such as Médecins du monde. The greatest inequity in the health system was, however, to be found elsewhere; it was (and is) the lack of universal supplementary insurance. The Sécu generally covers only 75 or 80% of "minor" medical costs, including visits to doctors and non-invasive tests and treatments. Major surgical interventions, care for diabetics and those with kidney problems, and others with chronic illnesses, are generally covered at 100%. But a portion of the costs associated with short hospital visits for minor procedures and many drugs are borne by the patient. Usually, it is the poorest paid who lack supplementary medical insurance. As this book went to press, Raffarin and Chirac were promising to provide supplementary insurance to all French citizens.

In 1980, 85% of cadres were covered by *mutuelles* (supplementary medical insurance groups). Two-thirds of workers, artisans, and *commerçants* were covered, but only 45% of farmers and 40% of farm laborers had supplementary insurance too.[65] *Cadres* were still twice as likely as farmers and the self-employed to see a specialist.[66] Parisians consumed 50% more medical care per person than the residents of rural areas.[67] To a certain extent cultural factors were at play here: the urban educated were more attuned to the latest medical advances and more likely to have the time and wherewithal to maneuver through the health-care system to their advantage. Again, this pattern is found in every rich nation.

By the late 1990s, over 90% of *cadres* had complementary medical coverage but only 68% of skilled workers were covered. Young, unskilled (and overqualified/underemployed) workers on short-term contracts rarely received complementary coverage. This is the chief form of inequality in the French medical system.[68] And coverage varies: one *mutuelle* might pay for this but not for that. Some companies have agreements with affiliated *mutuelles*; others do not. Sectors of the economy in full growth tended to have far better coverage than struggling sectors (it's an added cost to the employer).[69] Overall, in the allocation of health care resources, the top income quintile came out ahead; others more or less broke even; that is, they took out roughly what they put into the system with their taxes.[70]

Over-consumption

The financial side-effects of excessive consumption of pharmaceuticals are clear to everyone, yet the practice continues, driven by underpaid doctors eager to please pharmaceutical companies, who sometimes pay them bonuses and kick-backs based on the number of prescriptions they issue.[71] Of course the patients bear a share of responsibility: the French see a doctor more frequently than their European counterparts, and they consume more pills than any other people in Europe.[72]

From 70 to 100% of the cost of (most) prescription drugs as well as drugs like cough syrup (which are normally purchased privately by North Americans) is covered by social security – a key incentive to excessive drug consumption. As in Canada, "private practice, public payment" is the contradictory logic at the heart of the French health-care system. Most French physicians are not civil servants in the British or Greek fashion. But "private" practice is a somewhat inaccurate term: technically free of British-style bureaucratic interference, doctors are constrained by government-set price limits for consultations, the *convention*.

Consultation fees are extremely low by Canadian, American, or Dutch standards – at only thirty euros per basic visit, low fees are, perversely, a key component of health-care inflation in that they encourage a culture of the consultation. Doctors have an obvious incentive to get the patients into the office again and again to maximize fees. These fees are usually covered at up to 75% by social security; supplementary medical insurance covers the remaining 25%, so the up-front payment of thirty euros is, for most people, a minor nuisance and not a disincentive to regular medical visits.[73] But the state has set no limit on the number of prescriptions a doctor may issue, nor has it limited doctors' scope to treat, refer, and admit patients. In this sense, the French health-care system encourages a culture of "irresponsibility," to use the leading critic Jean de Kervasdoué's battle cry.[74]

Many doctors are amphibious, slipping in and out of the private and public sectors. Private doctors are paid for their consultations by patients (who in turn are reimbursed by social security). They represented 57% of the total medical profession in 1993. The full-time hospital doctors and public health service personnel are salaried employees of the state.[75] The French health-care system is of course a great success from a medical point of view, but from an administrative point of view it is a curious hybrid, and as a result it is difficult to control.[76] As one critic wrote in the mid 1990s, "France is the only country in the world where one could get eighteen electro-cardiograms in nine days – one in the morning, one in the evening, and be reimbursed without a single question asked."[77]

The Raffarin government is seeking to prevent such abuses from occurring in the future. Until very recently, general practitioners were not entrusted with a "gatekeeper" role, as they had for decades in Canada, Britain, Germany, and throughout Europe. With its inadequate controls, the French health-care system has encouraged self-diagnosis, hypochondria, and wasteful spending.

The handicapped

There are few more potent reminders of the historical lack of redistribution in France than the way in which the nation has treated (or not treated) its most "excluded" members. The social assistance sector, or "aide sociale" (what North Americans would call "welfare"), cares for those who do not contribute via payroll taxes to social security. It accounted for only 4% of all social expenditures in 1987.[78] In other words, 96% of all social benefits were linked in some way to past or current work experience (today this figure is closer to 90%). Who loses out in such a system? Elderly women who gave up many years (or their entire working-age life) to raising a family, and who are therefore shortchanged at pension time, the long-term unemployed, youth shunned by the labor market, those with long-term medical problems, and, above all, the disabled.

Historically, the French social security system has been driven by skilled and unionized male workers, by professionals, by civil servants. As a result, those who did not (and do not) work in good jobs have fewer links to benefits. There has never been a place in the mythic vision of worker-solidarity for a young unemployed female, a single parent working a minimum-wage job, an Algerian-born man living in a public housing ghetto on the outskirts of Lyon, a handicapped person shunned by the labor market, living alone in Paris on a pittance provided by the state. Citizenship-based access to social benefits, by contrast, ensures that those who are excluded from the workforce are not also marginalized within the social welfare system.

It was only in 1975 that the handicapped were integrated (on less than extravagant terms) into the French welfare state, fully twenty years after the handicapped were integrated into the US social security system.[79] France is still far behind Canada, Sweden, the Netherlands, and the USA in integrating the disabled into the workforce. In 1980, France trained only 5,000 handicapped adults for "re-insertion" into the economy. Another 4,650 people were placed in regular jobs. And 43,000 worked in subsidized jobs.[80] In 1981 a total of 65,309 handicapped people worked in France, representing just 6.5% of the handicapped population.[81] Today the handicapped of North America have a participation rate of over 30%.

In 2003, 37% of all companies in France employed no handicapped workers at all.[82]

In France, the allocation to the handicapped was around 60% of the SMIC (minimum wage) in 1987.[83] But the disabled were (and are) politically and socially invisible. To a certain extent, this is the accident of urban geography, the weight of the architectural past. It is a far greater challenge to navigate the unfriendly, narrow sidewalks of Paris or Lyon in a wheelchair than those of newer cities like Toronto or Seattle. Businesses have no ramps to accommodate the handicapped.[84] Most metro stations in Paris, including some built recently, are inaccessible. Motorists are extremely aggressive, and when they are not driving in Formula One fashion they park on the sidewalks, making it impossible for those in wheelchairs to live in older parts of cities (like the Marais in Paris). To a large extent the handicapped are marginalized from the workforce due to the absence of tough North American-style legislation mandating that firms hire them. Instead of subsidizing heavily (as in Sweden) or *forcing* firms to hire the disabled, the French state slaps companies' wrists with a fine of around 2000 euros for every worker they have not hired below their quota, which is set at 6% of large companies' personnel. Most firms simply pay the fine.

Attitudes die hard: the French have not made tolerance of difference a key priority. Even by European standards, France is behind the times: in 1998, the French spent, as a percentage of GNP, three times less than Germany, four times less than Denmark, seven times less than the Netherlands, and eight times less than Sweden on measures designed to integrate the disabled into the workforce.[85]

Only one-half of the nation's 36,000 city halls and other public buildings are accessible to those in wheelchairs. As a result, many people cannot vote. Nationwide protests in June 2000 centered on public offices, tax offices, and city halls drew attention to this state of affairs. The lack of facilities for handicapped persons in France perhaps explains why in the late 1980s, 12.4% of the aged dependent were incapable of leaving their home, whereas the same figure in the Netherlands and Denmark was 6.0%.[86] A study by the *Association des paralysés de France* in June 2001 found that in twenty-two major French cities, only 3% of bus lines, 34% of cinemas, and 30% of museums were accessible to wheelchairs. It also found that 42% of post offices were inaccessible. Dijon, Strasbourg, and Nantes were rated the most accessible cities; Toulon and Bastia, the least.[87] It is virtually impossible for handicapped people to go on vacation. The overwhelming majority of hotels are totally inaccessible – even those with elevators tend to have old, small elevators which will not accommodate wheelchairs.[88]

By all accounts, the French lag behind their European partners in integrating the disabled into the workforce and society in general.[89] There are over 660,000 disabled/elderly people in institutions – 1% of the entire population. Many of these people are cared for in old *refuges* or *asiles* which date back to the nineteenth century or earlier – and this is where many of the 14,000+ people died, in non-air conditioned rooms, during the heat wave of 2003, as their children and political leaders were vacationing.[90] As Jean-Marie Schléret, the President of the *Conseil national consultatif des personnes handicapées*, told *Le Monde* in 2003, the entire system is designed to "hide" the handicapped. "We must break with this logic," he argued.[91] Change will require a lot of money. Refuges run by religious orders and/or low-paid staff have low costs: providing the disabled with the means to support themselves in the workforce, providing them with Swedish-style modified apartments and transportation, costs much more money.

Between 1985 and 2001, spending on the handicapped fell by over 25%.[92] As *Le Monde* argued in 2002, the disabled are not and have never been a key concern of French governments – they do not bring the city of Paris to a halt several times a year in order to march in defence of "solidarity" (i.e., their unfunded pensions). It is the public-sector workers and the generally prosperous elderly who are the core supporters, and the core beneficiaries, of the French welfare state. The wealthy are still wealthy in France. But their wealth is generally not shared with those who need it the most. High spending on the retired squeezes out more redistributive options.

6   The protected people

As the Prime Minister has said, "la repartition" [pay-as-you-go, or pensions financed by current workers] is the symbol of the chain of solidarity which links the generations. *Repartition* is one of the most important
social pacts of the Nation. This is why the government has made the
clear choice to preserve this pact between the generations and to guarantee the continuation of pensions *par repartition*.

> Official statement from the Prime Minister's office,
> quoting Prime Minister Lionel Jospin, 21 March 2000.[1]

France remains, to an overwhelming degree, a gerontocracy . . . [political
and economic] power belongs mostly to those over the age of 60.

> Jacques Véron, researcher at the Institut national
> d'études démographiques, 1995.[2]

Pensions are the only social program with the potential to bring down a
French government and create a crisis on the order of May 1968. Pensions
constitute, by far, the largest government expense. As life expectancies
rise, the birth rate stagnates, and immigration to France is slowed by
politicians, the general population ages and pension spending threatens
to squeeze out other programs.

In every major Western industrial nation, pensions constitute by far
the largest government transfer program. With the exception of the UK,
no pension system today in Europe is fiscally solvent. By 1985, pensions
alone amounted to half of public social spending in the OECD and in
some nations this figure reached 60%. Health care for the elderly and
pensions together took up over 70% of social spending in France, Italy,
Austria, Germany, Greece, Spain, and other nations.[3]

No other nation's retired population is as rich (relative to the average salary), however, as the French. In 1993, France (and the world)
reached some sort of milestone, as French retirees, aged sixty and up,
became as rich as the workers supporting them.[4] By 2000, French
retirees were 15 to 20% richer, on average, than current workers. This
figure includes reported income but not other assets (real estate). The

Luxembourg Income Study, a widely used international data-gathering survey of income inequality, reported in 1992 that the low income rate for French elderly couples was, after Sweden and Canada, the lowest in the world. In a span of thirty years, France had come full circle, from a time when old-age poverty was rampant and the fortunes of youth were on the rise, to a time when old-age poverty was virtually non-existent and the fortunes of youth were falling rapidly. Even single elderly women, historically among the most vulnerable members of society, had the world's third lowest poverty rate, after the Netherlands and Sweden.[5]

Here was a great success story, to be sure. But there was also too much of a good thing. Nothing comes without a cost, and the costs to other groups in society of supporting unusually generous pensions have been high.[6] If payroll taxes added only 35% to the wage of the average worker instead of 40%, unemployment might fall, but poverty among the elderly need not rise.

During the 1990s, French pension spending as a percentage of GNP grew faster than in every other OECD nation except Denmark.[7] Unusually high pension increases by international standards would have made sense, from a redistributive point of view (one of the official operating principles of French governments) if the French middle-aged and elderly had been poor during the 1990s, but this was not the case. Politically motivated changes to benefit levels coupled with the low retirement age are the two key causes of runaway spending; the demographic scene has changed only since 2000, as the first wave of baby boomers employed in the public sector started to retire as of the age of fifty-five.

As in Italy, the French welfare state has been steered in the direction of the retired population; those over the age of fifty-eight consume at least 70% of social spending.[8] Depending on the pension fund, pensions distributed today in France are usually 50% and up to 400% more generous than they would be in a world in which actuarial discipline was observed. The publicly subsidized pensions of *cadres* and upper-level civil servants can amount to over 5,000 euros per month, or about seven times the maximum Canadian public pension and twice the maximum American public pension. This is the single largest source of income inequality, and it stems from the "welfare state" itself, not the market. These pensions have not been "earned" in their entirety; they are extracted from current workers. They go far and above the goal of reducing poverty among the elderly: they widen the generational imbalances which have divided France for thirty years.[9] As John Ambler concluded in a study of the issue, at the end of the 1980s, "the biggest winners were the elderly."[10]

The sustainability factor

By 1998, pension expenses accounted for 56% of French social spending.[11] Most pensioners who had worked in the private sector retired at the age of sixty-one on 60 to 70% of their net income at their career's end; many people retired on a net income above their pre-retirement one since they were no longer paying payroll taxes. In the public sector, most people retired at the age of fifty-seven but some retired as early as fifty, at up to 87% of their best six months' salary.

In France, public pensions are designed to be one's principal source of retirement income, and most people take home over $2,000 per month. In 1986, there were 3.38 million beneficiaries of family allowances but there were over 11.5 million pensioners, and more than one in three households had a pension(s) as the principal source of income.[12] With 95% of the electorate aged fifty and up inscribed on the voting rolls, with their well-documented above-average voting turn-out rate, and with their growing pressure groups inspired by the American Association of Retired Persons, the middle-aged and the elderly of France have become the single most important voting bloc.[13] France has never had a President below the age of sixty and the Senate is dominated by those over the age of sixty-five.

Forty years ago, there were 4.5 workers for every retiree in France. Today, in 2004, there are 1.5 (as against 4.0 in the USA and 3.6 in Canada).[14] By roughly 2016, France's demographic profile will mirror that of Florida's in the late 1990s (18.5% of the population will be sixty-five or older).[15] In 1990, France already had unfunded pension liabilities (that is, unfunded but promised pensions) to the tune of 216% of its annual GDP, a figure second only to Italy among major industrial nations. This is analogous to First World War debts.

Pension checks come in multiples of hundreds or thousands of euros; family allowance checks come in multiples of twenties or fifties. Pensions are also provided to many people for twenty to forty years of their lives – family allowances are generally available for only eighteen years and in a few nations until the age of twenty-one if the recipient is in university. Pensions are highly visible – and hence highly prone to political manipulation. They are provided to up to 15% or even 20% of the population in any given Western nation – and they are looked forward to, in the short to intermediate term, by at least another 15 or 20% of the population.[16] In other words, up to 40% of the electorate in many nations has become a single-issue voting bloc. Tens of millions of Europeans have framed their entire life expectations around the receipt of generous but unfunded pensions.

Most Europeans have all their eggs in one overburdened basket: the heavily indebted state. In 1993 in France, 74% of retirees' income came from their public pension; today the figure exceeds 80%. In the Netherlands that figure was 77%, and 80% in Germany. In Britain, though, where public pensions are now fully funded (and hence less generous than elsewhere), only 48% of pensioners' income comes from public sources and only 4% of GNP is spent on this. Private savings and pensions are, by necessity, more developed.

Many people believe that Britain has gone too far, too fast in the direction of "the private," and rising poverty among the elderly is the result. The poverty rate of retirees in Britain is over three times the European average. Canada has probably struck a better balance: Canadian retirees receive only 63.5% of their pension income from the state, but the rate of elderly poverty is very low (under 5%) thanks to (barely) adequate public pensions, tax-free pension accounts widely promoted by the federal government for twenty years, supplementary work-based pension plans, real estate gains, and other forms of capital gains.[17] The pension spending gap between Canada and France is an enormous eight to nine points of GNP but the gap between the poverty rates of the elderly in each nation is next to nil. The idea that a trimmed public pension system in France would necessarily lead to higher levels of poverty is simply false.[18]

In my view, state pensions are indeed superior to private ones – provided they are fully funded and are not overly generous and unsustainable over time. Presumably, state pensions, funded and supervised by "the public", in the context of a society committed officially to "solidarity," would operate according to more egalitarian principles than private pensions, and would not simply cement market-based inequalities and project sexual inequalities into retirement.[19]

For all the problems associated with the US Social Security system (which covers all workers) at least the Americans have a balanced portfolio, in the sense that 45% of them have both public and private pensions (as against less than 5% of French workers). If stock markets fall, as they do inevitably, individuals are still free to invest in treasury bonds and other secure forms of (low-yielding) investments. Regularly employed Americans do not (and will not) starve if they lose their company pension since they all have the basic Social Security payment. And company pensions rarely collapse; when things go sour it is more common for firms to trim and skim in piecemeal fashion. In any case, the American Social Security pension system still represented over 65% of all pension monies disbursed in the USA in the late 1990s, so the problems which have arisen with private company pensions should be put into perspective. Of course, this is cold comfort for those who have lost their private retirement savings, but the situation is not as cut and dried as European critics have argued. The problem is not private pensions *per se*; the problem is the weak regulation of them. Like European pension systems, the US public pension system will soon be insolvent, but US public pensions account for only 4% of GNP – less than one-third the French figure. Warnings about the dangers of US-style pensions might have helped to stall reform in France during the 1990s, but this diversionary tactic did not solve France's homegrown pension crisis.

The elderly's place in French society in historical perspective

This crisis was not inevitable; indeed it constitutes one of the greatest and most predictable blunders in the annals of social policy history.[20] In 1945, total spending on the elderly (pensions, old-age homes, etc.) in France took up less than 2% of Gross National Product (GNP). In 1960, the figure was still below 4%. Many old people were poor because they had also been poor as workers and they had not been able to save for their retirement. This was merely a continuation of age-old patterns: old people had always been among the most vulnerable and least affluent members of French (and European) society. The main pension system during the 1940s was comprehensive but basic and therefore sustainable. The state had aimed low, pegging benefits to contributions, the way the British state has since 1986. During the 1950s, French retirees could expect a replacement rate of no more than 40% of past income. Recall that real incomes tripled in France between 1945 and 1975, so during the immediate postwar era this was at best a 40% replacement of a low income by today's standards.

Towards the late 1950s to early 1960s, attitudes in the West towards old-age poverty changed swiftly and dramatically. What was once accepted with resignation was now seen as a problem which could be solved. Across the Western world, from Germany and Britain to Sweden and the USA, pension spending took off during the period 1955–75, as pension systems were reconfigured to reflect not the actual contributions made by retirees and soon-to-be retirees, but rather to reflect what was deemed to be an economically "just" (and/or politically attractive) level of pension income. As workers became richer and richer, governments acted to share their wealth with older people. The people who drew pensions during the period 1950 to 1975 took out far more than they had put into the system (as much as ten times more than they put in); this was a form of redistribution to the needier parts of the population. And it was inevitable that this occur in the early stages of pay-as-you-go pension system growth.

As Henri Mendras and Alistair Cole argue, "the generation of old people [in France] who lived out their retirement during the 1950s and 1960s was possibly the most disadvantaged of all generations during modern times."[21] These elderly people, born in the 1880s, 1890s, and 1900s, would have been hit hard by the two World Wars and by the Depression. Indeed, fate dealt this generation a particularly poor hand. Accordingly, public policy was redistributive towards the elderly, and if anyone was in need of help in 1960, it was the seventy-year-old worn-out worker, scarred by the World Wars and the Depression. By contrast, today's seniors enjoyed the career stability and real wage increases of the Golden Age of Capitalism – but their pensions are geared towards Great Depression-era notions of the elderly.

French retirees purchase 54% of all first-class train tickets and 46% of all first-class plane tickets leaving France. And they buy 52% of all new cars (often, with cash).[22] In 1999, those aged sixty to sixty-nine had an average income of 112,000 FF (French francs) and those seventy to seventy-nine had 109,000. Those under the age of fifty earned on average only 86,000 FF, and much of this went to paying debts and mortgages.[23] Those aged fifty and up were 30% richer than those below the age of fifty.

Policy designed for a completely different world – one in which young people were generally getting richer and old people were generally poor – remains on the books. Why does this continue? The origins of pension reform will provide some answers.

"Pensioneering": An international phenomenon

As Göran Therborn writes, "the basic social prerequisite of old age as a third age of human activity, rather than as one of decay and waiting for death, was the establishment of pensions as a sufficient source of income for a decent standard of living."[24] Pensions for certain privileged or protected sectors (some upper-level civil servants, sailors, soldiers, miners), have existed in Europe for roughly 250 years, but pensions providing a comfortable benefit for the majority of the elderly population date back only to the late 1950s or 1960s. In 1950, pensions in most Western European nations amounted to only 20 to 30% of an average worker's wage. Most pension systems were sound from an actuarial point of view – that is, they distributed benefits according to what people had contributed and according to life expectancies and projected birth rates. But by 1985, the average pension in Europe was worth 58% of a worker's wage. In France, Germany, Italy, and Austria, it was much higher – 60 to 87%. The result, Therborn argues, is that the social question "changed from being a 'workers' question to an 'old age question.'"[25]

Burned by the long memory of post-First World War inflation, suspicious of the stock market, and wary of risky business of all sorts, European retirees now rely on politically guaranteed pension payments. There is no balance between the public and private sectors in most of continental Europe. Without their unfunded public pensions – and all other things being equal – the vast majority of Europeans over the age of sixty-five would be poor. In Germany during the mid 1980s, 86% of the elderly would have been poor prior to government transfers.[26] The Dutch old-age poverty rate was 0% by the late 1980s but without public pensions this figure would have topped 70%.

Today, under 5% of the Canadian retired population is poor, but if public pensions were to disappear, this figure would jump to "only" about 50% because Canadian retirees have balanced pension portfolios. These figures indicate both the success of pension policy in preventing old-age poverty and the failure of the European elderly to put their own money aside voluntarily for their old age. In this sense, France is typical of the general Western European pattern, which was established by Germany forty-five years ago.

Before the famous reform of German pensions in 1957, the average German pension amounted to just 28% of net, after tax, average wages. Today, that figure is typically 65 to 75%, although recent reforms introduced by Chancellor Schroeder will see that figure decline to 60–65% within twenty years. There were two main reasons for reforming the German pension system during the late 1950s: first, to provide a similar level of material comfort for retirees as for workers, to let the elderly (and the soon to be elderly) share in the fruits of the postwar German "economic miracle."

Jens Alber argues that the German need for security and stability in the aftermath of a horrible war provided inspiration for this reform. The echoes of impoverished pensioners during the hyper-inflation of the 1920s and the Depression of the 1930s were surely a factor in the formulation of pension policy during the 1950s. Now that Germany was prospering, here was a way of paying back the elderly who had suffered thirty years earlier – or at least the few still alive.

Second, there was pressure from the Left wing of the CDU (Christian Democrats) to introduce a wage-related pension benefit. As Esping-Andersen and Korpi emphasize, Chancellor Konrad Adenauer went ahead with the idea to increase pensions in order to win votes for the Christian Democrats, the ruling party, and to steal the thunder from the Social Democrats on the eve of the 1957 elections. The law was passed in January 1957. It immediately boosted current pensions by a remarkable degree – in some cases, they were doubled in real terms overnight.[27]

Adenauer, of course, was re-elected. The German reforms set in motion a trend which is only now being arrested.[28] Between 1957 and 1982, there were twenty-two increases in the value of West German pensions. But there were only three increases in contribution rates.

The German reforms set a standard which other nations, including France and the UK, followed.[29] There were seventeen increases to British pensions between 1951 and 1978. Was there a link between pension increases and election years? Without a doubt. Two separate studies, by Heclo and by Kincaid, confirm this. The largest increases were in election years. In each and every election "manifesto" or pamphlet of election promises, issued by both the Labour and Conservative Parties between 1951 and 1978, pensions figured at the forefront of concerns and promises.

Pensioneering in France

French pension policy was not born in a vacuum; the same pattern is clearly visible.[30] In the year following the elections of 1958, 1974, and 1981, pension benefits were increased, by the Right and the Left alike, by 15 to 38%. At no time were contributions raised to cover more than one half of the added costs of these more generous pensions.[31] Between 1970 and 1992, the minimum pension, payable to all, whether they had worked and contributed or not, increased by 1400%, whereas the price index went up by 500%.[32]

The alarming demographic statistics have been well known for decades, but the political rewards associated with ignoring these statistics and increasing pensions were too hard for politicians to resist. The population of France grew from 39 million in 1900 to only 41 million in 1939, but then it jumped to 50 million in 1968. This massive baby boom – larger than in most other Western countries – has always been a well-documented fact. By the mid 1960s, government experts were well aware that projected population growth would not suffice to fund the pensions already in place. Meanwhile, the working population of France stagnated, at 19.4 million in 1949, 19.8 million in 1959, and 20.7 million in 1970.[33] Today it is still only 21 million – which is also the projected size of the pensioner population in 2030. Hence the urgency of further reform.

Between 1960 and 1980, the number of people over the age of sixty-five increased by only 2 million. But thanks to the "right" to retire at fifty to sixty, beginning in 2005, up to 800,000 people *per year* will retire. In the early 1980s, one did not need to be a rocket scientist to see that by 2005, precisely sixty years after the baby boom began, a huge wave of boomers would retire if the retirement age were lowered to sixty. Mitterrand went ahead and lowered the retirement age to sixty (in the private sector; it was already lower than this in the public sector) and increased the value of pensions.

The context within which Germany, Britain, and France embarked on this path was identical: rapid economic growth coupled with the intellectual ascendancy of planners fuelled a heady optimism, a faith in the economy's ability to absorb these unfunded promises. Keynesian economics – or at least a vulgarized version of it – eroded the traditional stigma against ongoing budget deficits. The result of this pensioneering has been the virtual elimination of old-age poverty, but huge debts left to later generations.

Delayed reaction: the French respond to old-age poverty

The German pension reforms hit the French media like Sputnik hit the US media. The frenzy of reform that followed still haunts governments today. The story really begins in 1960, when a highly publicized commission (the Commission d'étude des problèmes de la vieillesse) was struck to study the problem of old-age poverty. The commission included such academic luminaries as Professors Jean Fourastié (an economic historian), Louis Chevallier (a leading urban/social historian), the economist/demographer Alfred Sauvy, and the policy expert Nicole Questiaux. Each one of these experts would go on to an illustrious career.

The commission met in 1960–61. Chaired by Pierre Laroque, one of the architects of the 1940s social reforms, it published its report in 1962. As a recent report by the Commissariat Général du Plan noted, "this report inspired all that was done . . . during the 1960s and 1970s, in favor of the elderly," which is to say that the Laroque Report provided the intellectual underpinning and political rationale for overspending on pensions.[34]

To a certain extent, France's exceptionally generous pension policies of the 1960s to 1980s were a delayed overreaction against the manifest failure of past pension policy – or, at least, the relative "failure" of pensions in light of the smashing success of the economy. In the early 1960s, most old people in France were poor, as they were in Italy, in Spain, and in most European nations. This was a generation which had *not* been favored by the marketplace, in contrast to the generation which entered the workforce in the 1940s–60s. A government report in 1956 estimated that 90% of those aged sixty-five and over would qualify for the social minimum – that is, they had revenues below 2,010 francs per single person or 2,580 for a couple.[35]

Extreme problems tend to call forth extreme solutions. The French viewed the pension problem during the early 1960s as a sort of national crisis; *Le Monde* is filled with articles on the "Shame of the Nation: The Poverty of the Elderly" at this time. Younger workers seemed to be rolling along with the booming economy as the elderly were left behind. A major public opinion poll conducted in 1961 at the behest of the Laroque Commission revealed that the public believed that old-age issues were the most important ones facing the nation. Only 25% of those aged sixty and up were happy with their economic position.[36]

This opinion poll is important in several respects: first, it helped turn pensions into a major public, political issue, providing great impetus to raise them. Second, it reveals the very real economic problems of the time for many seniors; and third, it reveals the emergence of a growing sense of "rights" to economic comfort – regardless of contributions made to the system, regardless of the issue of finances and affordability.

Already, in 1962, the financial and actuarial writing was on the wall. The very first page of the Laroque Report noted that France had the largest proportion of people aged sixty-five and over in the world.[37] In 1901, 8.3% of the population was over the age of sixty-five; in 1960, 11.6% was.[38] The financial implications of caring for this unusually large demographic cohort via pay-as-you-go pensions were clear to the authors.[39] France was the world pioneer of the study of demography, a country with a decades-old tradition of keeping its official finger on the demographic pulse.[40] Laroque went ahead nonetheless. The report argued that French pensions were insufficient and that they needed to be increased significantly, regardless of the cost. The Laroque Commission concluded with a call to the nation's "dignity," arguing that the conditions of life of many of France's elderly citizens "are not worthy of a civilized nation."[41]

During the 1960s and 1970s, pension policy wiped out old-age poverty; if, in 1980, politicians had acknowledged this and frozen spending, France would be in much better shape today. Since roughly 1980, extra pension spending has, by and large, been non-redistributive and job-killing. By the time French pensions had become unusually generous by international standards – by 1980 – many retirees had also become wealthy and most had become reasonably comfortable, due to an unusually stable and prosperous career (those who worked during 1950–80) and due to asset inflation (gains they made in the housing market). During the 1980s pension policy was captured by the labor movement.

The Socialists and Communists, unable to bring about their much hoped for transformation of French capitalism on the shop floor, instead focused their energies on reducing the working week, increasing paid vacations, and rewarding workers at the end of their career. Throughout the 1960s and 1970s, momentum continued to build in support of more generous pensions and a younger retirement age – if you couldn't beat the system, then why not escape it earlier, on the best possible pension?

As early as 1960, the major unions were calling for retirement at sixty for all men, fifty-five for women, for those in "pénibles" or "insalubres" jobs, ones which exposed them to unusual degrees of hardship or danger.[42] In the public sector, where the unions were (and are) centered, this was achieved in small but regular steps, including a burst of success following the 1968 protests. The Laroque Commission was followed by the "Intergroupe personnes âgées," presided by Nicole Questiaux, which convened in 1969 and reported in 1971. A public opinion poll conducted in 1970 on workers' aspirations found that 25% were in support of the Socialists' program of nationalization of industries, 47% wanted more participation in the management of factories, 66% wanted a forty-hour week, but 89% wanted to lower the age of retirement.[43] French retirement policy did indeed stem from popular demand.

Several commissions concerned with old age followed during the 1970s, culminating in the creation under President Mitterrand, in 1982, of the Secrétariat d'Etat chargé des personnes agées (an under-Secretary, or junior Cabinet minister, in charge of seniors' affairs).[44] This subministry organized an annual national convention on retirement and the living conditions of the elderly. Old-age poverty was now at a historic low, under 5%, concentrated among women. Over three-quarters of those receiving the minimum pension were women.[45] In the absence of a citizenship-based right to pensions, women who had been paid, say, 50 to 70% of a man's wage for the same work, saw this job-based discrimination projected into their retirement. But the people most removed from regular wage labor, such as women who had raised families and not contributed for the period required for a full pension, or who had not worked outside the home at all, suffered the most. This situation was identical in Germany and elsewhere.

Solidarity is . . . theft?

By the mid 1970s and throughout the 1980s, the chief problem was that several pension funds were insolvent, bailed out regularly by the nation's regressive tax system. Since 1974, the French government has operated a "compensation" fund, to cover the deficits of the various insolvent "special" pension funds. These special funds got 30 to 35 billion francs each year during the mid 1980s, all taken from the general private-sector pension regime. The majority (those affiliated with the general regime),

Table 6.1 *Fewer contributors, more pensioners*

Period	Change in # of	Régime général	Special regimes
1970–73	contributors	+700,000	−400,000
	beneficiaries	+400,000	+400,000
1973–77	contributors	−500,000	−200,000
	beneficiaries	+800,000	+600,000

Source: Commissariat général du plan, *Vieillir demain* (Paris: La Documentation Française, 1980), p. 117.

whose pension payroll contributions were typically twice as high as the minority's (those affiliated with the special regimes), financed the privileged minority through transfers and through the tax system as well.[46] By the early 1980s, the cost of the SNCF's (railroad) pension system was greater than its annual labor costs; taxpayers footed the bill. And 80,000 miners were paying for the pensions of 200,000 of their retired colleagues. (In reality, of course, taxpayers did this.)[47] Farmers and the independents also received large transfers: their pension funds collected only 38 billion francs in contributions in 1979, but they got a state subsidy of 29.5 billion, which was equal to 78% of members' input.[48]

Table 6.1, taken from a 1980 government report published and widely distributed by the chief government printing office, shows that the sustainability problem has been apparent for decades. Pay-as-you-go pension systems operated on a corporatist basis (that is, covering one industry such as mining) could be sustained only as long as the industry grew at a constant rate. As industries died, there would, by definition, be fewer and fewer contributors paying for more and more retirees. The French taxpayer has been saddled with these bills for over thirty years.

In addition to the obvious inequities associated with the "special" pension funds, the wealthy in general got a better deal, no matter the fund in question.[49] As early as 1970 (and still today), a top-level *cadre supérieur* could receive a pension worth 950% more than the minimum pension.[50] As the French social policy expert Jean-Pierre Dumont reminds us, only six of Europe's fifteen major nations have redistributive pensions, and France is not among them (they are Sweden, Denmark, the Netherlands, Finland, Ireland, and the UK, with its stingy form of redistribution).[51]

In a report to the new "Minister of National Solidarity," Nicole Questiaux, the civil servant Catherine Blum-Girardeau presented a panoramic picture of French pensions. She painted an utterly grim demographic scenario and she revealed alarming inequities.[52] As Blum-Girardeau noted, in 1980, at the moment of his retirement, the typical male worker affiliated with the general private-sector pension regime received a pension of 3,000 francs per month. Usually still renting, his son was typically also a worker. He would probably die at the age of seventy, five to seven years after receiving his first pension check. His children would have had a 4% chance of going on to university.[53]

The average private-sector *cadre supérieur*, by contrast, would retire at sixty or even fifty-five, on a pension of 9,100 FF per month. He typically possessed his own apartment or house mortgage-free, and very likely had a cottage too. His children would probably have gone through university (a 72% chance), and he would have helped them buy their first apartment. His life expectancy was seventy-eight, so he was set to draw his costly pension for an average of eight years longer than the worker. This typical retiree drawn from the upper 10% of French society would benefit from a pension three times greater than the average total monthly income (wages and family benefits) of a twenty-one to twenty-five-year-old worker.[54] Rather than seeking to iron out the inequalities between the young worker and the retired *cadre* discussed above, Mitterrand increased the *cadre*'s underfunded, pay-as-you-go pension by over 25%. And he allowed him to retire even earlier than he would have during the late 1970s.

This is but one example of the many ways in which a government elected with an official commitment to redistributing the nation's wealth from the rich to the poor ended up exacerbating the existing inequalities of wealth between classes and generations. Reducing the retirement age was part of the government's job creation strategy; as the theory went, one fewer worker aged sixty would translate into one additional worker aged twenty to thirty. Of course there was no guarantee that this would happen.

Two things, however, were clear: first, those approaching the age of sixty were now going to get a full pension up to five years earlier than they had anticipated. Second, when Mitterrand came to power, France's elderly population was, after the Japanese and Italian, the largest, as a proportion of the general population, in the world. The impending demographic squeeze on state finances was a well-known fact. At the same time, in 1983, the USA raised the retirement age to sixty-seven (for those born after 1960). As John Myles notes, with a stroke of the legislative brush, France and the USA redefined their "elderly" populations.[55] But France did so in a way completely at odds with demographic trends and economic realities.

Between 1970 and 1985, the value of retirement pensions was increased by French governments both Left and Right by 260%; the typical worker's salary increased by only 140%. The civil service and the "special regime' pension funds saw the largest gains.[56] The period just before the 1974 elections witnessed massive pension increases and an overhaul of the terms of eligibility – which worked in favor of pensioners and to the detriment of the economy. Pension costs rose by 25% in real terms in two years.[57] The cost of business went up accordingly, job growth, in turn, declined.[58]

The "fiscal crisis of the welfare state," or the crisis of the pensioneering state?

Curiously, most scholarship and indeed the vast majority of informed opinion assumes that the large increases in social spending of the 1970s were due to the rising costs of unemployment, coupled with diminishing tax bases as economies went into decline, suffering from stagflation (economic stagnation coupled with inflation). This view has a touch of fatalism to it; politicians are portrayed as helpless victims tossed about by unfriendly sea changes in the globalizing and de-industrializing economy. This view is inaccurate.

Even during the economic "crisis" years following the OPEC oil embargo, pension costs rose three times faster than unemployment costs, and in the late 1970s they took up 43% of social spending as against the 6.6% devoted to unemployment costs.[59] By the late 1990s, pensions took up 56% of French social spending but unemployment payments, retraining and job subsidies combined took up just over 10%. The "fiscal crisis of the welfare state" is in fact the crisis of the pensioners' state.[60]

In 1980, even before the aging of the population had begun to set in, and at a time when there was a baby boom bulge (the children of baby boomers) putting strains on resources, most major OECD nations spent five to eleven times more (as a percentage of GNP) on pensions than on family allowances. Australia spent 1.1% of GNP on family allowances but 5.4% on pensions. Germany spent 1.1% on family allowances but 12.1% on pensions. Typically, in any given nation, the percentage of GNP devoted to pensions doubled between 1960 and 1984, but family allowance spending stayed constant or declined by as much as 50%. Between 1960 and 1994, the elderly population of France (those over the age of sixty-five) increased by 32% but pensions were increased by 300% in real terms (from 4% to over 12% of GNP).

In some OECD nations, real spending on pensions increased by over 400% between 1960 and 1985.[61] The general economic malaise coupled with a slowdown in the birthrate in the West might have underscored the unaffordable nature of large pension increases, especially since everywhere pensions were funded by current workers (and not by capitalization). Pensions were and are directly dependent upon the continuing health of the economy and upon a constant labor-force participation rate. But as productivity declined, and population growth slowed, politicians increased the real value of pensions and allowed people who were living longer to retire earlier.[62] Politicians pursuing short-sighted electoral gain are the root cause of the deficits: the OPEC embargo, the rise of Asian competition, the de-industrialization of Europe have comparatively little to do with the story. No other social expense has put such a heavy demand on the tax system, on employers and employees, as pensions.[63]

The crisis of the French pension system is a political, economic, and social issue of the greatest magnitude. It may well destabilize the Fifth Republic. Why has reform proven so difficult?

The people's choice?

"Public choice" economic theory provides us with *one part* of the picture. It cannot explain the emergence of unfunded pensions, but it certainly can explain their continuance. This theory dates back to the 1960s, but its relevance has probably never been greater than today. Public choice theory is associated primarily with the American economists Anne Krueger, James Buchanan, Gordon Tullock, and Mancur Olson. This school posits that modern liberal democracies are prone to abuse by special interest groups who extract a "rent" from the general population. Rent-seeking is "behaviour which improves the welfare of someone at the expense of the welfare of someone else."[64]

Such abuses might include corporations looking for special legislation and tax breaks; producers' associations looking for tariffs which protect their domestic market but harm consumers' pocketbooks; pensioners' associations which mobilize power in support of their own selfish, economically destructive aims; and lobby groups of the Right and the Left seeking to promote their narrow aims on the public dime. As the theory goes, such groups are usually powerful enough to have their interests pursued by legislators, yet small enough that the "rent" they extract is not a great burden on the rest of the population. As more and more "rent-seekers" accumulate, however, the economy will become sclerotic and nations will decline.[65]

Any political or economic model will necessarily fail to account for all the nuances that characterize real life. To be sure, as Robert Kuttner has argued, this theory tends to reduce democratic politics to interest group brokering, ignoring the possibility that democratic ideals might motivate most voters.[66] Unfortunately, many critics would dismiss this theory outright, viewing it as guilty by association with economists who would make a merchandise out of every idea, even democracy. To dismiss public choice theory flippantly would be a mistake, for it certainly does explain the ability that vested interests have had during the last fifteen years to thwart reform – reform in the name of the public good. If one plugs the insolvent pension funds of France, coupled with the rapidly aging population and the unusually low official retirement age into this formula, France's "social partners" and special pension regimes would clearly fall into the category of "rent-seekers."

Certainly, RATP workers, who take their retirement at fifty-three (on average) would qualify for this dubious label. And certainly the highly paid civil servant or *cadre* who takes his monthly pension of 4,500 euros at the age of fifty-five (and lives, on average to the age of eighty-two), after having accumulated a few hundred thousand euros in assets over his career, an apartment, and a cottage, would constitute a "rent-seeker." (The generosity of French pensions at the upper end of the income ladder is surely related to the fact that the French became the world leader in ownership of second homes during the 1980s and 1990s.) Finally, the upper-level manager from *La Poste* or Electricité de France/Gaz de France (invariably a male) who takes his pension at 85 to 87% of the average of his *final six months' salary* (typically he will be promoted to the highest possible rank during this final year) is a rent-seeker. His pension stands in stark contrast with that of the average worker in the private sector. He or she, by contrast, will get only a 60% replacement rate of the average of his/her *best twenty-five years of salary*.[67]

The cost of the special pension regimes to the public purse

As of early 2004, when this book went to press, Raffarin had not touched the special regimes with the broom of reform.[68] The average pension of RATP, SNCF, EDF-GDF pensioners is, over the life of the pay-outs, two to three times more generous than the average private sector pension.[69] These pensions are not a form of compensation for a life of gruelling labor and low wages, for this is not the story of the French public sector and the workers associated with the various special regimes. Generally speaking, the public sector is overstaffed in comparison with other nations. And in any case, it is usually the members of privileged pension regimes, whose rationale for an earlier than normal retirement is compensation for a "pénible" career (harsh working conditions), who take up new jobs upon retirement, allowing them to double their earnings (this happens in Italy too). The special regimes are so expensive that by 2015 the costs

Table 6.2 *Pension disbursements by percentile, 1998*

Top 15% (i.e. wealthiest) of retirees:	1/3 of all pension disbursements
next 25% "	1/3 "
next 60% "	1/3 "

Source: Xavier Gaullier, *Les temps de la vie. Emploi et retraite* (Paris: Editions Esprit, 1999), p. 56.

Table 6.3 *Strike days per 1000 employees*

Year	1995	1996	1997	1998	1999	2000
Public sector	1568	348	157	297	324	710
Private sector (500+ employees)	262	119	91	75	156	219
Private sector (all workers)	154	33	32	25	39	52

Source: Jacques Fournier, Rapport au ministre de la Fonction publique et de la réforme de l'Etat, *Livre blanc sur le dialogue social dans la fonction publique* (Paris: La Documentation Française, 2002), p. 163. For a historical view and a more sympathetic perspective than my own, see Jeanne Siwek-Pouydesseau, *Les syndicats des fonctions publiques au XXe siècle* (Paris: Berger-Levrault, 2001).

of supporting 2.7 million public-sector retirees may be the same as the costs of supporting 13.5 million private-sector retirees.[70]

In 2000, SNCF (railroad) workers, who made up 1% of all French workers, accounted for over 40% of the nation's strike days. In fighting the "neoliberal" management tactics being imposed on them, they claimed, the disruption caused to the nation was supposed to be in the general interest. Things are not so simple: as Jacques Fournier noted in an official report to Prime Minister Jospin in early 2002, throughout the 1980s and 1990s, the public sector, and particularly the SNCF, refused, with impunity, to play by the good faith rules of labor negotiations. Indeed, as Fournier concluded, the SNCF believed it stood above the law: politically motivated strikes aimed at combatting parliamentary legislation (as opposed to wage-specific, collective bargaining-related strikes) were the norm during the 1990s. Fearful of another December 1995-style strike, governments capitulated time and again. Table 6.3 is drawn from Fournier's report.

In 2003, there were 1.7 SNCF pensioners for every SNCF worker, which meant that the majority of the costs of paying for SNCF pensions are borne by the taxpayer.[71]

By the mid 1990s, the non-earned portion of all French pensions (the amount given to the nation's pensioners above and beyond what they contributed to the system as workers – or the "rent") amounted to an estimated 500 billion francs per year. This is a massive sum: at the time, it was equivalent to roughly $90 billion or $CDN 125 billion – three times the entire cost of the Canada Pension Plan. Divide the figure by two in order to account for France's population of 60 million as against Canada's 30 million, and we still have a figure greater than 1.5 times the value of the entire Canada Pension Plan – in unearned "rent" alone paid to French pensioners.[72]

The key line of demarcation, then, is not between the special regimes and the general regime; it is between the young and the middle-aged/elderly.[73] The largest single fund, the CNAV, which covers most private-sector workers, witnessed pension increases of 439% in real terms between 1960 and 1997. These increases in benefits, unmatched by adequate increases to contributions, have been legislated even as the number of contributors per retiree to the general fund dropped from 4.14 in 1960 to 1.54 in 1997.[74] Solidarity rhetoric is a device used to justify these gross inequities and this series of policy errors.

The generations: rhetoric and reality

Here is an example of the official line coming out of Matignon in early 1981, when Prime Minister Barre's office published a manual, the *Guide de la retraite*, explaining the nation's labyrinth of pension systems. It cost 25 francs and it sold tens of thousands of copies. In the preface, the Minister of Health and Social Security, Jacques Barrot, said: "After having contributed a great deal to the development of our country, 10 million Frenchmen over the age of 60 look forward to a happy retirement."[75] This was the first sentence of the book. Notice that it made an attempt to argue, indirectly, that pensions were owed for something more than simple contributions.

Since the French pension system bears little and often no relation to contributions made, some larger issue – larger than the actual fiscal contributions made by pensioners – needed, and needs, to be invoked to justify this situation. Hence the constant talk of "solidarity between the generations" in this and other documents, which is perhaps a bit of an exaggeration.

The Jospin government produced a pamphlet describing the French pension system in simple language, and with many pies and charts, widely

Table 6.4 *Generational accounting in France, baseline (in US $)*

Age, 1995	r = 3		r = 7	
	Male	Female	Male	Female
0	140,348	110,681	25,623	−3,714
5	174,584	138,844	63,904	17,299
10	211,835	170,319	113,065	47,738
15	243,973	195,695	164,013	82,022
20	290,671	234,637	235,394	138,292
25	306,148	253,627	284,190	184,112
30	263,625	227,146	278,405	190,447
35	199,287	185,985	246,843	180,957
40	115,108	130,656	188,989	154,209
45	23,743	67,894	112,966	112,738
50	−64,100	7,174	29,276	63,238
55	−184,251	−76,278	−91,104	−16,650
60	−232,282	−136,466	−164,612	−76,703
65	−225,530	−134,762	−175,435	−87,475
70	−168,734	−111,542	−134,820	−77,305
75	−177,047	−119,018	−148,190	−91,496
80	−101,447	−76,301	−86,935	−61,197
85	−109,300	−79,461	−96,974	−67,889
90	−99,988	−76,940	−89,642	−68,203
95+	−104,084	−76,387	−96,111	−70,623

Notes: Productivity growth assumed to be 1.5%; *r* is the discount rate (percent). A negative figure (e.g. −104,084, in the final row, means that individual members of this cohort have contributed the equivalent of $104,084 less to the French treasury than they have taken out in the form of services used, pensions, and debt accumulated on their watch, etc.).
Sources: Joaquim Levy and Ousmane Doré, "Generational Accounting for France," in Alan J. Auerbach, Laurence J. Kotlikoff, and Willi Leibfritz, eds., *Generational Accounting around the World* (Chicago: University of Chicago Press, 1999), p. 257; Legris and Lollivier, "Le niveau de vie par génération," p. 3. On the French deficit, in this vein, see Jean-Paul Fitoussi, "Des générations futures et du déficit budgétaire," *Le Monde*, 28 May 1998.

available to the public in bookstores in 1999 and 2000 for 15 francs (about $2.30). Here is a sample:

Solidarity. This principle lies at the heart of our pension system. In a pay-as-you-go system like ours [a current worker-financed, tax-based "régime par répartition"], solidarity is above all expressed between the generations . . . The functioning of the French pension system is founded on this contract between the generations.[76]

It is a "contract" written by the victors. Table 6.4, compiled by French economists in 1999 using standard international measures devised by

Table 6.5   *Projections of average workers' & cadres'*
pensions, as replacement rate of salary upon retirement
(normal age of retirement at 60) (French francs) (%)

Gross income, end of career	Age of worker in 1996		
	35 Yrs	45 Yrs	55 Yrs
100,000 FF	63.4%	67.3	86.5
200,000	50.0	52.4	66.1
300,000	36.3	38.3	50.1
	Age of *cadre* in 1996		
200,000	60.2	68.2	86.1
360,000	44.0	49.7	68.4
600,000	35.9	40.4	59.5

Sources: "Réformes des retraites, une projection inquiétante,"
Espace social européen 22, Supplément no. 361 (January 1997),
p. 29; Blanchet, "Population Aging and French Economic
Performance," in Bosworth and Burtless, eds., *Aging Societies*,
pp. 128–29; Laurence Assous, Carole Bonnet, and Christel Colin,
"Comparaison des régimes de retraite des cadres et des non
cadres," *Dossiers Solidarité et Santé* 3 (July–September 2000),
pp. 29–46.

the Boston University economist Laurence Kotlikoff and the US-based
National Bureau of Economic Research (a mainstream establishment run
by leading centrist economists), shows who in fact will be the net contributors and the net beneficiaries of state spending and taxation, if this
"contract" is not reformed radically. Raffarin's reforms of 2003 will only
add to the burdens of the younger cohorts (see Table 6.4) and current
retirees have not been asked to sacrifice at all.

These figures are based on a large mix of variables: projected interest
rates; economic growth; fertility rates; immigration rates; life expectancy;
age of retirement; taxation levels; various social security benefits; family
allowances; pension and health spending rates in the past and the future;
and so on. The corresponding figures for most other countries, from
Canada to the USA to Germany, are very similar.[77]

Table 6.4 includes the projected impact of the 1993 reforms introduced
by Prime Minister Edouard Balladur, but not Raffarin's 2003 reforms.[78]
Balladur changed the way in which pensions are calculated in the private
sector: until 1993, they were based on the best ten years of salary; now
they are based on the best twenty-five, which tends to cut the value of
pensions considerably.[79] The rules have already been changed, but not
enough to solve the pension problem.[80]

Perhaps the greatest indication of the lack of redistributive "solidarity" is the fact that the average female pensioner, in 1997, received a pension worth 43% less than the average male pensioner. Lifelong salary inequities born of different job experiences as well as sexual discrimination were (and are still) projected into retirement. Even in 2002, the average female worker earned 27% less than her male counterpart.[81] Women are indeed given "credits" towards pension contributions for raising children, and public-sector female workers have "special" benefits in this regard. But the credits do not fully close the gap.

Ninety percent of pension monies disbursed in 1997 were tied entirely to job experience and "rights" accumulated through work. The remaining 10% was given mostly to women who receive the minimum pension due to their short time in the workforce, and hence their paltry (or non-existent) earned pension. Unlike in Scandinavia, the UK, and Canada (where the non-contributory pension, the Old Age Security payment for those on low incomes, amounts to over 40% of all pension costs), the top-up part of French pensions, provided as a sort of social right, thereby helping women who have not worked as long as the average male worker, is next to nil.[82] The French system is one of the three least redistributive in Europe, along with those of Greece and Italy.[83]

The absence of private retirement savings

Since the rate of private savings for retirement is so low in France, with a small fraction of the population owning equities and other retirement assets, the country cannot offset spiralling public pension costs, as Canada, with its enormous RRSP industry and the USA, with similar 401K and IRA pension savings plans, might conceivably do one day.

During the late 1980s and 1990s, Canadian governments "clawed back" the Old Age Security payment (a top-up pension of roughly $ CDN 400 per month) from retirees with an annual income of over $ CDN 80,000 to 85,000. This was a cost-saving measure and it also freed up money for other pressing matters. Wealthy Canadians still receive the basic pension which runs as high as $ CDN 800 per month (the Canada Pension Plan or the Quebec Pension Plan). To a certain extent, wealthy Canadians were compensated with the RRSP (Registered Retirement Savings Plans) program, which allows individuals to put up to $14,500 away, tax-free, each year for their retirement.[84] This was a pragmatic move designed to free up scarce resources at a time of high taxes, large deficits, and falling productivity. Canadian politicians accepted the idea that they operated in a market economy, a world which imposed limits on profligate governments. They acted accordingly. Canada went from a budget deficit of 5 to 6% of GDP to budget surpluses in the span of six years. As governments cut spending, inequality increased (largely due to the shift towards a more service-oriented economy and tax cuts for the wealthy) but job growth topped the G7 growth rate for several years in a row and hundreds of thousands of people found work. Canada's labor-force participation rate is more than eleven points higher than France's, which is the single most important factor in an aging society. Canada still has serious social problems but its future looks brighter than France's.

The ideological hostility towards the market that dominated the Socialist Party prevented Mitterrand from taking a leaf from the Canadian story. With good reason, perhaps, the French also distanced themselves from the stock market mania that overtook North America during the 1990s. But the French probably went too far in this regard: they might have gone half-way, like the Dutch, and embraced the stock market in moderate measures.

The value of publicly traded companies listed on the French stock market increased by 283% between 1982 and 1987 (adding to the wealth of those few retirees whose generous state pensions were complemented by their investments) and it doubled again in value between 1994 and 1999.[85] The French *Bourse* has performed exceptionally well during the last thirty years, delivering a 1000% return. To be sure, it lost 40% of this value in 2001–02, but it has still delivered handsome returns over the long run. Yet there were (and are) very few state incentives to invest in it. Publicly, the Left dismissed capitalized (or simply partially capitalized) pension funds as being "unFrench," or "contrary to French values and traditions." In fact, Jospin quietly introduced a tax incentive for private retirement accounts, building upon his conservative predecessors' reforms, but, as John Gillingham puts it, "for the French left, capitalism remained an illicit pleasure," and Jospin refused to make his new relationship with the market "legit" by aggressively promoting these retirement accounts, by going public with them in the form of an advertising blitz (which is what Canadian politicians did during the 1980s and 1990s).[86]

This was a great missed opportunity. Ironically, the state's failure to whip up public support for the idea of tucking away some money in the Bourse (or simply in secure government bonds) meant that the majority of new stock market wealth, including stock in newly privatized firms, has accrued to a tiny slice of the population, and to foreign investors, who took advantage of an under-capitalized market.[87] Between 1987 and 1995, at a time when half a dozen major reports on the impending pension crisis were issued, pensions were increased at twice the rate of general wage increases.[88] While the Swedes and the Germans made private retirement accounts a central part of their reform platform during the mid 1990s and early 2000s, Jospin introduced this by stealth.

Small wonder that in 2000, only 10% of the adult French population owned mutual funds or stocks (the figure in the USA was 40%). And most French people who do own stocks have come late to the game and have very small sums invested. The French press portrayed the US stock market boom of the 1990s as a feast for the American super-wealthy, when in reality up to 20% of the population benefitted a great deal before the crash. In this sense, the French stock market, where equally large gains were made, still benefits only the top 5–10% of society, since the market has not been opened up through a large, private mutual fund industry.[89] The French distrust of the stock market is consistent with a more general distrust of private, non-governmental institutions. In 1990, only 22.4% of French people polled in a World Values Survey had "high" confidence in non-governmental institutions. In Canada, that figure was 34.1%, in the USA it was 38.2%.[90]

The Japanese, British, Americans, and Canadians are the most fiscally provident nations in the world. In these four nations, fully funded pension plans (solvent, actuarially sound), both private and public ones, had assets in 1995 of between 47 and 77% of GDP. In France that figure was only 4.4%, in Italy, 2.5%, in Germany, 6.3%. European pensioners are entirely dependent on the state. This is not solidarity – this is short-sighted public policy.[91] Little Canada, with one half the population of France, had $320 billion (US) in funded pension assets, mostly private but some public; this put Canada fourth in the world. The relative giants of France, Germany, and Italy had, respectively, only $60 billion, $120 billion, and $70 billion in funded pension assets.[92]

I am not blind to the potential dangers of private pension funds.[93] Mutual funds like Fidelity and Templeton have the potential to do damage (and good) around the world. High-flying managers like Mark Mobius can withdraw a couple of billion dollars of investment from a small country with the flick of a switch. But states are free to impose limits on the investment of pension assets outside of the home nation, as Canada does. Pension funds are potentially dangerous but not necessarily so. States still have the power to supervise them if they wish to do so.

The "welfare generation" of France? Deficits and the welfare state

By the mid 1990s, some critics like Alain Minc and Jacques Bichot were arguing that France had returned to the High Middle Ages, to a time when *seigneurs* (the parallel is with today's elderly) extracted an intolerable tax from the active population.[94] In 1994, 37% of all households received at least one pension.[95] By the year 2030, one-half of all households will be pensioner households.[96] Until Raffarin's reform takes effect in 2008, public sector workers who continue to retire at the age of fifty-five will typically draw a pension for twenty-three years (men) to twenty-six years (women).[97]

The concept of a "welfare generation" comes from the controversial work of the New Zealander David Thomson.[98] In his book, *Selfish Generations?*, Thomson demonstrated how Kiwis born during the period 1920–50 have been privileged by the state at every stage of their lives: generous family allowances (whose real value was five times greater in 1955 than in 1985) when they were young parents; regular funding for schools; the expansion of higher education; home loans and low real interest rates; low taxes in their early working years; and finally tax cuts for high earners, which benefit those over the age of fifty (at the peak of their careers) more than younger workers. At the same time as Thomson was writing, during the 1980s, a school of thought emerged, mostly in the USA, and centered at think tanks such as the Urban Institute, which argued that most state income support was being directed at a privileged generation. Critics like Timothy Smeeding argued that the state was standing on the sidelines while child poverty levels soared, even as it gave incredible returns on pension contributions to the elderly. According to Thomson, who wrote in the late 1980s and early 1990s,

the account of the evolution of social policy that is widely accepted still, and more important, that has served as a major underpinning of the expansive social-spending policies of the later twentieth century, is badly mistaken. This orthodox history is excessively, almost laughably Whiggish . . . simplistic, progressive, teleological, and determinist. It enshrines the welfare state as the ultimate goal toward which humankind has been groping. The tale is one of inexorable advance. From the grim Dark Ages, when individuals and families fended for themselves while the collectivity looked on with indifference, we have climbed toward the welfare state in which individuals and families increasingly share their resources for the uplift of all. In turn, this faith has bolstered the belief that the expanding welfare state is historically inevitable, proper, and right . . . and that any questioning of this is hopelessly or maliciously reactionary.[99]

The misinterpretation of the welfare state which Thomson criticizes persists in several nations, including France. As Thomson argues, during the last fifty years the general assumption that the "welfare state" has been redistributing resources to the needy, from rich to poor, from the haves to have-nots, has prevailed in most nations.'

Many scholars have operated under this assumption, but perhaps the most influential was the British scholar T. H. Marshall. In a famous 1949 lecture in Cambridge, England, Marshall argued that "the modern drive towards social equality is, I believe, the latest phase of an evolution of

citizenship which has been in continuous progress for some 250 years."[100]
Until roughly fifteen years ago, Marshall's paradigm inspired social scientists around the English-speaking world. Unfortunately, it is a grossly oversimplified conceptual lens through which to view the complexities of social policy. In fact, as Thomson demonstrates, social policy has been fundamentally concerned with saving for future need (protecting the elderly with current tax dollars) and protecting against risk (health insurance, unemployment insurance). And if taxes could not be raised to a sufficient level to bring about "solidarity" then they could simply be passed on to the next generation. Between 1950 and 1981, France had only five budget surpluses, and none since that date. In each and every year during the 1990s, the French state ran a budget deficit of between 150 and 500 billion francs – at one point, in the mid 1990s, this amounted to over 6% of GDP. Between 1990 and 1996 alone, the French state was so overextended that it accumulated 2.1 trillion francs in debt, for an average of 300 billion francs per year.[101] That 2.1 trillion was worth roughly $CDN 525 billion – which was almost the exact amount of the entire Canadian national debt. In other words, France, with double the Canadian population, had accumulated in seven years the same amount of debt that the Canadian state had taken 130 years to accumulate.

Rentiers vs. investment

Since the 1970s, increased payroll taxes and government spending have squeezed out private investment and corporate investment alike. Total investment as a percentage of GNP fell from 27% in 1973 to 21% in 1980, and kept falling rapidly during the 1980s as Mitterrand burdened French industry with more and more payroll charges.[102] In 1989 to 1994, the investment rate was down to 18% of GNP, which was 2.5 points lower than the German figure.[103] In 1993, if French firms had invested in job creation at the same rate as their German counterparts, they would have spent one trillion more francs – proof that high payroll taxes kill jobs. During the period 1980 to 1990, social expenditure as a percentage of GDP increased faster in France (by a full 4.0 points of GDP) than in Germany (−2.2 points); Denmark (+1.0 point); Italy (+3.3 points); the Netherlands (+0.5 of a point); Spain (+2.5 points); the USA (+1.2 points); and the OECD average of +1.9 points.[104]

Why did this occur? To a large extent, because of pensions and health-care inflation. Pension spending as a percentage of GNP increased by over 50% since 1980, and by 20% since 1990 alone; the percentage devoted to investment dropped accordingly.[105] In 1985, wages comprised 64.5% of household incomes in France; by 1995, this was down to 58.5%.

Pensions and assets (including stocks and bonds and interest-yielding assets) increased from 27.2% of the value of total incomes to 32.8%. France became not a socialist but a *rentier* society during the 1980s.[106] A huge flow of wealth from young to old was occurring, even as the young were being paid less and taxed more.[107] Pensioners represent one-fifth of the total population but they own more than 50% of all real estate in France.[108]

The young require a dynamic, vibrant economy with openings for them; the old have no such interest. Opinion polls tell us that the middle-aged and the elderly are far less likely than younger people in their twenties and thirties to support the following: the European Union; free-trade; the idea of labor market deregulation; the idea of opening up to the world in the cultural sense; and, unsurprisingly, pension reform.[109] The elderly, rather, seek (and receive) a comfortable, wage-indexed, and politically financed cushion against the uncertainties inherent to capitalism.

Pension reform

During the 1980s and 1990s, the German and British debates on pension reform came back down to earth. Substantial reform was achieved in Britain in the late 1980s and a partial reform in Germany in 2000. Canada achieved a wholesale reform of the Canada Pension Plan in 1996, phasing in contribution increases of over 70% in real terms over the next six years. Meanwhile, other nations, such as the USA, Japan, and Italy, reindexed their pension increases to prices, not wages. In 1984, Germany did the same. France waited until 1993 before it reindexed the *régime général*'s benefits to wages – but this main fund, covering 70% of the working population, accounts for only 40% of pension costs. The public sector and special regimes were not touched, and these were in the most need of reform. A couple of other nations used to permit retirement at sixty, but, seeing the writing on the wall, they have recently made reforms. By 2010, most Italians will not be able to retire on a full pension before the age of sixty-three to sixty-five.[110]

The longer nations delayed reform, the higher the final cost: Prime Minister Raffarin's reforms of 2003 will hurt all the more since his predecessor Lionel Jospin failed to acted. The government which could have moved with the least resistance – Jospin's Socialist government of 1997–2002 – chose to do nothing except establish a miniscule "reserve fund" out of general (regressive) taxes and to quietly introduce tax incentives for private savings.[111] Raffarin's 2003 pension reform will raise only one quarter of the monies required to meet France's pension promises by 2040.[112] As of 2008, public-sector workers will need to contribute the same number of years as private-sector workers to receive a full pension.

Further reform is imperative. But the French are torn between their desire for more pension spending and their knowledge that the system is broken.[113] Only one of France's five major unions, the CFDT, supported Prime Minister Raffarin's 2003 reform. The reason is that most union members share with Force Ouvrière the vision that: "The right to retire at sixty constitutes, in our country, an *acquis social* to which the population is particularly attached. Generations of men and women have fought to achieve this right."[114] The appeal is not to statistics, not to demographic facts. It is an appeal to ideology, to a mythic view of French history. This mythic view is framed around the male worker, well protected while at work, and well pensioned as of the age of fifty to sixty.[115] But unusually generous pay-as-you-go pensions require a dynamic economy with a high labor-force participation rate, not one of the lowest rates in Western Europe. The contrast between the comfort of French pensioners (the protected) and youth, women, and immigrants (the excluded) is the subject of the next chapter.

7 The excluded: immigrants, youth, women

I cannot count the number of times I have heard the same litany of complaints in the course of my conversations with shopkeepers, artisans, and the directors of small businesses: "Of course, I could expand, take on one or two young workers. But I won't do it. Too expensive. Too complicated."

The center-Right politician Pierre Lellouche, 1998.[1]

Things are booming at the moment, but I'll do anything to avoid taking on more workers.

A building contractor in Lille, 1999.[2]

With the spread of youth unemployment and poverty, the implicit acceptance by the popular classes and a good part of the middle classes of a certain period of personal sacrifice in exchange for a better future for the younger generation, seems to have evaporated.

Sociologist Jean-Marie Pernot, 1998.[3]

The spoiled children of May 68 [those born during the 1940s] have traversed the crisis [the crisis of unemployment of the 1980s–90s] practically unscathed, as if they still lived under the sign of the *trente glorieuses*. The growth escalator stopped as soon as the generation born after 1955 tried to get on board.

Bernard Préel, middle-aged author of the book, *Le choc des générations* (2000).[4]

Millions of young people remain trapped in the unemployment and underemployment ghetto. Hundreds of thousands of youth of North African descent, especially young women, have never had the chance to work. The victims of the expensive system of "solidarity" which protects older, "Frencher" workers, these abandoned youth are also the scapegoat of the far Right, which portrays them as leeches on the public purse. The reality is that immigrants receive very little social spending – with two clear exceptions, derelict public housing which can hardly be considered a great social gain, and the RMI ("welfare") payment. The lion's share of social spending, however, goes to pensions and health care, not to the "welfare" or housing costs associated with the immigrant unemployed. Still, the majority of public housing units are indeed occupied by non-French-born citizens and non-citizens, and this is a powerful image in the minds of Le Pen supporters.

Housing, immigration, and the French underclass ghetto

The immigrant experience sits uncomfortably in French history; until roughly 1988, when Gérard Noiriel published his landmark study, *Le creuset français* (translated as *The French Melting Pot*), it was whitewashed out of the books.[5] Along with the USA and Canada, France is a nation of immigrants, but until recently the grand narrative of French history has not incorporated this basic fact. In the realm of social policy, particularism is the guiding principle; where citizenship is concerned, French universalism spares no space for particularism.

The Republican creed holds that France is one and indivisible, that everyone's ancestors are the Gauls, that there is no room for the hyphenated French citizen, no place for an Antillean-French, an Algerian-French. In the French debate over immigration law reform during the late 1980s, many people expressed the view that "becoming French was an honor, not a bureaucratic convenience." To be truly French, one needed to be "French at heart." Those "unwilling or unable to assimilate" should be excluded.[6]

Insular French critics of the US model (the type of critics who fear and oppose what they do not understand) argue that multiculturalism tends to create ethnic ghettos and tear society apart; a trip to full-employment Toronto would show them how the model can succeed. Critics of the French approach to immigration and citizenship like John Ardagh and Jonathan Fenby argue that the universal Republican model fails to acknowledge the reality of mixed or divided loyalties and identities.

One thing is clear: whatever the reason, since the early 1990s, France has been in the midst of a racial crisis. During the last ten years there has been a palpable sense of fear among the French people, many of whom believe the social order is falling apart. As Loïc Wacquant has argued, French ghettos have a long way to go before they become as dangerous as their American counterparts.[7] Nevertheless, image is everything; annual rites such as the New Year's Eve burning of dozens of automobiles in Strasbourg (the apparent birthplace of this phenomenon) and hundreds more cars around the nation by rebellious unemployed youth do not help to calm things down.[8] In 1998, 82% of the 2,500 people surveyed by a top polling agency stated that they thought violence in the working-class suburbs was at an all-time high.[9]

If anything, the French are frank: more than 60% of respondents to polls regularly admit to harboring racist thoughts. A Eurobarometer opinion poll from 1990 revealed that more people favored reducing the rights of immigrants than extending them.[10] Over 75% of French people responded that there were "too many" Arabs in France. By contrast, 34% said there were too many people from the "Mediterranean" nations of Portugal, Spain, Italy, and Greece.[11]

These ideas translate into blatant discrimination in the hiring process. In the early 2000s, a young man (aged fifteen to twenty-four) of Algerian origins with the BAC+ (a BAC plus another diploma) had an unemployment rate of 32%. Young Algerian women with the same qualifications faced a 50% rate of unemployment. The national average for people (both sexes, all nationalities) with identical qualifications was "only" 15%. The overall unemployment rate of young, fifteen to twenty-four-year-olds of non-EU origins was 47%.[12] Taking all age groups, the total unemployment rate for people of non-EU origins was 31.4%.

There is a clear line of demarcation between North Africans and the rest of the population. They are the last hired and first fired. A survey of 360 large French firms in the late 1990s found that over the previous ten years they had laid off 41% of their foreign-born staff but only 12% of their French-born staff.[13] The level of discrimination that young job seekers of North African origins are forced to endure would be a national scandal in Canada (where unemployment among male immigrants is *below* the national average). A young North African is four to five times more likely to be unemployed than a young Frenchman or woman and two to three times more likely than a young immigrant from within the EU to be out of work.[14]

Racism explains some of the unemployment suffered by young French citizens of Arab descent.[15] But it is only one part of the larger story: after all, two-thirds of the nation's unemployed are native-born, "white" French. Racism *per se* is probably not the original problem – it is invoked (silently) by employers as a way to sort through job applicants; it is a device to sift through to the "worthy" unemployed at a time when job applicants overwhelm personnel departments. Racial discrimination in the job market is an old pattern, dating back at least to the 1930s, when firms fired foreigners first. In the context of a full-employment society and labor shortages, the incidence of job discrimination based on race would decline by necessity.

As Philippe Bernard shows in his comparative study of immigration in Western nations, the gap between the unemployment rate of immigrants and that of the general population is second highest in France. The other leaders in this regard are Finland, Belgium, and Italy.[16] During the late 1990s and early 2000s, as France was led by a Socialist government committed to equality and solidarity, precious little bandwidth on the

Table 7.1   *Unemployment rates in France, by nationality, 1980 and 1990*

	1980	1990
Algeria	15.2	28.1
Morocco	9.1	23.3
Spain	7.0	9.6
Portugal	5.6	8.3
All foreigners	9.3	16.8
All French	5.9	8.7

Source: Sophie Body-Gendrot, "Urban Violence and Community Mobilizations," in Body-Gendrot and Marco Martiniello, eds., *Minorities in European Cities* (London: Macmillan, 2000), p. 579.

political dial was set aside for discussion of this important problem (see Table 7.1); preserving the unfunded pensions of state employees got far more airtime.

Many of the structurally unemployed are of course immigrants from North Africa and their French-born children, who are trapped in the suburban public housing ghettos which surround Paris, Lyon, Marseille, and other large cities, where unemployment is typically 30% and can reach as high as 50%.[17] Foreigners account for 6 or 7% of the population of France (undocumented immigrants and the French refusal to ask ethnic origins in the census make the exact figure difficult to determine), but they account for one-third of all those unemployed.[18] By the late 1980s, there were at least 2.1 million immigrants from the "Third World" living in France.[19]

The vast majority of immigrants from North Africa had low skill levels when they arrived. For example, 83% of those who were at least fifteen years old when they arrived in France (before 1975), were unskilled workers.[20] From an educational point of view, their children were at a disadvantage; as INSEE showed in its 2002–03 report on the state of France, there is still a strong link between immigrant background and underutilization of the education system. Some 31% of youth from a recent immigrant background exits the education system without a diploma of any sort but only 14% of the French-born youth population does so.[21] It is not clear how this problem can be solved in the short term. Second generation immigrants' under-use of the education system is matched by their parents' below-average access to parts of the social security system, but in this case the reasons are more straightforward: the corporatist nature of the French welfare state, which ties good benefits to good jobs.

During the early 1990s, over 1 million people in France had no medical insurance. Many of these were of course undocumented immigrants, but many were also landed immigrants. In 1992, two-thirds of the people treated by the Paris chapter of Médecins du monde (who provide charitable medical care) were immigrants, most of them from North Africa. Many of them were older men who came to France during the 1960s and had few skills.[22] Likewise, an estimated 40% of Paris' homeless population in 1999 was born outside France.[23] Immigrants are underrepresented in the middle and upper ranks of the civil service and until a couple of years ago they were invisible in the media and in the cabinet. As Pierre Merlin, the dean of urbanism studies in France, argues, immigrants and second generation Frenchmen and women of North African origin experience segregation of all sorts: racial-geographic, demographic (the suburbs have a disproportionate number of younger people), wealth. They tend to have less access to community services and transportation, and so on.[24] Only in the realm of housing and "welfare" (the RMI, discussed below) do immigrants consume a disproportionate share of public resources.

Race and housing

From a distance, the French state's historic role in building millions of public housing units (Habitations à Loyer Modéré, or HLMs) seems like a concrete commitment to "solidarity." In fact, public housing construction grew out of an entirely practical and urgent motive: the need to address the crisis-like housing shortage in post-Second World War France. This housing shortage was the result, in the first instance, of a colossal state blunder: between the wars the state froze rents, providing no incentives for the private sector to build. By 1950, the French housing stock was in a shambles. As the rural exodus sped up and families were becoming larger due to the baby boom, most urban centers were faced with alarming overcrowding problems.

When the state corrected its errors during the 1950s to 1970s, it did so in such a rush that it built thousands of Soviet-style housing complexes. Up to one-quarter of a million people were living in shanty towns during the 1950s: these extreme conditions called for hurried, extreme solutions. In an age enamored with planning of all sorts, urban planners were given a great deal of power and responsibility and they failed in the worst way. Some of the housing estates were literally built in fields, but the jobs never came, and residents often had to wait a decade for a school and/or maternity clinic to be built nearby. A visitor from overseas, plopped down in the heart of Sarcelles on a cold winter night in the early 1960s, might well have imagined himself to be in Moscow.

Today, Sarcelles and other public housing complexes are far more racially segregated places than they were during the 1960s, when more "white" and lower-middle-class residents lived there. During the unemployment crisis of the 1980s and 1990s, spatial segregation increased dramatically. Where once many people had hoped to use the HLM as a stepping stone to a private house or apartment, this dream died for many people.[25] The increasing geographic segregation of North African immigrants confirms their social and economic segregation.[26]

French housing policy is a curious hybrid. On the one hand, there are very successful housing subsidies and credits for large families, which are portable, to be used where the beneficiary sees fit. This type of program was introduced during the 1970s and it is the best there is, since it enables people to choose where they wish to live, encouraging spatial mixing as opposed to segregation. Other nations have taken a leaf from this French policy. When governments have gone in the opposite direction, cramming the poor and immigrants into barren, isolated Le Corbusier-style tower block housing estates like Sarcelles, La Courneuve, or Les Tartarets, they have failed. Officially, 17.7 million of France's 60 million people live in "suburban" areas. At least 3 to 4 million people live in what the French euphemistically term "quartiers difficiles" like La Courneuve.[27] By some reckonings, up to one half of all declared crimes (mostly theft and vandalism) occurs in these forty-five "zones."[28] The low rents come at a high social cost.

Typically, Parisian public housing authorities offer apartments at 50% the market rate while provincial HLMs go for 50 to 80%.[29] In 1977, at the height of construction, 430,000 new housing units were built in France, 90,000 of which were public. By 1990, only 256,000 units were built, 60,000 of them public. Altogether, today there are five million social housing units in France; one-fifth of the population, or twelve million people, lives in them. Administered at the local level, many HLMs have fallen victim to local politics, financial scandals, and clientism. To be sure, some housing complexes, like the Cité Jean-Renaudie (in Villetaneuse, north of Paris), and several complexes in Grenoble and Montpellier, are success stories, but they are in the minority.

Over 70% of the French believe that housing estates are bad places to live.[30] Over 30% of residents are inactive. Increasingly, the poor are segregated in suburban housing complexes. This happens not as a result of official policy but through a gradual process of self-removal: as soon as people can afford to leave, they do. In 1973, 40% of the residents of HLMs had below-average incomes. By 1996, 67% did.[31] In the mid 1990s, a minority of the residents of "social housing" in France were French-born. Some cities, such as Venissieux, in the Lyon metropolitan region, put limits on the numbers of immigrants they would "tolerate" in social housing; most cities have no such restrictions.

The Haut conseil à l'intégration reported to Prime Minister Raffarin in June 2003 that there were two million youth, under the age of twenty-five, living in "priority zones," or "quartiers difficiles" characterized by high unemployment, high poverty, and high levels of crime.[32] In 1988, over 39% of the housing units occupied by immigrants were overcrowded, versus 9.7% of those occupied by French-born persons.[33] Even as things were getting better for much of French youth during the short-lived economic recovery of the late 1990s, they were getting worse for those in the banlieue: their unemployment rate increased at twice the rate of youth in general.[34] Over the course of the 1990s, unemployment became more and more "ethnicized," as the French say.[35]

Today, every French politician knows that the housing complexes which ring the major cities should be phased out, their residents reintegrated into viable communities of their own choosing with the help of portable housing subsidies. But this would require money which is not available. The process of destroying the very worst estates is indeed underway: by 2010, 3% of the total public stock will be demolished.[36] In July 2003, the Raffarin government launched a 30 billion euro "Marshall Plan" for "quartiers difficiles," which is, on the one hand, encouraging; on the other hand, it seems to portend a massive dose of statism. One can only hope that as 200,000 new housing units go up in the mid 2000s, to replace some of the units to be torn down, yesterday's lessons have been learned.

Demolishing dilapidated housing projects will not, of course, solve the problem of unemployment. What French immigrants need is a vibrant, full-employment society (and less racism, of course). Given this, most things will fall into place, and, in time, like previous waves of immigrants (Italians and Poles during the 1920s, Spaniards during the 1930s), today's unemployed immigrants will be absorbed into the mainstream. The Muslim–Christian divide has changed the dynamic of assimilation but it is not an unbridgable chasm, as the North American case would suggest. Full employment will not solve everything, but it will certainly ease tensions. What immigrants really need are jobs, even low-paying ones (the ones, which, after all, kept the unemployment statistics so low during the trente glorieuses). As in the Netherlands, low wages can be supplemented by housing credits and extra family support. Substantial cuts to regressive payroll taxes on low earners (in addition to the "exonerations" for employers) would also help.

McJobs or no jobs? Is *this* the question?

Are US-style McJobs the only way out? And would the French people accept this given the choice by their politicians and labor leaders? Since the 1980s, some authors, including the professor of management Philippe d'Iribarne, have argued that France's low-wage service sector is so small because this type of job offends the morals of many Frenchmen, who still attach a certain degree of "honor" to work, so these jobs are not created in the first place.[37] There is a kernel of truth to this argument but it cannot explain more than a small portion of France's unemployment problem.

The North American job market creates millions of positions in the economy for the unskilled. There is a risk of romanticizing this less-than-rosy situation: to be sure, wealth distribution in the USA is now more unequal than at any time since 1920. What many Europeans often ignore is that the vibrant American economy distributes *jobs* in a much more equitable fashion than the French economy. The failure of the US political elite to then redistribute to the working poor is another matter altogether, and far too often this fact is used to discredit the US model *in toto*.

Consider the US retail/hotel/restaurant industry, where many low-wage jobs are found. Anyone who has shopped or stayed in a hotel in Europe knows that the level of service is usually far inferior to that in North America. A small restaurant with a seating capacity of fifty to seventy will often have only one or two waiters – a similar restaurant in the USA or Canada would have three or four. There are two key reasons why this sector is understaffed in France (and "honor" isn't one of them): high wages and social benefits that come attached to all jobs, including low-skilled ones; and restrictive licensing and labor laws which protect those already employed and those businesses which already have a portion of the market cornered.

In a detailed 1997 study of these segments of the service industry in France and the USA, Thomas Piketty found that if France had the same percentage of workers in these sectors as in the USA, there would be three million more jobs in France – presto, unemployment problem solved.[38] But this would entail the creation of low-paid jobs, and French political elites refuse to allow this, out of concern for "solidarity." Concern for "solidarity" is, in this context, really concern for comfortably employed

Table 7.2 *Employment in selected service and other trades, USA and France, 1996, as % of total employment*

	USA	France
Wholesale and retail sales	17.5	13.6
Finance, banking, property	6.4	4.7
Hotel and food services	6.6	3.5
Personal and domestic services	1.9	2.5
Health care and social services	11.3	10.5
Total	43.7	34.8

Sources: Edward Luttwak, *Turbo Capitalism: Winners and Losers in the Global Economy* (New York: HarperCollins, 1999), p. 111. See also, Sophie Gherardi, "Mines d'emploi," *Le Monde*, 25 November 1997, "Economie" section, p. 1.

Table 7.3 *Occupations, USA and France, as % of total labor force, 1996*

	USA	France
Services	41.1	30.6
All other employment	52.9	57.4
Unemployed	6.0	12.0

constituents – at the expense of the "excluded." In other words, the very people who proclaim their concern for the excluded are the ones who are responsible for the problem in the first place.

As Piketty, Olivier Blanchard, and Jean-Paul Fitoussi have argued in convincing cross-national studies, low-skilled labor in the service sector is priced out of the job market in France. French firms cope by squeezing as much productivity as possible out of current workers, employing more labor-saving computer technology, and providing poorer service. A case in point: the American Toys-R-Us chain store employs one-third more people per square meter of shop floor in its US stores than in its French ones.[39] Surely French firms would provide better service – if they could be assured that the added labor costs would not erase the greater profits which might come from expansion.

Redistributive solidarity would require the sharing of the costs of France's expensive social model, not putting them on the shoulders of the young, women, immigrants, and the unemployed.

Youth unemployment and underemployment

To a greater extent than in most other large industrial nations, in France the wheel of fortune has smiled on those born during the period c. 1925 to 1955, only to turn quickly against those born afterward. And to a much greater extent than in North America, Sweden, or the Netherlands, the wheel of fortune has been rigged in favor of this cohort through the visible hand of state intervention.[40] Since the early 1980s, French labor law, taxation policy, pension policy, family policy, and monetary policy have worked to the detriment of young French women and men. By contrast, the state has cocooned the elderly and the majority of workers aged forty and up from economic insecurity. John Gillingham argues that

> it is easy to locate the most serious and persistent unsolved problem [of the period 1995–2002]: unemployment, especially of young people. The phenomenon gave rise to much tut-tutting about "social exclusion," but nothing really consequential was done to end it. Far from being either necessary or inevitable, the wretched problem resulted from two reversible decisions: to defend the overvalued franc and to protect labor markets. Not globalization but rigid protectionist policy making is what gave rise to *les exclus*.[41]

During the mid 1990s, a new social category was devised by French sociologists and demographers: the "génération galère," the "sacrificed generation," and the "orphans of the *trente glorieuses*."[42] Since the late 1990s, government report after report, news-magazine survey after survey, has noted that those born after 1960 have far worse economic and career prospects than those born between 1930 and the 1950s. Standard sociology textbooks, like *La société française* (Dalloz, 4th edn., 2001), by Charles Debbasch and Jean-Marie Pontier, include forty-five-page chapters devoted entirely to "Le Clivage Jeunes–Vieux."[43] The serious financial and employment problems of British and North American young adults during the 1980s and 1990s pale in comparison.[44]

Forty years ago, the unemployment rate in France was under 2%. Full employment was a strong social policy in and of itself, allowing the working class and middle class alike to bargain for a better deal and receive steadily rising real wages (alas, the tax system continued to take more from low-paid workers than from the rich). Full employment created opportunities for social advancement, ensured that young people found good jobs, and kept the public purpose grounded in the present and the future: politicians strove to build, to create new opportunities, to invest. Capital investment and infrastructure expansion was three times higher during the 1950s and 1960s than in the period 1995 to 2000.[45] By the 1990s, critics like Béatrice Majnoni d'Intignano, Jacques Julliard, and Laurent Joffrin argued that France was no longer prepared to invest in the future; politicians seemed more concerned with hanging onto the past and pleasing older voters.[46] Critics noted the discrepancy between health and pension inflation and the slow growth of family policy spending.[47]

At every single stage of their lives, and with regard to every single public policy issue, those born between 1925 and 1955 have taken priority over all others. In some regards this was the result of conscious decisions taken by politicians, labor leaders, and businesses; in other respects, the favoring of the 1925–55 cohort was unintentional, the product of secular economic trends. It happened in most Western nations, but the corporatist welfare states of France, Italy, and Spain witnessed the greatest youth unemployment problems. In any case, by the early 1980s it was clear that an Age Gap had emerged in France – and no government has sought to close it.[48]

A cynic could answer that the French government was simply giving its largest constituent group what it wanted, that democracy was being served. But if the principle of reciprocity is not observed, then the welfare state becomes nothing but a tax imposed by a more numerous, vocal, and organized generation on another less vocal, less numerous, and poorer generation.

Intergenerational inequality denial

Is this too cynical a view? Is it too simplistic? Some people would think so, especially the critics of the intergenerational inequality thesis, including the leading French exponent of this school, sociologist Claudine Attias-Donfut.[49] These critics deny a link between high pension spending and other social and economic problems. Since these critics are generally favorable toward social policy *per se*, they tend to ignore that one "social" program might cause serious problems elsewhere in the economy, that it might have perverse, unintended consequences. They fear that an attack on one social program is an attack on all.[50]

But if states like France, which already tax at the upper end of the spectrum, wish to provide more money to reduce child poverty, all other things being equal, some program must be cut. The extra money that will soon flow into French pension system coffers due to prolonged contributions mandated by Raffarin's partial reform is money that could have been spent on something else. Since spending on the elderly is the largest item of social spending in every Western nation, and since the elderly are generally prosperous, pensions are the obvious target for cutting. If money once spent on pensions is diverted to family programs, it will indeed reduce child poverty.

In recent years, critics like Attias-Donfut have turned to a new line of argument in their efforts to protect pensions from the chopping block: French families give a lot of money to their unemployed children.[51] Attias-Donfut has labelled this phenomenon "La Famille Providence" (in French, the term Welfare State is "Etat Providence"). She calculates that interfamilial "solidarity" amounted to at least 50 billion francs per year during the late 1990s (over 8 billion euros). That is, those aged sixty and over gave this amount to their children. Fair enough, but in reality, this is charity, since it occurs in only about one-half of families with unemployed youth. In addition, these families' children were paying the solidarity tax, either by standing in the unemployment line, or through high payroll taxes levied on their generally low incomes. Attias-Donfut's research is important insofar as it highlights the very strong links that still exist between family members in France and elsewhere; but she tries too hard to skip around the issue of the unfair treatment of one generation by the state.

The historian Louis Chauvel, author of the pathbreaking book *Le destin des générations* (1998), has torn this "Famille Providence" argument to shreds in a sharp article, referring to this supposed mass of "intergenerational solidarity" as nothing but a wafer-thin filling in the gaping "intergenerational divide."[52] Bringing in extraneous material such as the charity of parents towards their underemployed children (there is no guarantee that this exchange will take place), or invoking the phenomenon of intra-family wealth transfers through inheritance, clouds the main issue: the favoring of one generation over another as a matter of state policy.

To be sure, within many families, generational conflict is not the order of the day. But when individuals step into the public arena as workers, taxpayers, and pensioners, there are clear lines drawn between the older winners and the younger losers in the battle for an equitable distribution of national wealth. Finally, it is curious that a school of thought which is committed to "the social," to a state monopoly on pension provision as one of the cornerstones of "solidarity," invokes the accident of intra-family (private) charity in order to justify the continuation of high public spending on the richest demographic cohort in world history.

The middle-aged worker downsizing crisis?

The favoring of the elderly at the expense of the young is a Western-wide phenomenon; the heartless downsizing of middle-aged workers is not. (The latter is primarily a North American problem.) Some people argue that "la crise" has spared no one in France: no age group, no social class.

This is inaccurate: the young and the unskilled, and particularly young women, have borne the brunt of the unemployment crisis.

In 1984, 10.6% of those aged fifteen to twenty-four lost their jobs, as against 3.8% of those aged twenty-five to fifty and only 2.8% of those aged over fifty. By 1997, those figures were, respectively, 16.0%, 5.6%, and 4.0%.[53] The "crise" is experienced primarily by the long-term unemployed and the youth of France – and it is directly related to the comfort and stability of older workers. Indeed, older workers have never had it so good – whether in employment or in forced (but heavily subsidized) early retirement. At the same time, the French state has abandoned the social contract of the post-Second World War years; namely, upward generational mobility through policies designed to bring about full employment.

French youth, like their Italian counterparts, have no champions. The French labor movement has no history of bargaining for job creation; even as it has been generous with the verbal currency of compassion toward the unemployed, it has concentrated its efforts on defending existing jobs. The labor movement has sought wage increases above the European norm, pressed for a shorter work week, called for pre-retirement packages and increases in the value of pensions.[54] In a study of 6,100 annual collective bargaining sessions in 1990 and 1992, Guillaume La Chaise found that the issue of job creation occurred in only 2.6% to 4.6% of sessions, respectively. Salaries were the key issues negotiated, in 53 to 58% of the time.[55] Workers have not fought on behalf of those less fortunate than themselves – aspiring workers. And to the extent that they have expressed concern, labor leaders have recommended more powerful doses of failed statist policies. The protection of "droits acquis" has taken precedence over allowing young people to acquire those very "rights."

The typical younger household saw its combined annual income (including social transfers) fall from 86,000 francs per person in 1989 to 80,000 francs in 1994 (in constant 1994 francs). In 1984, a typical young couple reached the national average of household income at the age of twenty-four (their combined age average). Ten years later, in 1994, young households had to wait until they were on average twenty-nine years old before they reached the same level.[56]

For two decades, real wages have declined or stagnated for most of those under the age of 40.[57] In 1994, only 11.7% of French men aged seventeen to twenty-four were in stable, full-time, secure jobs, yet 85% of those aged forty to forty-nine were. Only 8.7% of young women had stable jobs.[58] Age and sex are the key factors determining success in the job market: young people with low levels of education in France were three times more likely to be out of work than their older counterparts with similar levels of education (this problem is even more pronounced in Italy).[59]

During the late 1990s, when over 25% of French youth was unemployed, and 12% of the general workforce was jobless, the average time spent at one particular full-time job was eleven years, as against eight in the UK and seven in the USA.[60] Older French workers do not like to change jobs, and they rarely have to, given the level of job protection afforded to them. In 1986, 90% of workers who had been polled the previous year were still in their position. The chances of those already employed *becoming* unemployed are far lower in France than in North America, but so too are the chances of young people finding jobs in the first place. In 1975, 75% of those who were unemployed had found work one year later; one decade later, that figure was only 45%.[61]

Since 1980, young people have had no bargaining power when they enter the job market. Accordingly, they saw their incomes fall by 15 to 25% between 1989 and 1994 alone.[62] As a CERC study showed, those aged eighteen to twenty who *were* able to find jobs during the year 1986 earned 56% less than they would have had they entered the job market ten years earlier.[63] More than one-half of all the new jobs which opened up in France during the 1980s and 1990s were short-term contracts.[64] Protecting existing jobs and mandating large wage increases for lower-paid workers at a time when companies had so many legitimate financial *dis*-incentives to do this on their own accord meant that companies would not create new permanent positions for youth.[65]

As a result, stable adult life, including marriage, children, and secure employment, generally does not begin in France until the age of thirty to thirty-five.[66] For the last twenty-five years, the typical twenty- to thirty-year-old – perhaps 75% of them – has experienced, at one point or other, unemployment, underemployment, internships which pay a pittance, and fixed-term contracts.[67] Career-track jobs are now the privilege of those aged thirty-five to sixty who have a good education – but even this is no longer a guarantee.

Full employment: an undervalued social policy

During the economic boom years, salaries rose regularly and rapidly. From the early 1950s until the early 1970s, workers of all sorts, aged eighteen to forty, from the unskilled to the skilled, to clerks, managers, and professionals, saw their income double in real terms.[68] In 1970, the vast majority of those earning high incomes were aged thirty to forty-five. This was true in France, as well as in Italy, Germany, and the Netherlands. But by 2000, the average French person with a university education got his or her first full-time, career-path job at the age of thirty-two, and they began a slow, arduous climb towards a good salary, which tends now to peak at the age of fifty-five.[69]

Today, younger workers begin their careers ten years later than their parents did, at a much lower real salary, and at a salary considerably lower relative to their fifty-five-year-old colleagues than would have been the case in 1970. Today workers in their twenties are taxed at over twice the rate their parents were taxed at a similar age. In 1996, only one in five of French youth aged twenty was working, and only one in four was living away from home. "Youth" was extended into the mid 20s, and the lucky Frenchman or woman under the age of thirty who secured a full-time, career-oriented job paying a decent salary was the talk of the dinner party.[70]

Young people who do not benefit from the assistance of their families (one-half of young households do not) are more or less on their own. In 1992, 41% of unemployed French youth whose families hailed from the bottom quartile of the income ladder received no help whatsoever – no help from their parents, no assistance from the state. The youth of the nation's modestly paid families was perhaps the most disadvantaged socio-economic group.[71]

To be sure, there is the RMI (Revenue Minimum d'Insertion) payment, but it is only available to those aged twenty-five and up. Introduced by Michel Rocard in 1988, the RMI is an inadequate check of 400 euros per month (for a single person) and higher for those with children, and it comes attached with stigma.[72] Some liken it to US-style welfare; others claim that in the general context of high and varied social spending in France, this is a misleading comparison.[73] In any case, the RMI is a program of last resort designed to help people who have no other form of assistance.

In effect, the RMI was a sign that the French state had capitulated, admitting its failure to offer a market-based solution to the problem of unemployment.[74] A more solidaristic approach would have consisted of fiscal and monetary policies aimed at restoring employment, even at the price of asking others (pensioners, investors) to take a cut.

Critics charge that the RMI is money that would be better spent on payroll tax deductions or on apprenticeships, and there are precious few of these in France.[75] Throughout the 1980s, there were only 220,000 apprenticeships: one-sixth the number in West Germany, a nation which had a much lower youth unemployment rate at the time (8% vs. 25% in France). By 1996, there were 310,000 apprenticeships in France, but, as *Le Monde* reported, the vast majority were dead-end jobs: 25% of apprentices never finished their stint, and of the remaining three-quarters who did finish, only 40% found a job at the end. Most French apprentice-ships are devices used by employers to skirt around high labor costs.[76] A Ministry of Labor study of 1992 concluded that apprenticeships were of "little significance" in the labor market as a whole.[77] During the 1990s, a few hundred thousand "contracts of solidarity" and "limited term con-tracts" were funded by the state, providing part-time jobs (a twenty-hour week was typical) for youth. Most of these jobs were dead-end, low-skilled positions in the public sector. Taken together, they never made more than a tiny dent in the overall employment picture.

In 1995 there were 500,000 unemployed youth (below the age of twenty-five) who had no unemployment benefits at all.[78] As the govern-ment statistics bureau CREDOC concluded in a review of French social policy that year, employed young adults under the age of twenty-five with no children got *nothing* from the French welfare state, even as they were taxed at high levels. They had no help in the housing market. Since they generally did not have secure, full-time jobs and the supplementary health insurance which generally comes with such jobs, they were obliged to pay for up to 25% of their medical bills.[79] The situation is unchanged today.

Solidarity's journeymen

Since secure work starts so late, younger adults will not be able to retire at fifty-five or sixty, like their parents. If today's average person, who starts full-time pension contributions at the age of thirty-two, must work forty-one years, they will not be able to retire on a full pension until they are seventy-three years of age. Longer life expectancies do not justify such a large gap.

There are very few career-path jobs available. Students prolong their studies, amassing degree after degree from overcrowded, under-funded universities, going from "stage" to "stage," from unpaid, so-called "internships" to yet more "internships," with little hope of full-time employment at the end of their contract.[80] Every year, over 500,000 young workers are hired as "stagiaires" (interns), paid nothing or perhaps up to 200 to 300 euros per month ($240 to $360) and then dispensed after a year of full-time labor has been extracted from them. Fewer than 20% of "stagiaires" are retained full time once their "stage" is completed. Here is another perverse consequence of the high cost of labor. Over 60% of interns were over the age of twenty-six in 1996; a remarkable 28% were over the age of thirty-five. This was a sign of just how desperate aspiring full-time workers had become.[81]

A typical example of how young people are affected can be seen in the case of "Jérôme," who was profiled in the magazine *Sciences humaines* in 2000 in a feature article on the declining fortunes of young people. Jérôme completed his degree at the age of twenty-one. For the next seven years, he floated in and out of poorly paid *stages*, punctuated by bouts of unemployment which lasted several months each time. He had no access to state assistance, so he had to move back home with his parents. Finally, Jérôme bounced between a few "emplois-jeunes," or state-financed fixed-term contract jobs for youth. At the age of twenty-eight, at long last, he landed a full-time job and was able to move into an apartment with his long-time girlfriend.[82] Jérôme was lucky: he secured his first career-path job four years ahead of average. His delayed career can explain why, if he and his girlfriend choose to start a family, they will do so at a much later stage than their parents did.[83]

Consider the case of Ariane, whose story does not have a happy ending. Born in Marseille in 1973, she grew up in public housing estates there and later in Metz. She completed lycée but did not go to a technical college or university. Between the age of eighteen and twenty-five, during the early and mid 1990s, she bounced between short-term, part-time CES contracts paying only 1,500 to 2,000 francs per month ($300 to $400) and bouts of unemployment. She had no hope for the future, and no sense of where she might be six months down the road. She landed a CES job at a major teaching hospital in Paris and this allowed her to study for the exams which might lead to a diploma which might in turn lead to a full-time position as a daycare *animatrice*. Ariane passed the exams, but there were 700 applicants for thirty-five training positions and she failed to get one of them, since there were far too many older people ahead of her in the line. So she continued to work her four-hour day and began to lose hope. In Paris, she took three different part-time jobs (all of them in the public sector) but failed to translate this work experience into a full-time contract. Despondent, Ariane quit her job and went on unemployment insurance, and started to make plans to emigrate to Australia. In her mid twenties, she had never had the opportunity to earn a living and stand on her own two feet – help from her mother and her mother's friends was the only thing that enabled her to pay her rent.[84]

To add insult to injury, politicians have reoriented French social spending away from Jérôme and Ariane's concerns. As the OECD concludes in an international study, to a greater extent than in any other European nation, during the 1980s and 1990s France shifted resources away from children, youth, and young adults towards the (already prosperous) elderly (see Table 7.4).[85]

The face of poverty was transformed in France during the 1970s and 1980s. Old-age poverty was wiped out by 1980, reduced to a small residual number, consisting, for the most part, of small pockets of widows of

Table 7.4 *Allocation of public transfers across age groups,*
change (%), 1984–94 (France)

	Age group					
0–17	18–25	26–40	41–50	51–65*	65–75
−3.6	−2.2	−0.1	0.8	−6.9*	9.1

* This statistic, for the 51–65 age group, is misleading. It is due, in large
part, to the termination of state-supported early retirement schemes, which
cost over 70 billion francs per year in the mid 1980s. Table 7.5 confirms the
general prosperity of those aged 51 to 65.
Source: Michael F. Forster, OECD, "Trends and Driving Factors in Income
Distribution and Poverty in the OECD Area," *OECD Occasional Papers*
no. 42 (2000), p. 92.

Table 7.5 *Relative disposable income, by age group, change*
(%) 1984–94 (France)

0–17	18–25	26–40	41–50	51–65	65–75
0.4	−5.0	−5.9	2.7	6.5	7.4

Source: Forster, "Trends and Driving Factors in Income Distribution and
Poverty," p. 78.

low-income earners and of unmarried elderly women living in high rent
areas.[86] From 1984 to 1994, poverty rates among the elderly fell by 50%.
Poverty rates of youth doubled.[87]

The elderly represented only 11% of the poor in 1975, under 5% in
1979 and under 3% by 2000. Serge Milano, a leading expert on French
poverty, concludes that even as the overall poverty level dropped in the
1970s to early 1980s (only to rise after that point) the nature of poverty
changed: it became a "caste-like situation," to be suffered by the young,
the unemployed, the de-skilled, and, much more rarely, the middle-aged
downsized. As jobs became more secure, better paying, and more protected by strict labor laws, the disappearance of the more casual, low-wage
labor force (which, it is usually forgotten, helped to keep unemployment
so low during the 1950s and 1960s) meant that those denied access to
the job market would now suffer longer.[88]

By the late 1990s, France's former above-average record of offsetting
child poverty through generous family allowances was a distant memory,
as the child poverty rate surpassed 7%. This was still much better than
the North American rate of at least 20%, but well behind the Swedish

rate of 2 to 3%.[89] Family allowances, which are tied to jobs, offer precious little support in the absence of a job. There are programs for "isolated" single parents – but they serve to confirm and trap these people in their isolation since they do not build links to employment. Allowances paid to unemployed parents, likewise, are inadequate to stave off poverty. And there is no allowance at all for the first child (although Prime Minister Raffarin had promised this as this book went to press).

In a sense, the Dutch, Canadian, and British economies are more egalitarian than the French economy. Unemployment is lower in these nations but job insecurity is higher for the average worker. The disruption associated with more flexible labor markets is offset by a lower unemployment rate and an abundance of jobs. Since so few North Americans (in particular) are sheltered from the vagaries of the market by corporatist privilege or by strict labor laws, risk and uncertainty are spread more equitably around the table, and above all between age groups. The North American model tends to put a higher premium on efficiency than on seniority. (As in Europe, a few groups such as civil servants, doctors, teachers, professors, and others are protected by guild-like bodies.) As Therborn wrote in his 1986 study, *Why Some Peoples are More Unemployed than Others*,

In Belgium, France and, above all, Italy, we have an *exclusivist unemployment*. Unemployment particularly befalls women and youth (to an extent unparalleled elsewhere). Long-term unemployment is very high. Unemployment compensation is also very exclusive in France and Italy, mainly geared to compensating people with long-term prior employment records who are unemployed for "economic" reasons [lay-offs]. . . The exclusivist unemployment pattern of these countries is also enhanced by their combination of high unemployment with a relatively favourable improvement of real wages for those employed.[90]

In some ways, the more flexible the labor market, the less likely the disruption of capitalist change will be shouldered by one specific group.[91]

Downward mobility of youth

During the 1960s and 1970s, the typical French woman gave birth at twenty-three or twenty-four years of age; now it is twenty-eight to twenty-nine.[92] Young French women with no diploma or degree, under the age of twenty-five, had an unemployment rate of 47% in 1998 – this statistic does not include those who have stopped looking for work.[93] The activity rate of young males under the age of twenty-five dropped by 57% between 1982 and 1990. The female activity rate dropped by 39%. Those lucky enough to find work often found the lowest-paying, part-time and/or, fixed duration jobs. Of the nation's 1.3 million working poor in 1996,

60% were under twenty-five years old, and almost all were under the age of forty.[94]

The very nature of the workforce was transformed: those under the age of twenty-five made up 14.4% of the French workforce in 1982, the year after Mitterrand came to power. By 1998, they represented only 7.0% of the workforce.[95] As Chauvel has demonstrated, the net effect of labor legislation of the early 1980s on the career-path chances of well-educated French men and women was to freeze one cohort's success in time – those born in 1930–55 – and to shelter it from insecurity.[96] This success story was made possible only by denying the fruits of economic growth to others.

The rate of downward social mobility was twice as high for those born in 1970 as for the cohorts born in 1920–50. The upward mobility rate was roughly 20% for those born in 1970, but close to 35% for those born in 1950.[97] The baby boomers in effect monopolized France's well-paying career-path jobs.[98] Almost all of the capital gains and real estate asset inflation has accrued to those over the age of fifty.

Chauvel's research is echoed by Christian Baudelot and Roger Establet. In their book comparing the fortunes of thirty-year-olds in 1968 with those of 1998, *Avoir 30 ans en 1968 et en 1998* (2000), they note that in 1964, the typical father aged fifty-five would make only 1,600 FF (in constant 2000 francs) more per month than his son, employed at the same socio-economic level; by 1993, that figure had jumped to 5,300 FF.[99] But in 1993, the typical cadre's son was better educated, with more schooling and more extensive computer and foreign-language training than his father.[100]

As the economy slowed down and as the cost of labor went up, French firms put the squeeze where they could, on those who were not yet protected by a sturdy coat of labor law armor – on young workers. French businesses have taken advantage of younger workers' precarious position: in 1970, those aged twenty-five to thirty earned 25% less than those aged fifty to fifty-five; today, they earn 50% less.[101] The gap between the average salary and the average starting salary of those aged twenty to twenty-five almost doubled between 1970 and 2000.[102]

Young people shared in France's economic growth during the 1950s to early 1970s because, in an environment of full employment, they had bargaining power when they entered the job market. But young workers began their careers when jobs were not as protected by strict labor legislation. Ironically, this meant that private firms were more likely than they are today to take on full-time, permanent employees, confident in the knowledge that if the employee did not succeed as hoped, he/she could be removed.

The golden age of secure, lifetime jobs (1950–75) is somewhat of a myth, certainly where blue-collar workers are concerned: consider the Renault automobile workers who, right up to 1968, could be dismissed for being two minutes late for their shift. But to the extent that this golden age of stable employment did exist, it was also an age without a firm legal right to such a benefit (in the private sector). Full employment, coupled with a corporate culture of social responsibility – which is more likely to exist during times of full employment – made lifelong white-collar careers possible. No laws were needed.[103] Since the early 1980s, market-generated full employment has been an under-valued social policy.[104]

During the 1960s and 1970s, new career models were constructed in the French civil service and in private firms. As Baudelot and Establet argue, until then there had been a sort of equilibrium between the salaries of younger and older workers. Coupled with economic growth, this had ensured that each successive generation could count on becoming a little (or a lot) wealthier than their parents. Since 1975, the salaries of middle-aged workers have grown faster than national wealth, and faster than the average salary raise. Age power has been translated – almost as a matter of policy – into wage power. As Guillemette de Larquier emphasizes, this salary pyramid benefitted, almost by definition, *male* workers born during the period 1930–50.[105] Age and sex rather than productivity or success on the job became the key criteria for advancement, and the key variables behind economic success. In a study of wage dispersion between younger and older workers in seven Western nations during the 1980s (France, USA, Canada, Netherlands, Australia, UK, Sweden), Peter Gottschalk and Mary Joyce found that the gap between the average salary of an older worker and a younger worker grew fastest in France. Sweden stood out as the one nation in which the young did not lose out to the old.[106]

The young and the restless: youth labor market turnover

In 1990 there were 1.2 million non-insured unemployed people; by 1997 there were 1.8 million. These people, most of them young, rejected by the labor market and the state alike, had fallen through the cracks of France's huge welfare state.[107] As Christine Daniel argues, where once the unemployment insurance system had been guided by a "logic of integration," in 1984, the system was reoriented to cushion the fall of middle-aged workers, redirected towards a "logic of segmentation."[108] More and more money, under the category "unemployment insurance expenses," was spent on a smaller and smaller number of (older) people.[109] Women working part-time jobs, balancing home and family life, who found themselves laid off, were the least likely to benefit from unemployment insurance.

Whereas a forty-year-old (or younger), earning the minimum wage prior to his/her bout of unemployment, saw a 24.3% *decrease* in his/her monthly unemployment benefits between 1981 and 1984, the fifty-five-year-old making four times the minimum wage saw an *increase* of 77.4% to his (invariably it was a "he") monthly unemployment check, which in reality became a costly form of early retirement.[110] The RMI should be placed in this context: in some ways it constitutes a mopping-up of past policy failures, or, less cynically, a reshuffling of resources. A change in the unemployment insurance law in 1984 allowed the unemployed aged fifty-five and up to keep their benefits right up to the time of retirement.[111] As Daniel and Tuchszirer conclude in their comprehensive study of unemployment in France: "Women and youth were affected more than others . . . The 'ligne de fracture' became more visible: on the one hand, a system of social protection for the most secure jobs and the best-paid workers; on the other, state public assistance [welfare, or the RMI, introduced in 1988] for all those camped on the periphery [of the job market]."[112]

The common image of the French labor market as a sclerotic, closed club is accurate – for the two-thirds of the labor force, generally aged forty to sixty, that is protected in secure jobs for life, or at least for the life of the company. Perversely, legislation designed to avoid the dog-eat-dog world of US capitalism creates structural, age-based unemployment, which in turn gives rise to US-style unemployment ghettos. The one-third of the French labor force which is left behind is subjected to American-style job insecurity, to an American-style revolving-door process of low wages, lower social benefits, and part-time work. Most of these people are young and a disproportionate number of them are women, immigrants, or the children of immigrants.

Critics of American-style "turbo-capitalism," like Edward Luttwak, argue that the US economy is far more ruthless towards workers than are the French, Italian, and German economic systems. Generally speaking this is true. But these critics also argue that Europeans choose lower growth and higher job stability in order to avoid the excesses of "turbo-capitalism," with its destructive effects on family and the social fabric. They argue that Europeans have been willing to sacrifice some efficiency in order to gain some equality.[113] By now, it should be clear that this argument is way off the mark since it equates "social" spending with social justice. And the Luttwak formula can work only if one limits the definition of "worker" to the "protected" worker aged forty to sixty, usually male. Surely ruthlessness to *aspiring* workers should figure into the equation?

The French economy is utterly ruthless towards youth, immigrants, and unskilled workers, who experience labor turnover of US proportions.[114] In the late 1990s, a young worker, under the age of twenty-five, was three to five times more likely to be fired during a twelve-month period than someone in their forties or fifties.[115] The youth unemployment rate was seven times higher the rate of those over the age of fifty. Part-time work was reserved for young people – especially young women. Part-time workers in France increased from 8.4% of the workforce in 1982 to 15.8% in 1995. Almost 60% of jobs created in 1995 were part time. But unlike in the Netherlands, most part-time jobs in France do not come with full social benefits attached and unlike in the Netherlands, the rise of part-time work in France corresponded with a rise in poverty because social policy did not adjust quickly enough to plug this market failure. Some 40% of new part-time workers in France would have preferred full-time work.[116]

Jobs – not help with the rent for one's thirty-year-old unemployed (or underemployed) daughter or son – are what provide people with structure, self-worth, and a network of friends. As the Commissariat Général du Plan concluded in a recent study of French unemployment, the problem of mass youth unemployment and underemployment has probably led to a rise in suicide among those in their twenties. The suicide rate has risen from 23 per 100,000 people aged fifteen to twenty-four in 1970 to 33 per 100,000 in 1986. Plotted on a graph, the jump in youth unemployment and suicide since the late 1970s follow the exact same upward slope.[117] Coincidence does not constitute causality, and it would be foolish to attribute this trend solely to higher unemployment. But many studies in several nations have made the case for some sort of link between long-term unemployment and suicide. By the late 1990s, the inactivity rate of French youth was higher than any other major Western nation: a remarkable 70.2%, as against 37.8% in Canada and 33.7% in the USA.[118]

French youth, like their counterparts elsewhere in Western Europe, have, on the whole, never had more schooling.[119] Yet the percentage of French youth with a university degree who had to take a non-skilled job doubled between 1986 and 1995.[120] Young French workers generally took what was offered to them by the marketplace.[121]

A recent study suggests that by expanding university enrollments so dramatically since 1980, the state has cheapened the value of a university degree (only one-third of undergraduates finish their degree). Those who do stay on to graduate enter the workforce tainted by association with the mass degree mill which has trained them. The other perverse effect is to enhance the cachet of the elitist *grandes écoles*, which have a poor record of attracting students from low-income and ethnic minority backgrounds (let alone recruiting, which generally cannot be done due to France's system of national entrance examinations).[122]

Table 7.6 *The revolving door of the labor market, USA and France, 1987*

	USA	France
Entries into the labor market (as % of total labor force)	25.3	28.9
Exits (jobs left)	26.5	30.7
Entries into unemployment	23.9	3.9
Long-term unemployed (as % of the total unemployed)	11.0	34.0

Sources: Daniel Cohen, "Les salaires ou l'emploi?" in Pierre Boisard and Olivier Mongin et al., eds., *Le travail, quel avenir?* (Paris: Gallimard, 1997), p. 89; Christine Erhel, "Emploi et chômage en France aujourd'hui," in Jean-Yves Capul, ed., *Emploi et protection sociale*, in *Cahiers français* 292 (July–September 1999), p. 5.

More is less (and worse)

National education spending as a percentage of the state budget fell from 18.5% in 1974 to 15.7% in 1986.[123] As with the drop in spending on family allowances, demographic changes (the lower birth rate of the last two decades) do not account for the majority of the fall in spending. As spending on health, pensions, and culture increased dramatically, the education sector was squeezed. To a certain extent, the failure of French universities is due to the unfulfilled, greater expectations of the 1990s. The baby boomers wished to perpetuate their economic success by sending their children to university, even if many parents had never attended themselves.[124]

Even as university enrollments have gone up by 1.4 million students since 1970, funding levels have remained the same in absolute terms (dropping substantially in real terms, and per student). The state refuses to allow tuition fees out of a commitment to "equality" and "accessibility." But this comes at a cost: universities are overcrowded, underfunded, underequipped, and many are dilapidated.

In the name of "solidarity," universities cannot make admissions decisions themselves. Anyone in France who passes the "bac" exam (and 70% of the university-age population passes it) taken usually at age 18, can go on to university. Most of those who pass the bac go on to the next level. As a result, with the unemployment crisis of the last twenty-five years, university enrollment doubled as more people feared the consequences of *not* having a degree, even as a degree became less valuable since more people earned one. It is truly a vicious circle.

Table 7.7 *The overcrowded French educational establishment*

Number of university students (below)		Percentage of overcrowded lycée classes (35+ students) (2nd cycle of lycée)[125]	
1950	136,700	1983	9.4
1960	213,100	1984	15.3
1970	625,600	1986	26.4
2000	2,100,000	1989	39.4
		1990	32.9

Source: Antoine Prost, *Education, société et politiques: Une histoire de l'enseignement de 1945 à nos jours* (Paris: Seuil, 1997), pp. 139, 214.

Half of all twenty-year-olds in France are in university, but a minority of them will graduate. Yes, higher education is free, but many degrees are of questionable value. Students in large cities like Paris must scramble to pay for living expenses. Very few students have scholarships or student aid of any sort, and in most cases it is a very small amount – a few hundred euros per year. Only students in the super-elite *grandes écoles* and other graduate schools earn valuable degrees. There are about 135,000 such lucky students – the other two million are left to fend for themselves. University housing is scarce. The majority of students live at home with parents and go to the local university. The situation is equally grim in Italy and Germany. Europeans have indeed expanded access to higher education, but of what quality? What would the youth unemployment rate have been if university admissions had not been allowed to jump by one million students between 1980 and 2000?

By the early 1990s, the French government's annual capital expenses for educational establishments were at 13.5 billion francs (in 1980 francs). In 1975 that figure was 15.9 billion francs (again, in 1980 francs). Capital expenditure, eroded by twenty-five years of inflation, resulted in buildings which were, quite literally, themselves eroding.[126] The decline of European universities is one of the great public policy failures of the past thirty years.

In his book *Après l'Empire: Essai sur la décomposition du système américain* (2002), leading public intellectual Emmanuel Todd notes that US university attendance has declined in recent years even as it has increased in France.[127] But he makes an oversimplified link between attendance ratios and utility to society. Todd ignores the quality–quantity issue altogether. And he ignores the fact that the majority of those who enroll in

French universities will not graduate. Rising attendance in the context of an already overcrowded and underfunded system can hardly be considered a social gain.

Moving on up? Access to home ownership among those under the age of forty

In 1999, three-quarters of retirees owned their residence, as against only 52% in 1982.[128] In 1982, 16% of households headed by those under the age of thirty owned their residence; in 2003, that figure had dropped to below 10%, which was less than one-half the rate in North America. Since the early 1980s, French youth have faced a radically different, unwelcoming housing market. Rents have increased rapidly. Mortgages have been nearly impossible to secure without a large down-payment of 25%. In other words, without family help, most young people simply could not buy homes or apartments. Low-interest loans are reserved for elite *cadres* and some privileged public-sector workers.

The average household headed by those aged under thirty-five devoted 3,000 to 4,000 more francs ($600 to $800 at 1995 exchange rates) per year, in real terms, for rents in 1994 than in 1984. Landlords and *rentiers* – who were and are overwhelmingly middle-aged and elderly – profited enormously. Higher housing costs account for a large portion of the rise in poverty among young families.[129] An enormous shift in wealth from younger renters and mortgage-holders to generally older landlords and vendors has occurred virtually undiscussed, perhaps because market mechanisms seemed responsible, making the whole situation appear "natural." But, to a large extent, the growing poverty of youth was the result of the high cost of housing (itself a by-product of high real interest rates), a reduction in the overall housing budget, and reductions in family allowances.

Nationwide, in 1970 the average household devoted only 15.3% of its budget to housing, heating, and electricity; by 1997, that figure had risen to 22.5%, but in the large cities it was often well over 50%. The lack of affordable housing for young, low- and mid-income families was a serious economic and social problem which affected millions of people, yet governments failed to introduce a meaningful program to address it. High social spending was locked into other, non-redistributive channels.

Since 1982, the overall home ownership rate has stagnated in France, at roughly 54 to 55%. Older richer people continue to buy; fewer younger people are able to buy. The social escalator is stalled, top-heavy with *rentiers* and retirees. Young people without family help have effectively been excluded from the housing market: those who buy before the age of thirty-seven to forty, and without family help, are rare indeed.[130] The home ownership rate of those aged under twenty-eight has dropped by 50% since the early 1980s.[131] The average age of first-time buyers rose from forty to forty-two years between 1984 and 1996. The difficulty that young people have with finding affordable housing, and the failure of the welfare state to adapt to this new social problem, is symptomatic of the "capture" of the welfare state. It is designed to serve yesterday's needy – who are today's affluent.[132]

Nationwide, total costs associated with lodging (rent/mortgage, taxes, heating, water, electricity, etc.) doubled during the 1980s and 1990s.[133] The number of subsidized mortgages for low-income families, however, dropped from a paltry 93,000 to a token 33,000 between 1984 and 1990. France's lack of government support for the mortgage industry sets it apart from the USA, Britain, Canada, and Australia (with its special mortgages for young, first-time home buyers). High interest rates were not offset by subsidies to low-income workers seeking to buy a home. One of the very architects of "sado-monetarism," Jacques Attali, admitted in 1998 to the widely read magazine, *L'Express*:

For at least twenty years, seniors have dominated the economic life of the West. The fight against inflation has taken priority over the fight for jobs. [The French state is obsessed] with the idea of providing, at every moment, the best possible rates of return ["rentes," to investors and seniors]. It is obsessed with the goal of fighting inflation, which favors lenders . . . even at the price of youth unemployment.[134]

Some economists estimate that the franc was 20 to 30% overvalued throughout the late 1980s and 1990s. This artificially high franc played no small role in the 5% drop in industrial production in France during the 1990s, as against an increase of 7% in Italy, 12% in the UK, and 25% in the USA.[135] French economists Olivier Blanchard, of MIT, and Jean-Paul Fitoussi, of the Institut d'Etudes Politiques in Paris, estimate that between 1987 and 1994, when real interest rates were over 6%, they could have been lowered to a point where no additional inflation would have resulted, but where unemployment would have dropped 3.5 points (from over 12% to just under 9%).[136] This figure of 3.5 points translates into almost one million jobs. The human costs were staggering. The official poverty rate of French youth doubled between 1984 and 1994.[137]

During the 1990s, over 35% of families with one child who were under the poverty line before state transfers were still poor after transfers (29% of poor families with three children were still poor after transfers).[138] Pension policy was six to seven times more effective in eliminating poverty than policies targeted at young families. In other words, social policy was directing more and more money at people who were, in any

Table 7.8 *Assets (real estate equity, stocks, bonds, liquid wealth, etc.) by age group, France 1986–98 (average person = 100)*

	1986	1998
under 40 years old	47.64	27.77
40 to 59	194.35	148.70
60 and over	90.00	124.54

Source: Christine Chambaz et al., "Le revenu et le patrimoine des ménages," in INSEE, *Données sociales. La société française* (1999) (Paris: INSEE, 1999), p. 281.

case, becoming wealthier and wealthier. As the nation's official statistics bureau, INSEE, reported, the vast majority of the gains made in the real estate and stock markets during the 1980s and 1990s accrued to those aged fifty to seventy.[139]

Critics of the intergenerational inequality thesis argue that the generous treatment of the elderly in most Western nations has *not* come at the expense of the young. Table 7.8 challenges this argument. In 1956, the minimum old-age pension, the *minimum vieillesse*, was introduced.[140] Old-age poverty was something that French politicians believed they could eliminate. To their credit, by the 1980s they did so. But they went too far, and they did it in part by taking money from family policy.[141]

The decline in spending on family policy

The USA is the yardstick which other academics, like Barbara Bergmann, Sheila Kamerman, and Alfred Kahn have used as they have taken the measure of the French welfare state's pro-child benefits.[142] Although I agree with the general tone of their argument (family support policy is a good thing due to its potentially redistributive effects), these authors present an incomplete picture in that they generally fail to acknowledge that French family policy has been in decline for forty years. They fail to measure French family policy against its own past. And in their avoidance of the unemployment crisis, these authors extract a few success stories out of the general context – which is Depression-like economic conditions for perhaps 30 to 40% of the working-age population.

As the French government taxed and spent more and more throughout the 1980s and 1990s, it spent less and less on family policy. During the 1940s and 1950s, 40 to 50% of social spending went to the "family" category. Having children on a low income is today, and usually has been, a sure way towards poverty. During the 1940s to 1960s, French social policy was geared toward reducing poverty by alleviating the high costs of raising children. A mixture of traditional depopulation concerns and redistributive concerns converged to produce a widespread political commitment to meaningful spending. By 1950, a working-class family of four with one earner would see its family income double as a result of the world's most generous family policy.[143]

During the 1950s, family benefits grew faster than all other sorts of benefits, although health spending was a close second. The year 1961 marks a clear turning point: after that date (a time during which pensions were becoming the most pressing public policy issue), family policy took a back seat to pension and health-care policy. In only five of the twenty-six years during the period 1960–85 did the state increase family benefits at a rate greater than that of old-age benefits (in 1960, 1973, 1978, 1980, and 1982), and this usually amounted to only two or three points over the increases to pensions. But there were several years when old-age benefits were increased at a rate four or six *times* greater than family benefits (as in 1976, when family benefits were increased by only 2.8% when inflation was 9.9%, but when old-age benefits were increased by 18.3%).[144]

During the late 1960s and early 1970s, under President Pompidou, family policy was pushed aside by other priorities, dropping to 25% of the social budget. Under Giscard d'Estaing and Mitterrand, family policy fell to under 10% of the social budget. Demographics had very little to do with it, since there were *more* people eligible for family allowances in 1970 than in 1950 (immigration overcame the declining birth rate). Until the 1970s, French family benefits were the most generous in the world.

The bleeding away of family policy began, officially, in 1969 when Jacques Chaban-Delmas announced to the National Assembly that henceforth the government's priorities would be health, pensions, housing, and the handicapped – he made no mention of family policy. Pompidou himself reiterated this list of priorities in 1970.[145] But the smoking gun is certainly the 1972 decision to pay for the new minimum pension for women of retirement age who had raised children from the coffers of the main family allowance fund. Jacques Bichot, a leading expert on French family policy, cites this as the moment at which family policy was deliberately sacrificed to other priorities.[146]

"Rendez-vous manqué"

According to a widely cited 1985 government report written by Pierre Laroque and Rémi Lenoir, family allowances in France had taken a back seat to all other forms of social spending during the period 1965–85. Family spending increased more slowly than all other categories of social spending during the 1960s and 1970s.[147]

Mitterrand failed to reverse this trend. Indeed, there was an obvious discrepancy between the resources devoted to middle-aged men, in the form of the pre-retirement packages for dying industries, and the stagnation of family policy. As Jane Jenson, Mariette Sineau, Margaret Maruani, and others have argued, a disproportionate part of the cuts to social policy during the U-Turn were inflicted upon daycare services and family policy in general.[148] Mitterrand's commitment to equality was not extended to income equality between the sexes. The gap between male and female earnings was almost as high in France in 1995 as it had been in 1980, but the Scandinavians managed to nearly eliminate the gap during this period.

As Jenson and Sineau show, under Giscard (1974–81), 43,000 new daycare and nursery places were created. Mitterrand promised to construct 300,000 new spots but delivered only 45,000 in his first seven-year mandate and another 42,000 in his second mandate (1988–95). Decentralization was used as an opportunity to "offload" this responsibility to the communes and departments. It was one of the precious few social services which was offloaded, signaling the government's willingness to allow local variation. As Mitterrand himself admitted, "the financial resources of the state are limited."[149] If family policy was expendable, pension policy was expandable.

Family allowances took a cut of 2.8 billion francs of the total 10 billion cut in September 1982 and still more during the larger cut of March 1983. This was 28% of the total cut, yet family allowances cost only 12% of all social spending at this time. Invalidity and widows' pensions took a hit of 800 million francs, and the brunt was borne by the health sector: 6.3 billion francs. Note that the key source of social spending, the general pension regime, took no cuts at all.[150] And the special regimes took no cuts either: the "protected people" came out of the "crise" unscathed. When Prime Minister Balladur made reforms to the general pension regime in 1993, he ensured that the people affected were those who would retire as of 2010 – once again protecting the "welfare generation." And the public sector pension regimes were not touched.[151]

During several years, especially during the Mitterrand governments (as in 1983, 1984, 1985, and beyond), annual family allowance increases were insufficient to match the inflation rate. This state of affairs did not go completely unnoticed. An important committee struck in 1989 at the Commissariat Général du Plan, presided by René Teulade, proposed that family allowances be increased substantially.[152] It noted that the pension and health-care sectors had siphoned off money that used to be spent on families. Teulade's call was not heeded. Under the Jospin government, pensions were given larger "boosts" than family allowances.[153]

As Alain Bihr and Roland Pfefferkorn argue in their important survey, *Hommes, femmes, quelle égalité?* (2002), the gender divide was not narrowed markedly after fifteen years of socialist rule. On every score – income levels, social mobility levels, access to senior positions in management and the civil service – France is either close to or below the European norm. The Conseil d'Analyse économique reported to Prime Minister Jospin in 1999 on the economic and social status of women. It painted a mixed picture of persistent inequalities between men and women over the age of fifty, but increasing equality among employed French men and women in their twenties and thirties, especially in the professional class.[154]

Why does the upper-middle class in France support the big welfare state?

Within this larger picture of the decline of family policy, during the last fifteen years spending has been reconfigured (for the better), to the point where over 60% of it is now means-tested, targeted at lower-income families. In the midst of rising child poverty, spending is indeed becoming more redistributive. But wealthier families have never had more help with childcare expenses.

A typical "special" benefit is the income tax deduction available to large families (three children or more). Since this benefit rises with income, it accrues overwhelmingly to the wealthy. Likewise, the extra benefit for stay-at-home mothers is something that only couples with one large income can enjoy. During 1997–98, when Lionel Jospin's government eliminated a few family benefits for the wealthy, those earning the equivalent of $100,000 per year stood to lose tax credits which were worth more than five times the value of the family allowance available to the average worker. Street protests forced Jospin to reverse this reform. Was "solidarity" defended? Over a million French children live in poverty but the protests ensured that tens of thousands of wealthy families continue to enjoy large tax breaks, often to the tune of tens of thousands of euros per family.

In 1981, a family with three children and an income of 3,500 francs per month received a family allowance of 1,600 FF per month. This constituted 40% of the pre-benefit income. This same family would receive a tax break of no more than 500 francs per month (6,000 FF per year).[155] By contrast, a family income of 600,000 FF per year, with three children, would gain 58,000 FF in tax reductions alone.[156] By 1998, the wealthy family with three children and an income of 700,000 FF would benefit from family benefits and family-related tax cuts to the tune of 67,100 FF; the family with three children and an income of only 100,000 FF would get only 30,000 FF in assistance.[157] These large child tax breaks, then, go overwhelmingly to the rich (and, some critics say, with a touch of conspiracy, to the white upper-middle class). And they are truly costly: tax breaks cost 50% of the total annual payments of France's main family allowance fund.[158] Small wonder the wealthy protested in 1998 when the Jospin government tried to eliminate their special benefits. French tax breaks for wealthy families have few parallels in Europe.[159]

Some would argue that supporting these privileges is worth the price if it means universal support for social policy in general. Some would argue that targeted, US-style social programs lead to stigmatization and ghettoization, and will fail to garner continuing political support.[160] Moving more in the direction of universal social programs and higher social spending is certainly an option in low-spending, low-taxing USA; substantially higher social spending is not possible in high-spending, high-taxing, high unemployment Europe.[161]

In a world of solidaristic overstretch, of millions of political blank checks written to (already prosperous) pensioners, of budget deficits, and a zero-sum fiscal environment, it is no exaggeration to state that the poverty of those million children *is* caused by the tax perks available to wealthy families. French family policy is not an example of redistribution in practice, because it generally consists, at the lower end of the income ladder, of a partial payback for high taxes. Young French parents receive the equivalent of $160 to $200 per month for raising two children, but they also lose one-fifth to one-third of their gross monthly income to pay for benefits they do not use: today's over-generous pay-as-you-go pensions. The tax rate on young families is over twice as high, in real terms, as it was thirty years ago. Regressive sales taxes are three times higher than they were thirty years ago; they eat into young families' incomes and negate many of the family benefits they receive. At 9% of all social spending, French family policy is a relatively small slice of solidarity; it should not serve as the key focus of comparative studies of welfare states.

But so much is spent in so many different venues, and everyone receives something; this, coupled with solidarity ideology, helps to ensure that the most generous benefits are not resented to the point that the public demands their abolition. The French public remains firmly committed to the idea of family allowances, even as their value has dropped. Equally popular are the maternity leave benefits (sixteen to twenty-six weeks at 100% pay, followed by one to three years of parental leave) and the ubiquitous state-funded daycare centers – which have also seen cuts in recent years. Although French family policy does indeed help those who choose to have children with their monthly expenses, permitting single women to venture into the workforce, it has not succeeded in its chief goal: to boost the birth rate substantially (since the 1990s, though, the French birth rate has been higher than the European average). Nonetheless, the relatively low level of single-parent and child poverty in France – which amounts to one-half the North American rates – should remind us that if there is one proven, effective poverty-reducing program, it is child welfare.

Taken together, family and housing allowances may provide up to 25% of many French working families' incomes, but regressive taxes claw much of this back. Over three million families benefit from family allowances. *Ecoles maternelles* dot the urban centers of France, in which the vast majority of the nation's three year-olds are enrolled. If there is a bright spot in the French social service landscape, this is certainly it.[162]

Despite the obvious success of French family policy, there is a tendency in North America to romanticize it, to portray it as the product of a more socially progressive, humane political culture. This is not necessarily the case. The roots of French family policy do not lie in some peculiarly French ideal of social justice or solidarity between the generations. Rather, they extend deep into the nation's past, to its 130-year-old collective concern over a rapidly falling birth rate and the dire military, cultural, and even racial implications of this. Of course, today, many people in France support family allowances out of a genuine sense of social solidarity towards those in their child-bearing years, but this sentiment did not give birth to the programs in the first place. These family programs are popular but like other social services, they don't come cheaply: they put a heavy burden on employers, who must pay for them (although the state now pays for the entire cost where low-income workers are concerned). Since women are now having their first baby at the average age of twenty-nine, and most have their second child in their early or mid-thirties, family benefits are not a boon to youth (defined in most cases as those sixteen to twenty-four years old).

The lack of support for the first child is a clear indication of the pronatalist, as opposed to social democratic, nature of French family allowances. Under Prime Ministers Balladur and Juppé, family policy was given a few years more to live: the increases they mandated slowed down thirty years of decline. If the cuts of 1982 to 1993 had continued, family policy was projected to take up only 5% of all social spending by 2040. Now it is set to take up 15% by that date.[163]

Table 7.9 *Family policy as a percentage of GNP*

	1980	1990	1993
Denmark	2,8%	3,0%	3.3%
UK	2.3	2.1	2.6
Luxembourg	2.2	2.0	2.7
Germany	2.6	1.9	1.8
France	2.6	2.2	2.4
Belgium	2.8	2.1	1.9
Ireland	1.7	2.0	2.2
Netherlands	2.6	1.7	1.6
Italy	1.2	1.0	0.8
Portugal	0.8	0.8	0.8
Spain	0.5	0.2	0.2
Greece	0.2	0.1	0.1

Note: The figure for France (above) includes hospitalization of women for childbirth – which is considered a normal health-care expense in most nations. So the French figure is exaggerated.
Source: Jean-Pierre Dumont, *Les systèmes de protection sociale en Europe* 4th edn. (Paris: Economica, 1998), p. 164.

The best way to correct for the drop in the birth rate, and to determine just how much allowances really have fallen, is to consider that at times during the 1940s and 1950s, family allowances might bring in 50% of the average wage into a household. Today they generally bring in less than 20%.[164] As Tables 7.9 and 7.10 show, the favoring of the elderly at the expense of young adults takes place throughout Europe.

Increased pension spending and decreased spending on the family is *not* explained primarily by demographics. It is the result of the politics of pensioneering and the politics of selective retrenchment. Italy, for example, now spends almost 16% of GNP on pensions, but only 0.8% on family allowances. In Italy, as in France and most other nations, the decline has been due, overwhelmingly, to political factors. France's share of GNP devoted to family allowances fell from 2.6% to 2.2% over the course of the 1980s, yet the number of families eligible for allowances *increased* by over 200,000.[165] In constant 1996 francs, the average family allowance dropped from 1,276 FF per month to 1,130 FF, or about one-eighth the amount of the average monthly pension in the general regime.[166] Despite this, France has been slipping from a very high point. French family policy can still be classified as a relative success, certainly in relation to Italian or North American family policy. But one wonders what might be done

Table 7.10 *Old-age pensions*
(excluding disability) as % of GNP

	1980	1993
Netherlands	9.5%	11.9%
Denmark	10.0	11.0
Luxembourg	12.0	11.2
France	10.5	12.7
Belgium	11.0	11.9
Italy	9.9	15.4
UK	8.5	10.8
Spain	7.2	9.4
Germany	11.9	11.0
Greece	6.1	10.2
Ireland	6.2	5.7
Portugal	4.6	7.0

Source: Dumont, *Les systèmes*, p. 213.

Table 7.11 *Relative well-being of*
single-mother families in four countries, 1990

	Income as percentage of average two-parent family income
USA	.47
Canada	.52
France	.74
Sweden	.87

Source: Sara McLanahan and Irwin Garfinkel, "Single-Mother Families and Social Policies," in Katherine McFate, Roger Lawson, and William Julius Wilson, eds., *Poverty, Inequality and the Future of Social Policy* (New York: Russell Sage Foundation, 1995) p. 370.

if, say, a mere 1% of pension expenditures were transferred over to the family support side of the ledger. Table 7.11 shows just what might be done – France could eliminate child poverty overnight.

Over the last decade, child poverty has risen in six of Europe's ten largest nations, most notably in Germany and Italy.[167] The poverty rates of families with children during the mid 1990s ranged as follows: Denmark, 2.9%; Finland, 2.1%; Norway, 3.4%; Sweden, 2.2%; France,

7.1%.[168] France could move closer to Scandinavian levels of success, if only the state could wrestle money away from other programs. A recent study by Esping-Andersen and Sarasa estimates that the cost of eliminating child poverty in France during the 1990s would have been only 0.04% of GDP.[169] Another 2003 study found that only 8 billion euros would be needed to raise everyone to the poverty line.[170]

By 2002, there were 1,361,000 (officially) working poor, roughly one million of whom were women, many of them working at part-time jobs in the service sector. As Margaret Maruani has argued, social policy has failed to recognize this problem.[171] Enormous sums of money would not be required to help this group; outdated corporatist social policy structures geared towards skilled male workers stand in the way. During the 1990s, the public debate surrounded programs targeted at generally wealthy people (retirees) instead of generally poor people (single parents working in the service sector).

In 1990, French social programs led to a 59% reduction of poverty among single-mother households; in Canada, that figure was only 19%, in Sweden, 81%. Single mothers in France and Sweden are able to work *and* receive social benefits; in North America, historically, it has been one or the other. Daycare facilities enable French women to work. This reduces their dependency rate. Here is one of France's most successful social policies. Unfortunately, it has not been expanded quickly enough, even as rising divorce rates and lower wages in the service sector (where more and more women are working) render this type of policy more and more essential. Rising pension and health spending are squeezing out all opportunities for experiments in other areas and monopolizing politicians' time.

By any measure, during the last thirty-five years, French social policy has been blown off its earlier, more redistributive, pro-family course. Higher poverty is the outcome. Globalization has nothing to do with it: political choices made by French politicians and tolerated by French voters are the cause.

8   The French exception

During the last fifty years, our social welfare institutions have developed with a complete disregard for the principle of reality which governs all human activity: the recognition of limits and the constraints imposed by a finite universe.

Sociologist Michel Crozier, in his Etat moderne, Etat modeste (1987).[1]

The future of Social Security is largely dependent on the prevailing psychological climate. In this respect, two opposing and contradictory elements can be identified: on the one hand, the French are strongly attached to the institution; on the other, they are not sufficiently aware of the responsibility they have towards [paying for] it.

Pierre Laroque, one of the "founding fathers" of the post-Second World War welfare state, 1985.[2]

Faithful to its [sense of being an] exception, France thought it could maintain public spending and salaries, reduce the working week, without touching social benefits either.

Michel Godet, referring to the Jospin years, in Claude Bébéar, ed., Le Courage de réformer (2002).[3]

In 1998, Martine Aubry succeeded in convincing her party to pass the 35-hour law, also known as the Loi Aubry or the RTT (Réduction du Temps de Travail). The law was phased in during 2000 to 2002.[4] The Loi Aubry was grounded in the idea that work is a finite thing and that it *must* be regulated and "shared" in order to reduce unemployment, but that wages need not be reduced. A quick look at the Dutch experience (work week reduced by 5%, wages reduced by 9%) would have shown that the Aubry law made promises it could not keep. Since the law raised the cost of salaried service labor, the unemployed will pay. And hourly wage workers, many of whom have lost four hours of wage labor per week, have sacrificed. Many of these people registered their disgust with France's out-of-touch politicians by voting for Le Pen in 2002.[5]

The wealthiest, most secure workers have come out even better off.[6] Only 59% of French workers had registered their support for this law in 2001 and 66% by the autumn of 2003.[7] I say "only" because the law was supposed to make *everyone* better off – less stressed, more vacationed, more secure in their jobs. In fact, as *Le Monde* discovered, in its first year, the 35-hour law caused widespread disruptions in the world of work. For many factory workers, the law has translated into accelerated, more stressful shifts. Low-skilled wage workers have had to adapt far more than sedentary office workers, who simply did the same job as before, but gained an extra three vacation days per month. In 2001, 28% of workers polled told *Le Monde* that their work environment had in fact deteriorated as a result of the law and 32% said they were now more stressed.[8] Only 49% of hourly paid workers supported the law but 69% of *cadres* (managers, professionals) were in favor. By 2003, 34% of workers were dissatisfied with the law and 23% wanted to return to the 39-hour week – most of these people were low-paid workers who had relied on overtime to augment their incomes.[9] In yet another way did "solidarity" add to the comforts of the already comfortable.[10]

Recent research suggests that some larger manufacturing companies did indeed use the law to introduce greater labor flexibility – not an original intention of the law's architects – and to restrain wages. The 35-hour law has enabled many (certainly not all) firms to introduce a decentralized form of Dutch-style wage restraint through the back door.[11] The government allowed employers to ask employees to work an *average* of 35 hours per week. Seasonal upswings can now be met with more flexibility; factory workers can be called in on weekends, companies can request shift-work at awkward times. If the law has indeed helped to mop up unemployment to a certain extent, it was precisely because it has rendered the manufacturing sector of France more "flexible," more adaptable – in a word, more American.[12]

But how many politicians would have dared to call for this publicly? Again, we see the failure of political elites to be honest with the electorate about the challenges facing the nation. The key critique of the 35-hour law, however, is *not* that it did not live up to its job-creating promises. It may well have led directly to the creation of 300,000 new jobs by mid 2003. But the job losses associated with the 35-hour week are impossible to quantify – they consist of positions which might have been created during France's mini-economic recovery of the late 1990s to 2001 had the law not increased the costs of business in certain sectors of the economy, such as the service sector. They consist of foreign companies which decided not to open or expand in France.

Above all, the law can be used by companies to justify wage moderation. But it will by definition lead to rising costs in the service sector, where thirty-five hours means thirty-five hours, where technological advances cannot lead to productivity increases which might offset the higher cost of labor. Inevitably, this has pushed companies in the service sector to urge wage restraint. And who works in the service sector? Many low-paid workers do. Instead of the state admitting that this would be necessary and taking responsibility for a lowering of service sector and low-skilled workers' wages, now workers can vent their sense of grievance toward their employer.

But the chief outcome of the 35-hour law was negative: born of a genuine concern for "solidarity," the Loi Aubry in fact increased social inequality in France. Philippe Manière writes:

in making current benefits more generous, we reinforce the isolation of those who do not enjoy such benefits . . . the idea of passing an extra week skiing with the children . . . or stretching out on the beach [in the name of job creation] is a joke. Two to three months [vacation]! Isn't it nice to think, as one goes off on vacation, that one is contributing to the noble cause of reducing unemployment? [The 35-hour law] has created new . . . divisions between the French. Divisions between those, like [hourly] wage workers, cashiers, manual laborers, for whom the law represents a pay cut and less desirable working hours, and the others, the [salaried] *cadres*, the civil servants . . . and other well-paid workers who had nothing to lose – but lots to gain. In the name of job creation, two classes of workers have been legally enshrined as of 1 January 2000.[13]

The divide between the protected, the well-vacationed, and the unwanted on the outside grows wider each year.

To a certain extent, the rhetoric of "solidarity" is indirectly responsible for the rise of Right-wing and Left-wing extremism because it helps to create a sort of intellectual impasse: if France spends so much on solidarity and tries to legislate, in such good faith, better working conditions and so on, yet there is still so much poverty and unemployment, then something bad, something sinister, must be at the root of the problem – foreign workers, the EU, "elites," globalization.[14] As Sophie Meunier has argued, if "globalization" is responsible for rising poverty and for unemployment, and if the real decisions are being made in Brussels and in New York, then why not vote for an extremist Left-wing anti-EU party?[15] Why not vote for the populist, nationalist, racist National Front? According to this logic, nothing is really decided in Paris, anyway. As the trade expert Brink Lindsey argues,

Without dynamism, without confidence in the future, modern society cannot sustain any sense of an all-embracing common interest. When the positive-sum game of continuing [job] growth gives way to the zero-sum game of stagnation and sclerosis, every group and faction comes to see all others as the enemy – as threats to its share of limited and dwindling spoils. Europe's backward looking labor restrictions have sought to tame the unruly process of creative destruction as it applies to employment. But the destruction continues, if more slowly; creation meanwhile, has ground to a halt – and with it, so has any basis for durable solidarity. The ugly resentment of immigrants so prevalent in Europe today is one obvious example of how lack of economic opportunity breeds division and rancor.[16]

The 35-hour law symbolizes the zero-sum approach to social problems so commonly seen in France: it started from the pessimistic premise that one person's loss of four working hours per week was necessarily another's gain. This is a dangerous approach to employment policy; politicians focus on sharing the pie instead of expanding it. So those who do not get a slice will tend to see those who do benefit as having gained at their expense. In other words, the loss of one person's full-time job (let's say this person is a supporter of Le Pen's National Front), might be seen as another's gain (say, a thirty-year-old woman of North African origins who finally lands a job after five years of searching).

Solidarity talk and legislation wins politicians points with parts of the electorate; it does not provide jobs to the unemployed. As the British journalist John Ardagh heard repeatedly in his interviews with French bosses and politicians, "No we do not want to move towards the American model."[17] Throughout the 1990s, this intransigence in the face of the American model, which was universally denounced as inhuman and anarchic, with its low wages and easy hiring and firing, was usually attributed to a desire to maintain the French system of "solidarity."[18] Take the words of none other than Jean-Luc Lagardère (who died in 2003), the arms industry magnate: "French business leaders, in general, have a much greater sense of their social responsibility than their Anglo-Saxon counterparts."[19] To a certain extent this is hollow rhetoric. Surely the fact that US and British companies were willing and able to provide jobs to most people who sought them during the 1990s amounted to some form of social good? Surely the fact that 45% of American workers still have a private, job-based pension (only 5% of French workers enjoy this benefit) in addition to Social Security indicates the survival of some sense of corporate social responsibility?

Rhetoric like Lagardère's helps French business and political elites to wash their hands of responsibility for the crisis of mass unemployment. The disruption associated with the relatively unregulated British, American, and Canadian labor markets would be unsettling to those who have come to expect a secure job for life, complete with seven to nine weeks of paid vacation. Above all, politicians can dispense "solidarity" and vow to "protect" jobs and then shrug their shoulders and claim that they have done everything within their power – it's a globalizing world, after all – to help the poor.

In fact, a freer labor market need not mimic the Anglo-American model – it could go halfway (Dutch) and accept even more part-time work. Or wages could be restrained, taxes could be reduced on low-income workers, and public-sector overspending could be curbed to offset the former. A freer labor market would help to absorb the unemployed – witness the success of recent Spanish reforms under Prime Minister Aznar. There is a trade-off, but it is rarely discussed in France, since this sort of nuanced argument gets squeezed out of the public arena by extremist, Marc Blondel- and Viviane Forrester-style rhetoric. France finds itself trapped between the US and Swedish models, enjoying very few of the benefits of either.

With a few exceptions, like Nicole Notat and later François Chérèque of the CFDT union, during the 1990s and early 2000s French labor leaders and their colleagues embedded in the headquarters of the various social funds retreated into a reflexive defence of all things "social." In 2003, labor was joined by François Hollande, the leader of the Socialist Party, who portrayed Prime Minister Raffarin's pension reforms as an attack on "solidarity," resisting them to the bitter end. A few old Socialist lights like Michel Rocard and Bernard Kouchner went on television to accuse their party and labor leaders of engaging in demagoguery.[20]

The French model stands associated with a quarter century of long-term unemployment. As I argued in Chapter Three, since the state became enormous precisely when the French economy was enjoying its glory age, many people cannot imagine prosperity without a high-spending state. In addition, since the public sector is so large, with 57% of the population working for it or the spouse, parent, or child of a civil servant, a large chunk of the French population is out of touch with the interests and concerns of the private sector.[21] When business leaders complain of the red tape, high social security payroll taxes, and other measures which weigh down on job creation, a large sector of the electorate simply cannot relate to their concerns, and they are disinclined to trust business leaders in the first place. But a trimmed-down state which tolerates more flexible labor markets need not mean an insensitive neoliberal state. Reform can be inspired just as easily by the Netherlands or Scandinavia as by the UK or the USA. France lacks a reformist discourse which emphasizes common goals, common sacrifices. The "social partners" fill the void, preventing change.

France was once willing to accept a great deal of change. During the 1950s and 1960s, France, along with Italy, partook in Europe's largest rural exodus. People were willing to move to where the jobs were; today they rarely do this (the Swedes, by contrast, *require* the unemployed to resettle).[22] As the *Nouvel Observateur* editor, Jacques Julliard, has argued, compared with the booming, geographically mobile, innovative 1940s–1960s, France has become a stagnant, immobile, *rentier* society, more concerned with hanging on to "droits acquis," more concerned with transferring existing wealth to the richest demographic cohort in world history, than with increasing the general level of economic productivity and national wealth.[23] As jobs were shed in the manufacturing sector during the 1980s and 1990s, the state used social spending to cushion the fall of those affected. A more long-term approach would have concentrated instead on macroeconomic policies which might have allowed the private sector to absorb those affected by job losses.

Since the 1980s, the entire public debate has focused on the maintenance or the expansion of social benefit levels, and on extending vacation time and reducing the work week, not on work itself, employment levels, productivity, investment, or innovation. In the minds of a large minority of the population, the leisure ethic, the *rentier* ethic, is favored over the work ethic: this is why opinion polls show that most people support strikes in favor of early retirement. During the late 1990s–early 2000s, Marc Blondel, the leader of the union Force Ouvrière, and Bernard Thibault, leader of the CGT union, spent more time defending pensions than anything else. French union leaders never contemplated the idea of labor market flexibility and wage restraint in the name of job creation. Intellectuals, unwilling to contemplate reform, instead wrote inflammatory polemics denouncing the outside neoliberal world. Intellectuals rarely concerned themselves with the effects of social spending; since they tended to equate all spending with "solidarity," they defended expensive, egregiously non-redistributive programs from reform. They told the public that a reform designed to eliminate retirement at fifty in the SNCF was a "neoliberal" plot to dismantle the great French social model. Politicians never asked the comfortably employed French people to make sacrifices and in any case the public showed no appetite for this.

Sweden, the cradle of social democracy, realized that there were limits to social spending, and the nation has been cutting public spending for fifteen years without increasing poverty in the process. The Swedes must now work longer – into their mid sixties – to receive a full pension. Germany realized that pension spending had to be controlled, and has recently (partially) reformed its pension system. Labor market reforms in Germany in early 2003 had created up to one million new jobs by late summer. If the unemployed, the poor, and the working poor of France are to see their situation improve, people with comfortable jobs and incomes will have to take some responsibility and make some sacrifices.

Today's most urgent priorities are the need to free up labor markets, to retrain unemployed workers, and to reduce the number of working poor, which usually means young families. But France's welfare state devotes under 15% of its resources to these problems. It is locked into providing benefits to people who are generally prosperous.

In the past, costly spending on the affluent may have been a price worth paying in order to ensure widespread political support for meaningful spending on all other groups, including the poor. When the affluent were but one small constituency, as they were during the 1940s to 1960s, this could be afforded. But today the affluent, who tend to be elderly, are becoming a larger and larger portion of society. Each year between 2004 and 2010, 600,000 to 800,000 people will retire.[24] Most of them are reasonably prosperous, many of them are wealthy; *none* has been asked to sacrifice as Prime Minister Raffarin introduced his pension reforms. Pensions will not be cut; public-sector workers have simply been asked to wait 2.5 more years before they retire on a full pension – and even this measure will free up only about one-fifth of the estimated 100 billion euros needed to keep pension promises over the next thirty-five years. The Raffarin reform is not a cut; it constitutes a partial realignment of benefits with longer life expectancies.

As the economic journalist Bernard Préel told the French news-magazine *Le Nouvel Observateur* in early 2001, the soon-to-be pensioners, most of them in their fifties, who marched *en masse* in January 2001 to defend their seventeen-year-old "right" to retire at sixty, were behaving as if they could and should be spared from experiencing what the French call "la crise," or the economic slowdown of the 1980s and 1990s. "La crise" has devastated the career prospects of French youth and eroded their economic status.[25] All of the pain (or simply loss of expected income) associated with the pension reforms of 1993 and 2003 has been inflicted upon: a) those who will retire after the year 2008; and/or b) those in the private sector. *Le Nouvel Observateur* has coined a label for the older/public sector workers and retirees who refuse to share in the nation's sacrifices: "les nouveaux réacs," the new reactionaries (of the Old Left, and of the over-fifty crowd).

As Préel notes, well-paid French workers who have recently retired or are about to retire within the next five years have experienced the following conditions over the course of their careers: regular real salary increases of 5.8% between 1955 and 1975; raises which were higher than anywhere else in the G7 during the 1980s and 1990s; good prospects for advancement early in their careers and an unprecedented level of social mobility; access to cheap credit and even negative real interest rates during the 1960s; affordable housing when they were young and massive returns on their housing investments when they cashed out; a world free of unemployment and job insecurity when they started their careers; and the promise (and reality) of pensions which are extravagant by North American standards. Having had it so good for most of their careers, many of these extraordinarily lucky people, born at the right time, could not fathom the idea that they might have to give up their "right" to retire at fifty to sixty, and work for a few more years in order to lighten the payroll tax burden on those beneath them.[26]

The world of work and generational fortunes has changed dramatically over the last thirty years, but the world of social policy has not adjusted to reflect this.[27] In fact, during the past twenty years, when economies have been made, they have targeted the programs which were in need of *more* funding, such as family policy and policy towards the disabled.

Why reform could lead to more solidarity

To contemplate a *different, reformed* French welfare state is not necessarily to advocate its dismantlement and the triumph of American-inspired "globalization." Reform need not entail turning France into a "corporation nation", with no sense of social justice or social purpose.[28] In *The Silent Takeover: Global Capitalism and the Death of Democracy*, Noreena Hertz argues that "by defining political power in terms of economic power, democratic politicians lose sight of the reason they are elected – to serve their constituents' needs, not solely the needs of big business."[29] I couldn't agree more. By the same token, by defining politics as the defense of vested "social" interests like the special pension funds and the special benefits of the public sector, the French Left lost sight of the reason *they* were elected: to eliminate unemployment, reduce inequality, and do other things which would have worked in the direction of the general interest. The Right's record on employment matters is no better.

A reformed, more streamlined French welfare state could be *more solidaristic*. The French welfare state could follow the road taken by the Dutch during the 1980s and 1990s. It could, like the Australian welfare state, focus its energies on the most needy, and means-test more than the current 6 to 8% of benefits which are pegged to income levels in France (the Australians, by contrast, means-test over 90% of social benefits, increasing their redistributive punch).[30] Like several other European welfare states, the French could do a much better job of redistributing income. French employment policy could, as in Switzerland and Norway, focus on integrating youth into the job market. The French could, as in Sweden reduce child poverty to 2%.[31]

The crisis of the French welfare state is linked to a general crisis of the corporatist/continental conservative welfare state regime.[32] For the first time in modern Western European history, poverty has grown steadily for a period of over twenty-five years, closely tied to joblessness. Long-term unemployment is epidemic in Western Europe. From Spain to Italy, from Germany to Belgium, unemployment is the scourge of the day.

But by the late 1990s, after the French public had been bombarded with extremist anti-globalization rhetoric and slogans for a decade, the marketplace had been so thoroughly discredited intellectually that no French government would dare to embrace it as the source of wealth and the potential solution to unemployment. Instead, throughout the 1990s, France chose short-term statist solutions. The Jospin government promised "emploi-jeunes," not a dynamic labor market – this was perceived as too "American" – which would, by definition, absorb young workers. No one was required to sacrifice. There were to be no trade-offs.

The trend continues: in early 2004, the Raffarin government proposed three-to five-year-long state-supported job contracts in a bid to reassure the public of its concern with unemployment. A more general macroeconomic solution is rarely considered, and until public deficits are under control, France will have no wriggle room to do this. France is prevented from reflating its economy by its own non-redistributive overspending, its bloated public sector, not by the EU's 3% deficit cap. At the end of the day, French politicians are constrained by their fear that public spending cuts will result in mass strikes. And this is a well-grounded fear.

Many French politicians cannot accept the idea that the market should be freed to destroy and create jobs. Above all, most French citizens do not trust the market to do this. Many people do not believe that the market is the root of prosperity; when over 50% of the population relies on the state for an income (civil servants, retirees, social welfare recipients), this sentiment is readily understood.[33] Until this hostility to the very system which funds the "social" is overcome, there is little hope of widespread reform. French leaders have a long road ahead: they could start by abandoning their obsession with globalization and focusing the public debate on France's homegrown problems.

If unemployment truly is a concern, the most "solidaristic" policy option would be a redistributive program to plug market gaps, to ensure a living wage, all the while deregulating the labor market in order to create jobs and to reduce the dependency ratio. This will also have the benefit of helping to pay for the growing pension costs of an aging society. But France is a long way from this scenario. In a recent study of labor market deregulation in Europe, France stands out as the one nation where the issue has never really become a popular concern: politicians (of both main parties) dare not broach it; the general public is unaware of the problem.[34]

There has been no German-style Hartz Commission on deregulating the labor market. This does not bode well for the future of the economy.

Point break?

As the unemployment rate dropped in France in 1998–2001 (only to begin rising once again in 2002), influential papers like *Le Monde* and *Libération* carried regular reports detailing this positive trend. Remarkably, the credit for the fall in unemployment was always put on the doorstep of the Jospin government. But the government was directly responsible for only one quarter of the new jobs created by that time (about 270,000 low-paid "emplois-jeunes" which will only ensure the long-term obesity of the overstaffed public sector). These newspapers also forgot that many of these jobs are simply replacements for retirements, which would have happened anyway. It is as if France were not a market society, and jobs were something created only by the government.[35]

Then again, the state is so immense in France that it is indeed a powerful rival actor to the market – and also a large, dependable source of votes for the Socialists, who have never contemplated cutting back the size of the civil service, as the Right did briefly during the mid 1980s. In any case, the "emploi-jeunes" program could enable the government to display its concern for the unemployed in the newspapers, at press conferences, in publicly distributed brochures, and on government websites. During the summer of 2001, the Ministry of Labor and Solidarity's website described the program in classic Newspeak: "New services for a more solidaristic society. Youth at the heart of society, master of its future."[36] Of course, if French youth really had been the captains of their fate under Jospin's government, they would not have needed low-paid, short-term twenty-hour per week "emplois jeunes" in the first place. In fact youth were being used as the pawns of the political process, the captives of solidarity.

In 2002, Paul Wallace predicted in an international survey of pensions that if European politicians did not bring about substantial reform within the next few years, they "will be guilty of failing to fend off one of the most predictable economic and social crises in history."[37] Raffarin has only taken one step away from this crisis scenario; the problem awaits a definitive reform. As *Le Figaro* asked its readership on 1 February 2003, on the eve of street demonstrations in favor of retaining retirement at fifty to sixty, "the question is simple: we must decide if we will change, or, defeated by corporatism, we remain mired in a suicidal status quo."[38] The longer French politicians put off meaningful reform, the more severe it will have to be, and the more likely the nation will be shut down by a long general strike comparable to that of May 1968.

Thirty-five years ago, when the country was paralyzed during the May 68 strikes, young baby boomers went to the barricades in the name (they believed) of social justice and in defence of lofty ideals like world peace. As the streets filled during the anti-pension reform protests of 2003, many of the same people were there, and once again they marched in defence of a lofty ideal – "solidarity." In reality, for many of them this meant their cushy pensions. As they marched in the millions through the streets of French cities, they talked the talk of "solidarity" but many were walking the walk of self-interest.

If the recent past is any indication of the future, reform will be frustrated and the barricades will go up again before the social welfare deficit comes down. In light of the aging population, the rise of the working poor and child poverty, the growing social spending deficit and the nation's high levels of taxation, one day spending will have to be contained and reoriented dramatically. In 1950, there were 200,000 French people over the age of eighty-five. By 2000, there were more than one million and by 2020 there will be at least two million (and up to four million by 2050).[39] France is doing very little to prepare for this scenario.

What is the French welfare state to those born between 1920 and 1950? Everything. A smashing success. For those born between roughly 1950 and 1960, French social policy is a mixed blessing. And what is it to those born since 1960? Nothing but a long wait in the job queue, a taxing burden, a system of insurance which overcharges them, and a lower standard of living than their parents enjoyed.

A thorough reform of French economic and social policy, steered in the direction of solidarity, might involve the following points:

- wage restraint (especially in the public sector) in the name of job creation; that is, wage restraint with direct provisions for job creation
- alignment of public-sector salaries with the private sector (except at the top level)
- reductions in payroll taxes, especially on low incomes
- increases in progressive income taxes and the CSG
- elimination of the so-called "social partners"; replacement with a universalistic system of social provision
- elimination of tax loopholes for independently employed people
- reductions in regulations inhibiting business start-ups
- a loosening of labor laws and licensing restrictions
- repeal of the 35-hour law, simplification of the Code du Travail

- enforcement of legislation prohibiting racial and sexual discrimination in the workplace
- increased funding for the handicapped; stronger measures to integrate them into the workforce
- supplementary health insurance for all residents
- a freezing of the minimum wage for several years followed by income supplements to low-income workers who suffer as a result
- a significant boost to family allowances, with even more targeting at low and middle incomes
- expansion of daycare facilities
- further cuts to tax breaks for wealthy families
- further cuts to pensions and the elimination of the special regimes
- retirement at sixty-five for all; higher for those who wish to continue working
- equal benefits for equal contributions (in all programs, but particularly pensions)
- elimination of public sector privileges (such as the eighteen free train trips allowed per year to SNCF employees and the subsidized housing provided to others)
- introduction of the "minimum service" in the public sector
- elimination of waste, redundancies, absenteeism in the public sector
- abolition of the ENA; integration of its staff into the general university system
- increased funding to universities and to research
- slightly lower enrollments in universities, offset by more funding for technical and vocational education
- an increase in housing allowances (portable) for those on low incomes

Even if only one-tenth of this wish list were tackled with a moderate degree of success, France would become a more solidaristic society. Globalization is not preventing French politicians from addressing these issues; the only obstacles are a lack of political will and a discourse which stresses egalitarianism and universal social programs as opposed to corporatist privilege.

In this book I have tried to lift the veil of "solidarity" which obscures the generational, sexual, and class-based inequalities embedded deep in the heart of the French welfare state.

Appendix
Some major pieces of social legislation, France, 1893–2003

1893	Free medical assistance for indigents (by 1920s, 6% of population benefits from this rudimentary program).
1898	Industrial accident insurance for workers (fails in practice).
1904	State grants to departments for maternal welfare programs (makes France a world pioneer in this regard).
1905	Modest system of assistance for the elderly indigent (expands considerably during the 1920s and 1930s).
1910	Pensions for workers (fails due to court challenges).
1913	Bonuses for large families (expanded considerably during 1920s).
1919	War pensions, various veterans' benefits; important public health legislation.
1923	Limited family allowance program (optional but pioneering).
1928	Loucheur Law. State support for public housing construction. Over 120,000 units built.
1928	Social Insurance Law. Implemented in 1930. Health insurance, maternity benefits, death benefits, modest and limited pension benefits. One-third of the population covered. By 1940, half of the population is covered, and millions of claims reimbursed.
1932	Mandatory employer-provided family allowances, non-means tested (universal).
1936	Forty-hour week and two weeks of paid vacations for workers (pioneering but negative from an economic point of view).
1939	Code de la Famille. Major increases to family allowances, etc.
1941	Hospital "charter." Hospitals declared open to all citizens. Vichy increases pensions and family allowances considerably.

A variety of sources were used to compile this table. The most useful (and readily available) source to consult is Jacques Bichot, *Les politiques sociales en France au XXe siècle* (Paris: Armand Colin, 1997).

1945   Social Security ordonnances (4 and 19 October). Creation of the régime général (the main pension fund). 70% of population has pension/health coverage by end of 1940s.

1946   Special regimes (pensions, etc.) declared autonomous by parliament. Ensures their survival to this day.

1947   Creation of pension system AGIRC, etc., for *cadres* (highly paid workers).

1948   Pensions for the "non-non" groups (non-salaried, non-agricultural).

1952   Pensions for agricultural workers.

1953   Reform of bureaux de bienfaisance. *Aide sociale* system created (social assistance).

1956   Minimum pension introduced (regardless of contributions made).

1958   Creation of UNEDIC (national unemployment insurance fund).

1961   ARRCO established. Complementary pension system for non-*cadres* (for workers affiliated with the main regime).

1966   Health insurance for the "non-non" groups (see above, 1948). (Confirms, once again, social separatism.)

1967   Social Security system redesigned. Creation of CNAM, CNAV, CNAF.

1971   Loi Boulin. Massive increases to pensions, via recalculation of eligibility and actuarial formula (general pension regime). (Origins of today's pension time-bomb.)

1972   Pension law change; complementary pensions, private sector.

1974   "Compensation démographique" between solvent and insolvent pension regimes introduced (i.e., some funds are raided to bail out insolvent ones).

1975   Law assisting the handicapped passed (finally). Fourth week of paid vacation added.

1981–82 Significant boosts (25 to 50%) to all social spending categories except education, which saw relatively small increases.

1982   Retirement age lowered from sixty-five to sixty. 37.5 years contribution required for full pension. Auroux Laws (governing labor relations, hiring, firing) go into effect.

1983   Hospital sector. "Budget global" introduced, designed to control costs. Fifth week of paid vacation added. Pensions increased by over 25%. Pre-retirement programs enable those aged fifty-five and up to retire early. Boost to family policy and housing. Some of this clawed back in U-Turn. Family allowances cut. Health care cut. Education funding squeezed. Disability benefits cut. Pensions *not* cut.

1988   Revenu Minimum d'Insertion (RMI). Like a form of minimum welfare, for those with no unemployment insurance, and with no other social benefits. Amounts to only a few hundred dollars per month.

1990   Small surtax introduced to fund social security deficits (the CSG).

1993   Balladur reform of private-sector pensions. Now forty years of contributions required, but only in the private sector (not in the public sector and in the special regimes). The main problems not solved.

1997   Loi Thomas, to promote private retirement savings. A baby step which Jospin seem ashamed to promote.

2000   Universal health insurance coverage (remaining 1% of population without coverage included).

2000   Thirty-five-hour work week phased in at the majority of businesses and in the public sector.

2003   Raffarin reforms to public sector pensions. As of 2008, forty years of contributions required for public sector workers (but special pension regimes unchanged). As of 2012, forty-one years required in public and private.

Notes

1 THE MISUNDERSTOOD FRENCH WELFARE STATE

1. Note on the euro: On 1 January 2002, the French adopted the euro. Three months later, the franc was officially laid to rest. The official conversion rate was set (in 2000) at 6.55957 francs per euro (or 0.152449 euros per franc). The chapter title, "The misunderstood French welfare state" is inspired by the title of Theodore R. Marmor, Jerry L. Mashaw and Philip L. Harvey's book, *America's Misunderstood Welfare State: Persistent Myths, Enduring Realities* (New York: Basic Books, 1990). Gorz is quoted from the English translation of the book: André Gorz, *Reclaiming Work: Beyond the Wage-Based Society*, trans. Chris Turner (Cambridge: Polity Press, 1999), p. 16.
2. Emmanuel Todd, *Après l'Empire: Essai sur la décomposition du système américain* (Paris: Gallimard, 2002), pp. 204, 205.
3. Nicole Notat, in Jean de Belot, ed., *Quelle ambition pour la France?* (Paris: Plon, 2002), p. 84.
4. A point stressed by Michel Godet, "Libérer l'activité et l'emploi," in Claude Bébéar, ed., *Le Courage de réformer* (Paris: Odile Jacob, 2002), p. 71.
5. Observatoire national de la pauvreté et de l'exclusion sociale, *Les Travaux de l'Observatoire national de la pauvreté et de l'exclusion sociale, 2001–2002* (Paris: La Documentation Française, 2002), p. 46.
6. See John Tuppen for the 1980s, *Chirac's France, 1986–88* (London: Macmillan, 1991). In many nations, the 10% unemployment threshold would signal a crisis of the highest order, and would lead to a wholesale reform of labor markets – as in the Netherlands, Canada, Britain, Sweden, the USA, etc.
7. World Health Organisation, *World Health Report 2000* (Geneva: WHO, 2000), p. 153 of statistical annex. See also Haut Comité de la Santé Publique, *La Santé des Français, 3e bilan* (Paris: La Découverte, 2002). Ironically, just weeks after the WHO ranked France number one, the leading French medical research group, INSERM, released a report on the persisting inequalities in access to health care and on the persisting links between class and health. See Annette Leclerc et al., INSERM, *Les inégalités sociales de santé* (Paris: La Découverte, 2000).
8. Paul Spicker, "Exclusion and citizenship in France," in Maurice Mullard and Simon Lee, eds., *The Politics of Social Policy in Europe* (Cheltenham, UK: Edward Elgar, 1997), pp. 219–36.

9. "L'image des Etats-Unis ne cesse de se dégrader en France," *Le Monde*, 31 October 1996, p. 2. For American views on France, see Barbara R. Bergmann, *Saving our Children from Poverty: What the United States can Learn from France* (New York: Russell Sage Foundation, 1996); Christopher Pierson, *Beyond the Welfare State: The New Political Economy of Welfare* (University Park, PA: Penn State University Press, 1998); Sheila B. Kamerman, "Child and Family Policies: An International Overview," in Sharon Lynn Kagan and Nancy W. Hall, eds., *Children, Families and Government: Preparing for the Twenty-First Century* (Cambridge: Cambridge University Press, 1996), pp. 31–48.

10. The term "neoliberal" is widely used in Europe and Britain, where "liberal" means laissez-faire, free market, pro-rich.

11. Guillaume La Chaise, *Crise de l'emploi et fractures politiques. Les opinions des Français face au chômage* (Paris: Presses de la Fondation National des Sciences Politiques, 1996), pp. 180–83.

12. There is a clear link between regions with high levels of unemployment and unusually high levels of support for Le Pen. See Zaki Laïdi, "La société française entre l'Europe et la mondialisation," in Robert Fraisse and Jean-Baptiste de Foucauld, eds., *La France en prospectives* (Paris: Odile Jacob, 1996), p. 287.

13. Sebastien Budgen, "The French Fiasco," *New Left Review* 17 (September–October 2002), p. 41.

14. Symbolized by the bestselling book by Nicolas Baverez, *La France qui tombe* (Paris: Perrin, 2003).

15. Baverez, *La France qui tombe*. For a discussion of the Baverez thesis, see "Le 'Portrait Social' de l'Insee contredit l'idée du déclin français," *Le Monde*, 30 October 2003; INSEE, *France, portrait social, 2003–2004* (Paris: INSEE, 2003); Sophie Meunier, "Free-Falling France or Free-Trading France?" *French Politics, Culture and Society* 22, no. 1 (Spring 2004); Alain Duhamel, *Le désarroi français* (Paris: Plon, 2003), and the numerous articles in *Commentaire* 103 (Autumn 2003) and in *Le Débat* 126 (September–October 2003).

16. Michael B. Miller, *The Bon Marché: Bourgeois Culture and the Department Store, 1869–1920* (Princeton: Princeton University Press, 1981).

17. *The Economist*, 22 August 1998, p. 80.

18. Philippe Manière, *La vengeance du peuple. Les élites, Le Pen et les Français* (Paris: Plon, 2002), pp. 28–33; *Le Monde*, 30 October 2003.

19. There have been cuts to these facilities in recent years but to this Canadian author the French family policy scene still appears remarkably generous.

20. On the problems of low-wage full employment, see, among many others, Katherine S. Newman, *No Shame in My Game: The Working Poor in the Inner City* (New York: Vintage Books/Russell Sage Foundation, 1999).

21. Philip H. Gordon and Sophie Meunier, *The French Challenge: Adapting to Globalization* (Washington, DC: Brookings Institution Press, 2001), p. 101; Olivier Duhamel, "Les Français et L'Etat," in Duhamel and Philippe Méchet, eds., *L'état de l'opinion 2000* (Paris: Seuil, 2000), p. 143.

22. For example, Jospin's speech at Epinay, 9 June 2001, quoted in *Le Monde*, 11 June 2001.

23. Gordon and Meunier, *The French Challenge*, p. 101; Sophie Meunier, "The French Exception," *Foreign Affairs* 79, no. 4 (2000).

24. Sophie Ponthieux, INSEE, "La pauvreté en termes de conditions de vie: quatre profils de ménages," *Données sociales. La société française, 2002–2003* (Paris: INSEE, 2002), pp. 417–26; Thomas Choffé, "Social Exclusion: Definition, Public Debate and Empirical Evidence in France," in David G. Mayes, Jos Berghman, and Robert Salais, eds., *Social Exclusion and European Policy* (Cheltenham, UK: Edward Elgar, 2001), pp. 204–29; "La société française et ses fractures," special edition of *Cahiers français* 314, no. 6 (May–June 2003); *Problèmes économiques* 2833 (26 November 2003), edition devoted to the working poor of France.

25. See Assar Lindbeck and Denis Snower, *The Insider–Outsider Theory of Unemployment* (Cambridge, MA: MIT Press, 1988).

26. OECD, *Employment Outlook* (Paris: OECD, June 2000), Tables A, C, G; OECD, *Employment Outlook* (Paris: OECD, July 1997), pp. 63–90; Franz Traxler, "Collective Bargaining and Industrial Change: A Case of Disorganization? A Comparative Analysis of Eighteen OECD Countries," *European Sociological Review* 12 (1996), pp. 271–87.

27. On the revolutionary period, see Alan Forrest, *The French Revolution and the Poor* (New York: St. Martin's, 1981) and Isser Woloch, *The New Regime: Transformations of the French Civic Order, 1789–1820s* (New York: Norton, 1994). On solidarity, see J. E. S. Hayward, "Solidarity: The Social History of an Idea in Nineteenth-Century France," *International Review of Social History* IV (1959), pp. 261–84, and "The Official Social Philosophy of the French Third Republic: Léon Bourgeois and Solidarism," *International Review of Social History* VI (1961), pp. 19–48; Judith F. Stone, *The Search for Social Peace: Reform Legislation in France, 1890–1914* (Albany, NY: SUNY Press, 1985); Allan Mitchell, *The Divided Path: The German Influence on Social Reform in France after 1870* (Chapel Hill, NC: University of North Carolina Press, 1991).

28. Göran Therborn, *Why Some Peoples are More Unemployed than Others* (London: Croom Helm, 1986).

29. Jelle Visser and Anton Hemerijck, *"A Dutch Miracle": Job Growth, Welfare Reform and Corporatism in the Netherlands* (Amsterdam: Amsterdam University Press, 1997).

30. Not one single bureaucratic head rolled due to the Crédit Lyonnais scandal, which continues to cost taxpayers billions of euros.

31. See John S. Ambler, "Preface," and Gary Freeman, "Socialism and Social Security," in Ambler, ed., *The French Socialist Experiment* (Philadelphia: Institute for the Study of Human Issues, 1985).

32. According to a 2001 poll, that figure was 56%: cited in John Andrews, "A Divided Self. A Survey of France," *The Economist*, 16 November 2002, p. 13 of survey.

33. See Bernard Préel, *Le choc des générations* (Paris: La Découverte, 2000). Préel also refers to the "protected people" in an interview with the magazine *Sciences humaines* 108 (August–September 2000), p. 15.

34. Mark Kleinman, *A European Welfare State? European Union Social Policy in Context* (London: Palgrave, 2002), pp. 182–83.
35. Tony Atkinson, Bea Cantillon, Eric Marlier, and Brian Nolan, *Social Indicators: The EU and Social Inclusion* (Oxford: Oxford University Press, 2002), pp. 7–13.
36. INSEE, *France, portrait social. 2000–2001* (Paris: INSEE, 2000), p. 118; Duncan Gallie and Serge Paugam, "The Experience of Unemployment in Europe: The Debate," in Gallie and Paugam, eds., *Welfare Regimes and the Experience of Unemployment in Europe* (Oxford: Oxford University Press, 2000), pp. 1–22.
37. Giuliano Bonoli and Bruno Palier, "From Work to Citizenship? Current Transformations in the French Welfare State," in Jet Bussemaker, ed., *Citizenship and Welfare State Reform in Europe* (London: Routledge, 1999), p. 49.
38. Dominique Méda, *Le travail. Une valeur en voie de disparition* (Paris: Flammarion, 1995); Sophie Pedder, "The Grand Illusion. A Survey of France," *The Economist*, 5 June 1999, p. 11 of survey; Gunnar Trumbull, "France's 35 Hour Work Week: Flexibility through Regulation," Brookings Institution, Washington, DC, *U.S.-France Analysis* (January 2001).
39. See Jean-François Revel's comments on the French tendency to dismiss the USA's state of full employment during the 1990s as a mirage of McJobs in *L'Obsession anti-américaine. Son fonctionnement, ses causes, ses inconséquences* (Paris: Plon, 2002), pp. 44–45.
40. Daniel Cohen, *Richesse du monde, pauvretés des nations* (Paris: Flammarion, 1997), p. 126, passim.
41. Sénat, Les Rapports du Sénat no. 504, Senator Bernard Barbier, reporter, *La persistence du chômage en Europe* (Paris: Senate of France, 1994), pp. 17, 35, 90.
42. Andrews, "A Divided Self. A Survey of France," p. 4.
43. Maurice Mullard, "The Politics of Unemployment in Europe," in Mullard and Lee, eds., *The Politics of Social Policy in Europe*, pp. 65–66.
44. Amartya Sen, *Development as Freedom* (New York: Anchor Books, 1999), p. 95; and Sen, "Inequality, Unemployment and Contemporary Europe," *International Labour Review* 135, no. 2 (1997), pp. 155–72.
45. Alain Degenne and Marie-Odile Lebeaux, "La précarité des jeunes sur le marché du travail," in Salvador Juan and Didier Le Gall, eds., *Conditions et genres de vie. Chroniques d'une autre France* (Paris: L'Harmattan, 2002), p. 39.
46. Premier Ministre to Edmond Malinvaud, 6 April 1998, in Conseil d'Analyse économique, Edmond Malinvaud, reporter, *Les cotisations sociales à la charge des employeurs: analyse économique* (Paris: La Documentation Française, 1998), p. 9.
47. Meunier, "Free-Falling France or Free-Trading France."
48. Valerie Symes, "Unemployment in Europe: A Continuing Crisis," in Valerie Symes, Carl Levy, and Jane Littlewood, eds., *The Future of Europe* (New York: St. Martin's Press, 1997).
49. In 1994, Denis Olivennes published a polemical article called "La préférence française pour le chômage" in the influential journal, *Le Débat*. Alain Minc and the Commissariat Général du Plan used Olivennes' language in their

report of 1994, saying that "France, consciously or not, has chosen unemployment," *La France de l'An 2000: Rapport au Premier Ministre* (Paris: La Documentation Française, 1994). In this instance, I have used the translation of Minc in John Grahl and Paul Teague, "Is the European Social Model Fragmenting?," *New Political Economy* 2, no. 3 (1997), pp. 405–26. Unless otherwise noted, all translations from the French are mine.

50. Sen, "Inequality, Unemployment and Contemporary Europe"; Symes, "Unemployment in Europe"; Stephen Nickell, "Unemployment and Labor Market Rigidities: Europe versus North America," *Journal of Economic Perspectives* 11, no. 3 (1997), pp. 55–74; Will Hutton, *A Declaration of Interdependence: Why America Should Join the World* (New York: Norton, 2003).

51. Daniel Cohen and Pascaline Dupas, "Trajectoires comparées des chômeurs en France et aux Etats-Unis," *Economie et statistique*, no. 332–33 (2000), p. 18; Lawrence Mishel, Jared Bernstein, and John Schmitt, Economic Policy Institute, *The State of Working America, 1998–1999* (Ithaca: Cornell University Press, 1999), ch. 1; Miguel A. Malo, Luis Toharia, and Jérôme Gautié, "France: The Deregulation that Never Existed," in Gøsta Esping-Andersen, ed., *Why Deregulate Labour Markets?* (Oxford: Oxford University Press, 2000), pp. 245–46.

52. Hugues de Jouvenel, "Le travail pourra-t-il financer le protection social demain?", in François Charpentier, ed., *Encyclopédie Protection Sociale. Quelle refondation?* (Paris: Economica, 2000), p. 268; "A manifesto to raise employment," *The Economist*, 20 September 2003, p. 74.

53. See Harold L. Wilensky, *Rich Democracies: Political Economy, Public Policy, and Performance* (Berkeley: University of California Press, 2002), pp. 376–77; Valérie Leselbaum-Stepler, "Le système de retraite," in Jean-Pierre Vesperini, ed., *Les problèmes actuels de l'économie française* (Paris: Presses Universitaires de France, 2001), p. 297, table 10; Nicolas Baverez, "A l'épreuve de la mondialisation," in Roger Fauroux and Bernard Spitz, eds., *Notre état* (Paris: Robert Laffont, 2000), p. 607, on activity rates.

54. For example, Jospin's speech at Epinay, 9 June 2001, quoted in *Le Monde*, 11 June 2001.

55. "Redistribution," editorial, *Alternatives économiques* 218 (October 2003), p. 5.

56. See the August 2003 edition of *Le Monde Diplomatique*. Fully one-third of the feature articles are devoted to criticizing the USA.

57. For example, "Retraites: le complot?", *Force Ouvrière* 8 (July 2002); Lorraine Millot, "Retraites: les allemands capitaliseront," *Libération*, 27–28 January 2001. See also Philippe Manière, *L'Aveuglement français* (Paris: Stock, 1998) and Claude Fouquet, *Délires et défaites. Une histoire intellectuelle de l'exception française* (Paris: Albin Michel, 2000).

58. See John Gray, *False Dawn: The Delusions of Global Capitalism* (London: Granta, 1998); Hutton, *A Declaration of Interdependence: Why America Should Join the World*. The latter is the US version of Hutton's book, *The World We're In*. See also Robert R. Geyer, *Exploring European Social Policy* (Cambridge: Polity Press, 2000).

59. "Germany's Labour-Market Reforms: Something Stirs," *The Economist*, 26 July 2003, p. 48.

60. See Ulrich Beck, *What is Globalization?* (Cambridge: Polity Press, 2000).

61. See Jacob S. Hacker, *The Divided Welfare State: The Battle over Public and Private Social Benefits in the United States* (Cambridge: Cambridge University Press, 2002).

62. This happens in Canada too: see Pat Armstrong and Hugh Armstrong, *Universal Health Care: What the United States can Learn from the Canadian Experience* (New York: New Press, 1998).

63. For a more positive vision of European social policy, see the various work of Linda Hantrais, Vic George, and Peter Taylor-Gooby in the UK and Barbara Bergmann, Alfred Kahn, and Sheila Kamerman in the USA. More specifically, see Hantrais, "France: Squaring the Welfare Triangle," in Vic George and Peter Taylor-Gooby, *European Welfare Policy: Squaring the Welfare Circle* (London: Macmillan, 1996).

64. Edward Luttwak, *Turbo Capitalism: Winners and Losers in the Global Economy* (New York: Harper Collins, 1999); Emmanuel Todd, *L'illusion économique* (Paris: Gallimard, 1998); Philippe d'Iribarne, *La logique de l'honneur. Gestion des entreprises et traditions nationales* (Paris: Seuil, 1989); Michel Albert, *Capitalisme contre capitalisme* (Paris: Seuil, 1990); Michael Porter, *The Competitive Advantage of Nations* (New York: The Free Press, 1990); Charles Hampden-Turner and Alfons Trompenaars, *The Seven Cultures of Capitalism* (New York: Doubleday, 1993).

65. Charles Goldfinger, *Travail et hors travail* (Paris: Odile Jacob, 1998), p. 22; Denis Clerc, *Condamnés au chômage?* (Paris: Syros, 1999), pp. 177–78; Vincent Chriqui, *A qui profite le libéralisme?* (Paris: Edition 1, 2003); pp. 38–64.

66. François Chatagner (*Le Monde*), *La protection sociale. Des réformes inachevées* (Paris: Le Monde, 1998), pp. 115–16.

67. Eileen Ciesla, "Laetitia's Lament," *The American Spectator* (June 2001), pp. 46–52.

68. Aside from the marginalized far-Right, racist fringe, there really is no economic "Right wing" to speak of in most of continental Europe.

69. Peter Katzenstein, *Small States in World Markets* (Ithaca: Cornell University Press, 1985); Assar Lindbeck et. al., eds., *Turning Sweden Around* (Cambridge: Cambridge University Press, 1994); Richard B. Freeman, Robert Topel, and Birgitta Swedenborg, eds., *The Welfare State in Transition: Reforming the Swedish Model* (Chicago: University of Chicago Press, 1997); Mikko Kautto, ed., *Nordic Social Policy: Changing Welfare States* (London: Routledge, 1999); Stig Hadenuis, *Swedish Politics during the Twentieth Century: Conflict and Consensus* (Trelleborg: The Swedish Institute, 1999); Gregg M. Olsen, *The Politics of the Welfare State: Canada, Sweden, and the United States* (Toronto: Oxford University Press, 2002), pp. 35, 41–44.

70. Martin Rhodes, "Globalization and West European Welfare States: A Critical Review of Recent Debates," *Journal of European Social Policy* 6, no. 4 (1996), pp. 305–27 and "Globalization, Labour Markets and Welfare States: A Future of 'Competitive Corporatism'?," in Rhodes and Yves Mény, eds., *The Future of European Welfare: A New Social Contract?* (London: Macmillan, 1998), pp. 178–203.

71. Philip Manow and Eric Seils, "The Employment Crisis of the German Welfare State," in Maurizio Ferrera and Martin Rhodes, eds., *Recasting European Welfare States* (London: Frank Cass, 2000), pp. 137–60.
72. "The Decline of Germany," *Business Week*, 17 February 2003, pp. 18–26.
73. See, for example, the numerous articles in *La Repubblica* and *Il Giornale* on 23 and 24 October 2003. Italians were protesting Berlusconi's plan to require forty years of contributions for a full pension (up from the current thirty-five).
74. Of course, the French intellectual class has no monopoly on anti-globalization doom and gloom. Witness Beck's *What is Globalization?*

2   CORPORATIST WELFARE STATES: THE RESIDUE OF THE PAST, OR THE WAVE OF THE FUTURE?

1. Jonathan Rauch, *Government's End: Why Washington Stopped Working* (New York: Public Affairs, 1994), pp. 154, 141.
2. Thierry Desjardins, *La décomposition française* (Paris: Albin Michel, 2002), p. 33. For the sake of accuracy, many of the people who voted to abolish privilege on the night of 4 August were themselves noble.
3. Michael Ignatieff, *The Rights Revolution* (Toronto: Anansi, 2000), p. 55. Ignatieff's statement refers to civil and political rights, not "social" rights, but it still seems apropos in this context.
4. Esping-Andersen, *The Three Worlds of Welfare Capitalism*; François-Xavier Merrien, *L'Etat-providence* (Paris: Presses Universitaires de France, 1997). For an amusing critique of welfare state typology, see Peter Baldwin, "Can We Define a European Welfare State Model?" in Bent Greve, ed., *Comparative Welfare Systems: The Scandinavian Model in a Period of Change* (London: Macmillan, 1996), pp. 29–44.
5. Maurizio Ferrera, "Il modello Sud-Europeo di welfare state," *Rivista Italiana di Scienza Politica* 1 (1996), pp. 67–101; Gøsta Esping-Andersen, *Social Foundations of Postindustrial Economies* (Oxford: Oxford University Press, 1999), pp. 90, 139–40. To complicate matters further, some scholars argue that the Australian or "Antipodean" welfare regime is a model unto itself. And then there is the East Asian model.
6. Fifteen years ago most English-writing observers would have used the term "corporatist" welfare state to describe France. Since the mid-1990s, Esping-Andersen's "continental conservative" term has also been used.
7. Philippe C. Schmitter and Gerhard Lehmbruch, eds., *Trends toward Capitalist Intermediation* (Beverly Hills: Sage, 1979).
8. Randall A. Hansen, "Against Social Solidarity and Citizenship: Justifying Social Provision in Britain and France," in Jet Bussemaker, ed., *Citizenship and Welfare State Reform in Europe* (London: Routledge, 1999), p. 32. See also Linda Hantrais, "Comparing Family Policy in Britain, France and Germany," *Journal of Social Policy* 23, no. 2 (1994), pp. 135–60.
9. Arthur M. Okun, *Equality and Efficiency, the Big Tradeoff* (Washington, DC: Brookings Institution, 1975), is the classic text on this issue.

10. John S. Ambler, "Ideas, Interests, and the French Welfare State," in Ambler, ed., *The French Welfare State: Surviving Social and Ideological Change* (New York: New York University Press, 1991), p. 26.

11. François de Closets, *Toujours plus!* (Paris: Grasset, 1982).

12. Douglas Ashford, *Policy and Politics in France* (Philadelphia: Temple University Press, 1982), p. 228.

13. The economist Yves Tinard, in his book, *L'Exception française: Pourquoi?* (Paris: Maxima, 2001), pp. 254–55, came close to making this argument, but in the context of a discussion of French resistance to competition and in favor of corporatist/oligarchistic restraints on business.

14. Thierry Tauran, *Les régimes spéciaux de Sécurité sociale* (Paris: Presses Universitaires de France, 2000); Bernard Zimmern, *Les profiteurs de l'état* (Paris: Plon, 2000), ch. 3; Jean-Marie Thiveaud, "Les régimes spéciaux hors régime des fonctionnaires de l'Etat," in Michel Laroque, ed., *Contribution à l'histoire financière de la Sécurité sociale* (Paris: La Documentation Française, 1999), pp. 117–42; Gérard Maudrux, *Retraites. Le mensonge permanent* (Paris: Les Belles Lettres, 2000), passim; François de Closets, *Le compte à rebours* (Paris: Fayard, 1998); Roger Fauroux and Bernard Spitz, eds., *Notre Etat. Le livre vérité de la fonction publique* (Paris: Robert Laffont, 2000). The special pension regimes conform to Mancur Olson's description of special interests in, *The Logic of Collective Action: Public Goods and the Theory of Groups* (Cambridge, MA: Harvard University Press, 1965), but they constitute a much larger group of special interests than he imagined possible.

15. Bernard Zimmern, *La dictature des syndicats* (Paris: Albin Michel, 2003), p. 116. Zimmern, of course, is extreme in his critique of the French state and unions, but he has unearthed a striking amount of material and his source base is reliable – *Cour des comptes* reports, INSEE reports, and the like.

16. See Andrew Jack, *The French Exception: Still so Special?* (London: Profile Books, 1999), pp. 158–59. Somehow Jack got his hands on the secretive EDF employee benefits manual, which the company tries to hide from the public. See also Zimmern, *La dictature des syndicats*, pp. 110–35.

17. "Les salaires de la fonction publique," in INSEE, *France, portrait social, 2003–2004* (Paris: INSEE, 2003), pp. 176–77.

18. For a whole slate of articles detailing the inefficient French public sector, see Fauroux and Spitz, eds., *Notre Etat.*

19. Jacques Chevallier, "Quel avenir pour les services publics 'à la française'?" in Serge Cordellier and Sarah Netter, eds., *L'Etat de la France. 2003* (Paris: La Découverte, 2003), p. 290; Marie-Christine Meininger, "The Development and Current Features of the French Civil Service System," in Hans A. G. M. Bekke and Frits M. van der Meer, eds., *Civil Service Systems in Western Europe* (Cheltenham, UK: Edward Elgar, 2000), pp. 188–211.

20. Sophie Meunier, "Free-Falling France or Free-Trading France?" *French Politics, Culture and Society* 22, no. 1 (Spring 2004).

21. See Walter Trattner, *From Poor Law to Welfare State: A History of Social Welfare in America*, 4th edn. (New York: The Free Press, 1989), chs. 6, 7, 10; Michael Katz, *In the Shadow of the Poorhouse: A Social History of Welfare in America* (New York: Basic Books, 1996), ch. 5.

22. Timothy B. Smith, *Creating the Welfare State in France, 1880–1940* (Montreal and Kingston: McGill-Queen's University Press, 2003). Full of nuts and bolts but not the most riveting read.

23. A point stressed by Colette Bec, *L'assistance en démocratie: les politiques assistancielles dans la France des XIXe et XXe siècles* (Paris: Belin, 1998) and by Bruno Palier, *Gouverner la sécurité sociale: Les réformes du système français de protection sociale depuis 1945* (Paris: Presses Universitaires de France, 2002).

24. Jean-Jacques Becker and Serge Berstein, *Victoire et frustrations, 1914–1929* (Paris: Seuil, 1990), p. 150; Young-sun Hong, *Welfare, Modernity, and the Weimar State, 1919–1933* (Princeton: Princeton University Press, 1998); Jurgen Kocka, *Facing Total War: German Society, 1914–1918*, trans. Barbara Weinberger (Leamington Spa, UK: Berg, 1984); Detlev J. K. Peukert, *The Weimar Republic: The Crisis of Classical Modernity*, trans. Richard Deveson (New York: Hill and Wang, 1989), ch. 6.

25. Tauran, *Les régimes spéciaux de Sécurité sociale.*

26. Susan Pedersen, *Family, Dependence, and the Origins of the Welfare State: Britain and France, 1914–1945* (Cambridge: Cambridge University Press, 1993).

27. Smith, *Creating the Welfare State in France*, ch. 3.

28. Conseil supérieur de l'assistance publique (CSAP) 127, séance du 25 juin 1925, p. 50.

29. CSAP 126 (1925), Annexe V, "Rapport sur l'assistance aux classes moyennes," p. 139.

30. See Rosemary Stevens, *In Sickness and in Wealth: American Hospitals in the Twentieth Century* (New York: Basic Books, 1989); Paul Starr, *The Social Transformation of American Medicine* (New York: Basic Books, 1982); Steven Cherry, *Medical Services and the Hospitals in Britain, 1860–1939* (Cambridge: Cambridge University Press, 1996), p. 57; Timothy B. Smith, "The Social Transformation of Hospitals and the Rise of Medical Insurance in France, 1914–1943," *The Historical Journal* 41, no. 4 (December 1998), pp. 1055–87.

31. M. Gauguery, "Les assurances sociales et les établissements hospitaliers," *Revue des hôpitaux* (1928), p. 381.

32. Jean-Jacques Lerosier and Maurice Baslé, "Les premières lois sociales," *Revue française des affaires sociales* 35, no. 1 (January–March 1981), p. 232.

33. Lerosier and Baslé, "Les premières lois sociales," p. 233; Jean-Marie Clément, *La mutation de l'hôpital, 1900–2000* (Paris: Berger-Levrault, 2001).

34. Paul Dutton, *Origins of the French Welfare State: The Struggle for Social Reform in France, 1914–1947* (Cambridge: Cambridge University Press, 2002), p. 219.

35. Philippe-Jean Hesse, "Les assurances sociales," in Philippe-Jean Hesse and Jean-Pierre Le Crom, eds., *La protection sociale sous le régime de Vichy* (Rennes: Presses Universitaires de Rennes, 2001), pp. 78–79.

36. Andrew Shennan, *Rethinking France: Plans for Renewal, 1940–1946* (Oxford: Oxford University Press, 1989), pp. 215–16; H. C. Galant, *Histoire politique de la sécurité sociale française, 1945–1952* (Paris: Armand Colin, 1955), pp. 29–38; Pierre Laroque, *Au service de l'homme et du droit. Souvenirs et réflexions*

(Paris: l'Association pour l'étude de l'histoire de la sécurité sociale, 1993); Nicole Kerschen, "L'influence du rapport Beveridge sur le plan français de Sécurité sociale de 1945," in Rencontres d'Oxford, *Comparer les systèmes de protection sociale en Europe* vol. I (Paris, 1994), pp. 127–59.

37. See Eric Jabbari's forthcoming book with Oxford University Press on Pierre Laroque and the post-Second World War welfare state in France.

38. Peter Baldwin, *The Politics of Social Solidarity: Class Bases of the European Welfare State, 1875–1975* (Cambridge: Cambridge University Press, 1990), pp. 185–86.

39. For a detailed account of the defeat of solidaristic reform see Baldwin, *The Politics of Social Solidarity*, pp. 163–86.

40. Ibid., p. 185.

41. G. Viatte, "Qui paie les charges sociales?" *Droit Social* (January 1951), pp. 41–42.

42. Georges Rottier and Jean-François Albert, "The Social Services and Income Redistribution in France," in Alan T. Peacock, ed., *Income Redistribution and Social Policy* (London: Cape, 1954), p. 129; Musée Social, Paris, 37.444, *Rapport concernant le fonctionnement des Services de la Caisse nationale de Sécurité sociale pendant l'année 1951*, dactylo report; "Le déficit budgétaire s'accroît," *Le Monde*, 31 March 1951. On postwar politics see Richard Vinen, *Bourgeois Politics in France, 1945–1951* (Cambridge: Cambridge University Press, 1995).

43. Musée Social, Paris, 52.088, Fédération nationale des organismes de Sécurité sociale, *Guide de l'assuré social* (Paris: FNOSS, 1963), p. 19.

44. Quoted in Jane Jenson, "The Liberation and New Rights for French Women," in Margaret Randolph Higonnet et. al., *Behind the Lines: Gender and the Two World Wars* (New Haven: Yale University Press, 1987), pp. 274–75. See also Claire Duchen, *Women's Rights and Women's Lives in France, 1944–1968* (London: Routledge, 1994), ch. 1.

45. Duchen, *Women's Rights and Women's Lives in France*, p. 143.

46. François Chatagner (Le Monde), *La protection sociale* (Paris: Le Monde, 1998), p. 211.

47. Wallace C. Peterson, *The Welfare State in France* (Lincoln, NB: University of Nebraska Press, 1960), p. 25.

48. Archives de l'Assistance Publique, Paris (AAP) B-6678/18, Ministère du Travail, *Social Security in France* (Paris: La Documentation Française, n.d., 1965?), p. 104.

49. Nicolas Tanti-Hardouin, *L'hospitalisation privée. Crise identitaire et mutation sectorielle* (Paris: La Documentation Française, 1996). A classic defense of corporatist privilege (in this case, public sector pensions and social benefits) is the editorial in *Syndicalisme, Fonction Publique* 184 (July 2003), p. 1. A CFTC publication.

50. Pierre Laroque, "La sécurité sociale de 1944 à 1951," *Revue française des affaires sociales* 2 (April–June 1971), p. 14; Elise Feller, "L'entrée en politique d'un groupe d'âge: la lutte des pensionnés de l'Etat dans l'entre-deux-guerres et la construction d'un 'modèle français' de retraite," *Le Mouvement Social* 190 (January–March 2000), pp. 33–59.

51. Roger Magraw, *France 1815–1914: The Bourgeois Century* (London: Fontana, 1983), p. 298.

52. Commissariat général du plan, *Vieillir demain* (Paris: La Documentation Française, 1980), p. 40; Tauran, *Les régimes spéciaux de Sécurité sociale*; B. Cochemé and F. Legros, *Les retraites: genèse, acteurs, enjeux* (Paris: Armand Colin, 1995); Francis Netter, "Les retraites en France au cours de la période 1895–1945," 2 parts, *Droit social* 7–8 and 9–10 (July-August and September-October 1965).

53. Michel Dreyfus, *Liberté, égalité, mutualité. Mutualisme et syndicalisme (1852–1967)* (Paris: Les Editions de l'Atelier, 2001), pp. 149–53.

54. Adam Steinhouse, *Workers' Participation in Post-Liberation France* (Lanham, MD: Lexington Books, 2001).

55. See Margaret Weir and Theda Skocpol, "State Structures and the Possibilities for 'Keynesian' Responses to the Great Depression in Sweden, Britain, and the United States," in Peter Evans, Dietrich Rueschemeyer, and Theda Skocpol, eds., *Bringing the State Back In* (Cambridge: Cambridge University Press, 1985), pp. 107–63; and Weir, "Ideas and Politics: The Acceptance of Keynesianism in Britain and the United States," in Peter A. Hall, ed., *The Political Power of Economic Ideas: Keynesianism across Nations* (Princeton: Princeton University Press, 1989), pp. 53–86.

56. Baldwin, *The Politics of Social Solidarity*; Peter Gourevitch, *Politics in Hard Times: Comparative Responses to International Economic Crises* (Ithaca: Cornell University Press, 1986).

57. Dutton, *Origins of the French Welfare State*, p. 224.

58. The historiography of the German welfare state tends to display a similar "crypto-deterministic bias." See R. Mayntz and F. W. Scharpf, "Der Ansatz des akteurzentrierten Institutionalismus," in their edited volume, *Gesellschaftliche Selbstregulung und politische Steuerung* (Frankfurt: Campus, 1995), p. 45.

59. On this "social" movement, there are, among others, Alain Touraine et al., ed., *Le grand refus, réflexions sur la grève de décembre 1995* (Paris: Fayard, 1996); Jean-Pierre Le Goff and Alain Caillé, *Le tournant de décembre* (Paris: La Découverte, 1996); Henri Vacquin and Yvon Minvielle, *Le sens d'un colère* (Paris: Stock, 1996); Jacques Julliard, *La faute aux élites* (Paris: Gallimard, 1997); de Closets, *Le compte à rebours*; Sophie Béroud, René Mouriaux, and Michel Vakaloulis, *Le mouvement social en France. Essai de sociologie politique* (Paris: La Dispute, 1998); and Claude Leneveu and Michel Vakaloulis, eds., *Faire mouvement. Novembre-décembre 1995* (Paris: Presses Universitaires de France, 1998). The journal *Espace social européen* provided some of the best minute-by-minute coverage of the crisis, in late 1995 and early 1996.

60. See Sidney Tarrow, *Power in Movement: Social Movements and Contentious Politics* (Cambridge: Cambridge University Press, 1998); and see *French Politics and Society* during 1996.

61. Dani Rodrik, *Has Globalization Gone Too Far?* (Washington, DC: Institute for International Economics, 1997), p. 1.

62. Philip H. Gordon and Sophie Meunier, *The French Challenge: Adapting to Globalization* (Washington, DC: Brookings Institution Press, 2001), p. 74.

See *Le Monde Diplomatique*'s portrayal of the strikes in the January and February 1996 editions.

63. Gilles Heuré, "La France est-elle 'out'?" *Espace social européen* (15 December 1995), pp. 28–29.
64. Marie-Thérèse Join-Lambert et. al., *Politiques sociales*, 2nd edn. (Paris: Presses de la Fondation Nationale des Sciences Politiques and Dalloz, 1997), p. 63; Bruno Palier, "A 'liberal' dynamic in the transformation of the French social welfare system," in Jochen Clasen, ed., *Social Insurance in Europe* (Bristol: Policy Press, 1997), p. 95.
65. On the subsidy given to the SNCF to fund retirement at fifty to fifty-five, see "Les scandales des caisses de retraite," and "La France des privilèges," *L'Expansion* 672 (February 2003), pp. 50–55.
66. Center Left by French standards; far Left by North American and British standards.
67. "Le bilan de la gauche restera marqué par la mise en place de la couverture maladie universelle," *Le Monde*, 7 May 2002.
68. Andrew Knapp, "What's Left of the French Right? The RPR and the UDF from Conquest to Humiliation, 1993–1998," *West European Politics* 22, no. 3 (July 1999), p. 121.
69. For this type of argument, see the discussion in Jean-Marie Domenach, "Interdits égoïstes et revendications morales," *French Politics and Society* 14, no. 1 (Winter 1996), pp. 1–3.
70. John Ambler, "Ideas, Interests and the French Welfare State," in Ambler, ed., *The French Welfare State*, p. 25.
71. Bourdieu, quoted in Gilles Heuré, Pascal Beau, and Christophe Vanackère, Espace Social Européen/Observatoire Européen de la Protection Sociale, *Le Siècle du social* (Paris: ESE, 2000), p. 170. For similar statements, see Bourdieu's two small books: *Contre-feux: Propos pour servir à la résistance contre l'invasion néo-libérale* (Paris: Raisons d'Agir, 1998) and *Contre-feux 2: Pour un mouvement social européen* (Paris: Raisons d'Agir, 2001).
72. Quoted in Catherine Mills, ed., *Protection sociale: quelle réforme?* A special edition of *Sociétés & Représentations* (September 1999), p. 301.
73. Cédric Mathiot, "Les 'seigneurs du rail' en leur royaume. Ils se sentent plus appartenir à leur métier qu'à la SNCF," *Libération*, 16 April 2002.
74. Julien Duval et. al., *Le "décembre" des intellectuels français* (Paris: Editions Liber-Raisons d'Agir, 1998); Mills, *Protection sociale: quelle réforme?*, pp. 300–04.
75. Adam Gopnik, *Paris to the Moon* (New York: Random House, 2000), pp. 31–32.
76. Jonah D. Levy, "France: Directing Adjustment?", in Fritz Scharpf and Vivien Schmidt, eds., *Welfare and Work in the Open Economy: Diverse Responses to Common Challenges*, vol. II (Oxford: Oxford University Press, 2000), pp. 308–50.
77. Jonah D. Levy, "Partisan Politics and Welfare Adjustment: The Case of France," *Journal of European Public Policy* (2001); Martin Rhodes, "The Political Economy of Social Pacts: 'Competitive Corporatism' and European Welfare Reform," in Paul Pierson, ed., *The New Politics of the Welfare State*

(Oxford: Oxford University Press, 2001), pp. 165–94; Paul Pierson, *Dismantling the Welfare State? Reagan, Thatcher, and the Politics of Retrenchment* (New York: Cambridge University Press, 1994).

78. Palier, *Gouverner la sécurité sociale*, p. 368; Giuliano Bonoli, "Pension Politics in France: Patterns of Cooperation and Conflict in Two Recent Reforms," *West European Politics* 20, no. 4 (1997), pp. 160–81; Mark Vail, "The Better Part of Valour: The Politics of French Welfare Reform," *Journal of European Social Policy* 9, no. 4 (1999), pp. 311–29.

79. From his editorial in *Droit social* 3 (March 1996), p. 755, n. 21. For an example of what Dupeyroux means, see *Le Monde*, 30 November 1995 (for a reprint of the magazine *Esprit*'s petition) and 6 December 1995 (for Pierre Bourdieu's petition). Both are printed in Duval et al., *Le "décembre" des intellectuels français*.

80. The full citation is: Alain Touraine, "L'ombre d'un mouvement," in Touraine et al., eds., *Le grand refus*, pp. 66–67. This 100-page article is probably the best critique of the selfish motives of those who led the anti-Juppé strikes.

81. Touraine, "L'ombre d'un mouvement," pp. 44–45.

82. Payroll taxes were slightly higher ten years ago and the overall tax burden is slightly lower. Other taxes (the CSG) have been added to offset the reduction in payroll taxes.

83. Similarly, the SNCF took over 1.16 billion euros from other pension regimes (its transfer) in 2000. See the report by the Cour des comptes, *La sécurité sociale* (Paris: Les Editions des Journaux Officiels, September 2002), p. 136.

84. On these perks and privileges, see the scathing critiques by Maudrux, *Retraites. Le mensonge permanent*; Zimmern, *Les profiteurs de l'Etat*, and Zimmern's second installment, *Les fabricants du chômage* (Paris: Plon, 2002); Louis Bériot, *Abus de bien public* (Paris: Plon, 1999); and Christian Julienne, *Le diable est-il libéral?* (Paris: Les Belles Lettres, 2001); Desjardins, *La décomposition française*, p. 148.

85. For examples of what I mean, see the interview with Denis Cohen, labor leader with the CGT, in "Les attentes qui ont mené à l'éviction de Jospin demeurent," *Le Monde*, 3 October 2002; "Les anciens du mouvement de 1995 réactivent leurs réseaux," *Le Monde*, 3 October 2002; "Journée test pour le gouvernement Raffarin," *Le Monde*, 3 October 2002; "Le gouvernement face à son premier mouvement social," *Le Figaro*, 3 October 2002; "EDF et GDF recherchent 60 à 70 milliards d'euros pour payer la retraite de leurs agents," *Le Monde*, 23 November 2002; "100,000 défenseurs des services publics défilent en France," *Le Figaro*, 26 November 2002.

86. John Andrews, "A Divided Self. A Survey of France," *The Economist*, 16 November 2002, p. 13. Conforming to a long tradition, some would argue. See Charles Tilly, *The Contentious French: Four Centuries of Popular Struggle* (Cambridge, MA: Harvard University Press, 1986).

87. The "frozen" and "defrosting" images are from Esping-Andersen and Palier, respectively. Giuliano Bonoli and Bruno Palier, "From work to citizenship? Current transformations in the French welfare state," in Bussemaker, ed., *Citizenship and Welfare State Reform in Europe*, pp. 42–43; Gøsta Esping-Andersen, ed., *Welfare States in Transition* (London: SAGE, 1996); Pierre

Rosanvallon, *La nouvelle question sociale: Repenser l'Etat-providence* (Paris: Seuil, 1995); Bruno Palier, "'Defrosting' the French Welfare State," in Maurizio Ferrera and Martin Rhodes, eds., *Recasting European Welfare States* (London: Frank Cass, 2000); Palier, "De la crise aux réformes de l'Etat-providence," *Revue française de sociologie* 43, no. 2 (2002), pp. 243–75. For the idea that the French welfare state divides the French as much as it unites them, see "Dossier: La France des Privilèges," *L'Expansion* 672 (February 2003), pp. 81–93. This magazine contains a full list of the various perks, exonerations, and tax breaks available to public-sector workers and special regime members.

88. Commissariat Général du Plan, Rapport de la Commission Protection Sociale, René Teulade, president, *Protection sociale. Xème Plan, 1989–1992* (Paris: La Documentation Française, 1989), p. 28. Hereafter cited as the "Teulade Report."

89. Teulade Report, p. 79.

90. Brink Lindsey, *Against the Dead Hand: The Uncertain Struggle for Global Capitalism* (New York: John Wiley & Sons, 2002), p. 217, has an excellent discussion of corporatist selfishness.

91. See Vivien A. Schmidt, *The Futures of European Capitalism* (Oxford: Oxford University Press, 2002).

92. On the barriers to job creation in Europe, see OECD, *The OECD Jobs Study* (Paris: OECD, 1994) and the regular OECD Country Surveys.

93. Bruno Palier, "Les différents modèles de protection sociale et leur impact sur les réformes nationales," in Christine Daniel and Bruno Palier, eds., *La protection sociale en Europe. Le temps des réformes* (Paris: La Documentation Française, 2001), pp. 33–46; Frank L. Wilson, *Interest Group Politics in France* (New York: Cambridge University Press, 1987); David Wilsford, "Path Dependency, or Why History Makes it Difficult but Not Impossible to Reform Health Care Systems in a Big Way," *Journal of Public Policy* 14, no. 3 (1994), pp. 251–83; Richard Rose, "Inheritance before Choice in Public Policy," *Journal of Theoretical Politics* 2, no. 3 (1990), pp. 263–90; Serge Paugam and François-Xavier Schweyer, "Transformations et inerties de l'Etat-providence," in Olivier Galland and Yannick Lemel, eds., *La nouvelle société française. Trente ans de mutation* (Paris: Armand Colin, 1998), pp. 146–80; David Wilsford, "Tactical Advantages versus Administrative Heterogeneity: The Strengths and Limits of the French State," *Comparative Political Studies* 21, no. 1 (April 1998); Michel Laroque, "L'administration de l'état providence," *Pouvoirs* 94 (2000), pp. 59–72

94. Jean-Daniel Reynaud, *Les règles du jeu. L'action collective et la régulation sociale* 3rd ed. (Paris: Armand Colin, 1997).

95. Gérard Moatti, "La France du 'quant-à-soi,'" *Sociétal* 39, no. 1 (2003), p. 3.

96. On the apparently positive effects of corporatism, see Harold L. Wilensky et al., "Comparative Social Policy: Theories, Methods, Findings," in Meinolf Dierkes et al., eds., *Comparative Policy Research: Learning from Experience* (Aldershot, UK: Gower, 1987), pp. 381–457. For a negative view, see Mattéi Dogan and Dominique Pélassy, *Le Moloch en Europe. Etatisation et corporatisation* (Paris: Economica, 1987). The key authors in the French case are Philippe Schmitter, Suzanne Berger, John Keeler, and Martin Schain.

97. AAP, B-6678/18, Ministère du Travail, *Social Security in France*, p. 75.
98. On this theme, Bruno Palier's excellent book is essential: *Gouverner la sécurité sociale*, p. 208, passim.
99. Inspection Générale des Affaires Sociales, *Tutelle et contrôle dans le domaine social. Rapport 1985–1986* (Paris: La Documentation Française, 1986), p. 28.
100. Rodney Lowe, *The Welfare State in Britain since 1945*, 2nd edn. (London: Macmillan, 1999), p. 298; Denis Clerc, *Condamnés au chômage?* (Paris: Syros, 1999), p. 53.
101. David Wilsford, "The State and the Medical Profession in France," in Frederic W. Hafferty and John B. McKinlay, eds., *The Changing Medical Profession* (New York: Oxford University Press, 1993), pp. 125–26.
102. Interview with Bruno Palier, in Palier, "A 'liberal' dynamic in the transformation of the French social welfare system," p. 102. For a classic apologia for the public sector's special pension perks see Editorial, *Syndicalisme, Fonction Publique* 184 (July 2003), p. 1.
103. In Palier, "A 'liberal' dynamic in the transformation of the French social welfare system," p. 102. For a critique of corporatist selfishness, see Moatti, "La France du 'quant-à-soi,'" p. 3.
104. Douglas E. Ashford, "The British and French Social Security Systems: Welfare States by Intent and by Default," in Ashford and Kelley, eds., *Nationalizing Social Security*, p. 269.
105. On the CSG, Palier, *Gouverner la sécurité sociale*, is fundamental.
106. Olivier Galland, *Les jeunes* (Paris: La Découverte, 1996), pp. 95–105. On the ignorance of the demographic structure of the nation, Brigitte Baccaïni and Léon Gani, "Concurrence ou solidarité entre 'jeunes' et 'vieux': les attitudes des lycéens en France," *Population* 5 (September–October 1997), pp. 1083–118, esp. p. 1086.
107. Jean Pisani-Ferry, *La bonne aventure. Le plein emploi, le marché, la gauche* (Paris: La Découverte, 2001), p. 37; "Economie" section, *Le Figaro*, 24 April 1996.
108. *Le Monde*, 27 February 2001, "Emploi" section, p. ix.
109. Polly Platt, *French or Foe?* 2nd edn. (London: Culture Crossings, 1998), p. 93.
110. Schmidt, *The Futures of European Capitalism*, pp. 84–85, passim; Vivien A. Schmidt, "The Politics of Adjustment in France and Britain: When Does Discourse Matter?," *Journal of European Public Policy* 8 (2001), pp. 247–64.
111. Andrews, "A Divided Self," p. 17 of survey.
112. "60% approuvent la mobilisation," *Libération*, 12 May 2003.
113. Paul Pierson, "Post-industrial Pressures on the Mature Welfare States," in Pierson, ed., *The New Politics of the Welfare State* (Oxford: Oxford University Press, 2001), pp. 82–104.
114. Interview with Marc Blondel, "Les Retraites: Je prends le dossier en main personnellement," *Le Parisien*, 2 December 2002; "Entretien avec Marc Blondel," *Le Monde*, 26 May 2003.
115. See "Retraites: le complot?" *Force Ouvrière* 8 (July 2002).
116. Jean-Jacques Chavigné and Gérard Filoche, *Retraites. Réponse au MEDEF* (Paris: Ramsay, 2001), p. 246.

117. Béatrice Majnoni d'Intignano, "Commentaire," in Conseil d'Analyse économique, Premier Ministre, Rapports, Olivier Davanne et al., *Retraites et épargne* (Paris: La Documentation Française, 1998), pp. 81–82; Majnoni d'Intignano, *La protection sociale* (Paris: Editions de Fallois, 1997), pp. 237–42.

118. "78% des Français favorables aux manifestations," *Le Parisien*, 28 January 2001; "Les cinq syndicats s'unissent pour défendre les retraites," *Le Monde*, 6 January 2001.

3   THE "TREASON OF THE INTELLECTUALS": GLOBALIZATION AS THE BIG EXCUSE FOR FRANCE'S ECONOMIC AND SOCIAL PROBLEMS

1. Quoted in Philip H. Gordon and Sophie Meunier, *The French Challenge: Adapting to Globalization* (Washington, DC: Brookings Institution Press, 2001), p. 74.

2. François de Closets, in *Le Compte à rebours* (Paris: Fayard, 1998), p. 41.

3. The most recent author to employ a spin on the "treason of the intellectuals" term is Jean-Claude Guillebaud, *La trahison des lumières. Enquête sur le désarroi contemporain* (Paris: Seuil, 1995).

4. Douglas Ashford, *Policy and Politics in France: Living With Uncertainty* (Philadelphia: Temple University Press, 1982), p. 230.

5. Gérard Lattès and Pierre Volovitch, "La protection sociale," *INSEE Première* 461 (June 1996), p. 1. Also available at www.insee.fr, and reprinted in Michel Laroque, ed., *Contribution à l'histoire financière de la Sécurité sociale* (Paris: La Documentation Française, 1999), pp. 51–23; Raymond Soubie, Commissariat général du plan, *Santé 2010. Equité et efficacité du système* (Paris: La Documentation Française, 1993), vol. III, p. 48.

6. Ashford, *Policy and Politics in France*, p. 230; Jean-Christophe Ulmer, in the newspaper *Libération*, 23 August 1994, quoted in Guillebaud, *La trahison des lumières*, p. 58. Economic nationalist Canadians have also constructed their identity around anti-Americanism. See the work of Maude Barlow, Richard Gwyn, Linda McQuaig, and James Laxer, as well as the more serious work of Gary Teeple, *Globalization and the Decline of Social Reform: Into the Twenty-First Century* (Aurora, Ont.: Garamond Press, 2000).

7. See "L'image des Etats-Unis ne cesse de se dégrader en France," *Le Monde*, 31 October 1996, p. 2; "Du modèle 'bismarckien' au modèle 'béveridgien,'" *Le Monde*, 22 March 2000; Hubert Védrine, *France in an Age of Globalization* (Washington, DC: Brookings Institution, 2001); Jean-François Revel, *L'obsession anti-américaine: Son fonctionnement, ses causes, ses inconséquences* (Paris: Plon, 2002); Philippe Roger, *L'Ennemi américain. Généalogie de l'antiaméricanisme français* (Paris: Seuil, 2002); Tony Judt, "Anti-Americans Abroad," *New York Review of Books* I, no. 7 (1 May 2003), pp. 24–27.

8. See, for example, "Le Conseil national des villes veut éviter les effets pervers 'à l'américaine,'" *Le Monde*, 7 November 1997. See also Philip H. Gordon and Sophie Meunier, "Globalization and French Cultural Identity," *French Politics, Culture & Society* 19, no. 1 (Spring 2001), pp. 22–41.

9. "Les altermondialistes défilent dans le calme à Annemasse," *Le Figaro*, 2 June 2003.

10. "Une menace ou une chance?" *Le Monde*, 19 July 2001. These statistics are from a Sofres poll. See Gordon and Meunier, *The French Challenge*, pp. 2, 119–20, for a discussion of these opinion polls.

11. "France's public sector," *The Economist*, 26 May 2001, p. 50.

12. "Conservative" by French standards, chameleon by any nation's standards!

13. Gordon and Meunier, *The French Challenge*, pp. 2–3. Since 2001, the *New York Times* has indeed published many more articles on the topic. For a discussion of this, see *The Nation*, 1 December 2003.

14. Quoted in Gordon and Meunier, *The French Challenge*, p. 3.

15. For a sample of one particular labor union's militant anti-globalization rhetoric, see Jean-Michel Denis, "Les syndicalistes de SUD-PTT: des entrepreneurs de morale?," *Sociologie du travail* 45, no. 3 (2003), p. 318.

16. Both Michelet and de Gaulle are quoted in Robert Gildea, *The Past in French History* (New Haven: Yale University Press, 1994), pp. 112, 138.

17. John Gillingham, *European Integration, 1950–2003: Superstate or New Market Economy?* (Cambridge: Cambridge University Press, 2003), p. 383; Philippe Legrain, *Open World: The Truth about Globalisation* (London: Abacus, 2002).

18. Quoted in Philippe Manière, *L'Aveuglement français. Le libéralisme contre la régression sociale* (Paris: Stock, 1998), p. 33.

19. Those who do not read French can consult, for example, the anti-American, anti-globalization articles by Bernard Cassen and Serge Halimi in the May 1997 issue of *Le Monde Diplomatique*, translated and reprinted in Frank J. Lechner and John Boli, eds., *The Globalization Reader* (Oxford: Blackwell, 2000).

20. Philippe Manière, *La vengeance du peuple. Les élites, Le Pen et les Français* (Paris: Plon, 2002), p. 139.

21. Vivien A. Schmidt, *From State to Market? The Transformation of French Business and Government* (Cambridge: Cambridge University Press, 1996), p. 437.

22. Erik Izraelewicz, *Ce monde qui nous attend* (Paris: Grasset, 1997).

23. Ignacio Ramonet, *Géopolitique du chaos* (Paris: Gallimard, 1997), p. 120.

24. Peter Baldwin, *The Politics of Social Solidarity: Class Bases of the European Welfare State, 1875–1975* (Cambridge: Cambridge University Press, 1990); David Vincent, *Poor Citizens: The State and the Poor in Twentieth-Century Britain* (London: Longman, 1991); P. E. Bryden, *Planners and Politicians: Liberal Politics and Social Policy, 1957–1968* (Montreal and Kingston: McGill-Queen's University Press, 1997).

25. Viviane Forrester, *L'Horreur économique* (Paris: Fayard, 1996).

26. As Jacques Généreux argues in a critique of *The Economic Horror*, the "horror" is political, not economic: *Une raison d'espérer. L'horreur n'est pas économique, elle est politique* (Paris: Plon, 1997).

27. Peter Karl Kresl and Sylvain Gallais, *France Encounters Globalization* (Cheltenham, UK: Edward Elgar, 2002), p. 6.

28. Kresl and Gallais, *France Encounters Globalization*, p. 6. Forrester's sequel to *The Economic Horror* was *Une étrange dictature* (Paris: Fayard, 2000).

29. For examples of this, see Pierre Rosanvallon, "France: The New Anti-Capitalism," *Correspondence* 7 (Winter 2000–2001); Bernard Cassen, "Non, la mondialisation n'est pas 'heureuse,'" *Le Monde*, 24 August 2001; Gordon and Meunier, *The French Challenge*, pp. 1–3 discuss anti-Americanism in the French media.

30. On the poverty of nationalist-protectionist approaches to globalization, see Gavin Kitching, *Seeking Social Justice through Globalization* (University Park, PA: Penn State Press, 2001), esp. pp. 242–43 and *Le Figaro*, 12 June 2001. On France and protectionism, see Jagdish Bhagwati, "The Poverty of Protectionism," in his *A Stream of Windows: Unsettling Reflections on Trade, Immigration, and Democracy* (Cambridge, MA: MIT Press, 1998), pp. 75–91.

31. "Les altermondialistes embarrassent le PS," *Le Figaro*, 12 August 2003; "Après Larzac," *Le Monde*, 11 August 2003.

32. "Jean-Pierre Chevènement se pose en candidat de l'antimondialisation," *Le Monde*, 28 May 2001.

33. See my article on this theme, "The Ideology of Charity, the Image of the English Poor Law, and Debates over the Right to Assistance in France, 1830–1905," *The Historical Journal* 40, no. 4 (December 1997), pp. 997–1032.

34. Neil Nevitte, *The Decline of Deference: Canadian Value Change in Cross-National Perspective* (Toronto: Broadview Press, 1996), p. 98.

35. Quoted in Gordon Wright, *France in Modern Times*, 5th edn. (New York: Norton, 1995), p. 435.

36. On the conflict between change and stasis, see Virginia Postrel, *The Future and its Enemies: The Growing Conflict over Creativity, Enterprise, and Progress* (New York: The Free Press, 1998).

37. Jospin, speech at Epinay, 9 June 2001, quoted in *Le Monde*, 11 June 2001.

38. Philippe Frémeaux, *Sortir du piège. La gauche face à la mondialisation* (Paris: Plon, 1998); Jacques Commaille, *Les nouveaux enjeux de la question sociale* (Paris, Hachette, 1997), pp. 59–67.

39. A point emphasized by Anton Brender, *La France face à la mondialisation* (Paris: La Découverte, 2002), p. 120. See also Jean-Pierre Le Goff and Alain Caillé, *Le Tournant de décembre* (Paris: La Découverte, 1996).

40. See the magazine *Politis* 734 (2003). The cover story was called "Retraites. Préserver la solidarité."

41. For an example of how pension reform gets caught up in discussions of different types of "civilization," see Lorraine Millot, "Retraites: les allemands capitaliseront," *Libération*, 27–28 January 2001. More generally, there is Manière, *L'Aveuglement français*; Claude Fouquet, *Délires et défaites. Une histoire intellectuelle de l'exception française* (Paris: Albin Michel, 2000); and Thierry Leterre, *La gauche et la peur libérale* (Paris: Presses de Sciences Po, 2000).

42. Pierre Khalfa and Pierre-Yves Chanu, *Les retraites au péril du libéralisme* (Paris: Editions Syllepse, 2000), esp. pp. 17–18.

43. For cliché-views of the USA, see Emmanuel Todd, *Après l'Empire: Essai sur la décomposition du système américain* (Paris: Gallimard, 2002), *L'invention de l'Europe* (Paris: Seuil, 1990), *La nouvelle France* (Paris: Seuil, 1988) and *L'illusion économique* (Paris: Gallimard, 1998); Pierre Bourdieu, ed., *La Misère du monde* (Paris: Seuil, 1993); and some of the essays in Remi Lenoir,

ed., CREDHESS, *Société & Représentations* 5 (December 1997), special edition, "Le social en questions."

44. Philippe Labarde and Bernard Maris, *La Bourse ou la Vie: La grande manipulation des petits actionnaires* (Paris: Albin Michel, 2000).

45. See Marc Blondel's editorials in *Force Ouvrière (Hebdomadaire)*: 2615, 7 May 2003; 2619, 4 June 2003; 2621, 18 June 2003, and his book *Qu'est-ce que Force Ouvrière?* (Paris: L'Archipel, 2002).

46. David Miliband, "Ne pas caricaturer la 'troisième voie,'" *Le Monde*, 25 November 1999.

47. Christian Saint-Etienne, *L'Etat mensonger* (Paris: Les Belles Lettres, 1996); Laurent Joffrin, *La Régression française* (Paris: Seuil, 1992), p. 224; Généreux, *Une raison d'espérer*.

48. Cazettes, interviewed by Jacques Huguenin, in *Seniors: l'explosion* (Paris: Gallimard, 1999), p. 147; Jean-François Revel, *The Flight from Truth: The Reign of Deceit in the Age of Information* (New York: Random House, 1991), p. 228. See also Thomas Sowell, *The Vision of the Anointed: Self-Congratulation as a Basis for Social Policy* (New York: Basic Books, 1995), ch. 9.

49. Jean-Michel Charpin, Commissaire au Plan, Rapport au Premier ministre, *L'avenir de nos retraites* (Paris: La Documentation Française, 1999); *Le Monde*, 26 February 1999; "Le rapport Charpin, c'est la rupture programmée du contrat social," *Le Monde*, 24 May 1999.

50. Charpin, *L'avenir de nos retraites*; "Le Rapport Charpin," *Le Monde*, 24 May 1999. See also *Le Monde*, 26 February 1999. A more balanced view was provided in "Retraite. Un guide pour trois générations," *Le Nouvel Observateur* no. 1798 (22 April 1999).

51. The term belongs to Nicolas Baverez, *Les Trente piteuses* (Paris: Flammarion, 1998).

52. See the threat made by the CFTC in Rémi Barroux, "La concertation sur les retraites s'ouvre sur fond de désaccord entre les syndicats et le gouvernement," *Le Monde*, 1 March 2003, p. 8.

53. "Raffarin, c'est Thatcher," *Le Nouvel Observateur*, no. 1986, 28 November 2002.

54. "De Lille à Marseille, des défilés fleuves pour la retraite et pour l'emploi," *Le Monde*, 14 May 2003.

55. Michel Husson, *Les casseurs de l'Etat social. Des retraites à la Sécu: La grande démolition* (Paris: La Découverte, 2003), p. 1.

56. Sophie Meunier, The Brookings Institution, "France and Globalization in 2003," *US-France Analysis Series* (May 2003), pp. 1–2; "The World's Best Big Companies," *Forbes*, 10 April 2003.

57. Meunier, "France and Globalization in 2003," p. 5.

58. Vivien Schmidt, *The Futures of European Capitalism* (Oxford: Oxford University Press, 2002).

59. Meunier, "France and Globalization in 2003," p. 5; Jacques Généreux, *Chroniques d'un autre monde* (Paris: Seuil, 2003), pp. 49–53.

60. Tony Judt, *Past Imperfect* (Berkeley: University of California Press, 1992); "L'Utopie est le pire des refuges," *Le Figaro*, 27 December 1997; Pierre Lellouche, *La république immobile* (Paris: Grasset, 1998), pp. 118–21.

61. Judt, *Past Imperfect*, pp. 308–09.
62. For an earlier period, see Judt, *Past Imperfect*. For more recent times, there is Manière, *L'Aveuglement français*; Fouquet, *Délires et défaites*; and Michel Winock, *Le siècle des intellectuels* (Paris: Seuil, 1997).
63. Judt, *Past Imperfect*, p. 310.
64. "CSG: Jospin paiera en septembre," *Libération*, 11 January 2001; "Le gouvernement et le PS divisés sur l'aide fiscale aux ménages modestes," *Le Monde*, 9 January 2001. Simple things like a child income-tax credit generate debates over the "neoliberal American" origins of the proposed reform.
65. Alain Duhamel, *Le désarroi français* (Paris: Plon, 2003), pp. 160–61.
66. See Amy Chua, *World on Fire: How Exporting Free Market Democracy Breeds Ethnic Hatred and Global Instability* (New York: Doubleday, 2003), ch. 11.
67. Fouad Ajami, "The Falseness of Anti-Americanism," *Foreign Policy* (September–October 2003), pp. 56–58; Revel, *L'Obsession anti-américaine*.
68. See Bill Ashcroft, Gareth Griffiths, and Helen Tiffin, eds., *The Post-Colonial Studies Reader* (London: Routledge, 1995).
69. Richard F. Kuisel, *Seducing the French: The Dilemma of Americanization* (Berkeley: University of California Press, 1993), p. 236.
70. Kuisel, *Seducing the French*, p. ix.
71. Tyler Cowen, *Creative Destruction: How Globalization is Changing the World's Cultures* (Princeton: Princeton University Press, 2002), p. 2.
72. Gordon and Meunier, *The French Challenge*, p. 47.
73. On the MAI, see Edward M. Graham, *Fighting the Wrong Enemy: Antiglobal Activists and Multinational Enterprises* (Washington, DC: Institute for International Economics, 2000), pp. 11–12, 33.
74. Schmidt, *The Futures of European Capitalism*, p. 286.
75. William R. Cline, *Trade and Income Distribution* (Washington, DC: Institute for International Economics, 1997); Torben Iversen and Anne Wren, "Equality, Employment, and Budgetary Restraint: The Trilemma of the Service Economy," *World Politics* 50, no. 4 (July 1998), p. 507; Torben Iversen and Thomas Cusack, "The Causes of Welfare State Expansion: Deindustrialization or Globalization?," *World Politics* 52, no. 3 (April 2000), p. 313; Mark R. Brawley, *The Politics of Globalization: Gaining Perspective, Assessing Consequences* (Peterborough, Ontario: Broadview Press, 2003), ch. 4.
76. Several of Jospin's speeches and newspaper articles are gathered in Lionel Jospin, *My Vision of Europe and Globalization* (Cambridge: Polity Press, 2002).
77. I have borrowed this line from an argument made by John Gillingham regarding Delors. As Gillingham argues, what Delors had failed to do in France, he would offer as the solution for Europe: *European Integration: 1950–2003*, ch. 7.
78. The economic historian Andrew Shonfield wrote: "Going right back to Colbert, there were important economic gains which the master of seventeenth-century *dirigisme* had achieved," *Modern Capitalism: The Changing Balance of Public and Private Power* (New York: Oxford University Press, 1965), p. 77.

79. Quoted in Sophie Pedder, "France. The Grand Illusion," *The Economist*, 5 June 1999, p. 1 of survey. For another example of the Colbert myth, see Diana Green, "Individualism versus Collectivism: Economic Choices in France," in Vincent Wright, ed., *Conflict and Consensus in France* (London: Frank Cass, 1979), pp. 81–82.

80. On this theme, see Keith Dyson, *The State Tradition in Western Europe: A Study of an Idea and Institution* (Oxford: Martin Robertson, 1980), as well as Cécile Laborde's critique of Dyson, "The Concept of the State in British and French Political Thought," *Political Studies* 48 (June 2000), p. 542. On the pejorative connotations of the word "liberal" in France see Yves Tinard, *L'Exception française: Pourquoi?* (Paris: Maxima, 2001), p. 109.

81. See Richard Kuisel, *Capitalism and the State in Modern France* (Cambridge: Cambridge University Press, 1981), ch. 1, "The Liberal Order of 1900." On French poor relief during the nineteenth century, see André Gueslin, *Gens pauvres, pauvres gens dans la France du XIXe siècle* (Paris: Aubier, 1998); André Gueslin and Pierre Guillaume, eds., *De la charité médiévale à la sécurité sociale* (Paris: Les Editions Ouvrières, 1992); Jacques-Guy Petit and Yannick Marec, eds., *Le social dans la ville, en France et en Europe (1750–1914)* (Paris: Les Editions Ouvrières, 1996).

82. Pierre Rosanvallon, *L'Etat en France de 1789 à nos jours* (Paris: Seuil, 1990), pp. 243–76.

83. Pierre Rosanvallon, "The Development of Keynesianism in France," in Peter A. Hall, ed., *The Political Power of Economic Ideas: Keynesianism across Nations* (Princeton: Princeton University Press, 1989), pp. 171–93.

84. The French move towards the religion of planning was part of a Western-wide trend, visible in Canada (as of the 1960s), Britain, Italy, and elsewhere. None of these nations has needed to harken back to a Colbert. See, for example, Robert Skidelsky, *The World after Communism: A Polemic for our Times* (London: Macmillan, 1995), ch. 3.

85. Quoted in Daniel Yergin and Joseph Stanislaw, *The Commanding Heights: The Battle between Government and the Marketplace that is Remaking the Modern World* (New York: Simon and Schuster, 1998), p. 28.

86. Peter Lange, George Ross, and Maurizio Vannicelli, *Unions, Change and Crisis: French and Italian Union Strategy and the Political Economy, 1945–1980* (London: George Allen & Unwin, 1982), pp. 17–23.

87. Peter A. Hall, *Governing the Economy: The Politics of State Intervention in Britain and France* (Cambridge: Polity Press, 1986), p. 152.

88. Yergin and Stanislaw provide a concise account of these events in their popular *The Commanding Heights*.

89. Charles S. Maier, "The Two Postwar Eras and the Conditions for Stability in Twentieth-Century Western Europe," *American Historical Review* 86, no. 2 (April 1981), pp. 327–53.

90. "1947 Année Sociale," *Annales de la médecine sociale* (January 1947), p. 2. The parallels with the idealism of the Attlee government in Britain are striking, but, as yet, unexplored. On Britain, see Corelli Barnett, *The Lost Victory: British Dreams, British Realities, 1945–1950* (London: Macmillan, 1995), chs. 7, 8.

91. "1947 Année Sociale," *Annales de la médecine sociale* (January 1947), p. 2.

92. Douglas E. Ashford, "In Search of the Etat Providence," in James F. Hollifield and George Ross, eds., *Searching for the New France* (New York: Routledge, 1991), p. 162.

93. For example, Jean Estève, "Tendances de la médecine aux Etats-Unis," *Bulletin d'Information et de documentation de l'Assistance Publique* (July–August), 1952.

94. Pierre Rosanvallon, *L'Etat en France de 1789 à nos jours* (Paris: Seuil, 1990), ch. 4.

95. Gordon and Meunier, *The French Challenge*, pp. 16–17.

96. Paul Krugman, *Pop Internationalism* (Cambridge: MIT Press, 1996).

97. Jean Fourastié, *Les trente glorieuses* (Paris: Hachette, 1979), p. 130; Krugman, *Pop Internationalism*, ch. 11.

98. Daniel Cohen, *Les infortunes de la prospérité* (Paris: Julliard, 1994), pp. 9–11.

99. Kresl and Gallais, *France Encounters Globalization*, pp. 128–29; Peter Kenen, *Economic and Monetary Union in Europe* (Cambridge: Cambridge University Press, 1995).

100. Valérie Leselbaum-Stepler, "Le système de retraite," in Jean-Pierre Vesperini, ed., *Les problèmes actuels de l'économie française* (Paris: Presses Universitaires de France, 2001), p. 297, table 10, on activity rates.

101. J. R. McNeill and William H. McNeill, *The Human Web: A Bird's-Eye View of World History* (New York: W.W. Norton, 2003), pp. 309–12; Angus Maddison, *The World Economy: A Millennial Perspective* (Paris: OECD, 2001); and Brink Lindsey, *Against the Dead Hand: The Uncertain Struggle for Global Capitalism* (New York: John Wiley & Sons, 2002).

102. Jay R. Mandle, *Globalization and the Poor* (Cambridge: Cambridge University Press, 2003), pp. 106–07.

103. Jonah D. Levy, *Tocqueville's Revenge: State, Society, and Economy in Contemporary France* (Cambridge, MA: Harvard University Press, 1999), p. 22.

104. Jean Pisani-Ferry, Conseil d'Analyse économique, *Plein emploi* (Paris: La Documentation Française, 2000), part I.

105. On the Left and the Right's invocation of "globalization" as the excuse (or the rationale) for everything, see Legrain, *Open World*, ch. 6.

106. Renaud Dely, "Le PS se grime en altermondialiste," *Libération*, 22 October 2003.

107. Claudine Padieu, *RMI et SMIC. Etude sur l'apport financier de l'accès à l'emploi par types de ménages* (Paris: ODAS, 1997), p. 27.

108. Sabine Ferrand-Nagel, "Sécurité sociale. La réforme permanente," in Serge Cordellier and Elisabeth Lau, eds., La Découverte, *L'état de la France, 2000* (Paris: La Découverte, 2000), pp. 546–50; Robert Holcman, *Le chômage: Mécanismes économiques, conséquences sociales et humaines* (Paris: La Documentation Française, 1997), p. 79; Daniel Cohen, Arnaud Lefranc, and Gilles Saint-Paul, "French Unemployment: A Transatlantic Perspective," *Economic Policy* 25 (October 1997), pp. 267–85.

109. I agree with Elmar Rieger and Stephan Leibfried, who conclude in their monumental new study, *Limits to Globalization: Welfare States and the World Economy* (Cambridge: Polity Press, 2003), p. 335, that "globalization will

mean more rather than less social policy." This is the concluding sentence to this remarkable book.

110. On the fall of tariffs in the USA since the Second World War, from 60% of the value of imports to 6%, see Robert Gilpin, *The Challenge of Global Capitalism* (Princeton: Princeton University Press, 2000), ch. 2.

111. On the myth of the declining state, see Clive Crook, "The World Economy. The Future of the State," *The Economist*, 20 September 1997; Legrain, *Open World*; John Micklethwait and Adrian Wooldridge, *A Future Perfect: The Challenge and Hidden Promise of Globalization* (New York: Crown Business, 2000).

112. For discussions of the debate in other nations, see T. Notermans, "The Abdication of National Policy Autonomy: Why the Macroeconomic Policy Regime has Become so Unfavorable to Labor," *Politics and Society* 21, no. 2 (1993), pp. 133–67; Paul Pierson, "Irresistible Forces, Immovable Objects: Post-Industrial Welfare States Confront Permanent Austerity," *Journal of European Public Policy* 5, no. 4 (1998), pp. 539–60; and Martin Rhodes, "Globalization, Welfare States and Employment: Is there a European 'Third Way'?" in Nancy Bermeo, ed., *Unemployment in the New Europe* (Cambridge: Cambridge University Press, 2000).

113. Charles Derber, *Corporation Nation: How Corporations Are Taking Over Our Lives and What We Can Do About It* (New York: St. Martin's, 1998).

114. Gillingham, *European Integration*, p. 478.

115. Conseil d'Analyse économique, Premier Ministre, Jean-Paul Fitoussi et al., reporters, *Réduction du chômage: Les réussites en Europe* (Paris: La Documentation Française, 2000), p. 75.

116. On this theme see Gordon and Meunier, *The French Challenge*, pp. 30–32.

117. Michael Hart, *A Trading Nation: Canadian Trade Policy from Colonialism to Globalization* (Vancouver: UBC Press, 2002), pp. 427, 437; Deborah Mabbett, *Trade, Employment, and Welfare: A Comparative Study of Trade and Labour Market Policies in Sweden and New Zealand, 1880–1980* (Oxford: Clarendon Press, 1995); World Trade Organization, *International Trade Statistics* (Geneva: WTO, 2001), table II.1; Jean-Claude Milleron, "La France et la mondialisation," *Commentaire* no. 100 (Winter 2002–03), p. 807;

118. "Measuring Globalization," *Foreign Policy* (January–February 2003), pp. 61, 65.

119. Premier Ministre to Edmond Malinvaud, 6 April 1998, in Conseil d'Analyse économique, Edmond Malinvaud, reporter, *Les cotisations sociales à la charge des employeurs: analyse économique* (Paris: La Documentation Française, 1998), p. 9.

120. Larry Siedentop, *Democracy in Europe* (London: Penguin, 2000), p. 222; Rod Phillips, *A Short History of Wine* (London: Penguin, 2000); Kym Anderson, "Wine's New World," *Foreign Policy* (May–June 2003), pp. 46–54.

121. "Farmers," *Le Point* 1588 (21 February 2003), p. 80.

122. See J. F. V. Keiger, *France and the World since 1870* (London: Arnold, 2001), ch. 1.

123. Jean-Hervé Lorenzi, "L'intégration européenne, moteur de la compétitivité française," in Benoît Ferrandon, ed., *Vingt ans de transformations de l'économie française* (*Cahiers français*, 311, no. 6 (November–December 2002), p. 8); Siedentop, *Democracy in Europe*, p. 137.

124. Patrick Artus, "La France à l'heure de la mondialisation: Le déclin de la France, mythe ou réalité," in Ferrandon, ed. *Vingt ans de transformations de l'économie française*, pp. 11–19.

125. Keith G. Banting, "Social Policy," in G. Bruce Doern, Leslie A. Pal, and Brian W. Tomlin, eds., *Border Crossings: The Internationalization of Canadian Public Policy* (Toronto: Oxford University Press, 1996), pp. 27–54; John Gerard Ruggie, "Taking Embedded Liberalism Global: The Corporate Connection," in David Held and Mathias Koenig-Archibugi, eds., *Taming Globalization: Frontiers of Governance* (Cambridge: Polity Press, 2003), pp. 93–129.

126. Herman Schwartz, "Small States in Big Trouble: State Reorganization in Australia, Denmark, New Zealand, and Sweden in the 1980s," *World Politics*, 46, no. 4 (July 1994); Lewis Evans, Arthur Grimes, Bryce Wilkinson, and David Teece, "Economic Reform in New Zealand, 1984–1985: The Pursuit of Efficiency," *Journal of Economic Literature* 34 (December 1996); Gillingham, *European Integration*, pp. 182–84.

127. Mary Ruggie, *Realignments in the Welfare State* (New York: Columbia University Press, 1996); Duane Swank, *Global Capital, Political Institutions, and Policy Change in Developed Welfare States* (Cambridge: Cambridge University Press, 2002); Geoffrey Garrett and Deborah Mitchell, "Globalization, Government Spending, and Taxation in the OECD," *European Journal of Political Research* 39 (2001); Vito Tanzi and Ludger Schuknecht, *Public Spending in the Twentieth Century* (New York: Cambridge University Press); Paul Pierson, "The New Politics of the Welfare State," *World Politics* 48 (January 1996), pp. 143–79. For a dissenting view, see Evelyne Huber and John D. Stephens, *Development and Crisis of the Welfare State: Parties and Policies in Global Markets* (Chicago: University of Chicago Press, 2001).

128. Paul Pierson, *Dismantling the Welfare State? Reagan, Thatcher and the Politics of Welfare Retrenchment* (New York: Cambridge University Press, 1994); Rhodes, "Globalization, Welfare States and Employment," in Bermeo, ed., *Unemployment in the New Europe*.

129. On the flight of capital and the brain drain, see Denis Badré and André Ferrand, Les Rapports du Sénat, no. 386, *Mondialisation: Réagir ou subir? La France face à l'expatriation des compétences, des capitaux et des entreprises* (Paris: Senate of France, 2001).

130. Bill Emmott, *20:21 Vision: Twentieth-Century Lessons for the Twenty-first Century* (New York: Farrar, Straus and Giroux, 2003), p. 71.

131. Figures from Dani Rodrik, *Has Globalization Gone Too Far?* (Washington, DC: Institute for International Economics, 1997), p. 50.

132. See Gøsta Esping-Andersen, ed., *Welfare States in Transition* (London: SAGE, 1996).

133. Linda Weiss, *The Myth of the Powerless State: Governing the Economy in a Global Era* (Ithaca: Cornell University Press, 1998). Layna Mosley, "Room to Move: International Financial Markets and National Welfare States," *International Organization* 54, no. 4 (Autumn 2000), pp. 737–73; Mosley, *Global Capital and National Governments* (Cambridge: Cambridge University Press, 2003), pp. 3, 27.

134. Rhodes, "Globalization, Welfare States and Employment," in Bermeo, ed., *Unemployment in the New Europe.*

135. Jean Picq, Rapport au Premier ministre, *L'Etat en France. Servir une nation ouverte sur le monde* (Paris: La Documentation Française, 1995), p. 148. For cuts in other nations, see Richard Clayton and Jonas Pontusson, "Welfare State Retrenchment Revisited," *World Politics* 51 (1998), in Christopher Pierson and Francis G. Castles, eds., *The Welfare State Reader* (Cambridge: Polity Press, 2000), p. 329.

136. Richard B. Freeman, Robert Topel, and Birgitta Swedenborg, eds., *The Welfare State in Transition: Reforming the Swedish Model* (Chicago: University of Chicago Press, 1997).

137. "L'Europe invite la France à mieux cibler ses dépenses," and "L'Europe exige de M. Chirac l'équilibre des comptes publics en 2004," *Le Monde*, 15 May 2002.

138. Geoffrey Garrett, "Capital Mobility, Trade, and the Domestic Politics of Economic Policy," *International Organization* 49, no. 4 (Autumn 1995), pp. 659–61.

139. Schmidt, *The Futures of European Capitalism*, p. 24.

140. Schmidt, *The Futures of European Capitalism*, p. 25; Duane Swank, "Withering Welfare? Globalisation, Political Economic Institutions, and Contemporary Welfare States," in Linda Weiss, ed., *States in the Global Economy: Bringing Domestic Institutions Back In* (Cambridge: Cambridge University Press, 2003); Fritz W. Scharpf and Vivien A. Schmidt, eds., *Welfare and Work in the Open Economy* (Oxford: Oxford University Press, 2000), 2 volumes.

141. This figure is from Gordon and Meunier, *The French Challenge*, p. 40.

142. On this theme, see François Charpentier, "Avant-propos," in Charpentier, ed., *Encyclopédie Protection Sociale. Quelle refondation?* (Paris: Economica, 2000), p. 7.

143. Olivier Marchand, *Plein emploi, l'improbable retour* (Paris: Gallimard, 2002), p. 108.

144. Krugman, *Pop Internationalism.*

145. Daniel Cohen, *Richesse du monde, pauvretés des nations* (Paris: Flammarion, 1997), p. 64; H. Bonnaz, N. Courtot, and D. Nivat, INSEE, "Le contenu en emplois des échanges industriels de la France avec les pays en voie de développment," *Economie et Statistique* 279 (1994); Paul Hirst and Grahame Thompson, *Globalization in Question: The International Economy and the Possibilities of Governance* (Cambridge: Polity Press, 1999), pp. 68–77.

146. Olivier Marchand and Claude Thélot, *Le travail en France, 1800–2000* (Paris: Nathan, 1997), p. 202.

4   FRANCE'S BREAK WITH SOCIALISM

1. Quoted in Robert Mundell, "Unemployment, Competitiveness and the Welfare State," in Mario Baldassarri, Luigi Paganetto, and Edmund S. Phelps, eds., *Equity, Efficiency and Growth: The Future of the Welfare State* (London: Macmillan, 1996), p. 129.
2. Giscard, quoted in Pierre Favier and Michel Martin-Rolland, *La décennie Mitterrand. Les ruptures (1981–1984)* (Paris: Seuil, 1990), vol. i, p. 38.
3. The European Monetary System.
4. Quoted in Jean Lacouture, *Mitterrand. Une histoire de français* (Paris: Seuil, 1998) vol. ii, p. 85. The original source is Jacques Attali, *Verbatim, I, 1981–1986* (Paris: Fayard, 1993). On the issue of "external constraints," see Jean-Charles Asselain, "L'expérience socialiste face à la contrainte extérieure (1981–1983)," and Olivier Feiertag, "Finance publique, 'mur d'argent,' et génèse de la libéralisation financière en France de 1981 à 1984," both in Serge Berstein, Pierre Milza, and Jean-Louis Bianco, eds., *François Mitterrand. Les années du changement, 1981–1984* (Paris: Perrin, 2001).
5. Jonah D. Levy, "Partisan Politics and Welfare Adjustment: The Case of France," *Journal of European Public Policy* (2001).
6. Jonah D. Levy, "France: Directing Adjustment?" in Fritz Scharpf and Vivien Schmidt, eds., *Welfare and Work in the Open Economy: Diverse Responses to Common Challenges* (Oxford: Oxford University Press, 2000), vol. ii, pp. 308–50.
7. Peter Gourevitch, *Politics in Hard Times: Comparative Responses to International Crises* (Ithaca: Cornell University Press, 1986), pp. 9–10.
8. INSEE, *Données sociales. Edition 1981* (Paris: INSEE, 1982), p. 119.
9. INSEE, *Données sociales. Edition 1981*, p. 122.
10. Jonah D. Levy, *Tocqueville's Revenge: State, Society, and Economy in Contemporary France* (Cambridge, MA: Harvard University Press, 1999), pp. 42–43; Vivien A. Schmidt, *From State to Market? The Transformation of French Business and Government* (Cambridge: Cambridge University Press, 1996), p. 88; Alain Lipietz, *L'audace ou l'enlisement: Sur les politiques économiques de la gauche* (Paris: La Découverte, 1984).
11. Robert Boyer, "Wage Labor, Capital Accumulation, and the Crisis, 1968–1982," in Mark Kesselman and Guy Groux, eds., *The French Workers' Movement: Economic Crisis and Political Change* (London: George Allen & Unwin, 1984), p. 24.
12. William James Adams, *Restructuring the French Economy: Government and the Rise of Market Competition since World War II* (Washington, DC: Brookings Institution Press, 1989), p. 105.
13. On the huge gap between promises and results, see Alain Fonteneau and Pierre-Alain Muet, *La Gauche face à la crise* (Paris: Presses de la Fondation nationale des sciences politiques, 1985).
14. Mitterrand is quoted in John S. Ambler, "Preface," in Ambler, ed., *The French Socialist Experiment* (Philadelphia: Institute for the Study of Human Issues, 1985), p. vii. The original is from Parti Socialiste, *Changer la vie: Programme de gouvernement du Parti Socialiste* (Paris: Flammarion, 1972), p. 8.

15. Gérard Grunberg, *Le Long Remords du pouvoir. Le parti socialiste français, 1905–1992* (Paris: Fayard, 1992); René Mouriaux, "Trade Unions, Unemployment, and Regulation: 1962–1989," in James F. Hollifield and George Ross, eds., *Searching for the New France* (London: Routledge, 1991), pp. 173–92.

16. See David Wilsford, *Doctors and the State: The Politics of Health Care in France and the United States* (Durham, NC: Duke University Press, 1991).

17. Jean-Paul Thomas, *Les politiques économiques au XXe siècle*, 2nd edn. (Paris: Armand Colin, 1994), p. 164.

18. Göran Therborn, *Why Some Peoples are More Unemployed than Others* (London: Macmillan, 1986), p. 141.

19. Commissariat Général du Plan, *Rapport sur les principales options du VIIIe Plan*, pp. 38–39; Peter Karl Kresl and Sylvain Gallais, *France Encounters Globalization* (Cheltenham, UK: Edward Elgar, 2002), p. 22.

20. Denis Olivennes and Maryvonne de Saint-Pulgent, "L'Etat en crise," *Le Débat* 112 (November–December 2000); Vincent Giret and Bernard Pellegrin, *Vingt ans de pouvoir, 1981–2001* (Paris: Seuil, 2001), p. 212.

21. Peter A. Hall, "Socialism in One Country: Mitterrand and the Struggle to Define a New Economic Policy for France," in Philip Cerny and Martin Schain, eds., *Socialism, the State and Public Policy in France* (London: Pinter, 1985).

22. Howard Machin and Vincent Wright, eds., *Economic Policy and Policy-Making under the Mitterrand Presidency* (London: Pinter, 1985); Schmidt, *From State to Market?* pp. 107–08.

23. Douglas Ashford, *Policy and Politics in France: Living with Uncertainty* (Philadelphia: Temple University Press, 1982), p. 245; Jean-Pierre Jallade, "Redistribution and the Welfare State: An Assessment of the French Socialists' Performance," *Government and Opposition* 20, no. 3 (1985), pp. 343–55; Gary Freeman, "Socialism and Social Security," in Ambler, ed. *The French Socialist Experiment*, pp. 92–115; George Ross, "The Mitterrand Experiment and the French Welfare State," in M. Brown, ed., *Remaking the Welfare State* (New York, 1988), pp. 119–38; Serge Halimi, Jonathan Michie, and Seumas Milne, "The Mitterrand Experience," in Jonathan Michie and John Grieve Smith, eds., *Unemployment in Europe* (London: Academic Press, 1994), pp. 97–115. Two earlier accounts of Mitterrand's initial social reforms were remarkably astute: George Ross and Jane Jenson, "French Socialism in Crisis," *Studies in Political Economy* 11 (Summer 1983) and Volkmar Lauber, *The Political Economy of France: From Pompidou to Mitterrand* (New York: Praeger, 1983), ch. 13.

24. Gary P. Freeman, "Financial Crisis and Policy Continuity in the Welfare State," in Peter A. Hall, Jack Hayward, and Howard Machin, eds., *Developments in French Politics*, rev. edn. (London: Macmillan, 1994), pp. 199–200.

25. John S. Ambler, "Ideas, Interests, and the French Welfare State," in Ambler, ed., *The French Welfare State: Surviving Social and Ideological Change* (New York: New York University Press, 1991).

26. W. Rand Smith, *The Left's Dirty Job: The Politics of Industrial Restructuring in France and Spain* (Pittsburgh: University of Pittsburgh Press, 1998), p. 37.

27. Schmidt, *From State to Market?* p. 108.
28. Kresl and Gallais, *France Encounters Globalization*, p. 177; "Brevets: le gouvernement prêt à autoriser l'anglais," *Le Parisien*, 10 June 2001.
29. OCDE, Etudes économiques de l'OCDE, *France* (Paris: OCDE, 2000), p. 30. OCDE is the French acronym for OECD (Organization for Economic Cooperation and Development).
30. Jacques Mistral, "L'heure des choix," in Roger Fauroux and Bernard Spitz, eds., *Notre état* (Paris: Robert Laffont, 2000), p. 315.
31. Pascal Lamy and Jean Pisani-Ferry, *The Europe We Want* (Cambridge: Polity Press, 2002), p. 61. Published in tandem with Lionel Jospin's *My Vision of Europe and Globalization* (Cambridge: Polity Press, 2002).
32. Daniel Cohen, *Les infortunes de la prospérité* (Paris: Julliard, 1994), p. 116; Jean-Paul Fitoussi, *Le débat interdit. Monnaie, Europe, pauvreté* (Paris: Seuil, 2000).
33. David Calleo, *Rethinking Europe's Future* (Princeton: Princeton University Press, 2001), p. 195.
34. Calleo, *Rethinking Europe's Future*, pp. 167–70, 186–94; Jean-Paul Fitoussi, "'Competitive Disinflation': An Assessment of French Macroeconomic Policy since 1987," in Fitoussi, ed., *Competitive Disinflation: The Mark and Budgetary Policy in Europe* (Oxford: Oxford University Press, 1993), pp. 17–30.
35. One option was to devalue earlier: see David Cameron, "Exchange Rate Politics in France, 1981–1983: The Regime-Defining Choices of the Mitterrand Presidency," in Anthony Daley, ed., *The Mitterrand Era: Policy Alternatives and Political Mobilization in France* (London: Macmillan, 1996).
36. Conseil supérieur de l'Emploi des revenus et des coûts, *Les inégalités d'emploi et de revenu* (Paris: La Découverte, 1996), p. 37. From OECD statistics.
37. Fitoussi, *Le débat interdit*, pp. 84–86. Fitoussi and I present a completely different picture of French monetary policy than that found in Robert Gilpin's *The Challenge of Global Capitalism: The World Economy in the 21st Century* (Princeton: Princeton University Press, 2000), pp. 198–213. On earlier times, and the trade-off between higher inflation and growth, see Stephen S. Cohen, *Modern Capitalist Planning: The French Model* (London: Weidenfeld and Nicolson, 1969), ch. 9.
38. Frédérick Lordon, "The Logic and Limits of *Désinflation Compétitive*," in Andrew Glyn, ed., *Social Democracy in Neoliberal Times: The Left and Economic Policy since 1980* (Oxford: Oxford University Press, 2001), p. 110.
39. The originator has not been identified, but Elie Cohen and Jean-Paul Fitoussi have used the term. See Elie Cohen, *L'ordre économique mondial. Essai sur les autorités de régulation* (Paris: Fayard, 2001), p. 189, n. 1.
40. The same is true of Canada's national debt. See Jim Stanford, *Paper Boom* (Ottawa: Canadian Centre for Policy Alternatives, 1999), ch. 9.
41. Saint-Etienne, *L'Etat mensonger*, p. 43.
42. For a view of deficits in time, see Niall Ferguson, *The Cash Nexus: Money and Power in the Modern World, 1700–2000* (New York: Basic Books, 2001), ch. 4. For a former insider's view of France's social security deficits, see Gilles Johanet, *Sécurité Sociale: L'échec et le défi* (Paris: Seuil, 1998).
43. Ronald Tiersky, *François Mitterrand: A Very French President* (Lanham, MD: Rowman and Littlefield, 2003), p. 145.

44. Conseil d'Analyse économique, Premier Ministre, Olivier Blanchard and Jean-Paul Fitoussi, reporters, *Croissance et chômage* (Paris: La Documentation Française, 1998), p. 17; Larry Elliot and Dan Atkinson, *The Age of Insecurity* (London: Verso, 1998), p. 239; Robert M. Solow and John B. Taylor, eds., *Inflation, Unemployment, and Monetary Policy* (Cambridge, MA: MIT Press, 1998), pp. 8–11. On Canada, and the policy of zero-inflation and high real interest rates: Lars Osberg and Pierre Fortin, eds., *Hard Money, Hard Times: Why Zero Inflation Hurts Canadians* (Toronto: Lorimer, 1998); Stanford, *Paper Boom*. For a more positive spin on the Bank of Canada, there is Ben S. Bernanke, Thomas Laubach, Frederic S. Mishkin, and Adam S. Posen, *Inflation Targeting: Lessons from the International Experience* (Princeton: Princeton University Press, 1999). Some recent research is summed up in "The Price of Profligacy," *The Economist*, 25 January 2003, p. 73.

45. Bernard Lassudrie-Duchêne, "L'économie française depuis 1967: de l'inflation au chômage," *Revue d'économie politique* 99, no. 6 (November–December 1989), pp. 797–809; Jean-Pierre Vesperini, *Le Franc dans le système monétaire international* (Paris: Economica, 1989).

46. Philippe Sigogne, "L'inflation," in OFCE, *L'Economie française, 2000* (Paris: La Découverte, 2000). See p. 46 for the table on inflation.

47. See also Anne Laferrère, "L'occupation des logements depuis 1945," in INSEE, *Données sociales. La société française* (1999 edition) (Paris: INSEE, 1999), p. 336; Conseil d'Analyse économique, Premier Ministre, Blanchard and Fitoussi, reporters, *Croissance et chômage*, p. 21.

48. Gøsta Esping-Andersen, "After the Golden Age? Welfare State Dilemmas in a Global Economy," in Esping-Andersen, ed., *Welfare States in Transition: National Adaptations in Global Economies* (London: Sage, 1996), p. 11.

49. Jean-Pierre Vesperini, *L'Economie de la France sous la Ve République* (Paris: Economica, 1993). Delors admitted in an interview in *Le Monde*, 5 May 2001, that his economic policy was a failure. See also "Quand les socialistes voulaient rompre avec le capitalisme," *Le Monde*, 4 May 2001, and "Quand la relance socialiste devait vaincre le chômage," *Le Monde*, 5 May 2001.

50. Pierre Rosanvallon and Jean-Paul Fitoussi, *Le nouvel âge des inégalités* (Paris: Seuil, 1996), p. 155.

51. A point stressed by Nathalie Martin-Papineau, *Les familles monoparentales. Emergence, construction, captations d'un problème dans le champ politique français (1968–1998)* (Paris: L'Harmattan, 2001).

52. Peter A. Hall, *Governing the Economy: The Politics of State Intervention in Britain and France* (Cambridge: Polity Press, 1986), p. 194.

53. Jean-Gabriel Fredet and Denis Pingaud, *Les patrons face à la gauche* (Paris: Editions Ramsay, 1982).

54. George Ross, "French labor and economic change," in Stephen S. Cohen and Peter A. Gourevitch, eds., *France in the Troubled World Economy* (London: Butterworth, 1982), p. 157.

55. For example, Keith G. Banting and Charles Beach, eds., *Labour Market Polarization and Social Policy Reform* (Kingston, Ont.: School of Policy Studies, 1995).

56. Robert Holcman, *Le chômage: Mécanismes économiques, conséquences sociales et humaines* (Paris: La Documentation Française, 1997), p. 79.

57. William Julius Wilson, *When Work Disappears: The World of the New Urban Poor* (New York: Vintage, 1996), p. 154; Emmanuel Todd, *L'illusion économique* (Paris: Gallimard, 1998), p. 335; *Le Monde*, 26 September 1996.

58. Dominique Meurs, "Salaires réels et emplois dans les pays OCDE," in Jean-Yves Capul, ed., *Emploi et chômage* in *Cahiers français* 246 (May–June 1990), p. 35.

59. André Masson, "Equité ou solidarité intergénérationelle?" in François Charpentier, ed., *Encyclopédie Protection Sociale. Quelle refondation?* (Paris: Economica, 2000), p. 359.

60. Jeremy Atack, "Long-Term Trends in Productivity," in Julian L. Simon, ed., *The State of Humanity* (Cambridge, MA: Blackwell, 1995), p. 169.

61. Daniel Cohen, *Richesse du monde, pauvretés des nations* (Paris: Flammarion, 1997), pp. 64–65.

62. Serge Marti, ed. (*Le Monde*), *Questions économiques et sociales* (Paris: Le Monde, 2000), p. 164.

63. See Gérard Duthil and Estelle Paquet-Vaultier, *Le chômage des jeunes en Europe* (Paris: L'Harmattan, 1999), p. 85; Denis Olivennes, "La préférence française pour le chômage," in Patrice Bourdelais, ed. (*Le Débat*), *Etat providence. Arguments pour une réforme* (Paris: Gallimard, 1996); Jean-Claude Guillebaud, *La trahison des lumières: Enquête sur le désarroi contemporain* (Paris: Seuil, 1995), pp. 57–60; Christian Gros-Jean and Claudine Padieu, "La montée de l'exclusion par l'emploi," *Revue française des affaires sociales* 49, nos. 2–3 (April–September 1995), p. 9. On wage restraint in other European nations, see Fritz W. Scharpf, *Crisis and Choice in European Social Democracy*, trans. Ruth Crowley and Fred Thompson (Ithaca: Cornell University Press, 1991), especially ch. 9.

64. Bruce Western and Kieran Healy, "Wage Growth, Recession, and Labor Decline in the Industrialized Democracies, 1965–1993," in Nancy Bermeo, ed., *Unemployment in the New Europe* (Cambridge: Cambridge University Press, 2001), p. 123.

65. Xavier Timbeau, "Le partage de la valeur ajoutée," in OFCE, *L'économie française, 2002* (Paris: La Découverte, 2002), p. 90, using INSEE data. A theme raised by Jean Pisani-Ferry in his controversial report, *Plein emploi* (Paris: La Documentation Française, 2000).

66. Alain Minc, "Les salaires contre l'emploi," *Futuribles* 201 (September 1995); Jean-Philippe Cotis and Elisabeth Rignols, "Le partage de la valeur ajoutée: quelques enseignements tirés du 'paradoxe franco-américain,'" *Revue de l'OFCE* 65 (April 1998); Denis Clerc, *Condamnés au chômage?* (Paris: Syros, 1999), pp. 140–43; Premier Ministre, Conseil d'Analyse économique, Edmond Malinvaud, reporter, *Les cotisations sociales à la charge des employeurs: analyse économique* (Paris: La Documentation Française, 1998), p. 9; Yves Crozet et al., *Les grandes questions de la société française* (Paris: Nathan, 2000), p. 5.

67. Danièle Demoustier, "France: Voluntary Sector Initiatives for Work Integration," in Roger Spear, Jacques Defourny, Louis Favreau, and Jean-Louis Laville, eds., *Tackling Social Exclusion in Europe: The Contribution of the Social Economy* (Aldershot, UK: Ashgate, 2001), pp. 114–15.

68. All quoted in Sophie Pedder, "France: The Grand Illusion," *The Economist*, 5 June 1999, p. 12 of survey.

69. Therborn, *Why Some Peoples are More Unemployed than Others*, p. 31; Michael Mandelbaum, *The Ideas that Conquered the World: Peace, Democracy, and Free Markets in the Twenty-first Century* (New York: Public Affairs, 2002), p. 283.

70. Xavier Gaullier, *La deuxième carrière. Ages, emplois, retraites* (Paris: Seuil, 1988), p. 39; Editorial, *Droit social* 8 (June 1970), p. 326; François Sellier, "L'évolution des négociations collectives dans la sidérurgie et la métallurgie en France (1950–1969)," *Droit social* 9/10 (September–October 1970), pp. 431–49; François Lenormand and Gérard Magnier, "Le développement des dispositifs de cessation anticipée d'activité," *Travail et emploi* 15 (January–March 1983), p. 48.

71. Quoted in Xavier Gaullier, *L'avenir à reculons, chômage et retraite* (Paris: Les Editions Ouvrières, 1982), p. 228. For similar statements to the cabinet, see *Liaisons sociales* 66/81 (17 June 1981).

72. Jean Pisani-Ferry, *La bonne aventure. Le plein emploi, le marché, la gauche* (Paris: La Découverte, 2001), pp. 38–39.

73. Quoted in Gaullier, *L'avenir à reculons*, p. 230.

74. Xavier Gaullier, "Crise économique et vieillissement. La période critique de la pré-retraite," in Ministère de la Santé, Institut national de la Santé et de la Recherche médicale, *Santé publique et vieillissement* (colloquium proceedings) (Paris: INSERM, 1982), p. 396.

75. Gaullier, "Crise économique et vieillissement," p. 400.

76. Gaullier, *La deuxième carrière*, pp. 40–41.

77. Conseil supérieur de l'Emploi, des revenus, et des coûts (CSERC), *Les inégalités de l'emploi et de revenu* (Paris: La Découverte, 1996), p. 112.

78. Levy, *Tocqueville's Revenge*, p. 251.

79. Gaullier, *La deuxième carrière*, p. 17.

80. Charles Debbasch and Jean-Marie Pontier, *La société française*, 4th edn. (Paris: Dalloz, 2001), p. 671.

81. Gaullier, *La deuxième carrière*, p. 54; and, most recently, his article "La protection sociale et les nouveaux parcours de vie," *Esprit* 272 (February 2001), pp. 93–111. Anne-Marie Guillemard, "The Social Dynamics of Early Withdrawal from the Labour Force in France," *Ageing and Society* 5, no. 4 (December 1985), pp. 381–412. Another fierce critique of the pré-retraites is Philippe Garraud, *Le chômage et l'action publique: Le "bricolage institutionnalisé"* (Paris: L'Harmattan, 2000), pp. 81, 196–97.

82. Gaullier, *La deuxième carrière*, p. 42.

83. Ibid., p. 55.

84. Duthil and Paquet-Vaultier, *Le chômage des jeunes en Europe*, p. 85.

85. Gaullier, *La deuxième carrière*, p. 53.

86. Xavier Gaullier, "Politiques sociales, emploi et gestion des âges," *Revue française des affaires sociales* 44, no. 4 (October–December 1990), pp. 115–21.

87. Therborn, *Why Some Peoples are More Unemployed*, p. 44.

88. For example, Banting and Beach, eds., *Labour Market Polarization*.

89. Some critics argue that France's high minimum wage accounts for only one point more of unemployment (i.e., it raises unemployment from, say, 9% to

10%). In any case, one point equals a few hundred thousand people, so it is a serious issue. See Cohen, *Richesse du monde, pauvretés des nations*, esp. pp. 104–05 and Hedva Sarfati, *Flexibilité et création d'emplois: Un défi pour le dialogue social en Europe* (Paris: L'Harmattan, 1999), esp. pp. 185–90; Pascal Pochet, *Les personnes âgées* (Paris: La Découverte, 1997); Jacques Huguenin, *Seniors: L'explosion* (Paris: Gallimard, 1999); Holcman, *Le chômage*, p. 79.

90. Philip H. Gordon and Sophie Meunier, *The French Challenge: Adapting to Globalization* (Washington, DC: Brookings Institution, 2001), p. 35.

91. Assar Lindbeck and Dennis J. Snower, *The Insider-Outsider Theory of Employment and Unemployment* (Cambridge, MA: MIT Press, 1988); Numa Murard, *La protection sociale* (Paris: La Découverte, 1996), p. 87; Sébastien Jean, "Emploi: les enseignements de l'expérience néerlandaise," INSEE, *Economie et statistique* 332–33 (2000), pp. 133–57; Michel Fouquin, Sébastien Jean, and Aude Sztulman, "Le marché du travail britannique vu de France," INSEE, *Economie et statistique* 332–33 (2000), pp. 97–115. See also Richard B. Freeman, "War of the Models: Which Labour Market Institutions for the 21st Century?" *Labour Economics* 5, no. 1 (1998), pp. 1–24; Gøsta Esping-Andersen, "Who is Harmed by Labour Market Regulations? Quantitative Evidence," in Esping-Andersen, ed., *Why Deregulate Labour Markets?* (Oxford: Oxford University Press, 2000).

92. Michel Coffineau, Rapport au Premier Ministre, *Les lois Auroux, dix ans après* (Paris: La Documentation Française, 1993).

93. Editions Dalloz, *Code du travail*, 64th edn. (Paris: Editions Dalloz, 2002), p. 133; Philippe Auvergnon, "L'Etat créateur et gardien du droit des relations du travail," in Auvergnon, ed., *L'Etat à l'épreuve du social* (Paris: Editions Syllepse, 1998). For a full discussion of the Auroux Laws, see Chris Howell, *Regulating Labor: The State and Industrial Relations Reform in Postwar France* (Princeton: Princeton University Press, 1992).

94. Mark Kesselman, "The New Shape of Industrial Relations: Ce n'est plus la même chose," in Paul Godt, ed., *Policymaking in France: From de Gaulle to Mitterrand* (London: Pinter, 1989); W. Rand Smith, "Towards *Autogestion* in Socialist France: The Impact of Industrial Relations Reform," *West European Politics* 10, no. 1 (January 1987); Duncan Gallie, "Les lois Auroux: The Reform of French Industrial Relations?," in Machin and Wright, eds., *Economic Policy and Policy-Making under the Mitterrand Presidency*.

95. For example, see D. S. Parker, *The Idea of the Middle Class: White-Collar Workers and Peruvian Society, 1900–1950* (University Park, PA: Pennsylvania State University Press, 1998). For a comparison with German labor relations, see Michel Lallement, *Les gouvernances de l'emploi: Relations professionnelles et marché du travail en France et en Allemagne* (Paris: Desclée de Brouwer, 1999).

96. On the byzantine world of French labor regulations and red tape, see the journalistic account (with the unfortunately flippant title, given the seriousness of his scholarship) by Thierry Desjardins, *"Arrêter d'emmerder les Français!"* (Paris: Plon, 2000). A more serious work is Michel Crozier, *Etat modeste, Etat moderne* (Paris: Seuil, 1987). A recent study of the negative economic impact

of the overstaffed civil service is Bernard Zimmern, *Les profiteurs de l'Etat* (Paris: Plon, 2000). Nothing compares with going to the source: Editions Dalloz, *Code du travail*, 64th edn., pp. 113, 2016; Editions Francis Lefebvre, *Le droit au travail en France*, 8th edn. (Paris: Editions Francis Lefebvre, 1997), pp. 170–75.

97. OCDE, Etudes économiques de l'OCDE, *France*, p. 96.

98. "Economics focus: The white heat of technology," *The Economist*, 25 May 2002, p. 76.

99. See *Les Echos*, 22 June 1999, for a summary of the report and see Kresl and Gallais, *France Encounters Globalization*, pp. 171–72, for a thorough discussion. The French state receives a good survey in Robert Graham, "Economy. France Survey," *Financial Times*, 10 November 2000 and in Andrew Jack, *The French Exception* (London: Profile Books, 2000).

100. Eric Heyer, "Le commerce extérieur," in OFCE, *L'économie française, 2002* (Paris: La Découverte, 2002), pp. 43–44.

101. See the special edition of *L'Express*, 1–7 March 2001, "Comment les 35 heures changent notre vie."

102. See Jill Andresky Fraser, *White Collar Sweatshop: The Deterioration of Work and its Rewards in Corporate America* (New York: Norton, 2001).

103. Quoted in Pedder, "France. The Grand Illusion," p. 12.

104. Duane Swank, "Withering Welfare? Globalisation, Political Economic Institutions, and Contemporary Welfare States," in Linda Weiss, ed., *States in the Global Economy: Bringing Domestic Institutions Back In* (Cambridge: Cambridge University Press, 2003), pp. 69–70.

105. Schmidt, *From State to Market?*

106. Jean-Pierre Azéma, "La campagne présidentielle de François Mitterrand," and Serge Berstein, "Le programme présidentiel: les 110 propositions," both in Berstein et al., *François Mitterrand. Les années du changement*, pp. 45–56 and pp. 77–90.

107. Levy, "France: Directing Adjustment?" pp. 308–50.

108. Levy, "France: Directing Adjustment?"

109. Assar Lindbeck et al., eds., *Turning Sweden Around* (Cambridge, MA: MIT Press, 1994).

110. Denis Clerc, *Déchiffrer l'économie*, 13th edn. (Paris: Syros, 1999), p. 252.

111. Quoted in Jelle Visser and Anton Hemerijck, *A Dutch Miracle: Job Growth, Welfare Reform and Corporatism in the Netherlands* (Amsterdam: Amsterdam University Press, 1997), p. 9. See also Robert H. Cox, *The Development of the Dutch Welfare State: From Workers' to Universal Entitlement* (Pittsburgh: University of Pittsburgh Press, 1993) and Anton Hemerijck, "Corporatist Immobility in the Netherlands," in Colin Crouch and Franz Traxler, eds., *Organized Industrial Relations in Europe: What Future?* (Aldershot: Avebury Press, 1995), pp. 183–226.

112. I owe "attention to deficit disorder," to the satirical newspaper, *The Onion* (August 2003). It was a reference to George W. Bush's fiscal policy.

113. See Gøsta Esping-Andersen's two articles, "After the Golden Age?" and "Welfare States without Work," in Esping-Andersen, ed., *Welfare States in Transition*, pp. 1–31 and 66–87.

114. Although there is a large black market in Italy, so the true figure is probably closer to the French.
115. Jean, INSEE, "Emploi: Les enseignements de l'expérience néerlandaise," p. 135.
116. The Netherlands was not alone in this. See M. Kohli, M. Rein, A.-M. Guillemard, and H. van Gunsteren, eds., *Time for Retirement: Comparative Studies of Early Exit from the Labour Force* (Cambridge: Cambridge University Press, 1991).
117. Mark Kleinman, *A European Welfare State? European Union Social Policy in Context* (London: Palgrave, 2002), p. 48.
118. Visser and Hemerijck, *A Dutch Miracle*, p. 23.
119. Jonah D. Levy, "Vice into Virtue? Progressive Politics and Welfare Reform in Continental Europe," *Politics and Society* 27, no. 2 (June 1999), pp. 261–62.
120. John Gillingham, *European Integration, 1950–2003: Superstate or New Market Economy?* (Cambridge: Cambridge University Press, 2003), p. 377.
121. Ibid., pp. 376–77.
122. Jean, INSEE, "Emploi: Les enseignements de l'expérience néerlandaise," p. 139.
123. See, most recently, the English translation of his 1997 book, André Gorz, *Misères du présent, richesse du possible* (Paris: Editions Galilée, 1997): *Reclaiming Work: Beyond the Wage-Based Society*, trans. Chris Turner (Cambridge: Polity Press, 1999).
124. On the declining work ethic see Guillaume La Chaise, *Crise de l'emploi et fractures politiques. Les opinions des Français face au chômage* (Paris: Presses de la Fondation Nationale des Sciences Politiques, 1996), pp. 72–80.
125. Quoted in Kleinman, *A European Welfare State?* p. 48.
126. Jean, INSEE, "Emploi: Les enseignements de l'expérience néerlandaise," p. 142. The economist Elie Cohen provides a spirited critique of the *franc fort* policy in *L'Ordre économique mondial.* pp. 188–96.
127. Evelyne Huber and John D. Stephens, *Development and Crisis of the Welfare State: Parties and Policies in Global Markets* (Chicago: University of Chicago Press, 2001), p. 279.
128. Robert C. Kloostermann, "Three Worlds of Welfare Capitalism? The Welfare State and the Post-industrial Trajectory in the Netherlands after 1980," *West European Politics* 17, no. 4 (October 1994), p. 172.
129. Christopher Pierson, *Hard Choices: Social Democracy in the Twenty-First Century* (Cambridge: Polity Press, 2001), pp. 121–22; OECD, *The Jobs Study* (Paris: OECD, 1994).
130. Vivien A. Schmidt, *The Futures of European Capitalism* (Oxford: Oxford University Press, 2002), p. 26. Schmidt uses a 1999 Eurostat report.
131. See "Miracle ou mirage aux Pays-Bas?" *Le Monde Diplomatique*, July 1997. The supreme example of this is Ministère de l'Emploi et de la Solidarité, *Exclusion sociale et pauvreté en Europe* (Paris: La Documentation Française, 2001). See also the work by two Dutchmen: Paul De Beer and Ronald Luttikhuizen, "Le 'modèle polder' néerlandais: miracle ou mirage?," in Jean-Claude Barbier and Jérôme Gautié, eds., *Les politiques de l'emploi en Europe et aux Etats-Unis* (Paris: Presses Universitaires de France, 1998), pp. 113–34.

132. Levy, "Vice into Virtue?" p. 259.

133. Viviane Forrester, *L'Horreur économique* (Paris: Fayard, 1996).

134. OECD, *Industry Productivity: International Comparisons and Measurement Issues* (Paris: OECD, 1997); Freeman, "War of the Models," pp. 1–24; B. B. Bakker and I. Halikias, "Policy Reforms and Employment Creation," in International Monetary Fund, "The Netherlands: Transforming a Market Economy," *Occasional Papers*, no. 181 (Washington, DC: IMF, 1999), pp. 16–41; L. Aarts and P. de Jong, *Curing the Dutch Disease* (Aldershot: Avebury Press, 1996); F. Van den Ploeg, "The Political Economy of a Consensus Society: Experience from Behind the Dykes," *The Economic and Social Review* 28, no. 3 (1997), pp. 307–32.

135. Willem Adema, OECD, "Net Social Expenditure," *OECD Labour Market and Social Policy Occasional Papers*, no. 39 (1999); Gregg M. Olsen, *The Politics of the Welfare State: Canada, Sweden, and the United States* (Toronto: Oxford University Press, 2002), p. 67.

136. Joel F. Handler, "Social Citizenship and Workfare in the US and Western Europe: From Status to Contract," *Journal of European Social Policy* 13, no. 3 (August 2003), p. 236; Uwe Becker, "Welfare State Development and Employment in the Netherlands in Comparative Perspective," *Journal of European Social Policy* 10, no. 3 (2000), pp. 219–31; Philippe Bernard, *Immigration: le défi mondial* (Paris: Gallimard, 2002).

137. Ministère de l'Emploi et de la Solidarité, *Exclusion sociale et pauvreté en Europe*.

138. David Held, Anthony McGrew, David Goldblatt, and Jonathan Perraton, *Global Transformations: Politics, Economics, Culture* (Stanford: Stanford University Press, 1999).

139. Olsen, *The Politics of the Welfare State*, p. 45.

140. Sherwin Rosen, "Public Employment and the Welfare State in Sweden," *Journal of Economic Literature* 34, no. 2 (June 1996), pp. 729–37.

141. Marie-Odile Gilles and Michel Legros, "Politiques Sociales. L'épreuve de la pauvreté," CREDOC, *Collection des rapports*, no. 159 (April 1995), p. 51.

142. "Les retraites," *Questions de Sécurité Sociale* 588 (March 2003), p. 21; Ministry of Health and Social Affairs, Sweden, *Pension Reform: A Short Summary* (Stockholm: Ministry of Health and Social Affairs, 1994); Ann-Charlotte Stahlberg, "Pension Reform in Sweden," *Scandinavian Journal of Social Welfare* 4, no. 1 (1995), pp. 267–73.

143. Peter A. Hall, "Organized Market Economies and Unemployment in Europe: Is it Finally Time to Accept Liberal Orthodoxy?" in Bermeo, ed., *Unemployment in the New Europe*, pp. 52–86; Peter A. Hall and David Soskice, eds., *Varieties of Capitalism: The Foundations of Comparative Institutional Advantage* (Oxford: Oxford University Press, 2001).

144. Vivien A. Schmidt, "Values and Discourse in the Politics of Adjustment," in Scharpf and Schmidt, eds., *Welfare and Work in the Open Economy*, vol. I, pp. 229–309.

145. In this way, such nations have avoided the pitfalls of "Baumol's cost-disease": the tendency of service-sector wages to lag behind manufacturing. If service-sector wages are allowed to stagnate or rise merely according to

low productivity increases (as in North America), there will be jobs aplenty for the victims of manufacturing downsizing. See Gøsta Esping-Andersen's succinct discussion of Baumol (who devised this theory in 1967) in his *Social Foundations of Postindustrial Economies* (Oxford: Oxford University Press, 1999).

146. See John Grahl and Paul Teague's important article, "Is the European Social Model Fragmenting?" *New Political Economy* 2, no. 3 (1997), pp. 405–26.

147. See John M. Hobson, "Disappearing Taxes or the 'Race to the Middle'? Fiscal Policy in the OECD," in Weiss, ed., *States in the Global Economy*, pp. 37–57.

5 PERSISTING INEQUALITIES

1. Quoted in R. D. Anderson, *France 1870–1914: Politics and Society* (London: Routledge & Kegan Paul, 1977), p. 98.

2. François Bourguignon, Conseil d'Analyse économique, *Fiscalité et redistribution* (Paris: La Documentation Française, 1998), p. 46, all italics except the first series are in the original text. This study puts France in a less than favorable international spotlight. See also *Cahiers français* 292 (July–September 1999), special edition on "Emploi et protection sociale," pp. 66–68, for a discussion of the lack of redistribution in the French welfare state.

3. Mancur Olson, *The Rise and Decline of Nations: Economic Growth, Stagflation, and Social Rigidities* (New Haven: Yale University Press, 1982), p. 174; Arthur M. Okun, *Equality and Efficiency, the Big Tradeoff* (Washington, DC: Brookings Institution, 1975). Good discussions of Olson, both favorable and unfavorable, can be found, respectively, in Jonathan Rauch, *Government's End: Why Washington Stopped Working* (New York: Public Affairs, 1994) and in Robert Kuttner, *Everything for Sale: The Virtues and Limits of Markets* (Chicago: University of Chicago Press, 1996).

4. Gøsta Esping-Andersen, *The Three Worlds of Welfare Capitalism* (Princeton: Princeton University Press, 1990), p. 23; Robert E. Goodin, Bruce Headey, Ruud Muffels, and Henk-Jan Dirven, *The Real Worlds of Welfare Capitalism* (Cambridge: Cambridge University Press, 1999).

5. The best study of inequality in France is Alain Bihr and Roland Pfefferkorn, *Déchiffrer les inégalités*, 2nd edn. (Paris: Syros, 1999). See also the Conseil supérieur de l'Emploi des revenus et des coûts, *Les inégalités d'emploi et de revenu* (Paris: La Découverte, 1996). Some of the egregious tax privileges enjoyed by some French citizens are exposed in Bernard Zimmern, *Les profiteurs de l'Etat* (Paris: Plon, 2000). John Ardagh, *France in the New Century: Portrait of a Changing Society* (London: Viking, 1999), is a very useful journalistic account which relies on INSEE reports. For some recent INSEE statistics on poverty, see www.insee.fr, and "Quatre millions de pauvres en France," *Le Monde*, 22 March 2001.

6. Walter Korpi, "Social Policy and Distributional Conflict in the Capitalist Democracies. A Preliminary Comparative Framework," *West European Politics* 3, no. 3 (October 1980), p. 311.

7. Malcolm Sawyer, OECD, "Income Distribution in OECD Countries," *OECD Economic Outlook: Occasional Studies* (July 1976), pp. 34–35; John D. Stephens, *The Transition from Capitalism to Socialism* (Urbana: University of Illinois Press, 1979), p. 98.

8. John Ambler, "Ideas, Interests, and the French Welfare State," in Ambler, ed., *The French Welfare State: Surviving Social and Ideological Change* (New York: New York University Press, 1991), p. 13.

9. "Inequality," *The Economist*, 6 September 2003, pp. 28–29; Jean-Paul Fitoussi and Patrick Savidan, eds., "Comprendre les inégalités," special edition of the *Revue de philosophie et de sciences sociales* 4 (2003).

10. Thomas Piketty, *Les hauts revenus en France au XXe siècle. Inégalités et redistributions, 1901–1998* (Paris: Grasset, 2001).

11. Luigi Barzini, *The Europeans* (Harmondsworth, UK: Penguin, 1983), p. 154.

12. Ardagh, *France in the New Century*, pp. 194–95; Serge Berstein and Jean-Pierre Rioux, *La France de l'expansion. L'apogée Pompidou, 1969–1974* (Paris: Seuil, 1995), p. 197; Franz Kraus, "The Historical Development of Income Inequality in Western Europe and the United States," in Peter Flora and Arnold J. Heidenheimer, eds., *The Development of Welfare States in Europe and America* (New Brunswick, NJ: Transaction Publishers, 1984), p. 193.

13. Bruno Palier, *Gouverner la sécurité sociale* (Paris: Presses Universitaires de France, 2002), p. 341.

14. "D'où vient l'argent de la collectivité?" *Alternatives économiques* 211 (February 2003), p. 45; Louis Maurin, "Tous salariés et tous inégaux," *Alternatives économiques* 207 (October 2002), pp. 36–39.

15. Catherine Blum-Girardeau, *Les tableaux de la solidarité* (Paris: La Documentation Française, 1981), p. 9.

16. I owe the term "hidden welfare state" to the book by Christopher Howard, *The Hidden Welfare State: Tax Expenditures and Social Policy in the United States* (Princeton: Princeton University Press, 1999).

17. See Arnold J. Heidenheimer, Hugh Heclo, and Carolyn Teich Adams, *Comparative Public Policy*, 3rd. edn. (New York: St. Martin's, 1990); "Fisc. Les nouvelles ruses des riches," *Le Point* 1588 (21 February 2003), pp. 71–74.

18. Maurice Baslé, *Le budget de l'Etat* (Paris: La Découverte, 1997), p. 26.

19. John Ardagh, *France Today* (London: Penguin, 1990), p. 366; Jonathan Fenby, *On the Brink: The Trouble with France* (London: Warner Books, 1998), pp. 151–52.

20. Piketty, *Les hauts revenus en France au XXe siècle*, pp. 437–38.

21. Ardagh, *France in the New Century*, p. 195; "M. Mitterrand admet avoir été léger en ne déclarant pas 13 millions de francs au fisc," *Le Monde*, 15 January 2001. The man in question is the deceased President's son.

22. Carolyn Webber and Aaron Wildavsky, *A History of Taxation and Expenditure in the Western World* (New York: Simon & Schuster, 1986), pp. 547–50.

23. For a discussion of this concept of "trust," putting France in international perspective, see Francis Fukuyama, *Trust: The Social Virtues and the Creation of Prosperity* (New York: The Free Press, 1995), especially ch. 11.

24. Heidenheimer et al., *Comparative Public Policy*, pp. 202–16.

25. Alain Tourret, *Fonds spéciaux, primes et autres dérives* (Paris: Albin Michel, 2002), p. 268. The funds amounted to 536 million francs in 1995 and 473 million in 1994. Not even the Socialists, officially committed to cracking down on tax evasion, could resist the temptation of the secret funds. Most major Socialist politicians accepted them. On Chirac's spending habits, see "Paris: L'Imprimerie de Fortune de Chirac," *Libération*, 9 May 2002.

26. See "Let them eat foie gras," *The Economist*, 21 June 2003. Chirac and his wife spent 2.1 million euros on "food" between 1987 and 1995. This alleged abuse of public money is under investigation.

27. "Canada Ranks High for Lack of Corruption," *Globe and Mail* (Toronto), 28 August 2002. The group which tracks corruption is called Transparency International.

28. Charles de Gaulle, *Memoirs of Hope* (New York: Simon and Schuster, 1971), p. 342.

29. Interview with Marc Blondel, "Les Retraites: Je prends le dossier en main personnellement," *Le Parisien*, 2 December 2002.

30. On this theme, see Jacques Julliard, "La société de méfiance," *Nouvel observateur*, no. 2012, 29 May 2003 and "Une si moderne peur de l'avenir," *Nouvel observateur*, no. 2014, 12 June 2003.

31. Theodore Zeldin, *France, 1848–1945: Taste and Corruption* (Oxford: Oxford University Press, 1980), p. 332.

32. Béatrice Majnoni d'Intignano, *L'Usine à chômeurs* (Paris: Plon, 1998), p. 198.

33. Ardagh, *France in the New Century*, p. 189.

34. Eric Maurin and Christine Chambaz, INSEE, "Pauvreté persistante, pauvreté transitoire: une évaluation sur données françaises, 1987–1994," *Solidarité Santé* 2 (April–June 1996), p. 80.

35. For examples of how corporatist pressure groups have gained special status and benefits, see Suzanne Berger, "Regime and Interest Representation: the French Traditional Middle Classes," in Berger, ed., *Organizing Interests in Western Europe: Pluralism, Corporatism, and the Transformation of Politics* (Cambridge: Cambridge University Press, 1981), pp. 83–101.

36. Some of the best insights into this problem often come from foreigners, including the famous British expert on all things French, Theodore Zeldin, *The French* (London: Harvill, 1983), pp. 192–93, 285.

37. Based on Sawyer's widely-cited 1976 study for the OECD, from B. Guy Peters, "The Development of the Welfare State and the Tax State," in Douglas E. Ashford and E. W. Kelley, eds., *Nationalizing Social Security in Europe and North America* (Greenwich, CT: JAI Press, 1986), p. 227. On France's position in 1980, see INSEE, *Données sociales. Edition 1981* (Paris: INSEE, 1982), p. 227; Thomas Wilson, "The Finance of the Welfare State," in A. Peacock and F. Forte, eds., *The Political Economy of Taxation* (New York: St. Martin's, 1981), pp. 94–117. For earlier years, see Gabriel Ardant, *Histoire de l'impôt* (Paris: Fayard, 1971) and OECD, *Long-Term Trends in Tax Revenues of OECD Member Countries, 1955–1980* (Paris, OECD Studies in Taxation, 1981), tables B and 8.

38. Didier Maillard, "Tax Policies in the 1980s and 1990s: The Case of France," in Anthonie Knoester, ed., *Taxation in the United States and Europe: Theory and Practice* (New York: St. Martin's, 1993), p. 313.

39. Michael F. Forster, OECD, "Trends and Driving Factors in Income Distribution and Poverty in the OECD Area," *OECD Occasional Papers*, no. 42 (2000), p. 86; Bourguignon, *Fiscalité et redistribution*, chs. 1, 2; Zimmern, *Les profiteurs de l'Etat*, p. 26.

40. Emmanuel Suard, "Le financement de la protection sociale," in Jean-Yves Capul, ed., *Emploi et protection sociale* in *Cahiers français* 292 (July–September 1999), p. 45.

41. Zimmern, *Les profiteurs de l'Etat*, p. 31.

42. Surjit S. Bhalla, *Imagine There's No Country: Poverty, Inequality, and Growth in the Era of Globalization* (Washington, DC: Institute of International Economics, 2002), p. 223; Andrew Jackson and David Robinson, Canadian Centre for Policy Alternatives, *Falling Behind: The State of Working Canada, 2000* (Ottawa: Canadian Centre for Policy Alternatives, 2000), p. 43; OECD, Economics Department, Working Paper no. 189, *Income Distribution and Poverty in Selected OECD Countries* (Paris, 1998), tables 5.4 and 5.7. Poverty in this case is defined as less than half the median income.

43. Ardagh, *France in the New Century*, p. 195.

44. Joseph Berliner, *The Economics of the Good Society* (Oxford: Blackwell, 1999), p. 409; Christophe Fourel, "Tableau social. Les inégalités se portent bien," in *L'Etat de la France, 95–96* (Paris: La Découverte, 1995), p. 153; "Plus de retraites en haut de l'échelle," *Espace social européen* (10 January 1997), p. 19.

45. Alissa Goodman, Paul Johnson, and Steven Webb, *Inequality in the UK* (Oxford: Oxford University Press, 1997), p. 207; Bourguignon, *Fiscalité et redistribution*, p. 46. See also *Cahiers français* 292 (July–September 1999), special edition on "Emploi et protection sociale," pp. 66–68.

46. Gary Freeman, "Socialism and Social Security," in John S. Ambler, ed., *The French Socialist Experiment* (Philadelphia: Institute for the Study of Human Issues, 1985), p. 112.

47. Baslé, *Le budget de l'Etat*, p. 26.

48. A. B. Atkinson, *Incomes and the Welfare State: Essays on Britain and Europe* (Cambridge: Cambridge University Press, 1995), p. 55; Howard H. Davis, "Social stratification in Europe," in Joe Bailey, ed., *Social Europe*, 2nd edn. (London: Longman, 1998), pp. 17–35.

49. Esping-Andersen has ranked France in this category in his *The Three Worlds of Welfare Capitalism*. See also Goodin, Headey, Muffels, and Dirven, *The Real Worlds of Welfare Capitalism*, pp. 82–85.

50. See Patrick de La Morvonnais' article in Marion Segaud, Catherine Bonvalet, and Jacques Brun, eds., *Logement et habitat. L'Etat des savoirs* (Paris: La Découverte, 1998), p. 152.

51. Thomas Amossé, "Vingt-cinq ans de transformation des mobilités sur le marché du travail," in INSEE, *Données sociales. La société française, 2002–2003* (Paris: INSEE, 2002), p. 236.

52. Alain Garrigou, *Les élites contre la République. Sciences Po et l'ENA* (Paris: La Découverte, 2001), p. 149; Serge Bose, *Stratification et transformations sociales. La société française en mutation* (Paris: Nathan, 1993).
53. Eric Maurin, *L'égalité des possibles: La nouvelle société française* (Paris: Seuil, 2002), p. 75; R. Erikson and J. O. Jonsson, *Can Education be Equalized? The Swedish Case in Comparative Perspective* (Boulder: Westview Press, 1996).
54. Dominique Merllié and Jean Prévot, *La mobilité sociale*, 2nd edn. (Paris: La Découverte, 1997); Maria Vasconcellos, *Le système éducatif* (Paris: La Découverte, 1999), pp. 74–75; Yves Crozet et al., *Les grandes questions de la société française* (Paris: Nathan, 2000), p. 183; D. Goux and E. Maurin, "Meritocracy and Social Heredity in France: Some Aspects and Trends," *European Sociological Review* 13, no. 2 (1997), pp. 159–77; Zeldin, *The French*, p. 192; Stephens, *The Transition*, pp. 168, 170; Richard Musgrave, *Fiscal Systems* (New Haven: Yale University Press, 1969), p. 183.
55. World Health Organisation, *World Health Report 2000* (Geneva: WHO, 2000), p. 153; "Les Français inégaux face à la santé," *Le Monde*, 13 September 2000, pp. 1, 15; INSERM, *Les inégalités sociales de la santé* (Paris: INSERM, 2000); Nathalie Blanpain et al., "L'assurance complémentaire maladie: une diffusion encore inégale," *INSEE Première* 523 (June 1997) (at www.insee.fr).
56. E. Van Doorslaer, A. Wagstaff, and F. Rutten, *Equity in the Finance and Delivery of Health Care: An International Perspective* (Oxford: Oxford University Press, 1993).
57. Fenby, *On the Brink*, pp. 150, 281.
58. François Steudler, *L'Hôpital en observation* (Paris: Armand Colin, 1974), p. 9; Jacques Bichot, *Les politiques sociales en France au XXe siècle* (Paris: Armand Colin, 1997), p. 117; Maurice Rochaix, *Les questions hospitalières de la fin de l'Ancien Régime à nos jours* (Paris: Berger-Levrault, 1996), p. 375; Christian Maillard, *Histoire de l'hôpital de 1940 à nos jours* (Paris: Dunod, 1986).
59. Archives de l'Assistance Publique, Paris (AAP), C-1522, Emile Lévy, director (CNRS), *Hospitalisation publique, hospitalisation privée* (Paris, 1977), p. 79.
60. Ibid.
61. Ibid.
62. Ibid.
63. "Les dépenses de santé ont atteint 2,579 euros par Français en 2002," *Le Monde*, 24 July 2003.
64. Raymond Soubie, Commissariat général du plan, *Santé 2010. Equité et efficacité du système* (Paris: La Documentation Française, 1993) vol. III, p. 28; Marc Duriez and Simone Sandier, CREDES, *Le système de santé en France* (Paris: Presses Universitaires de France, 1994), p. 7.
65. Alain Charraud and Pierre Mormiche, INSEE, *Disparités de consommation médicale. Enquête santé 1980–1981* (no. 118, *Les Collections de l'Insée*) (Paris, January 1986), pp. 42–43.
66. Ibid., p. 47.
67. Ibid., p. 131.
68. Soubie, *Santé 2010*, vol. III, p. 139.
69. Ibid., p. 140.

70. Ibid., pp. 175–76.
71. David Wilsford, "Reforming French Health Care Policy," in John T. S. Keeler and Martin A. Schain, eds., *Chirac's Challenge: Liberalization, Europeanization and Malaise in France* (New York: St. Martin's, 1996), p. 243.
72. "Les dépenses d'assurance-maladie en hausse de 6.3% en 2000," *Le Monde*, 16 February 2001; "Médicaments: les mauvais comptes de la Sécu," *Le Parisien*, 15 September 2000; "France: A Headache," *The Economist*, 8 March 1997, p. 57; Serge-Allain Rozenblum, "Santé: enjeux et défis," *Revue politique et parlementaire* 987 (March-April 1997), pp. 28–34; Renaud Fabrykant, "Médicaments: le cas français," in Ibid., pp. 53–54; Philippe Austruy and Philippe Rollandin, *Santé volée. Une faillite sur Ordonnances* (Paris: Editions Le Cherche Midi, 1999).
73. A.-M. Brocas and C. Zaidman, "Perspectives financières du système du santé," in Soubie, *Santé 2010*, vol. I.
74. Jean de Kervasdoué, "Economie de la santé," in Jean-Pierre Vesperini, ed., *Les problèmes actuels de l'économie française* (Paris: Presses Universitaires de France, 2001), pp. 329–78; and his widely read polemic, *La santé intouchable* (Paris: J.-C. Lattès, 1996).
75. David Wilsford, "The State and the Medical Profession in France," in Frederic W. Hafferty and John B. McKinlay, eds., *The Changing Medical Profession: An International Perspective* (New York: Oxford University Press, 1993), pp. 124–37. p. 125; Jean-Philippe Buisson and Dominique Giorgi, *La politique du médicament* (Paris: Editions Montchrestien, 1997).
76. Haut comité de la santé publique, *La santé des français*, rev. edn. (Paris: La Découverte, 1998), chs. 5, 6.
77. Christian Saint-Etienne, *L'Etat mensonger* (Paris: Editions J.-C. Lattès, 1996), p. 80; Wilsford, "Reforming French Health Care Policy," p. 233.
78. Ambler, "Ideas, Interests," p. 15.
79. Amédée Thévenet, *L'Aide sociale aujourd'hui, après la décentralisation*, 10th edn. (Paris: ESF, 1994), pp. 307–18.
80. Marie-Claire Villeval, "Politique sociale et emploi des personnes handicapées," *Revue française des affaires sociales* 37, no. 3 (July–September 1983), p. 12.
81. Villeval, "Politique social et emploi des personnes handicapées," p. 15.
82. Sar Levitan et al., *Programs in Aid of the Poor*, 8th edn. (Baltimore: Johns Hopkins University Press, 2002); "Handicapés: 'Nous avons un énorme retard depuis deux décennies,'" *Le Monde*, 25 June 2003.
83. Jean-Michel Charbonnel et al., Documents du Centre d'étude des revenus et des coûts (CERC), *Protection sociale et pauvreté* (Paris: CERC, 1988), pp. 10–11.
84. Pascale Roussel and Jésus Sanchez, "La compensation des incapacités au travers de l'enquête Handicaps-Incapacités-Dépendance," in INSEE, *Données sociales. La société française, 2002–2003* (Paris: INSEE, 2002), pp. 365–71.
85. Antoine Parent, "Minima sociaux et retour à l'emploi," in Capul, ed. *Emploi et protection sociale*, p. 36. For the relatively weak French commitment to integrate the handicapped into the labor force see: Jean-Claude Barbier and

Jérôme Gautié, *Les politiques de l'emploi en Europe* (Paris: Presses Universitaires de France, 1997), for a comparison with other European nations; and DARES, *Quarante ans de politique de l'emploi* (Paris: La Documentation Française, 1996).

86. Thévenet, *L'Aide sociale*, p. 158.
87. "Les paralysés dénoncent les difficultés de la ville," *Libération*, 13 June 2001.
88. Jacques Trémintin, "Les personnes à mobilité réduite ont-elles accès aux vacances ordinaires?," *Lien social* 673 (10 July 2003), pp. 4–8.
89. "Handicapés: 'Nous avons un énorme retard depuis deux décennies,'" *Le Monde*, 25 June 2003.
90. Natacha Czerwinski et al., "Maisons de retraite. Ce qu'on ne veut plus voir," *L'Express*, 30 September 2003.
91. Sandrine Blanchard, "La France tente de rattraper son retard vis-à-vis des handicapés," *Le Monde*, 3 February 2003. See also the polemic by Pascal Gobry, *L'Enquête interdite. Handicapés: Le scandal humain et financier* (Paris: Editions Le Cherche Midi, 2002), which illustrates the French lag behind northern European nations.
92. Blanchard, "La France tente de rattraper son retard vis-à-vis des handicapés."

6   THE PROTECTED PEOPLE

1. This statement was widely reported in the press and it was displayed, from March 2000 into 2001, on Prime Minister Lionel Jospin's official website, at www.premier-ministre.gouv.fr.
2. Jacques Véron, "L'âge du pouvoir," *Gérontologie et société* 74 (October 1995), quoted in Jacques Huguenin, *Seniors: l'explosion* (Paris: Gallimard, 1999), p. 163.
3. Thai Than Dang, Pablo Antolin, and Howard Oxley, OECD, "Fiscal Implications of Ageing," OECD Economics Department Working Papers, no. 305, 19 September 2001, p. 26.
4. Patricia Lormeau, "Des anciens plus riches que les actifs," *Le Monde*, 2 April 1997; *Espace social européen* 360 (3 January 1997), pp. 14–17.
5. Theodore R. Marmor, Timothy M. Smeeding, Vernon L. Greene, and Deborah A. Chassman, "The North American Context and Volume Overview," in Marmor, Smeeding, and Greene, eds., *Economic Security and Intergenerational Justice: A Look at North America* (Washington, DC: Urban Institute, 1994), pp. 8, 9.
6. Bernard Préel, *Le choc des générations* (Paris: La Découverte, 2000), p. 224; Jean Hervé Lorenzi, "Consolider la retraite en respectant un nouvel équilibre," in Conseil d'Analyse économique, Premier Ministre, Rapports, Olivier Davanne et al., *Retraites et épargne* (Paris: La Documentation Française, 1998), pp. 45, 35; Henri Sterdyniak, "Retraites: l'état du débat," in OFCE, *L'Economie française, 2000* (Paris: La Découverte, 2000), p. 102.
7. Michael F. Forster, OECD, "Trends and Driving Factors in Income Distribution and Poverty in the OECD Area," *OECD Occasional Papers* no. 42 (2000), p. 40.

8. Xavier Gaullier, "Pour un new deal entre générations," *Esprit* (October 1998), p. 21; Gaullier, "Transferts publics et privés entre générations: incidences sur les inégalités sociales," *Retraites et société* 20 (1997); Claudine Attias-Donfut, ed., *Les solidarités entre générations. Vieillesse, familles, Etat* (Paris: Nathan, 1995).

9. For example, "Retraites: inventaire avant réforme," *Le Monde*, 15 February 1999; Gaël Dupont and Henri Sterdyniak, *Quel avenir pour nos retraites?* (Paris: La Découverte, 2000), p. 80; Jean-Jacques Rosa, "France," in Rosa, ed., *The World Crisis in Social Security* (San Francisco: Institute for Contemporary Studies, 1982), pp. 9–28; Archives de l'Assistance Publique, Paris (AAP), B-6201, Pierre Schopflin, Inspecteur général des Affaires sociales, *Evaluation et sauvegarde de l'assurance vieillesse. Rapport au Ministre des Affaires sociales et de l'Emploi* (Paris: La Documentation Française, 1987), p. 7 (hereafter cited as Schopflin Report).

10. John Ambler, "Ideas, Interests, and the French Welfare State," in Ambler, ed., *The French Welfare State: Surviving Social and Ideological Change* (New York: New York University Press, 1991), p. 26; Laurence Lautrette, *Le droit de la retraite en France* (Paris: Presses Universitaires de France, 1999); Bernard Legris and Stephan Lollivier, "Le niveau de vie par génération," *INSEE Première* 423 (January 1996), pp. 1–4; Pierre-Alain Greciano, ed., *Retraites: réformes et débats, France, Italie, RFA, Royaume-Uni* (Paris: La Documentation Française, nos. 817–18, 1999), pp. 30–37.

11. Georges Dorion and André Guionnet, *La Sécurité Sociale*, 6th edn. (Paris: Presses Universitaires de France, 1997), p. 83; François Chatagner *(Le Monde)*, *La protection sociale: des réformes inachevées* (Paris: Le Monde, 1998), p. 207.

12. Jean-Michel Charbonnel et al., Documents du Centre d'étude des revenus et des coûts (CERC), *Protection sociale et pauvreté* (Paris: CERC, 1988), p. 29.

13. Jean-Michel Normand, "Les retraités découvrent le lobbying," *Retraite et société* 4, no. 4 (1993); Huguenin in *Seniors: l'explosion*, pp. 151–62; Vincent Drouin, *Les effets de génération dans l'électorat français* (Paris: L'Harmattan, 1995).

14. Didier Blanchet and Florence Legros, "France: The Difficult Path to Consensual Reforms," in Martin Feldstein and Horst Siebert, eds., *Social Security Pension Reform in Europe* (Chicago: University of Chicago Press, 2002), p. 117; "Synthèse du Rapport Charpin," at www.plan.gouv.fr/retraites (site visited in March 2000). The Commissariat Général du Plan's website.

15. Sénat, Les Rapports du Sénat no. 459, presented by Senator Alain Vasselle, *Réforme des retraites: peut-on encore attendre?* (Paris: Senate of France, 1999), pp. 9, 20.

16. "La structure de la protection sociale," *Espace social européen* 360 (3 January 1997), p. 16, and author's calculations; Ministère du Travail et des Affaires sociales, *Les revenus sociaux, 1981–1995* (Paris: La Documentation Française, 1996).

17. Martial Delignon and Jean-Marie Saunier, "Les revenus sociaux," in INSEE, *Données sociales. La société française. Edition 1999* (Paris: INSEE, 1999), p. 399.

18. Richard Hauser, OECD, "Adequacy and Poverty among the Retired," *Ageing Working Papers*, Working Paper AWP 3.2, 1998 (consulted at www.oecd.org), pp. 17, 18.
19. See Denis Kessler, "L'avenir de la protection sociale," *La Revue des entreprises MEDEF*, no. 616 (November–December 1999), pp. 38–39.
20. We have known for forty years of the coming pension crisis. See Jacques Bichot, "Retraites: ajustement ou réforme?," *Futuribles* 286 (May 2003), p. 5.
21. Henri Mendras and Alistair Cole, *Social Change in Modern France* (Cambridge: Cambridge University Press, 1991), p. 190.
22. Serge Guérin, *Le boom des seniors* (Paris: Economica, 2000), p. 52.
23. Guérin, *Le boom des seniors*, p. 48; Robert Rochefort, *Vive le papy-boom* (Paris: Odile Jacob, 2000), pp. 93–96. Rochefort belongs to the intergenerational inequality denial school. Another recent example of this school of thought is Sara Arber and Claudine Attias-Donfut, eds., *The Myth of Generational Conflict: The Family and State in Ageing Societies* (London: Routledge, 2000).
24. Göran Therborn, *European Modernity and Beyond* (London: Macmillan, 1995), p. 94.
25. Therborn, *European Modernity*, p. 94.
26. Bruce Headey, Robert E. Goodin, Ruud Muffels, and Henk-Jan Dirven, "Welfare over Time: The Three Worlds of Welfare Capitalism in Panel Perspective," *Journal of Public Policy* 17 (1997), p. 349.
27. Gøsta Esping-Andersen and Walter Korpi, "Social Policy as Class Politics in Post-War Capitalism: Scandinavia, Austria, and Germany," in John H. Goldthorpe, ed., *Order and Conflict in Contemporary Capitalism* (Oxford: Oxford University Press, 1984), p. 197.
28. Frank L. Wilson, *European Politics Today: The Democratic Experience*, 2nd edn. (Englewood Cliffs, NJ: Prentice Hall, 1994), p. 256.
29. Ken Judge, "The Growth of Social Security in Britain: Spending on Pensions," in Douglas E. Ashford and E. W. Kelley, eds., *Nationalizing Social Security in Europe and North America* (Greenwich, CT: JAI Press, 1986), p. 203.
30. Helga Michalsky, "The Politics of Social Policy," in Klaus Von Beyme and Manfred G. Schmidt, eds., *Policy and Politics in the Federal Republic of Germany* (New York, 1985); Catherine Mills, *Economie de la protection sociale* (Paris: Dalloz, 1994), p. 275; Geneviève Canceill, INSEE, "Ressources et niveau de vie des personnes âgées: les pensions de retraite ont fortement progressé de 1970 à 1984," *Economie et statistique* 222 (June 1989).
31. Commissariat général du plan, *Vieillir demain* (Paris: La Documentation Française, 1980), p. 42.
32. Ibid., p. 42; Dupont and Sterdyniak, *Quel avenir pour nos retraites?*, p. 48.
33. Peter Coffey, *The Social Economy of France* (London: Macmillan, 1973), p. 11.
34. Commissariat général du plan, *Vieillir demain*, p. 13.
35. Quoted in Commissariat général du plan, *Vieillir demain*, p. 59.
36. Anne-Marie Guillemard, *Le déclin du social: Formation et crise des politiques de vieillesse* (Paris: Presses Universitaires de France, 1986), p. 143.

37. AAP B-764, Pierre Laroque, *Rapport de la commission d'étude des problèmes de la vieillesse* (Paris: La Documentation Française, 1962), p. 3. Hereafter cited as the "Laroque Report."
38. Laroque Report, p. 18.
39. Ibid., pp. 3–4.
40. Robert Hugonot, *Politiques municipales du vieillissement et de la vieillesse* (Paris: Erès, 1989), p. 7.
41. Laroque Report, p. 259.
42. Ibid., p. 157.
43. *Droit social* (May 1970), p. 240. The poll was conducted by the Fondation nationale des sciences politiques.
44. Hugonot, *Politiques municipales du vieillissement*, p. 9.
45. Observatoire Régional de Santé d'Ile-de-France and Institut National de la Santé et de la Recherche Médicale (INSERM), *Conditions de vie et état de santé des personnes âgées en Ile-de-France* (Paris: INSERM, 1985), pp. 38–39, 53.
46. Dominique Thouvenin, "Sécurité sociale = solidarité, ou le 'Manifeste mutualiste pour la Sécurité sociale,'" *Revue du droit sanitaire et social* 22, no. 2 (April–June 1986), pp. 282–88; "Les scandales des caisses de retraite," *L'Expansion* 672 (February 2003), pp. 50–54.
47. Schopflin Report, p. 7.
48. Catherine Blum-Girardeau, *Les tableaux de la solidarité. Rapport au Ministre de la Solidarité nationale* (Paris: La Documentation Française, 1981), p. 237.
49. Commissariat général du plan, *Vieillir demain*, pp. 42–43.
50. Ibid., p. 43.
51. Jean-Pierre Dumont, *Les systèmes de protection sociale en Europe*, 4th edn. (Paris: Economica, 1998), p. 209.
52. Blum-Girardeau, *Les tableaux de la solidarité*, p. 189.
53. Ibid., pp. 48–49.
54. Ibid., pp. 50–51.
55. John Myles, *Old Age in the Welfare State: The Political Economy of Pensions*, rev. edn. (Lawrence, Kansas: University of Kansas Press, 1989), pp. 5–6.
56. Commissariat général du plan, *Vieillir demain*, p. 35.
57. Françoise Cribier, "Changes in Life Course and Retirement in Recent Years: The Example of Two Cohorts of Parisians," in Paul Johnson, Christoph Conrad, and David Thomson, eds., *Workers versus Pensioners: Intergenerational Justice in an Ageing World* (Manchester, UK: Manchester University Press, 1989), p. 190.
58. Xavier Gaullier, *L'avenir à reculons, chômage et retraite* (Paris: Les Editions Ouvrières, 1982); Anne Marie Guillemard, *La vieillesse et l'état* (Paris: Presses Universitaires de France, 1980).
59. Bruno Palier, *Gouverner la sécurité sociale* (Paris: Presses Universitaires de France, 2002), p. 129.
60. In 1995, the cost of all passive "unemployment" expenses was only one-ninth the cost of pensions, and one-twentieth the total social budget: Palier, *Gouverner la sécurité sociale*, p. 202.

61. OECD, *Reforming Public Pensions* (Paris: OECD, 1988), p. 49. Like all OECD publications, this one appeared simultaneously in French.

62. François Mercereau, "Raisons et leçons des déficits chroniques," *Pouvoirs* 94 (2000), pp. 51–52.

63. Jean-Claude Henrard, Commissariat général du plan, *Les systèmes d'aides aux personnes âgées* (Paris: La Documentation Française, 1992), p. 156, table 17; Didier Blanchet and Louis-Paul Pelé, "Social Security and Retirement in France," in Jonathan Gruber and David A. Wise, eds., *Social Security and Retirement around the World* (Chicago: University of Chicago Press, 1999), p. 105; J.-C. Chesnais, "Evolution démographique et charge de financement des retraites," *Revue française des affaires sociales* (June 1983), pp. 85–102; Guillemard, *Le déclin du social*, pp. 316–21.

64. G. Bannock, R. E. Baxter, and E. Davis, *Penguin Dictionary of Economics*, 6th edn. (London: Penguin, 1998), p. 355; Dennis C. Mueller, *Public Choice III* (Cambridge: Cambridge University Press, 2003).

65. See James M. Buchanan and Gordon Tullock, *The Calculus of Consent: Logical Foundations of Constitutional Democracy* (Ann Arbor, MI: University of Michigan Press, 1962), pp. 286–87.

66. For a critique of this school of economic thought, see Robert Kuttner, *Everything for Sale: The Virtues and Limits of Markets* (Chicago: University of Chicago Press, 1996), pp. 333–45. An earlier critique is Terry M. Moe, "Toward a Broader View of Interest Groups," *The Journal of Politics* 43 (1981), pp. 531–43 and his earlier book, *The Organization of Interests* (Chicago: University of Chicago Press, 1980).

67. See Béatrice Majnoni d'Intignano, *L'Usine à chômeurs* (Paris: Plon, 1998), pp. 200–02, for a critique of the replacement rates enjoyed by certain public-sector employees.

68. Gérard Maudrux, *Retraites. Le mensonge permanent* (Paris: Les Belles Lettres, 2000), p. 72; François Charpentier, *Les fonds de pensions* (Paris: Economica, 1996), p. 33.

69. In 1998, the general treasury was raided to the tune of 75 billion francs (roughly 11 billion euros) to pay for the unfunded pension "rights" of public-sector pensioners. According to the Institut français de recherche sur les administrations publiques, by 2005 the annual cost will be 20 billion euros: Christian Julienne, *Le diable est-il libéral?* (Paris: Les Belles Lettres, 2001), p. 60.

70. Maudrux, *Retraites*, p. 76; Bernard Zimmern, *Les profiteurs de l'état* (Paris: Plon, 2000), p. 73. This calculation was made before Raffarin's 2003 reforms so the figure would have to be lowered somewhat.

71. "Les régimes siphonnés . . . ," *L'Expansion* 672 (February 2003), p. 52.

72. Maudrux, *Retraites*, p. 83. On the special family allowances, housing, and other taxpayer-subsidized perks of the civil service, see Commissariat général du plan, Alain Blanchard, reporter, *L'Action sociale de l'Etat en faveur de ses agents* (Paris: La Documentation Française, 1995); Jean-Marc Dupuis and Claire El Moudden, "Une mesure de la contributivité et de la redistribution des retraites en France de 1947 à 1999," *Revue française des affaires sociales*, nos. 3–4 (July–December 2000), pp. 64–65; Christian Saint-Etienne, *L'Etat mensonger* (Paris: Les Belles Lettres, 1996), pp. 95–96, 100; "Le problème des

retraites," in Serge Marti, ed. (Le Monde), *Questions économiques et sociales* (Paris: Le Monde, 2000), p. 205.

73. World Bank, *Averting the Old Age Crisis: Policies to Protect the Old and Promote Growth* (Washington, DC: World Bank, 1994), Box 1, p. 11.

74. Caisse nationale de l'assurance vieillesse, website, www.cnav.fr/recherche/ evolutionprestations.htm, pp. 1–2. Consulted in late 2000.

75. Premier Ministre. Service d'Information et de diffusion, *Guide de la retraite*, 3rd edn. (Paris: La Documentation Française, 1981), p. 2.

76. Commissariat général du plan, Premier Ministre, *La Retraite en 10 questions, 10 réponses* (Paris: La Documentation Française, 1999), p. 6.

77. For other nations, see the high-quality articles in Auerbach, Kotlikoff, and Leibfritz, eds., *Generational Accounting around the World.*

78. Yves Cannac and Armand Laferrère, "La dépense publique," *Commentaire* 19, no. 74 (Summer 1996), pp. 354–55; John Myles and Jill Quadagno, "Recent Trends in Public Pension Reform: A Comparative View," in Keith G. Banting and Robin Boadway, eds., *Reform of Retirement Income Policy: International and Canadian Perspectives* (Kingston, Ont.: School of Policy Studies, 1997), pp. 247–71.

79. Schopflin Report, p. 55.

80. Didier Blanchet, "Population Aging and French Economic Performance," in Barry Bosworth and Gary Burtless, eds., *Aging Societies: The Global Dimension* (Washington, DC: Brookings Institution, 1998), p. 130.

81. "Les inégalités salariales hommes/femmes," *Questions de Sécurité Sociale* 588 (March 2003), p. 10; Odile Dangerfield and Danièle Prangère, "Les Retraites en 1997," in *Solidarité, Santé* 1 (January–March 1998), p. 11.

82. Dangerfield and Prangère, "Les Retraites en 1997," p. 12.

83. Philippe Montigny and Jean-Marie Saunier, "Les systèmes de retraite en Europe," *Solidarité, Santé* 1 (January–March 1998), pp. 35–44.

84. Ken Battle, "Sustaining Public Pensions in Canada: A Tale of Two Reforms" (2003). Paper available at the Caledon Institute of Social Policy's website and published in Noriyuki Takayama, ed., *Taste of Pie: Searching for Better Pension Provisions in Developed Countries* (Tokyo: Maruzen Co., 2003).

85. Robert J. Shiller, *Irrational Exuberance* (New York: Broadway Books, 2000), pp. 4, 127–28. On the lack of interest in the stock market, see the articles in *Le Monde*, 25 November 1999; Jean-Marie Poursin, "Rigidité de la répartition et turbulences de la démographie," and "La rupture entre générations," in Patrice Bourdelais, ed., *Etat-providence: Arguments pour une réforme* (Paris: Gallimard, 1996).

86. John Gillingham, *European Integration, 1950–2003: Superstate or New Market Economy* (Cambridge: Cambridge University Press, 2003), p. 386; "Still a Dirty Word: Private Pension Funds in France," *The Economist*, 8 June 2002.

87. Denis Kessler, "Introduction générale," in *Economie et statistique* 233 (June 1990), pp. 4–5. A special edition, published by INSEE. See also Eurostat, *Dépenses et recettes de protection sociale, 1980–1989* (Brussels: Eurostat, 1990); OECD (OCDE in French), *La réforme des régimes publics de pensions* (Paris: OCDE, 1988); OCDE, *L'avenir de la protection sociale* (Paris: OCDE, 1988), esp. pp. 42–45. Prime Minister Michel Rocard sounded the same alarm in a 1991 report, *Livre blanc sur les retraites* (Paris: La Documentation Française,

1991). Eric Szij, ed., *Retraites et vieillissement démographique. Comparaisons internationales* (Paris: La Documentation Française, no. 715, 1993), is a useful collection.

88. Gaël Dupont and Henri Sterdyniak, *Quel avenir pour nos retraites?* (Paris, La Découverte, 2000), p. 32.

89. "Stock market lingo Greek to most French," *The Globe and Mail* (Toronto), 27 May 1999; Philip H. Gordon and Sophie Meunier, *The French Challenge: Adapting to Globalization* (Washington, DC: Brookings Institution, 2001), p. 23; Alain Minc, *www.capitalisme.fr* (Paris: Grasset, 2000), pp. 166–68.

90. Neil Nevitte, *The Decline of Deference: Canadian Value Change in Cross-National Perspective* (Toronto: Broadview Press, 1996), p. 72; Joseph S. Nye Jr., Philip Zelikow, and David C. King, eds., *Why People Don't Trust Government* (Cambridge, MA: Harvard University Press, 1997); Pippa Norris, *Critical Citizens: Global Support for Democratic Governance* (Oxford: Oxford University Press, 1999).

91. Peter G. Peterson, *Gray Dawn* (New York: Three Rivers Press, 1999), p. 163.

92. Claude Bismut and Najat El Mekkaoui-de Freitas, *Fonds de pension. Aspects économiques et financiers* (Paris: Economica, 2000), p. 11; Peterson, *Gray Dawn*, p. 164; R. Herd and P. Van der Hoord, "Estimating Pension Liabilities: A Methodological Framework," *OECD Economic Studies* 23 (Winter 1994) (also at www.oecd.org); World Bank, *Averting the Old Age Crisis*.

93. See Adam Harmes, *Unseen Power: How Mutual Funds Threaten the Political and Economic Wealth of Nations* (Toronto: Stoddart, 2001).

94. Jacques Bichot, *Retraites en péril* (Paris: Presses de la Fondation Nationale des Sciences Politiques, 1999), p. 119; Christian Saint-Etienne, *Génération sacrifié: les 20–45 ans* (Paris: J.-C. Lattès, 1993); Jean-Pierre Cendron, *Le monde de la protection sociale* (Paris: Editions Nathan, 1996), p. 116; Pierre Rosanvallon, *La nouvelle question sociale* (Paris: Seuil, 1995), p. 43; Isabelle Chapellière, *Où va la protection sociale?* (Paris: Syros, 1989).

95. Alain Bihr and Roland Pfefferkorn, *Déchiffrer les inégalités*, 2nd edn. (Paris: Syros, 1999), p. 130; Journal Officiel de la République Française, Avis et rapports du Conseil économique et social, Séance des 11 et 12 janvier 2000, *L'Avenir des systèmes de retraite*, presented by René Teulade (Paris, 2000), p. 8.

96. By the mid 1990s, the typical retiree in the private sector used up his or her pension contributions in seven years and drew on the public purse for thirteen years: Pierre Rosanvallon and Jean-Paul Fitoussi, *Le nouvel âge des inégalités* (Paris: Seuil, 1996), p. 86.

97. Between 1958 and 1976, 55% of French parliamentarians were former state employees, including teachers. Only 11.4% hailed from business. See Maurice Larkin, *France since the Popular Front: Government and People, 1936–1986* (Oxford: Clarendon Press, 1988), p. 307.

98. David Thomson, *Selfish Generations? How Welfare States Grow Old*, rev. edn. (Cambridge: White Horse Press, 1996). For a contrasting view of this generation see the excellent study on Canada (with frequent comparisons to the USA) by Doug Owram, *Born at the Right Time: A History of the Baby Boom Generation* (Toronto: University of Toronto Press, 1996).

99. David Thomson, "Generations, Justice, and the Future of Collective Action," in Peter Laslett and James Fishbin, eds., *Justice between Age Groups and Generations* (New Haven: Yale University Press, 1992), p. 208.
100. T. H. Marshall, "Citizenship and Social Class," in David Held, ed., *States and Societies* (New York: New York University Press, 1983), p. 249. Originally published in *Citizenship and Social Class, and other essays* (London, 1950).
101. Saint-Etienne, *L'Etat mensonger*, p. 32.
102. Robert Gildea, *France since 1945* (Oxford: Oxford University Press, 1997), pp. 95–96.
103. Saint-Etienne, *L'Etat mensonger*, p. 47.
104. Vic George, "The Future of the Welfare State," in Vic George and Peter Taylor-Gooby, eds., *European Welfare Policy: Squaring the Circle* (London: Macmillan, 1996), p. 10.
105. See James K. Galbraith, *Created Unequal: The Crisis in American Pay* (New York: The Free Press, 1998), pp. 82–83.
106. Christine Chambaz et al., "Le revenu et le patrimoine des ménages," in INSEE, *Données sociales. La société française* (1999) (Paris: INSEE, 1999), p. 275.
107. Nicolas Baverez, *Les Trente piteuses* (Paris: Flammarion, 1998).
108. Ibid., p. 53; Douglas E. Ashford, "Advantages of Complexity: Social Insurance in France," in Ambler, ed., *The French Welfare State*, p. 49; Ministère de l'Emploi et de la Solidarité, *Les comptes de la protection sociale, 1990–1997* (Paris: La Documentation Française, 1998), p. 61. Retirees also benefit from half-price train tickets at most times of the year; retirement homes; free access to public transit in many cities; exoneration from the annual television tax; reductions in the residence tax, and so on. See Hugonot, *Politiques municipales du vieillissement et de la vieillesse*; Commissariat Général du Plan, Rapport de la Commission Protection Sociale, René Teulade, president, *Protection sociale. Xème Plan, 1989–1992* (Paris: La Documentation Française, 1989), p. 27; Arnaud Parienty *(Le Monde)*, *Fiscalité. L'impossible réforme?* (Paris: Le Monde, 1997), p. 87.
109. Pippa Norris, "Global Governance and Cosmopolitan Citizens," in Joseph S. Nye Jr. and John D. Donahue, eds., *Governance in a Globalizing World* (Washington, DC: Brookings Institution Press, 2000), pp. 162–63, 168–73. The French statistics are usually folded into general "northwestern European" ones.
110. Stéphanie Toutain, *Les systèmes de retraites en Italie. Une interminable réforme* (Paris: L'Harmattan, 2001), ch. 7; Alberto Martinelli, Antonio M. Chiesi, and Sonia Stefanizzi, *Recent Social Trends in Italy, 1960–1995* (Montreal and Kingston: McGill-Queen's University Press, 1999), chs. 1, 8.
111. Schopflin Report, pp. 62–63.
112. See the special edition, "La réforme des retraites," of *Regards sur l'actualité* 295 (November 2003) for the reforms and "Santé et retraite. 2003, l'Année des réformes," *Problèmes économiques* 2801–02 (19–26 March 2003) for the background.

113. In a 1993 cross-national survey conducted by Eurobarometer, the level of support for generous pensions in France was close to the European average: Alan Walker, ed., *The New Generational Contract* (London: University College London Press, 1996), p. 3, table 1.1. See also Giuliano Bonoli, Vic George, and Peter Taylor-Gooby, *European Welfare Futures: Towards a Theory of Retrenchment* (Cambridge: Polity Press, 2000), pp. 93, 94; Tito Boeri, Axel Börsch-Supan, and Guido Tabellini, "Welfare State Reform: A Survey of what Europeans Want," *Economic Policy* 32 (April 2001), p. 42; "Voting for Welfare," *The Economist*, 2 June 2001, p. 76.

114. Teulade Report, pp. 182, 186.

115. See the language used to describe the "struggle" for the right to retire at sixty, in "Retraites: le complot?" *Force Ouvrière* 8 (July 2002). The FO's online magazine, viewed at www.fo-com.com in December 2002.

7 THE EXCLUDED: IMMIGRANTS, YOUTH, WOMEN

1. Pierre Lellouche, in his book, *La République immobile* (Paris: Grasset, 1998), p. 76.

2. Quoted in Sophie Pedder, "France. The Grand Illusion," *The Economist*, 5 June 1999, p. 11 of survey.

3. The full citation is: Jean-Marie Pernot, "Deux années de luttes sociales dans le privé," *Cahiers de Ressy* 1 (1998), p. 4, quoted in Sophie Béroud, René Mouriaux, and Michel Vakaloulis, *Le mouvement social en France. Essai de sociologie politique* (Paris: La Dispute, 1998), p. 109.

4. Préel, in an interview with *Sciences humaines* 108 (August–September 2000), p. 15.

5. Gérard Noiriel, *Le creuset français. Histoire de l'immigration XIXe–XXe siècles* (Paris: Seuil, 1988) and "Immigration: Amnesia and Memory," *French Historical Studies* 19, no. 2 (Fall 1995), pp. 367–80.

6. These are the words of Rogers Brubaker, *Citizenship and Nationhood in France and Germany* (Cambridge, MA: Harvard University Press, 1992), pp. 182–83.

7. Loïc J. D. Wacquant, "Banlieues françaises et ghetto noir américain: de l'amalgame à la comparaison," *French Politics and Society* 10, no. 4 (Fall 1992), pp. 81–103.

8. Sophie Body-Gendrot, "Urban Violence and Community Mobilizations," in Body-Gendrot and Marco Martiniello, eds., *Minorities in European Cities* (London: Macmillan, 2000), pp. 75–87.

9. Sophie Body-Gendrot, *Les villes face à l'insécurité. Des ghettos américains aux banlieues françaises* (Paris: Bayard, 1998), p. 202.

10. Ian Gordon, "The Impact of Economic Change on Minorities and Migrants in Western Europe," in Katherine McFate, Roger Lawson, and William Julius Wilson, eds., *Poverty, Inequality and the Future of Social Policy* (New York: Russell Sage Foundation, 1995), p. 535. See also the articles in the same volume by Loïc Wacquant, "The Comparative Structure and Experience of Urban Exclusion: 'Race,' Class, and Space in Chicago and Paris," pp. 543–70 and Sophie Body-Gendrot, "Immigration, Marginality and French Social Policy," pp. 571–83.

11. Alain Policur, "Racisme et antiracisme," in Gilles Ferreol, ed., *Intégration et exclusion dans la société française contemporaine* (Lille: Presses Universitaires de Lille, 1992), p. 55; Patrick Weil, *La France et ses étrangers* (Paris: Gallimard, 1995).

12. Mohammed Rebzani, *Des jeunes dans la discrimination* (Paris: Presses Universitaires de France, 2002), pp. 45–47.

13. Jonathan Fenby, *On the Brink: The Trouble with France* (Paris: Warner Books, 1998), p. 208.

14. "La galère des jeunes blacks et beurs face à l'emploi," *Lien social* 666 (15 May 2003), p. 5.

15. Michel Wieviorka, *La France raciste* (Paris: Seuil, 1992).

16. Philippe Bernard, *Immigration: le défi mondial* (Paris: Gallimard, 2002), p. 148.

17. Fenby, *On the Brink*, p. 204.

18. For estimates, see the chapter, "La politique d'intégration des populations immigrées," in Marie-Thérèse Join-Lambert et al., *Politiques sociales*, 2nd edn. (Paris: Presses de la Fondation Nationale des Sciences Politiques and Dalloz, 1997), p. 662.

19. Martin A. Schain, "Immigration and Politics," in Peter A. Hall, Jack Hayward, and Howard Machin, eds., *Developments in French Politics*, rev. edn. (London: Macmillan, 1994), p. 254.

20. Michèle Tribalat, *Faire France. Une enquête sur les immigrés et leurs enfants* (Paris: La Découverte, 1995), p. 160; Vincent Viet, *La France immigrée. Construction d'une politique, 1914–1997* (Paris: Fayard, 1998).

21. Library of the Ministère de l'Emploi et de la Solidarité, Paris, Haut conseil à l'intégration, "La promotion sociale des jeunes dans les quartiers en difficulté," report, June 2003, p. 10; INSEE (Institut national de la statistique et des études économiques), *Données sociales 2002–2003* (Paris: INSEE, 2002).

22. Olivier Mazel (Le Monde), *L'Exclusion. Le social à la dérive* (Paris: Le Monde, 1996), p. 150. On the subculture of older, single men from North Africa, many of whom live in hostels, see Gilles Ascaride and Salvatore Condro, *La ville précaire. Les "isolés" du centre-ville de Marseille* (Paris: L'Harmattan, 2001).

23. Jacques Guillou and Louis Moreau de Bellaing, *Misère et pauvreté. Sans domicile fixe et sous prolétaires* (Paris: L'Harmattan, 1999), pp. 255–57. An estimated 80 to 90% of Paris' homeless were men.

24. Pierre Merlin, *Les banlieues des villes françaises* (Paris: La Documentation Française, 1998), pp. 91–112; Haut conseil à l'Intégration, *Liens culturels et intégration* (Paris: La Documentation Française, 1995).

25. Michel Glaude, "Où va la cohesion sociale?," in Robert Fraisse and Jean-Baptiste de Foucauld, eds., *La France en prospectives* (Paris: Odile Jacob, 1996), pp. 128–29; "Les méandres d'une France inégale," *Alternatives économiques* 218 (October 2003), pp. 52–53.

26. Joëlle Bordet, *Les 'jeunes de la cité'* (Paris: Presses Universitaires de France, 1998); Hervé Vieillard-Baron, *Les banlieues françaises ou le ghetto impossible* (Paris: Editions de l'Aube, 1996); Joël Roman, ed., *Ville, exclusion et citoyenneté. Entretiens de la ville II* (Paris: Editions Esprit, 1993); Alain Gauthier, ed.,

Aux frontières du social. L'Exclusion (Paris: L'Harmattan, 1997); Jean-Claude Abric, ed., *Exclusion sociale, insertion et prévention* (Saint-Agne: Erès, 1996).

27. Merlin, *Les banlieues des villes françaises*, p. 7.
28. Body-Gendrot, "Urban Violence and Community Mobilizations," pp. 75–87; "Le grand ensemble, coupable idéal du mal urbain," *Le Monde*, 6 December 2003.
29. Gilles Horenfeld, "L'univers des HLM," in Marion Segaud, Catherine Bonvalet, and Jacques Brun, eds., *Logement et habitat. L'Etat des savoirs* (Paris: La Découverte, 1998), p. 143.
30. Yan Maury, *Les HLM. L'Etat providence vu d'en bas* (Paris: L'Harmattan, 2001), p. 86.
31. Michel Glaude, "La pauvreté, sa mesure et son évolution," in Conseil d'Analyse économique, Premier Ministre, Tony Atkinson et al., reporters, *Pauvreté et exclusion* (Paris: La Documentation Française, 1998), p. 64.
32. Haut conseil à l'Intégration, "La promotion sociale des jeunes dans les quartiers en difficulté," p. 3.
33. Weil, *La France et ses étrangers*, p. 433; Tribalat, *Faire France*, cited by Merlin, *Les banlieus*, p. 117. Serge Paugam, *La société française et ses pauvres* (Paris: Presses Universitaires de France, 1993), p. 59.
34. Haut conseil à l'Intégration, "La promotion sociale des jeunes dans les quartiers en difficulté," p. 4.
35. Michèle Tribalat, "Immigration et concentration urbaine," in Daniel Cohen, ed., *France: les révolutions invisibles* (Paris: Calmann-Lévy, 1998), pp. 193–203.
36. Jean-Marc Stébé, *Le logement social en France*, 2nd edn. (Paris: Presses Universitaires de France, 2002), pp. 112–24.
37. Philippe d'Iribarne, *Le chômage paradoxal* (Paris: Seuil, 1990) and *La logique de l'honneur. Gestion des entreprises et traditions nationales* (Paris: Seuil, 1989). For a discussion of this literature, see Denis Clerc, *Condamnés au chômage?* (Paris: Syros, 1999), pp. 34–36.
38. Thomas Piketty, "Les créations d'emploi en France et aux Etats-Unis," *Notes de la Fondation Saint-Simon* (December 1997); Edmond Malinvaud, "The Rise of Unemployment in France," *Economica* 53, no. 210 (supplement) (1986); Jean-Paul Fitoussi, "Minimum Wages and Unemployment," *American Economic Review* (May 1994).
39. Edward Luttwak, *Turbo Capitalism: Winners and Losers in the Global Economy* (New York: HarperCollins, 1999), p. 112.
40. A recent report by the Commissariat Général du Plan admits as much: *Rapport sur les perspectives de la France* (Paris: La Documentation Française, 2001), "Synthèse," pp. 1–42 of online version. Consulted at Commissariat Général du Plan's website, June 2001.
41. John Gillingham, *European Integration, 1950–2003: Superstate or New Market Economy?* (Cambridge: Cambridge University Press, 2003), p. 382.
42. Pierre Mayol, "Quelques cadrages sur les jeunes," *Esprit* (October 1996), pp. 8–23. The influential journal *Esprit* ran a series of articles in 1996 under the rubric, "Les orphelins des trente glorieuses," or the "Orphans

of the Golden Age." See also Mireille Elbaum, "Pour une autre politique de traitement du chômage," in Pierre Boisard and Olivier Mongin et al., eds., *Le travail, quel avenir?* (Paris: Gallimard, 1997), p. 143; "The Politics of Unemployment," *The Economist*, 5 April 1997, p. 22; Serge Paugam, *La disqualification sociale* (Paris: Presses Universitaires de France, 1991).

43. Charles Debbasch and Jean-Marie Pontier, *La société française*, 4th edn. (Paris: Dalloz, 2001), pp. 633–77.

44. The fortunes of North American youth (but particularly Americans) have been on the rise since the mid 1990s, despite well documented reversals to their fortunes in the 1980s and early 1990s. See James E. Côté and Anton L. Allahar, *Generation on Hold: Coming of Age in the Late Twentieth Century* (Toronto: Stoddart, 1994); Katherine S. Newman, *Declining Fortunes: The Withering of the American Dream* (New York: Basic Books, 1993), esp. chs. 7–8; and Jeffrey Madrick, *The End of Affluence* (New York: Random House, 1995).

45. Nicolas Baverez, *Les Trente piteuses* (Paris: Flammarion, 1998), pp. 51–53, 83–86; OCDE, *Pour un monde solidaire. Le nouvel agenda social* (Paris: OCDE, 1999), p. 78. The English version of this OECD report was called *A Caring World: The New Social Policy Agenda*; Norbert Holcblat, "La politique de l'emploi en France," in Jean-Claude Barbier and Jérôme Gautié, eds., *Les politiques de l'emploi en Europe et aux Etats-Unis* (Paris: Presses Universitaires de France, 1998), p. 85.

46. Béatrice Majnoni d'Intignano, "Vers la lutte des âges?" *Commentaire 21*, no. 81 (Spring 1998), p. 95; Claude Thélot and Michel Villac, Rapport au Ministre de l'Emploi et de la Solidarité, *Politique familiale. Bilan et perspectives* (Paris: La Documentation Française, 1998), p. 87; Jacques Commaille and François de Singly, eds., *La question familiale en Europe* (Paris: L'Harmattan, 1997).

47. INSEE, *Les comptes de la protection sociale de 1959 à 1985* (January 1987), pp. 24–25. For the period 1985–95, I have used Bruno Palier, *Gouverner la sécurité sociale* (Paris: Presses Universitaires de France, 2002), p. 202.

48. Eric Maurin, *L'égalité des possibles: La nouvelle société française* (Paris: Seuil, 2002), p. 51.

49. Prominent members of this school include Jill Quadagno and Theda Skocpol (of the USA), Alan Walker (of the UK), and Ellen Gee (of Canada).

50. Ellen M. Gee, "Population and Politics: Voodoo Demography, Population Aging, and Canadian Social Policy," in Gee and Gloria M. Gutman, eds., *The Overselling of Population Aging: Apocalyptic Demography, Intergenerational Challenges, and Social Policy* (Toronto: Oxford University Press, 2000), p. 13; Theda Skocpol, *The Missing Middle: Working Families and the Future of American Social Policy* (New York: Norton, 2000).

51. See Claudine Attias-Donfut, ed., *Les solidarités entre générations. Vieillesse, familles, État* (Paris: Nathan, 1995).

52. Louis Chauvel, "Comment se manifeste la solidarité intergénérationelle?" in François Charpentier, ed., *Encyclopédie Protection Sociale. Quelle refondation?* (Paris: Economica, 2000), p. 388.

53. Maurin, *L'égalité des possibles*, p. 22.
54. François-Xavier Merrien, "Nouveau régime économique international et devoirs des états providence," in Pierre de Senarclens, ed., *Maîtriser la mondialisation* (Paris: Presses de la Fondation Nationale des Sciences Politiques, 2000), pp. 110–11.
55. Guillaume La Chaise, *Crise de l'emploi et fractures politiques. Les opinions des Français face au chômage* (Paris: Presses de la Fondation Nationale des Sciences Politiques, 1996), p. 263.
56. "Niveau de vie des jeunes ménages," in INSEE, *Les jeunes* (Paris: INSEE, 2000), pp. 88–89; "Les dix leviers pour doper l'emploi," *Liaisons sociales* 47, no. 7 (December 2003), pp. 14–18.
57. Jean-Pierre Terrail, *La dynamique des générations. Activité individuelle et changement social (1968/1993)* (Paris: L'Harmattan, 1995), pp. 60–61, 66–69.
58. Robert Holcman, *Le chômage* (Paris: La Documentation Française, 1997), p. 69.
59. Gilles Saint-Paul, INSEE, "L'anatomie du chômage en Espagne: une comparaison avec la France et les Etats-Unis," *Economie et statistique*, no. 332–33 (2002–2003), p. 162.
60. Denis Olivennes, "Pour une politique publique de l'emploi," in Roger Fauroux and Bernard Spitz, eds., *Notre Etat. Le livre vérité de la fonction publique* (Paris: Robert Laffont, 2000), p. 345.
61. Jacques Freyssinet, *Le chômage*, 2nd edn. (Paris: La Découverte, 2000), pp. 40–41, 53; Dominique Gambier and Michel Vernières, *L'Emploi en France* (Paris: La Découverte, 1998), p. 49, for part-time work and under-employment.
62. John Ardagh, *France in the New Century* (London: Viking, 1999), p. 196; Observatoire national de la pauvreté et de l'exclusion sociale, *Rapport 2000* (Paris: La Documentation Française, 2000), ch. 4.
63. Centre d'étude des revenus et des coûts (CERC), *Les rémunérations des jeunes à l'entrée dans la vie active* (Paris: CERC, 1991), pp. 61–62.
64. Guy Standing, "Labor Insecurity through Market Regulation: Legacy of the 1980s, Challenge for the 1990s," in McFate, Lawson, and Wilson, eds., *Poverty, Inequality and the Future of Social Policy*, p. 164.
65. Join-Lambert et al., *Politiques sociales*, p. 595; Conseil supérieur de l'Emploi, des revenus et des coûts (CSERC), *Inégalités d'emploi et de revenu, les années 1990* (Paris: La Découverte, 1996); Commissariat général du Plan, Groupe de travail présidé par Raoul Briet, *Perspectives à long terme des retraites* (Paris: La Documentation Française, 1995), pp. 33, 21.
66. Martine Fournier, "Générations: volées, dorées, sacrifiées?" *Sciences humaines* 108 (August–September 2000), p. 15; Chrystelle Carroy and Laurent Joffrin, "La guerre des 30 ans," *Le Nouvel Observateur*, no. 1888 (11 January 2001); Jeanne Fagnani and Marie-Thérèse Letablier, eds., "Famille et travail: contraintes et arbitrages," in the series, *Problèmes politiques et sociaux* 858 (8 June 2001).
67. Martine Segalen, "Familles et générations: Grandes tendances," in Serge Cordellier and Elisabeth Lau, eds., La Découverte, *L'Etat de la France, 2000–2001* (Paris: La Découverte, 2000), p. 65.

68. Christian Baudelot, "Effets d'âge et de génération dans l'évolution du salaire individuel," in Denis Kessler and André Masson, eds. *Cycles de vie et générations* (Paris: Economica, 1985), p. 11.

69. Baudelot, "Effets d'âge et de génération," p. 10; Christian Baudelot and Roger Establet, *Avoir 30 ans en 1968 et en 1998* (Paris: Seuil, 2000).

70. Olivier Galland, *Les jeunes* (Paris: La Découverte, 1996), p. 81.

71. Claudine Attias-Donfut, "Rapports de générations. Transferts intrafamiliaux et dynamique macrosociale," *Revue française de sociologie* 41, no. 4 (September–October 2000), p. 666.

72. Gilbert Clavel, *La société d'exclusion* (Paris: L'Harmattan, 1998); Chantal Guérin-Plantin, *Génèses de l'insertion* (Paris: Dunod, 1999); Jean-Michel Belorgey, *La gauche et les pauvres* (Paris: Syros, 1988); Marie-Christine Palicot and Louis Thibout, *L'Europe et la lutte contre l'exclusion* (Paris: Racine, 1995); Claudelle Guyennot, *L'insertion. Un problème social* (Paris: L'Harmattan, 1998); and above all Isabelle Astier, *Revenu minimum et souci d'insertion* (Paris: Desclée de Brouwer, 1997).

73. See, for example, Sylvie Morel's fine comparative study, *Les logiques de la réciprocité. Les transformations de la relation d'assistance aux Etats-Unis et en France* (Paris: Presses Universitaires de France, 2000), pp. 127–29.

74. Attias-Donfut, "Rapports de générations," p. 666.

75. DARES, *La politique de l'emploi* (Paris: La Découverte, 1997), p. 39; Commissariat général du Plan, Rapport au Premier ministre, directed by Robert Castel, *Chômage: le cas français* (Paris: La Documentation Française, 1997), p. 113.

76. Jonah D. Levy, *Tocqueville's Revenge: State, Society and Economy in Contemporary France* (Cambridge, MA: Harvard University Press, 1999), p. 248.

77. Quoted in Levy, *Tocqueville's Revenge*, p. 248.

78. *Le Monde*, 12 January 1995; Susan Milner and René Mouriaux, "France," in Hugh Compston, ed., *The New Politics of Unemployment: Radical Policy Initiatives in Western Europe* (London: Routledge, 1997), p. 50.

79. Marie-Odile Gilles and Michel Legros, CREDOC, *Politiques sociales: l'épreuve de la pauvreté* (Paris: CREDOC, 1995), especially p. 364.

80. Join-Lambert et al., *Politiques sociales*, p. 197.

81. Nicole Péry, *La formation professionnelle* (Paris: La Documentation Française, 1999), cited in Paul Santelmann, ed., *Politique d'emploi et formation des chômeurs* (Paris: La Documentation Française, 2000), p. 19.

82. Fournier, "Générations: volées, dorées, sacrifiées?" p. 18.

83. Dominique M. Gross, "Unemployment Persistence in France and Germany," in Brian K. MacLean and Lars Osberg, eds., *The Unemployment Crisis: All for Nought?* (Montreal & Kingston: McGill-Queen's University Press, 1996), pp. 207–25.

84. Ariane's story as well as several other vignettes can be found in Sebastien Schehr, *La vie quotidienne des jeunes chômeurs* (Paris: Presses Universitaires de France, 1999), pp. 98–110.

85. Michael F. Forster, OECD, "Trends and Driving Factors in Income Distribution and Poverty in the OECD Area," *OECD Occasional Papers* no. 42 (2000), pp. 1–40.

86. Serge Milano, *La pauvreté absolue* (Paris, 1988), pp. 17–19, 35–37, 44–45, cited in Emmanuel Hirsch, *Nouvelles pauvretés, nouvelles solidarités* (La Documentation Française, "Problèmes politiques et sociaux," no. 588) (July 1988), p. 12; Forster, "Trends and Driving Factors in Income Distribution and Poverty," p. 139; Commissariat Général du Plan, Rapport du Groupe "Europe Social," Joël Maurice, ed., *Emploi, négociations collectives, protection sociale: vers quelle Europe sociale?* (Paris: La Documentation Française, 1999), ch. 2.

87. Forster, "Trends and Driving Factors in Income Distribution and Poverty," p. 114; Commissariat général du Plan, Rapport au Premier Ministre, *Rapport sur les perspectives de la France* (Paris: La Documentation Française, 2000), pp. 57–62; Xavier Gaullier, "Ages mobiles et générations incertaines," *Esprit* (October 1998); Louis Chauvel, *Le destin des générations. Structure sociale et cohortes en France au XXe siècle* (Paris: Presses Universitaires de France, 1998); Carine Burricand and Nicole Roth, INSEE, "Les parcours de fin de carrière des générations 1912–1941," *Economie et statistique* 335 (2000), pp. 63, 69.

88. Milano, *La pauvreté absolue*, pp. 17–19, 35–37, 44–45.

89. Atkinson, "La pauvreté et l'exclusion sociale en Europe," in *Pauvreté et exclusion*, p. 14.

90. During the early 1990s, Sweden devoted five times more per capita than France to job re-training programs. See Olivier Marchand, *Plein emploi, l'improbable retour* (Paris: Gallimard, 2002), pp. 157–58; Dominique Anxo and Christine Erhel, "La politique de l'emploi en Suède: nature et évolution," in Barbier and Gautié, eds., *Les politiques de l'emploi en Europe et aux Etats-Unis*, 1998), p. 190; Göran Therborn, *European Modernity and Beyond: The Trajectory of European Societies, 1945–2000* (London: Macmillan, 1995). On the distribution of risk and exposure to hardship in France's labor market, see Olivier Mazel, *La France des chômages* (Paris: Gallimard, 1999), ch. 3; Didier Demazière, *La sociologie du chômage* (Paris: La Découverte, 1995); Daniel Cohen et al., "French Unemployment: A Transatlantic Perspective," *Economic Policy* 25 (1997), pp. 267–91; Daniel Cohen and Pascaline Dupas, "Trajectoires comparées des chômeurs en France et aux Etats-Unis," *Economie et statistique* 332–33 (2000), pp. 17–26; and Charles R. Bean, "European Unemployment: A Survey," *Journal of Economic Literature* (June 1994), pp. 573–619.

91. Joseph S. Berliner, *The Economics of the Good Society* (Oxford: Blackwell, 1999), p. 272.

92. Anne Laferrère, "L'occupation des logements depuis 1945," in INSEE, *Données sociales. La société française* (1999 edition) (Paris: INSEE, 1999), p. 336; François Dubujet and David Le Blanc, "Accession à la propriété: le régime de croisière?", *INSEE Première* 718 (June 2000), pp. 1–4; Margaret Maruani, "Féminisation du monde du travail," in Jean-Yves Capul, ed., *La société française contemporaine*, in *Cahiers français* 291 (May–June 1999), pp. 16–20.

93. Mazel, *La France des chômages*, p. 92.

94. Christine Lagarenne and Nadine Legendre, INSEE, "Les travailleurs pauvres en France: facteurs individuels et familiaux," *Economie et statistique* 335 (2000), p. 5.

95. Nicole Roth, "L'activité après 50 ans: évolutions récentes," in Conseil d'Analyse économique, Premier Ministre, Rapport, Dominique Taddei, *Retraites choisies et progressives* (Paris: La Documentation Française, 2000), pp. 149–50.

96. Chauvel, *Le destin des générations*, p. 269. For a discussion of the concept of generation, see Henry Colombani and Xavier Lionet, "Vie sociale, générations et territoires," *Vie sociale* 1 (January–February 2001), pp. 71–80.

97. Chauvel, *Le destin des générations*, p. 211; Olivier Brossard, "L'emploi et le chômage," in OFCE, *L'Economie française, 2000* (Paris: La Découverte, 2000), p. 55.

98. Michel Coffineau, *Les lois Auroux, dix ans après, février 1993* (Paris: La Documentation Française, 1993).

99. Baudelot and Establet, *Avoir 30 ans en 1968 et en 1998*; Fournier, "Générations: volées, dorées, sacrifiées?" p. 17.

100. And, as some would argue, to *male* workers, almost by definition. See Guillemette de Larquier, "Dynamiques des marchés du travail, chômage et inégalités," in Christian Bessy, ed., *Des marchés du travail équitables? Approche comparative France/Royaume-Uni* (Brussels: Peter Lang, 2001).

101. Majnoni d'Intignano, "Vers la lutte des âges?" p. 95; Véronique Sandoval, "Les transformations du marché du travail des jeunes et des femmes en France et dans trois autres pays européens," in INSEE, *Données sociales. La société française* (1999 edition) (Paris: INSEE, 1999), p. 187.

102. Baudelot and Establet, *Avoir 30 ans*, p. 90.

103. Consider how well high-tech firms on the US West Coast treated their employees during the 1990s boom. They had no other choice.

104. Chauvel, "Comment se manifeste la solidarité intergénérationelle?" in Charpentier, ed., *Encyclopédie Protection Sociale*, p. 387; Baudelot, "Effets d'âge et de génération," p. 22.

105. See de Larquier, "Dynamiques des marchés du travail, chômage et inégalités."

106. Peter Gottschalk and Mary Joyce, "The Impact of Technological Change, Deindustrialization, and Internationalization of Trade on Earnings Inequality: An International Perspective," in McFate, Lawson, and Wilson, eds., *Poverty, Inequality and the Future of Social Policy*, p. 210.

107. Olivier Galland, *Sociologie de la jeunesse. L'entrée dans la vie* (Paris: Armand Colin, 1991), and Galland, "Une entrée de plus en plus tardive dans la vie adulte," INSEE, *Economie et statistique* 283–84 (1995), pp. 33–52. Robert Castel, *Les métamorphoses de la question sociale* (Paris: Gallimard, 1995); Michel Lemoine, "Les difficultés d'intégration professionnelle des jeunes étrangers ou d'origine d'étrangère," *Revue française des affaires sociales* (December 1992), pp. 174–77; Yves Lichtenberger, "L'emploi des jeunes," in Boisard and Mongin et al., eds., *Le travail, quel avenir?* p. 126; Christine Daniel and Carole Tuchszirer, *L'Etat face aux chômeurs. L'indemnisation du chômage de 1884 à nos jours* (Paris: Flammarion, 1999), p. 326; Marie-Thérèse Join-Lambert, Rapport au Premier Ministre, *Chômage: mesures d'urgence et minima sociaux* (Paris: La Documentation Française, 1998).

284 Notes to pages 196–98

108. Christine Daniel, "L'indemnisation du chômage depuis 1974: d'une logique d'intégration à une logique de segmentation," *Revue française des affaires sociales*, nos. 3–4 (July–December 2000), pp. 29–45.
109. Daniel, "L'indemnisation," p. 41.
110. Daniel and Tuchszirer, *L'Etat face aux chômeurs*, p. 291.
111. See www.assedic.com, "Données et chiffres" section. The official website of UNEDIC and ASSEDIC. Consulted in early 2001; OCDE, *Pour un monde solidaire. Le nouvel agenda social* (Paris: OCDE, 1999), p. 59. The English version of this OECD report was called *A Caring World: The New Social Policy Agenda*.
112. Daniel and Tuchszirer, *L'Etat face aux chômeurs*, p. 292. Jacques Bichot, *Les politiques sociales en France au XXe siècle* (Paris: Armand Colin, 1997), p. 131, agrees with Daniel.
113. Luttwak, *Turbo Capitalism*, p. 183; John Gray, *False Dawn: The Delusions of Global Capitalism* (London: Granta, 1998).
114. Horst Siebert, "Labor Market Rigidities: At the Root of Unemployment in Europe," *Journal of Economic Perspectives* 11, no. 3 (1997), pp. 37–54; Miguel A. Malo, Luis Toharia, and Jérôme Gautié, "France: The Deregulation that Never Existed," in Gøsta Esping-Andersen and Marino Regini, eds., *Why Deregulate Labor Markets?* (Oxford: Oxford University Press, 2000), pp. 245–70.
115. Premier Ministre, Conseil d'Analyse économique, Jean Pisani-Ferry, ed., *Plein emploi* (Paris: La Documentation Française, 2000), p. 156.
116. Danièle Demoustier, "France: Voluntary Sector Initiatives for Work Integration," in Roger Spear, Jacques Defourny, Louis Favreau, and Jean-Louis Laville, eds., *Tackling Social Exclusion in Europe: The Contribution of the Social Economy* (Aldershot, UK: Ashgate, 2001), pp. 114–15.
117. Castel, *Chômage*, pp. 15, 23, 75. The graph is on p. 154. Chauvel, *Le destin des générations*, p. 193. On the widespread fatalism in the face of youth unemployment, see Christophe Dejours, *Souffrance en France: La banalisation de l'injustice sociale* (Paris: Seuil, 1998).
118. Castel, *Chômage*, p. 75.
119. Lichtenberger, "L'emploi des jeunes," in Boisard and Mongin et al., eds., *Le travail, quel avenir?* pp. 115–33. For the classic, misguided notion that the high rate of youth unemployment is the result of poor training, see Claude Malhomme, "Protection et fracture sociales," *Commentaire* 19, no. 75 (Autumn 1996), p. 675.
120. Gérard Forgeot and Jérôme Gautié, "Insertion professionnelle des jeunes et processus de déclassement," INSEE, *Economie et statistique* no. 304–05 (4 May 1997), p. 56; Clerc, *Condamnés au chômage?*, pp. 32–33.
121. Clerc, *Condamnés au chômage*, pp. 160–61.
122. Miguel A. Malo, Luis Toharia, and Jérôme Gautié, "France: The Deregulation that Never Existed," in Esping-Andersen and Regini, eds., *Why Deregulate Labour Markets?* p. 265. In 2002, Sciences Po broke with regulations and began to take socio-economic and ethnic factors into consideration in the admissions process.

123. Michel Forsé et al., *Recent Social Trends in France, 1960–1990* (Montreal & Kingston: McGill-Queen's University Press, 1993), p. 171.

124. Antoine Prost, *Education, société et politiques: Une histoire de l'enseignement de 1945 à nos jours* (Paris: Seuil, 1997), p. 211; Cordellier and Lau, *L'Etat de la France, 2000–2001*, p. 145.

125. Prost, *Education*, pp. 139, 214.

126. Ibid., p. 211.

127. Emmanuel Todd, *Après l'Empire: Essai sur la décomposition du système américain* (Paris: Gallimard, 2002).

128. Jean-Claude Driant, "Logement. Grandes tendances," in Serge Cordellier and Sarah Netter, eds., *L'Etat de la France, 2003* (Paris: La Découverte, 2003), pp. 86–88.

129. Chauvel, *Le destin des générations*, p. 179.

130. Laferrère, "L'occupation des logements," pp. 337, 342.

131. Dubujet and Le Blanc, "Accession à la propriété," p. 2.

132. "Beaucoup de bruit pour peu de choses," *Espace social européen* (21 March 1997), p. 7; Marceline Bodier, INSEE, "Les effets d'âge et de génération sur le niveau et la structure de la consommation," *Economie et statistique* 324–25 (1999), pp. 163–65; Claude Louvot, Minister of Transport, "Les dépenses de logement de 1984 à 1996," *INSEE Première* 611 (October 1998), pp. 1–4.

133. Louvot, "Les dépenses de logement de 1984 à 1996," pp. 1–4.

134. Jacques Attali, editorial in *L'Express* (22–28 October 1998).

135. Baverez, *Les Trente piteuses*, p. 128. Chapter 5, on deflation, is a blistering condemnation of French monetary policy during the 1990s. See also Bichot, *Les politiques sociales en France au XXe siècle*, pp. 95–97.

136. Olivier Blanchard and Jean-Paul Fitoussi, reporters, *Croissance et chômage* (Paris: La Documentation Française, 1998), p. 28.

137. Castel, *Chômage*, pp. 140, 127; Olivier Galland, "Les jeunes et l'exclusion," in Serge Paugam, ed., *L'exclusion. L'état des savoirs* (Paris: La Découverte, 1996), pp. 183–92.

138. Jean-Michel Charbonnel et al., Documents du Centre d'étude des revenus et des coûts (CERC), *Protection sociale et pauvreté* (Paris: CERC, 1988), p. 54; Nadine Lefaucheur, "French Policies Towards Lone Parents: Social Categories and Social Policies," in McFate, Lawson, and Wilson, eds., *Poverty, Inequality and the Future of Social Policy*, pp. 257–89.

139. Christine Chambaz et al., "Le revenu et le patrimoine des ménages," in INSEE, *Données sociales. La société française* (1999) (Paris: INSEE, 1999), p. 281.

140. Charbonnel et al., *Protection sociale et pauvreté*, pp. 41, 45.

141. Alain Bihr and Roland Pfefferkorn, *Déchiffrer les inégalités*, 2nd edn. (Paris: Syros, 1999), p. 139; Jean-Pierre Dumont, *La Sécurité Sociale toujours en chantier. Historique, bilan, perspectives* (Paris: Les Editions Ouvrières, 1981), p. 43.

142. Barbara Bergmann, *Saving our Children from Poverty: What the United States can Learn from France* (New York: Russell Sage Foundation, 1996).

143. Susan Pedersen, *Family, Dependence, and the Origins of the Welfare State* (Cambridge: Cambridge University Press, 1993), pp. 391–92; Jacques Hochard, *Aspects économiques des prestations familiales* (Paris: UNCAF, 1961), pp. 22, 175.

144. INSEE, *Les comptes de la protection sociale de 1959 à 1985* (January 1987), pp. 24–25, 9.

145. Jacques Bichot, *La politique familiale* (Paris: Editions Cujas, 1992), p. 86.

146. Ibid., pp. 88–9.

147. Pierre Laroque, Rémi Lenoir, Commissariat général du plan, *La politique familiale en France depuis 1945* (Paris: La Documentation Française, 1985), pp. 225–31.

148. See Jane Jenson and Mariette Sineau, *Mitterrand et les Françaises. Un rendez-vous manqué* (Paris: Presses de la Fondation nationale des sciences politiques, 1995); Jane Jenson, Jacqueline Laufer, and Margaret Maruani, eds., *The Gendering of Inequalities: Women, Men and Work* (Aldershot, UK: Ashgate, 2000); Margaret Maruani, *Travail et emploi des femmes* (Paris: La Découverte, 2000).

149. Jane Jenson and Mariette Sineau, "France: Reconciling Republican Equality with 'Freedom of Choice,'" in Jenson and Sineau, eds., *Who Cares? Women's Work, Childcare and Welfare State Redesign* (Toronto: University of Toronto Press, 2001), p. 96.

150. Catherine Mills, "Le système social à l'épreuve de la crise," *Revue française des affaires sociales* 37, no. 3 (July–September 1983), pp. 128–29.

151. Margaret Maruani, *Les mécomptes du chômage* (Paris: Bayard, 2002); Alain Bihr and Roland Pfefferkorn, *Hommes, femmes, quelle égalité?* (Paris: Les Editions de l'Atelier, 2002).

152. Commissariat Général du Plan, Rapport de la Commission Protection Sociale, René Teulade, president, *Protection sociale. Xème Plan, 1989–1992* (Paris: La Documentation Française, 1989).

153. "Entre 1.7% et 2.2% de relèvement des prestations sociales," *Le Monde*, 29 December 2000.

154. Béatrice Majnoni d'Intignano, Conseil d'Analyse économique, *Egalité entre femmes et hommes: Aspects économiques* (Paris: La Documentation Française, 1999).

155. Michel Laroque, "Systèmes familiaux et politiques de la famille en France," *Revue française des affaires sociales* 35, no. 2 (April–June 1981), p. 135.

156. Catherine Blum-Girardeau, *Les tableaux de la solidarité. Rapport au Ministre de la Solidarité nationale* (Paris: La Documentation Française, 1981), p. 54.

157. François Chatagner, *La protection sociale. Des réformes inachevées* (Paris: Le Monde, 1988), p. 215; *Le Monde*, 14 October 1997.

158. See *Libération*, 2 October 1998; Join-Lambert et al., *Politiques sociales*, pp. 566–67.

159. A. B. Atkinson, *Incomes and the Welfare State: Essays on Britain and Europe* (Cambridge: Cambridge University Press, 1995), p. 244.

160. Theda Skocpol, "Targeting within Universalism: Politically Viable Policies to Combat Poverty in the United States," in Christopher Jencks and Paul E. Peterson, eds., *The Urban Underclass* (Washington, DC: Urban Institute, 1991), pp. 411–36; Skocpol, *The Missing Middle*, pp. 27–43.

161. "Les cadres n'hésitent plus à s'engager dans les conflits sociaux," *Le Monde*, 5 February 1997.

162. Jane Jenson and Ruth Kantrow, "Labor Market and Family Policy in France," in Gertrude S. Goldberg and Eleanor Kremen, eds., *The Feminization of Poverty: Only in America?* (New York: Praeger, 1990), p. 119; Michel Messu, "Les politiques familiales," in François de Singly, ed., *La famille. L'état des savoirs* (Paris: La Découverte, 1997), p. 278.

163. Philippe Steck, "De la loi Veil au plan Juppé: l'évolution de la branche famille," *Droit social* 4 (April 1996), p. 408; Blum-Girardeau, *Les tableaux de la solidarité*, p. 113. On the decline in the real value of family allowances, see Thélot and Villac, *Politique familiale*, tables on pp. 184–85.

164. Commissariat Général du Plan, *Protection sociale et famille. Préparation du Huitième Plan* (Paris: La Documentation Française, 1980), p. 135; Jacques Commaille, *Misères de la famille, question d'Etat* (Paris: Presses de la Fondation Nationale des Sciences Politiques, 1996); Commaille, *Les enjeux politiques de la famille* (Paris: Bayard, 1998), pp. 111–12.

165. Dominique Lamiot and Pierre-Jean Lancry, *La protection sociale. Les enjeux de la solidarité* (Paris: Nathan, 1989), p. 80; Sheila B. Kamerman and Alfred J. Kahn, "Social Policy and Children in the United States and Europe," in John L. Palmer, Timothy Smeeding, and Barbara Boyle Torrey, eds., *The Vulnerable* (Washington, DC: Urban Institute, 1988), pp. 372–73.

166. Thélot and Villac, *Politique familiale*, pp. 184–87; Gérard Abramovici et al., "La protection sociale dans l'Union Européenne," *Solidarité Santé* 1 (January–March 1998), p. 49.

167. Gøsta Esping-Andersen and Sebastian Sarasa, "The Generational Conflict Reconsidered," *Journal of European Social Policy* 12, no. 1 (February 2002), p. 11.

168. Matt Barnes, "Social Exclusion and the Life Course," in Barnes et al., eds., *Poverty and Social Exclusion in Europe* (Cheltenham, UK: Edward Elgar, 2002), p. 15; Esping-Andersen and Sarasa, "The Generational Conflict Reconsidered," p. 9.

169. Esping-Andersen and Sarasa, "The Generational Conflict Reconsidered," p. 16.

170. Pierre Concialdi, "Les politiques anti-pauvreté ont-elles réussi?" *Sociétal* 39, no. 1 (2003), p. 83.

171. Most recently, see Margaret Maruani, "Les *working poor*, version française," *Droit social* 7–8 (July–August 2003), pp. 696–702.

8   THE FRENCH EXCEPTION

1. Michel Crozier, *Etat moderne, Etat modeste* (Paris: Seuil, 1987), p. 145.

2. Pierre Laroque, "Quarante ans de Sécurité sociale," *Revue française des affaires sociales* 39 (July–September 1985) (special issue), pp. 7–35. The translation of Laroque is from Linda Hantrais, "France: Squaring the Welfare Triangle," in Vic George and Peter Taylor-Gooby, *European Welfare Policy: Squaring the Welfare Circle* (London: Macmillan, 1996), p. 51.

3. Michel Godet, "Libérer l'activité et l'emploi," in Claude Bébéar, ed., *Le courage de réformer* (Paris: Odile Jacob, 2002), p. 92.

4. "L'impact des 35 heures jugé majoritairement positif par les salariés," *Le Monde*, 14 May 2001; Jean-Louis Quermonne, *L'Appareil administratif de l'Etat* (Paris: Seuil, 1991), p. 135; Yves Crozet, *Analyse économique de l'état* (Paris: Armand Colin, 1997); Denis Kessler and Philippe Trainar, "Les 35 heures et l'emploi: Illusions et effets pervers," *Commentaire* 23, no. 92 (Winter 2000–01), pp. 785–97.

5. See Philippe Manière, *La vengeance du peuple. Les élites, Le Pen, et les Français* (Paris: Plon, 2002).

6. See *L'Express* 2591 (1–7 March 2001). The cover story is "Comment les 35 heures changent notre vie."

7. "L'impact des 35 heures jugé majoritairement positif par les salariés," *Le Monde*, 14 May 2001; "Les salariés sont attachés aux 35 heures," *Le Monde*, 12 October 2003.

8. "Une intensification du travail et un plus grand sentiment de stress," *Le Monde*, 14 May 2001.

9. "Les salariés sont attachés aux 35 heures," *Le Monde*, 12 October 2003.

10. On this theme, see "Loisirs, famille: l'effet 35 heures enfin mesuré," *Le Parisien*, 14 May 2001; "Les 35 heures en mouvement: chiffres et enjeux," *L'Express*, 13 December 2001 (web version). For a collection of articles on the law, see Catherine Bloch-London and Jérôme Pélisse, eds., *La réduction du temps de travail. Des politiques aux pratiques* (Paris: La Documentation Française, 2003).

11. See John Gillingham, *European Integration, 1950–2003: Superstate or New Market Economy* (Cambridge: Cambridge University Press, 2003), pp. 385–86; Christopher Caldwell, "Europe's Social Market," *Policy Review* (October–November 2001), pp. 29–37. In my view, both authors above exaggerate the importance of the 35-hour law. Over 500,000 people retired in France each year between 1999 and 2002. Surely this was partly responsible for job creation.

12. On this theme, see "France's shorter week. Unintended results," *The Economist*, 3 April 1999, p. 44; "How to extract flexibility from rigidity," *Financial Times*, 29 July 1999, p. 25; and Gunnar Trumbull, Brookings Institution, "France's 35 Hour Work Week: Flexibility Through Regulation," *US-France Analysis* (January 2001), pp. 1–4.

13. Manière, *La vengeance du peuple*, pp. 20, 30, 31, 32.

14. Laurent Joffrin, *La Régression française* (Paris: Seuil, 1992), p. 224. The capital R is symbolic, as in République. (Except for the first word, French book titles are not capitalized.)

15. Sophie Meunier, Brookings Institution, "France and Globalization in 2003," *US-France Analysis Series* (May 2003), pp. 4–5.

16. Brink Lindsey, *Against the Dead Hand: The Uncertain Struggle for Global Capitalism* (New York: John Wiley & Sons, 2002), p. 243.

17. John Ardagh, *France in the New Century: Portrait of a Changing Society* (London: Viking, 1999), p. 187; Henri Mendras, *L'Europe des Européens: Sociologie de l'Europe occidentale* (Paris: Gallimard, 1987), pp. 259–65.

18. See, for example, Michel Albert, *Capitalisme contre capitalisme* (Paris: Seuil, 1991) and Viviane Forrester, *L'Horreur économique* (Paris: Fayard, 1996). For an amusing dissection of Forrester, see Jacques Julliard, *La faute aux élites* (Paris: Gallimard, 1997).
19. Quoted in Sophie Pedder, "France. The Grand Illusion," *The Economist*, 5 June 1999, p. 4 of survey.
20. Renaud Dely, "Retraites: 'Il n'est pas temps de brouiller de débat," *Libération*, 31 May 2003.
21. Andrew Jack, *The French Exception: Still so Special?* (London: Profile Books, 1999), p. 67, citing a study by the magazine, *Le Revenu Français*.
22. Gregg M. Olsen, *The Politics of the Welfare State: Canada, Sweden, and the United States* (Toronto: Oxford University Press, 2002), p. 115; Margaret Gordon, *Social Security Policies in Industrial Countries: A Comparative Analysis* (Cambridge: Cambridge University Press, 1990).
23. Jacques Julliard, former politician, labor union advisor, and now contributing editor to *Le Nouvel Observateur*, in his book, *La faute aux élites*, p. 48, passim.
24. See *Le Monde*, 5 December 2002 and *The Economist*, 8 February 2003, p. 49.
25. Préel, quoted in Patrick Williams, "Les nouveaux réacs, c'est vous!" *Le Nouvel Observateur*, 11 January 2001.
26. Bernard Préel, *Le choc des générations* (Paris: La Découverte, 2000), pp. 224–25. *Le Nouvel Observateur* ran a few articles on this theme in April 2003.
27. On this theme, see Gøsta Esping-Andersen, "Quel Etat-providence pour le XXIè siècle?" *Esprit* 272 (February 2001), pp. 122–50.
28. See the convincing book on this theme, as it applies to the US, by Charles Derber, *Corporation Nation: How Corporations are Taking Over Our Lives and What We Can Do About It* (New York: St. Martin's Griffin, 1998).
29. Noreena Hertz, *The Silent Takeover: Global Capitalism and the Death of Democracy* (New York: Arrow Books, 2001), p. 112.
30. Francis G. Castles, "Changing Course in Economic Policy: the English-speaking Nations in the 1980s," in Castles, ed., *Families of Nations* (Aldershot: Dartmouth, 1993); Castles, "Needs-Based Strategies of Social Protection in Australia and New Zealand," in Gøsta Esping-Andersen, ed., *Welfare States in Transition: National Adaptations in Global Economies* (London: SAGE, 1996), pp. 88–115.
31. Anton Brender, *La France face à la mondialisation*, 3rd edn. (Paris: La Découverte, 2002), pp. 115–17.
32. Tony Judt, "Europe: The Grand Illusion," *New York Review of Books*, 11 July 1996, p. 7; Thai Than Dang, Pablo Antolin, and Howard Oxley, OECD, "Fiscal Implications of Ageing," OECD Economics Department Working Papers, no. 305, 19 September 2001, p. 26.
33. As witnessed, for instance, in the regular banners and statements at the official website of the Ministry of Labor and Solidarity (www.nsej.travail.gouv.fr), especially the "Emplois jeunes" section, during the period 1999–2002.

34. Miguel A. Malo, Luis Toharia, and Jérôme Gautié, "France: The Deregulation that Never Existed," in Gøsta Esping-Andersen, ed., *Why Deregulate Labour Markets?* (Oxford: Oxford University Press, 2000), p. 266.
35. For example, "Emplois-jeunes: poursuite de l'effort financier," *Le Monde*, 6 June 2001, and "Emplois-jeunes," *Libération*, 6 June 2001.
36. Consulted in June 2001, at www.nsej.travail.gouv.fr/home.html.
37. These are the words of Paul Wallace, in his general survey of pensions in the Western world, "Pensions: Time to Grow Up," A Survey of Pensions, *The Economist*, 16 February 2002, p. 21.
38. "Le faux-semblant des cortèges," *Le Figaro*, 1 February 2003.
39. According to INSEE statistics. Cited by Jean-Michel Charpin, "Le vieillissement de la population," in Assistance Publique-Hôpitaux de Paris, *L'Hôpital au XXIe siècle. Actes du colloque national, Cent-cinquantenaire de l'AP-HP* (Paris: Assistance Publique-Hôpitaux de Paris, 2000), p. 143.

Index